NINE BATTLES
TO
STANLEY

NINE BATTLES
TO
STANLEY

by

Nick van der Bijl

with a foreword by
Major General Julian Thompson

LEO COOPER

First published in Great Britain in 1999 by
LEO COOPER

an imprint of
Pen & Sword Books Ltd
47 Church Street, Barnsley,
South Yorkshire, S70 2As

A CIP record of this book is available from
the British Library

ISBN 0 85052 619 1

Typeset in 10/12.5pt Sabon by
Phoenix Typesetting, Ilkley, West Yorkshire.

Printed and bound by Mackays of Chatham PLC, Chatham, Kent

TO PENNY AND IMOGEN

Contents

Maps

Foreword

by

Major General Julian Thompson, CB, OBE

Intelligence is a vital commodity to any commander engaged in war. Of course good intelligence work also forms the basis of all successful anti-terrorist and counter-insurgency operations, or, to give them the current vogue name, operations other than war. Gathering and assessing strategic and other forms of high-level intelligence continues in peacetime. But, in the British Army and Royal Marines, intelligence at the tactical and operational level is hardly ever played realistically in the peacetime exercises which are supposed to be rehearsals for a 'real war'. The troops must be put through their paces in the all-too-short time available, so the commanders and staff are spoon-fed with information on which to base their plans, and the intelligence sections get little opportunity to practise the painstaking skills involved in collecting and collating the snippets of information which go to make up the intelligence picture in a real war situation, and disseminating it. The collection of intelligence, of course, includes the art of prisoner interrogation. False lessons are learned on exercises. The intelligence staffs fall prey to succeeding rounds of defence cuts, and when a proper war comes along there is a great deal of hurried 'reinventing the wheel'.

Nine Battles to Stanley is an account of the fighting on land in the Falklands War of 1982 by Nick van der Bijl who was the sole Intelligence Corps representative on the staff of my brigade, 3rd Commando Brigade. His post was all that remained after a Whitehall decision ten years earlier had removed the professional intelligence staff just as I arrived as Brigade Major (Chief of Staff) of this Brigade.

Nick van der Bijl tells a fascinating tale as a result not only of being at the centre of events, or thereabouts, throughout the war, and the run-up to it, but also because he has thoroughly researched the Argentine side, and has revealed some hitherto unknown (to the British anyway) facts. He is extremely modest in the telling. Little of the tremendous efforts he had made to overcome years of playing at intelligence on exercises is included. He was fortunate in having a talented team, albeit none of them intelligence personnel by profession, and a highly experienced, battle-wise boss, Captain Viv Rowe, Royal Marines.

I can not resist a wry smile when I remember the efforts needed to persuade the Royal Navy to spare sufficient space in which to allow the Intelligence Section to work as we sailed south to battle. The compartment originally allocated was no larger than a couple of decent-sized built-in cupboards – quite enough to assemble the predigested intelligence pap handed out on the exercises which constituted the sole operational experience of all but the most senior naval officers in 1982, Commodore Clapp excepted. The information collaged by my Intelligence Section during the voyage south quickly convinced any doubters among the Navy of the worth of giving them adequate quarters in which to work. Soon they demanded that room be found for their own staff reassigned from other duties or hurriedly flown-in from the United Kingdom to work on naval intelligence. The naval staffs were in an even worse state regarding trained intelligence personnel than my headquarters; at the start of the war they had none.

Nick's fascinating book pulls no punches and is one of the best assessments of the Argentine Army I have read. After the war someone in my Brigade described the Argentine Army as 'military pygmies'. This is probably fair; they were about on a par with the Italian Army at its best in the Second World War. This was not, of course, the fault of the soldiers, nor anything to do with their being Argentine as opposed to British. It was because they were not properly trained and motivated. The blame for those deficiencies must be laid on the senior officers, all the way to the top of their Army.

The Argentines were also militarily naïve, again all the way to the top. Their officers and troops wrote and sang what we regarded as childishly jingoistic songs, and expressed sentiments that would have been greeted with jeers by any self-respecting British soldier or marine. This was also not the Argentines' fault. The blame again lay with Argentine senior officers, like the one that boasted that he would be proud if his son died fighting for the Malvinas. They failed to prepare their troops, perhaps because they had no national memory of war and what it entails, and certainly no practical experience. They were up against soldiers and marines whose fathers, grandfathers and great-grandfathers had fought in two world wars, and whose army had been fighting non-stop since 1945, except for one year, 1968. Some of the fighting had been small beer, some of it, like Korea, Suez, the Radfan and Dhofar had not. Most of the British soldiers and marines who fought in the Falklands had served in Northern Ireland. Many had experienced the crack and thump of incoming fire. Few had any illusions.

Experience, however, is not enough. One US Secretary of State for War is supposed to have remarked, 'Frederick the Great had a mule that went on twenty-seven campaigns with him. After twenty-seven campaigns it still remained a mule'. Good training combined with experience proved a winning combination for the British in the Falklands. Lack of either did for the Argentines.

But, as Nick van der Bijl makes clear in this excellent book, intelligence was one area in which the British had a great deal of catching-up to do. Let us hope the lesson has been learned.

Julian Thompson

Glossary

Advanced Forces	Naval term for Special Forces. In the context of this book, the SAS, SBS and Mountain and Arctic Warfare Cadre RM.
AML 90	French Panhard AML 90. A four-wheeled armoured car with a 90mm main armament.
AOR	Amphibious Operations Room. The floating command post on board the LPDs.
ARA	*Armada de la Republica Argentina.* Argentine equivalent to Her Majesty's Ship.
BAS	British Antarctic Survey.
Bergen	Large backpack.
Blowpipe	Shoulder-launched optically guided surface-to-air missile. Very heavy and entirely unsuited to being carried. Used by both sides.
"Blue on blue"	An engagement between friendly forces i.e. friendly fire. So-called because allied forces are marked in blue, as opposed to the enemy which are in red, on maps.
BMA	Brigade Maintenance Area. The main brigade-level logistic centre.
BV	Volvo Bandwagon 202. A Swedish tracked oversnow prime mover towing a small covered trailer. Sometimes known simply as a BV.
C-130	Transport aircraft. Known to the British as a Hercules and nicknamed "Fat Albert".
"Camp"	The area outside Stanley.
Carl Gustav	Infantry 84mm medium anti-tank weapon.

CB	Citizens' Band.
CBU	Cluster Bomb Unit. A case filled with several hundred small bomblets. Two versions used by the British: Hunting BL 755 cluster bomb unit and Matra BLG 66, which was known to both sides as "Beluga".
CH-47	Large troop-carrying helicopter with two rotors. Known to the British as a Chinook.
Chief of Staff	Senior staff officer. In a British brigade used to be known as a Brigade Major. Usually a major.
Close target recce	A reconnaissance in which the patrol gets as close to the target as practical without being compromised.
CPO	Chief Petty Officer. Royal Navy SNCO.
CO	Commanding Officer. In the Army, the commander of a battalion, usually a lieutenant colonel.
CP	Command Post.
CTF	Combined Task Force.
CTG	Combined Task Group.
CTU	Combined Task Unit.
CVR(T)	Combat Vehicle Reconnaissance (Tracked). A light armoured vehicle with several variants, including the Scorpion mounting a 76mm, Scimitar with a 30mm, Samson recovery and Samaritan ambulance. Has a ground pressure lighter than a person.
DF	Direct fire.
Deputy Chief of Staff	Second most senior staff officer, usually responsible for disciplinary, personnel and logistic matters. Used to be known as Deputy Adjutant General and Quartermaster General.
DMS	DeMarcated Sole. Patterns on the rubber sole of the boot.
Embarked Force	The military personnel on board ships. Usually regarded by the Royal Navy as more people to keep their ships clean.

	Differs from the Ship's Detachment who are Royal Marines and part of the ship's complement.
EW	Electronic Warfare.
FAC	Forward Air Controller. An officer responsible for directing air operations to assist ground troops. Often air force.
FAL	Argentine-manufactured 7.62mm rifle made under licence by *Fabriaca Militar de Armas Portatiles*. Standard rifle of the Argentine Armed Forces. Has a shorter barrel than the SLR and can come with a folding butt.
FIBUA	Fighting in Built-Up Areas.
FIC	Falkland Islands Company.
FIDF	Falkland Islands Defence Force. A military volunteer unit of company strength based in a drill hall in Stanley. Its equivalent in the camp was the Settlement Volunteers
FOO	Forward Observation Officer. A small party of gunners, usually one officer and four other ranks, who organize artillery fire support to the infantry and armour. Each team was given a number e.g. FOO2
FTV	*Fearless* Television.
Go about	Naval terminology meaning to turn around.
"Grey Funnel Line"	The fleet oilers, fleet auxiliary and landing ships supporting warships and amphibious forces. So called because the ships are painted grey.
GPMG	7.62mm General Purpose Machine Gun used by the British.
GPMG SF	GPMG in the Sustained Fire role. As opposed to being fired from a bipod, the gun is fitted to a tripod with sights and is more accurate over long distances.
GSO3 G2	General Staff Officer Grade 3 General 2, the NATO name for the most junior

	Intelligence officer. Also responsible for military security. In the British Army and Royal Marines, usually a captain.
GSO3 G3	General Staff Officer Grade 3 General 3, the NATO name for the most junior Operations officer.
Hercules	C-130 transport aircraft.
Hirundo	Argentine name for the Italian Agusta A-109A helicopter. Heavily armed with machine guns and rockets; highly manoeuvrable.
HQ	Headquarters.
HE	High Explosive.
HF	High Frequency.
Installaza	Spanish 88.9mm anti-tank rocket launcher. Portable and often known as a "bazooka". Found in an Argentine infantry platoon.
Iroquois	US manufactured UH-IH helicopter. Used extensively in Vietnam for troop-carrying and as a close support gunship.
ICRC	International Committee of the Red Cross.
JFIT	Joint Forward Interrogation Team. An interrogation team designed to support a brigade.
JNCO	Junior non-commissioned officer. In the Army and Royal Marines, corporals and lance corporals.
JSIU	Joint Service Interrogation Unit. An interrogation team designed to support a division.
"Kelper"	Nickname for the Falkland Islanders who lived in the "camp".
KFS	Knife, fork and spoon. Military terminology, sometimes known as "irons" or "eating irons".

LADE	*Linea Aerea Del Estado.* The state airline servicing internal flights to remote parts of Argentina, including to the Falklands. It had an office in Stanley which also doubled up as the Argentine consul's office.
LARC-5	Lighter Amphibious Resupply and Cargo Series 5. US wheeled amphibious vehicle.
LAW 66mm	66mm Light Anti-Tank Weapon. One-time throwaway portable tube containing a projectile. Very useful against bunkers.
LCU	Landing Craft Utility. 100-ton landing craft designed to carry two tanks or about 150 troops in full kit. Four to a LPD.
LCVP	Landing Craft Vehicle and Personnel. A ten-ton plywood landing craft capable of carrying thirty fully-equipped troops or a small vehicle and a trailer. Four to a LPD and slung on davits.
LFFI	Land Forces Falkland Islands.
LMG	Light Machine Gun. The modern 7.62mm version of the highly accurate .303 Bren. Still has the familiar curved magazine.
LPD	Land Platform Dock. HMS *Fearless* and *Intrepid*, the two Royal Navy assault ships capable of launching an assault either by landing craft or helicopter.
LS	Landing site. A landing place for heli-borne troops as opposed to DZ (Dropping Zone) for parachute troops
LSL	Landing Ship Logistic.
LVTP-7	Landing Vehicle Tracked Personnel Series 7. Development of tracked infantry APC used extensively by US forces in the Pacific campaign.
M113	US tracked armoured personnel carrier.
MA	Medical Assistant. Medic in the Royal Navy.

MAG	7.62mm machine gun used by the Argentines, equivalent to the British GPMG.
M&AW	Mountain and Arctic Warfare Cadre Royal Marines. Specialist troops trained in above the tree-line mountain and winter warfare in support of 3rd Commando Brigade. Subject of television BBC TV documentary *Behind The Lines*. SAS equivalent is Mountain Troop
MEZ	Maritime Exclusion Zone. The 200-mile exclusion zone around the Falklands imposed by Great Britain on 12 April 1982 with the threat to sink any ship in the area.
MRR	Maritime Radar Reconnaissance.
NAS	Naval Air Squadron.
NGFO	Naval Gunfire Officer. Similar to a FOO but directing naval bombardment. Found with 148 (Meiktila) Commando Forward Observation Battery.
NGS	Naval Gunfire Support.
NP	Naval Party. A group of Royal Navy or Royal Marine personnel on detached duties. A number of Naval Parties supplemented Merchant Navy crews to provide communications, liaison and defence and help integrate merchant ships into the Task Force.
OC	Officer Commanding. An officer of any rank commanding a unit below battalion level.
OP	Observation Post.
Panhard AML 90	French wheeled armoured car with a 90mm main armament.
Para	Short for parachute or paratrooper.
Puma	Troop-carrying helicopter.
RAMC	Royal Army Medical Corps.
RAP	Regimental Aid Post. The first place

	where the wounded receive medical treatment, as opposed to first aid at the point of being wounded or injured. Normally manned by unit medics as opposed to RAMC.
Recce	Reconnaisance.
RFA	Royal Fleet Auxiliary. Part of the "grey funnel line".
RM	Royal Marine.
RMP	Royal Military Police.
RN	Royal Navy.
RRS	Royal Research Ship.
RSRM	Raiding Squadron Royal Marines. A small unit equipped with light assault boats. In 1982 these were Rigid Raiders fitted with either one or two powerful outboard engines.
SAM-7	Soviet manufactured surface-to-air missile.
Samson	The recovery vehicle of the CVR(T) series.
SEAL	Sea, Air and Landing Team. US amphibious Special Forces.
Scimitar	Part of the CVR(T) series firing a Raden 30mm quick-firing cannon.
Scorpion	Part of the CVR(T) series firing a 76mm gun.
Sea Harrier	Naval version of the Harrier vertical take off aircraft equipped with Sidewinder air-to-air missiles, 30mm Raden cannons and rockets; could carry bombs. Principal roles were air defence, close air support to ground forces and combat air patrol.
Sea King	Royal Navy support helicopter used by the Fleet Air Arm. Troop-carrying version, the Mark IV, sometimes known as the Sea Commando, can carry about twenty fully equipped men.
Senior rate	A naval term for a senior non-commissioned officer, i.e. an other rank above Petty Officer.
SLR	Self-Loading Rifle. British version of the

	7.62mm semi-automatic rifle FN and used between 1960 and 1990. A little cumbersome for the jungle and internal security.
SMG	Sub-machine gun.
Sterling	9mm SMG. Argentine equivalents were the 9mm PA3-DM and .45 M3 A1 SMG.
Stick	In military terms, a group of troops to be landed from the air, for instance a stick of paras or a stick of heliborne soldiers.
Tac HQ	Tactical headquarters. A small mobile or manpack HQ operating from the main HQ.
TEZ	Total Exclusion Zone imposed on 30 April. This expanded the MEZ to include aircraft and was an attempt by the British to seal off the Falklands. Aircraft on the ground were liable to be attacked.
Troop	In British Army, equivalent to an infantry platoon and applied to mounted units (cavalry, gunners and transport) but includes engineers. For the Royal Marines the term originated in the Second World War from army commando platoon-level units. The nomenclature is thought to originate from the mounted Boer commandos of the Boer wars, remembering that it was Winston Churchill who sanctioned the name 'Commando' for the British and Commonwealth Special Service battalions.
VHF	Very High Frequency.
Wasp	A small helicopter found on Royal Navy destroyers and frigates used for anti-submarine warfare, over-the-horizon observation and ship to ship

	and ship to shore liaison.
Wessex	Medium support helicopter used by the Royal Navy and the RAF, for, amongst other roles, transporting troops and equipment. In naval role had an anti-submarine warfare role.
YPF	*Yacimientos Petroliferos Fiscales*, the Argentine State Oil Company. There was an oil storage dump outside Stanley.

REAR ADMIRAL BUSSER'S ADDRESS

The address given to the Argentine Landing Force by Rear-Admiral Carlos
Busser on the *Cabo San Antonio* on 1 April, 1982.

'I am the Commander of the Landing Forces, made up of the Argentinian
Marines and Army on this ship, of units aboard the destroyer *Santisima
Trinidad* and the icebreaker *Almirante Irizar* and the divers on board the
submarine *Santa Fe*. Our mission is to disembark on the Malvinas and to
dislodge the British military forces and authorities installed there. That is
what we are going to do. Destiny has wished us to be the instigators of
making good the 150 or so years of illegal occupation. In those islands we
are going to come across a population with whom we must develop a special
relationship. They live on Argentine territory and consequently they must be
treated as though they are living on the mainland. You must be punctilious
in respecting the property and integrity of each of the inhabitants. You will
not enter into any private residence unless it is necessary for reasons of
combat. You will respect women, children, old people and men. You will be
hard on the enemy, but courteous, respectful and pleasant in your dealings
with the population of our territory and with those we have to protect. If
anyone commits rape, robbery or pillage, I shall impose the maximum
penalty.And now, with the authorisation of the Commander of the
Transport Division, I am sure the Landing Force will be the culmination of
the brilliant planning other members of the group have already achieved.
Thank you for bringing us this far and thank you for landing us tomorrow
on the beach. I have no doubts that your courage, honour and capability of
you will bring us victory. For a long time we have been training our muscles
and our hearts for the supreme moment when we shall come face to face with
the enemy. That moment has now arrived. Tomorrow you will be
conquerors. Tomorrow we shall show the world an Argentine force valorous
in war and generous in peace. May God protect you! Now say with me Long
live the Fatherland!

In comparison, shortly before the British Landing Group entered the exclusion zone around the Falklands on 19 May, 1982, Commander John Kelly
RN, Executive Officer on board HMS *Fearless,* read the austere Articles of
War on FTV and over the tannoy, reminding everyone that war is fought to
a set of rules. One person on board described it as vaguely Nelsonian.

RECOVERY

When captured, many Argentine prisoners were found to have a poem dedicated to Marine Infantry Lieutenant Commander Pedro Eduardo Giachino, who was killed during the Amphibious Commando Grouping assault on Government House. He was also the first Argentine to be killed during the campaign.

The poem was written by Nidia AG Otbea de Fontanini of Santa Fe

The Malvinas Are Argentine

RECOVERY

Many hued skies, majestic above the sea,
A rapid flight of white seagulls
Fleeing from the infernal thunder of guns,
Eternal witness, the Southern Cross,

Imposing white and blue standard,
May you bless it, may all-powerful God,
There is the silence of death round about us,
The blood of brothers lives in grief.

Struggle of the people, fervour, lamentations,
Voices of the Anthem, Flag on the balcony!'
A song of the brotherhood, glory and unction.

Impassioned verses of Pedroni,
Have anchored at your port, SOLEDAD . . .
"Come home to the Fatherland, to eternity!

In analysing some aspects of the poem, the *white and blue standard* refers to the Argentine flag, which commemorates the white and blue uniforms of 1st 'Los Patricios' Regiment which defeated the British in 1807. The remainder were a rag-bag of ununiformed militia and included a battalion of Africans. *Soledad* in the final verse has a double meaning of literally translated as *Loneliness* and the name given by the Argentines to *Puerto Soledad,* the Argentine name for Port Louis, the first place they colonised in 1820.

Acknowledgements

It is a fact that wars are fought by thousands but recorded by very few and they are usually commanders. It also a fact that those who fight wars probably know less about what happened than those who followed them. During the research for this book, I learnt more about the Falklands campaign than I gathered during it, in particular about the Argentines, confined as I was to a ship, a hole in the ground and, finally, a building. Since I was involved in intelligence, there was also one burning question to answer 'Did we get it right?' As I dived back into my memory, my notes and recollections written during 1982 and 1983, while in Northern Ireland, the answer was 'Just about' which wasn't bad, considering how poorly we were prepared for a war 8000 miles from home in a region few knew anything about against a country whose claim to fame was *coup d'états* and football. To the veterans, I hope I can answer some of their questions because, as someone commented about an article in an Army periodical on the short engagement at Port San Carlos, it is always good to know who the enemy were.

It is said we all have a book in us but very few have the privilege of having one published. I am indebted to Leo Cooper. I regard it a privilege that as a participant, he gave me this opportunity to contribute to the history. Without his positive encouragement and support in the early stages, it would have gathered dust. I am also most grateful to Tom Hartman, my editor, who gave me firm but fair encouragement and patience to a new author keen to see his work published, and to Brigadier Henry Wilson, Pen and Sword managing editor, for his guidance. I would also like to mention Reg Davis-Poynter, who guided me through my early incursions into the world of publishing.

I am indebted to David Aldea, an Australian who was in Chile at the time of the Falklands campaign. David sacrificed his draft of the Argentine side of the war and allowed me to include substantial parts in this book. On more than one occasion, his telephone call was our alarm clock. Most of the material he sent was enlightening but, as is often the case, there was too much to include it all.

Others who I must thank for their help include Major-General Julian Thompson CB OBE, for writing the Foreword and putting me right where I was wrong; Richard Bethell MBE, for explaining what happened during the Scots Guards important diversionary attack below Tumbledown Mount; Chris Davies MBE for giving me an insight into HQ 5th Infantry Brigade; Colonel Harry Massey, Naval/Military Attaché Buenos Aires, for liaising with the Argentine Army; former colleague in 7th Field Force, Major Gary Bullivant, HQ British Forces Falkland Islands and Lieutenant Jim Finch, Falkland Islands Logistic Unit, for helping with information on the war that is still available 'down south'; Will Fowler for providing me with information he gathered as a newshound in 1982 and also for proof-reading; Neil Hislop and Jayne Murray of Murraygraphics for their patience as we made the maps; John Glauert for helping with translations; the Household Cavalry, Royal Artillery, Royal Engineer and Airborne Museums and Steve Walton at the Imperial War Museum for providing me with information.

Finally, I must mention three people. First, my wife, Penny, who during the war, like all our wives, parents, brothers, sisters and girlfriends watched and listened to the news and knew it was only part of what was happening on those distant islands. I am grateful to the Intelligence Corps for their support to her during the campaign. Secondly, Imogen, who was six months old when I left and just over nine months when I returned, but that smile from her cot will remain with me for the rest of my life, much to her embarrassment! Their support and patience each evening and most weekends were more than invaluable. Thirdly, my Mother, who sent me 'Red Cross' parcels, which were a welcome break from rations, and also collected for the South Atlantic Fund.

Nick van der Bijl
Somerset

I

The Road to War

"It looks as though the silly buggers mean it". Governor Hunt on being advised an Argentine invasion was imminent.

8000 miles from Great Britain and 350 miles from South America lies an archipelago of two large islands and over 200 smaller ones, mostly treeless, with a total area of about 4700 square miles. The distance east to west equates roughly from London to Cardiff and north to south from Oxford to the Isle of Wight. There are many good anchorages but no significant lakes and the terrain is generally hilly moorland, not dissimilar to Dartmoor and with an abundance of wildlife – the Falkland Islands.

At the height of their maritime power Spain and Portugal, through the 1494 Treaty of Tordesillas, divided the unknown world, Spain claiming everything to the west of an imaginary line running from pole to pole, including this desolate archipelago. Portugal took the rest. But the two countries had not appreciated the audacity of English naval influence and soon Spain's claim looked decidedly vulnerable. Great Britain's association began in August, 1592, when the Elizabethan Arctic explorer John Davis sighted the islands after his ship the *Desire* was driven off course in a storm. The Italian Amerigo Vespucci may have seen them in 1509 when storms also blew his tiny ship into the distant reaches of the South Atlantic, but neither landed. The Dutchman Sebald de Weert, returning home after passage through Cape Horn, plotted Jason Islands in 1600, but it was not until 1690 that the English privateer John Strong named the islands after Anthony Carey, 5th Viscount Falkland, then First Lord of the Admiralty. In Strong's wake, visitors were frequent, in particular Frenchmen from St Malo, the Iles Malouines. In 1764 colonists led by Louis Antoine de Bougainville, largely inspired by the loss of Canada to the British, settled at Port Louis in Berkeley Sound and, as French influence in the region was taken over by Britain, these isolated colonists became a focus of resistance.

After Captain George Anson returned from his epic circumnavigation in 1745, he suggested a station be found in the South Atlantic to counter Spanish domination. Great Britain was then engaged in a trade war with her continental competitors and the Admiralty despatched Commodore John Byron, grandfather of the poet, who raised the Union flag at Port Egmont on Saunders Island on West Falklands on 12 January, 1765, and claimed the islands for George III. He was unaware of the colonists at Port Louis. The

1

Admiralty was keen to cement its influence and in January the following year Captain John McBride with 100 men established a garrison at Settlement Cove. He charted the coast and either ejected anyone found on the islands or persuaded them to swear allegiance to Great Britain. The French were given six months to leave. McBride was not enamoured with the Falklands, nor were his men, nor indeed the French, one of whom wrote, 'I tarry in this desert.' Strange words for a land full of water and edible wildlife. The French then sold their settlement to the Spanish, who christened East Falklands as "Isla Soledad", the West Falklands as "Isla Gran Malvina" and the islands as a whole "Las Malvinas".

For the next three years the British and Spanish were undisturbed by each other's presence until Captain Anthony Hunt met a Spanish ship. Both sides demanded each other's surrender and the incident was only resolved in June, 1770, when five ships from the Spanish-governed province of Buenos Aires arrived off Settlement Cove. The British could muster only a sloop, four 12-pounders in shore positions and twenty-three Royal Marines. Both sides negotiated each other's departure, but Admiral Madariaga landed with 1600 men and forced the tiny garrison to surrender. Hunt's force returned to Great Britain to find their defeat had first been broadcast by Spain. In London there was outrage that national honour had been disgraced, particularly as the threat had not been predicted. Foreign Secretary Lord Weymouth resigned and, although Prime Minister Lord North did not want hostilities with Spain, he was urged by the Earl of Chatham to consider war. By the end of the year this seemed inevitable, until Louis XV told his Spanish ally Charles III that he would not support Spain in a conflict with Great Britain. Britain agreed to Spain's sovereignty of Las Malvinas but omitted this clause from their copy of the declaration. Nevertheless the government was unable to convince sceptics it had secretly agreed to abandon Port Egmont to the Spanish. How history would repeat itself!

In 1771 Spain returned Settlement Cove to the British, but three years later the colonists pulled out completely, largely at the instigation of the venerable Dr Johnson, who questioned the need to colonize such an inhospitable place. Lieutenant S.W. Clayton RN, the garrison commander, hammered a lead plaque, carved by a shipwright on HMS *Endurance*, on the fort door declaring:

Be it known to all nations, that Falkland Island, with this Fort, Stonehouse, Wharf, Harbour, Bays and Creeks thereunto belonging, are the Sole Right of His Most Sacred Majesty George III, King of England, France and Ireland, Defender of the Faith etc. In witness whereof this plate is set up, and his Britannic Majesty's colours left flying as a mark of possession.

The interesting aspect of this statement is the use of Falkland Island in the singular, referring only to West Falklands, so does Britain have a valid claim?

Great Britain recognized Spain's claim to East Falkland and their settlement in Berkeley Sound remained unmolested until it was abandoned in 1811. By this time British traders were also influential in the region.

In 1816 a network of South American provinces around the River Plate won independence, formed themselves into the United Provinces of the Rio de la Plata and claimed the Spanish colonies in the region, which included the Falklands. Four years later they sent a small force to re-occupy Port Louis, renamed Soledad. In 1826 colonists from the newly-created republic of Argentina arrived under Louis Vernet to develop the settlement and, despite British protests, he was appointed governor. Keen for the islands to be self-sufficient, in 1831 he arrested three American schooner skippers for poaching seals, one of whom was taken to Buenos Aires to stand trial. However, the USS *Lexington,* which happened to be in the River Plate, sailed to the Falklands, flattened Soledad, captured the colonists and declared the islands free of all government. The Americans had arrived on the global scene. Argentina objected to the American act and sent Governor Mestivier to set up a penal settlement, but he was promptly murdered by the convicts. An Argentine naval force rounded them up.

On 2 January 1833, a small British flotilla commanded by Captain John Onslow in HMS *Clio* appeared offshore and, having forced the garrison to surrender, deported Governor Pinedo to Montevideo and replaced the Argentine tricolour with the Union flag, much to the fury of the Argentines. This humiliation was to underscore much of Argentina's foreign policy relationship with Great Britain. Argentina claimed she owned the islands because they had been inherited from Spain after France had sold them. Also Britain had first abandoned its claim in 1771 and then in 1774 had abandoned Egmont. But the young Argentina found it could do little to counter the growing imperialism of Great Britain.

By this time cattle was the main industry and Soledad was a rough place. Onslow left two administrators but they were later murdered. In January, 1834, a naval party from HMS *Tyne* rebuilt the fort at Port Egmont and captured the killers. Nine years later, Lieutenant Richard Moody RE arrived with some sappers and, on being appointed Governor, moved to Stanley and set up the Legislative Council, which was to play an important role in the governing and development of the Falkland Islands. He is commemorated by the barracks. In 1849 a detachment of pensioned Royal Marines, aged between twenty-six and fifty-three, replaced the sappers and, although technically civilians, they were expected to provide a military presence. Military pensioners were elderly, severely wounded or injured servicemen unfit for active service and used for garrison duties in quiet areas. They were expected to train annually for twelve days.

In January, 1858, regular Royal Marines, who were accompanied by their families, took over the pensioners' duties and were known as the Falkland Islands Garrison Company. Stanley quickly established itself as a port essential not for coaling but as a respite after rounding Cape Horn. As a cost-cutting measure, the Garrison Company was withdrawn in December, 1878. The islands were largely unaffected by the two world wars, although the Battle of the Falklands in 1914 is commemorated by a public holiday and a large memorial overlooking Stanley Harbour. During this engagement Admiral Graf von Spee's squadron was decisively defeated by Vice Admiral Sir Doveton Sturdee flying his flag in the battlecruiser HMS *Invincible*.

Although her relations with Great Britain were generally good, Argentina still grumbled. In 1933, after Britain had issued a set of commemorative stamps, Argentina issued its own showing the Falklands as part of its territory and laid claim to other dependencies in the region, including South Georgia. The disagreement simmered until September, 1964, when an Argentine pilot landed on Stanley Racecourse, planted an Argentine flag and took off. This prompted the ice patrol ship *Protector* to land her Royal Marine ship's detachment as a defence against the threat of an Argentine landing. This was replaced by a permanent Royal Marine garrison, Naval Party 8901, whose duties included training the reservist Falkland Islands Defence Force and the militia Settlement Volunteers outside Stanley, whose role was a cadre for guerrilla groups, an absurd notion given the open nature of the terrain, the tiny population and the difficulties of finding a secure base from which to operate.

At the United Nations, Argentina found sympathy for her claim and in 1965 Resolution 2065 was passed. This listed the Falklands as a colony and members were reminded that under the Resolution 1514, passed in 1960, it had undertaken to 'bring to an end everywhere colonialism in all its forms', but in the case of the Falklands, much to the frustration of Argentina, only 'in the interests of the population'. The problem was no one really knew what the islanders thought.

Great Britain took little interest in the development of the Falklands, leaving this to the Falkland Island Company. Founded in 1852 by a debt-ridden Argentine, Samuel Lafone, he bought Lafonia to develop the islands through his public company, the Royal Falkland Land, Cattle, Seal and Whale Fishery Company, and quickly cleared his debts by introducing sheep to replace the wild cattle. With the sheep came shepherds from Scotland, Wales and the West Country, including from the hamlet of Goose Green in Somerset, all of whom lived in Company-owned settlements in the "camp", the interior outside Stanley. Colloquially sheep are known as "365" because lamb and mutton, and not much else, is available 365 days each year. The Company dominated life on the islands, in much the same way as the East India Company had done in India, and the settlers developed into stubborn pro-British colonialists, to the frustration of successive post-1945 governments, most of whom wanted to be rid of the islands.

In 1967 the nationalist Condor Gang hijacked a Dakota and landed on the racecourse with the intention of capturing the islands. They were arrested and later imprisoned in Argentina, which led to the perception that it was an Argentine matter and enhanced the view that the British Government had little interest in the islands. By the 1970s Argentina had developed into a powerful South American nation but then degenerated into a shameful period in her history – the Dirty War. In common with other South American nations, she had found herself under siege from reactionary and revolutionary groups campaigning to overthrow the government. President Jorge Videla suppressed them in a vicious campaign in which military and police covert operations became a feature of Argentine life and thousands of young men and women disappeared from interrogation and detention centres, some of the worst run by the Navy. Within two years the back of the revolutionary movements had been broken, but Argentina's appalling human rights record rebounded on her and she found herself a political and economic pariah. Commercial sanctions bit hard and the faltering economy collapsed.

In 1976, to deflect attention from internal security issues, Argentina occupied South Thule and, since there was a very muted reaction from Great Britain, the following year she threatened invasion of the Falklands. Although the British response was to say nothing publicly, Prime Minister James Callaghan discreetly sent a small naval task force south and the threat dissipated. The following year the roles of Naval Party 8901 were expanded to include the protection of the Governor, the representative of British sovereign authority, and to buy a three-week bargaining window in the UN, the time needed to assemble a task force. It must be left to bureaucratic imagination to conceive quite how about fifty Royal Marines were to resist for three weeks.

In 1980 President Roberto Viola undertook to return Argentina to democracy and, after a visit to the USA, the hand of forgiveness was extended with joint exercises, known as UNITAS. Heir apparent to Viola was General Leopoldo Galtieri, son of a poor Italian immigrant, extrovert cavalry officer and commander of 2nd Army Corps. In December, 1981, Viola announced his retirement and Galtieri, backed by Admiral Jorge Anaya, Commander-in-Chief of the Navy and a former school friend, was appointed President. They joined with Brigadier General Lami Dozo, head of the Air Force, to form a Junta, but found they had inherited a disastrous economy. Needing a diversion as signs of political and popular upheaval surfaced, they renewed the Beagle Channel dispute with Chile.

Irresistible to Anaya was the recovery of the Falklands. The Navy was responsible for planning against potential regional conflict and consequently their recovery was continually updated and exercised at the Naval and Army War Schools in much the same way as the British frequently practised the defence of West Germany, something for which most thought they would never be called on to do. The Navy were also enthusiastic about removing British regional influence, because, for the first time, it, and not the Army, could make a significant contribution to Argentine history. The Air Force was not as keen as the other two services, but, as the junior partner, it emerged from the war with enhanced credibility. To Galtieri the proposition was also tantalizing, especially as January, 1983, was the 150th anniversary of the humiliating deportation of Governor Pinedo. He also believed Argentina's new relationship with the USA would favour him rather than the US's NATO ally, Great Britain.

Critically, the Junta believed Britain to be complacent about the islands. The ice patrol ship HMS *Endurance* was about to be decommissioned and there were no plans to replace her; the British Antarctic Survey (BAS) base at South Georgia was due to close and the islanders had recently been denied full British citizenship by Prime Minister Margaret Thatcher. Most important, though, was the fact that, although he was experiencing considerable opposition in Parliament, Nicholas Ridley, Under-Secretary of State at the Foreign Office, seemed sympathetic to leasing the islands to Argentina for ninety-nine years. He had made similar proposals to Guatemala over Belize, but, by the close of 1981, Ridley had left the Foreign Office. To the plotters in Buenos Aires, the British Government had again recoiled from resolving the crisis and seemed to show little interest in the islands.

It appeared to the Junta that the only way to force Great Britian to negotiate was military intervention and on 15 December, 1981, Anaya, convinced that war was inevitable, flew to the main Argentine Navy base at Puerto Belgrano and instructed the newly-installed Chief of Naval Operations, Vice Admiral Juan Lombardo, to update the plans to liberate the Falkland Islands. By early January, 1982, a top secret group, consisting of Lombardo, Major General Osvaldo Garcia, commander 5th Corps which covered the Atlantic Littoral and included the Falklands and its dependencies, and Brigadier General Siegfriedo Plessl of the Air Force, had begun planning. It was initially envisaged that, if the current political negotiations were unsuccessful, then military operations would begin about mid-September, 1982, that is after the southern hemisphere winter and to allow the conscripts inducted in February to be more fully trained. Planning was on a strict need-to-know basis with only a very few senior officers, barely a dozen, given access to relevant information. Among them was Rear Admiral Carlos Busser, who commanded the Argentine Marine Corps, and was a keen 'Malvinist'. He would plan the landings. From the very start the Argentines wanted the operation to be bloodless to fit her new global philosophy. The Dirty War was history. The strategy was that on the same day the Falklands were being invaded South Georgia was to be captured.

On 29 January, 1982, Commander Alfredo Weinstabl, who commanded 2nd Marine Infantry Battalion, was summoned from leave to see Busser and was passed a piece of paper on which was written: 'Mission: To recover the Falkland Islands and to restore it in perpetuity to the sovereignty of the Nation'. Busser told him to start planning an amphibious operation. Weinstabl and his operations officer, Lieutenant Commander Nestor

Carballido, spent several sessions at HQ Marine Infantry where they analysed the mass of topographical, social and military intelligence about the Falklands, including recent photographs of Royal Marine Barracks at Moody Brook. On 2 February Busser agreed that the battalion should be ready by 15 April and, when it assembled, after a period of leave, Weinstabl briefed his second-in-command, Lieutenant Commander Guillermo Santillan, about the plan. Since only about half the battalion was amphibious-trained, Santillan worked out a four-week training programme, much of it taking place on the former US tank landing ship, the ARA *Cabo San Antonio*. Not only did the marines become thoroughly familiar with life on board but the full range of amphibious operations was also practised, including night and day landings in LVTP amtracs. The secrecy was such that no one, including the ship's captain, Jorge Acuna, knew the purpose behind the training. The battalion Logistics Officer, Lieutenant Commander 'Fatty' Payba, worked hard to resolve the complexities of supporting the operation, which had been named Operation *Carlos*.

It is not intended to relate in detail the events which pitched Argentina into war, except to mention the Navy's interest in the Argentine scrap metal merchant Constantino Davidoff's negotiations with Christian Salvesen of Leith, Scotland, not to be confused with Leith, South Georgia, to remove the derelict whaling settlements on South Georgia. The island lies about 600 miles to the east of the Falkland Islands and about 2000 miles south of Ascension Island. With some mountains as high as the Alps, the valleys are filled with huge glaciers glowing blue, grey and green. On the leeward side, among the jagged bays and coves, are the five derelict sealing and whaling stations, once a hive of activity. The weather is treacherous and in winter snow is deposited by unpredictable winds and sudden gales.

The Argentine Navy saw Davidoff's contract as an opportunity to further its regional influence by occupying South Georgia, as had been achieved with South Thule, and lent him the support of the sophisticated Naval Transport Service naval icebreaker ARA *Almirante Irizar*, skippered by Captain Cesar Trombetta, commander of the Antarctic Squadron. On 20 December, 1981, the ship arrived off Leith after a four-day voyage in which Trombetta maintained radio silence and then deliberately flouted international convention by not reporting to the port of entry, Grytviken. While Davidoff could be excused for not presenting his credentials to Peter Witty, the BAS base commander, whose constitutional responsibilities included immigration, judicial and consular duties, reporting directly to Governor Rex Hunt, Governor of the Falkland Islands and its Dependencies, the same cannot be said of Trombetta. Substantial evidence of the visit was reported to Hunt, including someone chalking on a wall '*Las Malvinas es Argentina*', but the Foreign Office were inclined 'not to provoke proceedings which could escalate and have an unforseeable outcome'. On 4 January, 1982, the British Government's formal protest to Argentina about the violation of its sovereignty was rejected, to no one's surprise. Other incidents indicated close Argentine interest in South Georgia. On board the Panamanian-registered yacht *Carmen*, found at Leith by BAS scientists on 21 January, was an Argentine named Adrian Machessi, who claimed to be an employee of the bank funding Davidoff's contract. Three powerful radios of a type not normally associated with business trips were found on board.

By February protracted diplomatic negotiations were underway, but in March Foreign Minister Costa Mendez became so impatient by the lack of progress that he declared 'Argentina reserves the right to put an end to this process and freely elect whatever path may serve her interests'.

In this diplomatic maelstrom sailed the 'Red Plum' – *Endurance,* which every October for fifteen years had sailed to the South Atlantic where her arrival in Port Stanley was part of the colony's social calendar. Each summer she carried out scientific and hydrographic work, supported BAS bases and liaised with other nations' ships in the region, including Argentina and the Soviet Union. *Endurance* carried two Wasp helicopters, was armed with two 20mm Oerlikon anti-aircraft guns and, since she was a warship, had a Ship's Detachment of twelve Royal Marines, who in 1982 were commanded by Lieutenant Keith Mills RM. In October, 1981, without fanfare, except from the complement's families, the ship had slipped out of Chatham on her last voyage and she was now preparing to return home.

In command since 1980 was Captain Nick Barker, an experienced seaman, who had formed a rapport with the Argentine Navy, something about which Foreign Office seemed not entirely comfortable. In January, 1982, he had reported tension amongst Argentine naval officers, one whom Captain Russo, the deputy Puerto Belgrano base commander, told him, 'There is to be a war against the Malvinas. I don't know when, but I think quite soon'. Chilean naval officers also warned Barker that Argentine intentions were hostile and British diplomats in the region also began to identify tension. But all these indications of increased Argentine hostility were passed to London where they were studiously filed.

In early March the British Embassy authorized Davidoff to begin work at Leith and he and forty-one workmen embarked in the naval transport *Bahia Buen Suceso*, which he had chartered from the Argentine Navy and whose commander, Captain Briatore, would supervise the work. Infiltrated on board pretending to be scientists were several *Buzo Tactico*, literally Tactical Divers, members of a naval Special Forces unit based at Mar del Plata with an operational role similar to that of the US Navy SEAL's beach and coastal reconnaissance and underwater demolition. They were commanded by Lieutenant Commander Alfredo Astiz, who was wanted by both Sweden and France for the murder of a girl and three nuns at a naval interrogation centre during the Dirty War.

Davidoff told British officials he would be in Leith for about four months. On 11 March, shortly before he sailed, his lawyer was reminded by the

British Embassy that, when the *Bahia Buen Suceso* arrived, her captain must report to Grytviken to complete immigration formalities. On the same day Lieutenant Veal RN, a member of a Joint Services expedition on South Georgia, watched an Argentine Air Force C-130, on a photo-reconnaissance mission, fly from Bird Island to Calf Head. Within three weeks he was back in England advising the Task Force about South Georgia. The aircraft made a genuine forced landing at Stanley Airport but such was the tension among the Argentine plotters that the Air Force was accused of staging the landing and alerting the British. Faced by Foreign Office complacency, they need not have worried.

Into the midst of the deteriorating situation sailed three Frenchman in their yacht *Cinq Pars Pour*. Damaged off Cape Horn, they ran on bare poles to Grytviken where they received a frosty reception from the British scientists, to say the least. After they had shot a reindeer, Steve Martin, the new base commander, confiscated their rifle and warned them to obey local laws. The French were a little nonplussed.

The *Bahia Buen Suceso* arrived at Leith on 19 March. Captain Briatore failed to report to Martin and, while Davidoff's workmen brought equipment ashore, Astiz paraded his men in uniform, raised the Argentine flag on a mast on a derelict tower and fired a volley over British territory. The findings of four BAS scientists, who had seen the Argentine activity, were relayed to London. Next morning, Trefor Edwards, the BAS team leader, visited Leith and read a message from London to Briatore:

> You have landed at Leith without obtaining proper clearance. You and your party must go back on board the *Bahia Buen Suceso* immediately and report to the Base Commander at Grytviken for further instructions. You must remove the Argentine flag from Leith. You must not interfere with the British Antarctic Survey depot at Leith. You must not alter or deface the notices at Leith. No military personnel are allowed to land on South Georgia. No firearms are to be taken ashore.

Explicit and to the point, there was no room for misunderstanding, but Buenos Aires denied all knowledge of the *Bahia Buen Suceso's* military activities.

In Stanley the tension overflowed when someone broke into the office of Linea Aerea Del Estado (LADE), the state-owned airline. Argentina treated the incident as deeply humiliating. After the Argentine surrender the offices were used by an HQ LFFI intelligence team and upstairs in a concealed room they found four radios far more powerful than one would expect in a consular office. They were packed by two paroled Argentine prisoners and despatched to the United Kingdom for technical examination.

On 15 March *Endurance* collected the Joint Services expedition from Grytviken and four days later was in Port Stanley preparing for the long voyage back to Chatham. However, Governor Hunt had concerns about the developing crisis in the region and persuaded London to send *Endurance* back to South Georgia to evict the Argentines. Barker was ordered to keep his destination confidential for fear of 'escalating the incident'. The man who had reported Argentine belligerence over the Falklands and had caused some disquiet in the dusty corridors of the Foreign Office must have smiled wryly.

Five days later Lieutenant Keith Mills was looking forward to a few days ashore when he was told to embark his detachment on *Endurance*. Disappointed, because everyone was looking forward to some ground training after months at sea, at Moody Brook he was briefed by Major Gary Noott RM, commanding Naval Party 8901, on the situation and given a re-inforcement of a NCO and eight Royal Marines, which brought his detachment to nearly troop strength. To accommodate them, Barker disembarked an officer and ten sailors with instructions to complete the scientific records gathered during the summer. Early next day *Endurance* left Stanley

Although the BAS had agreed to pass information to Barker, throughout the crisis Steve Martin was careful not to jeopardize the civilian status of his team. Nevertheless Bob Headland, Peter Stark and, later, Neil Shaw established an observation post on Jason Peak overlooking Stromness Bay but could not see what was happening in Leith. Then, much to Martin's annoyance, because of the information they could share with the Argentines, the three Frenchmen, tired of their frosty reception at Grytviken, left for Leith where they were made welcome. They became unlikely witnesses to the hostilities between Argentina and Great Britain.

Barker arrived off South Georgia on the 23rd and waited for orders. When the Junta were briefed at their regular weekly meeting that she was still in the region, Foreign Minister Mendez was instructed to advise the British that any attempt to remove the Argentines would not be tolerated. For the next week *Endurance* continued hydrographic and charting work while the Royal Marines prepared her for action and took over manning the Jason Peak observation post. By now it was clear the Junta were not prepared to be humiliated by a forced removal from South Georgia; indeed it had become a convenient vehicle on which to escalate the crisis and give them an opportunity to regain the Falkland Islands.

During the night of the 24 March the naval transport *Bahia Paraiso*, which had been diverted from scientific work in the Antarctic, glided into Stromness Bay and landing craft disembarked about twelve naval technicians dressed as marines, who quickly moved out of sight into the derelict buildings. On board the ship was an Army 601 Combat Aviation Battalion Puma and a 1st Helicopter Squadron Alouette. That evening the three French dined with the Argentines in the whaling station's hospital, one of whom introduced himself as Alfredo Astiz.

As dawn broke on 25 March the observation post reported the *Bahia Paraiso* anchored in Stromness Bay. Because of the difficulty of seeing into

Leith, the observation post was moved next day to Grass Island, deep inside Stromness Bay, but even this was only a marginal improvement. Mindful of the need for information, Mills decided to carry out a close target recce. He and his highly experienced Detachment Sergeant Major, Sergeant Peter Leach, were landed from the BAS launch at the foot of Olsen Valley and, plodding through freezing rain, they scouted the abandoned whaling stations of Husvik and Stromness before concealing themselves in a rocky outcrop on Harbour Point, about 600 metres from Leith, and watched not only stores being unloaded from the *Bahia Paraiso* but also men in Argentine marine uniform milling around the jetty.

Meanwhile Captain Barker had joined Lieutenant Commander Tony Ellerbeck and his observer Lieutenant Wells in one of *Endurance's* Wasps for a flight over Olsen Valley. Landing on Tonsberg Point, they walked up a small hill to observe Leith. Buzzing around the harbour was the Alouette flown by Lieutenant Remo Busson who had been tasked to shadow *Endurance* and its helicopters. Unknowingly he had already forced Mills and Leach to seek cover. Meanwhile the two Royal Marines met Barker's party. However, it seems that Ellerbeck's blue Wasp had been seen and Busson was scrambled. Joined by Trombetta, he made one pass over the helicopter and then, hovering above the five Britons, Trombetta gave Barker the two-fingered archer's salute. Fully alerted that the British were watching them, Busson then found two tents used by the Royal Marines on Green Island. British surveillance operations were thereupon transferred to Busen Peninsula.

Argentina's sabre-rattling about South Georgia was not having the desired effect of forcing Britain to negotiate and the chiefs of staff advised the Junta that they were not in favour of a protracted engagement. Intelligence assessments, mostly from media comment in London, indicated British military preparations. Two reports were regarded to be significant, namely the cancellation of Exercise *Spring Train*, a large naval exercise in the Mediterranean, and the despatch of the nuclear submarine *Spartan* from Gibraltar to the South Atlantic. The sailing of two other submarines from Faslane was discounted. Political and popular attitudes in Great Britain were also hardening. The Junta considered it critical to bring forward the invasion date before Great Britain had time to mobilize sufficient forces to reinforce its interests in the South Atlantic. If it had to be mounted in early winter, the earliest date was 15 May although the preferred one was 9 July, Independence Day, but, with the crisis quickly deepening, D-Day was set for evening 2 or 3 April with the option of bringing it forward to the evening of 31 March.

During the afternoon of 26 March First Lieutenant Oscar Outlon, who commanded A Company 1st Marine Infantry Battalion, was ordered to attend a briefing at 2nd Marine Infantry Battalion. Expecting to receive orders for a forty-five day exercise in the barren Tierra del Fuego's Grand

Isle, he was shocked to be given orders for Operation *Carlos* and then instructed to form a sixty-strong composite platoon of a rifle section, an 81mm mortar section, a MAG section and a Tigercat surface-to-air missile detachment and blister it on to 2nd Marine Infantry Battalion. He was also instructed to form a second composite platoon to consist of two rifle sections, a 60mm mortar and a MAG section and place it under the command of Second Lieutenant Guillermo Luna for another operation.

The A69 frigate *Guerrico,* commanded by Commander Carlos Alfonso, was hurriedly withdrawn from dry dock, made ready for sea and loaded with Luna's platoon. Together with the *Bahia Paraiso*, she would form Task Force 60 to capture South Georgia.

Apart from those involved in the planning, very few were aware that Argentina, a country whose international experience was largely confined to South America and who hadn't fought a major war for 120 years, was about to declare war on Great Britain, whose international experience extended over several centuries across the world and who had the long habit of losing battles but winning wars.

Argentina's decision to opt for a winter campaign is briefly worth examining because it was so ill-judged. Most of the *Spring Train* ships were in Gibraltar preparing to return to the United Kingdom. A few days more, they would be tied up in their home ports and their complements on Easter leave but to the Argentine's cost, the ships simply turned left after leaving the Straits of Gibraltar and headed for the South Atlantic where the long winter nights would give them plenty of time to close inshore for bombardments and landings and withdraw unmolested. Equally, most of the Argentine Air Force could not operate at night and, critically, the February 1982 intake of conscripts were barely trained.

For the invasion of the Falklands, the Argentine force was divided into four separate elements. Providing an outer naval and air screen was Supporting Task Force 20 commanded by Captain Sarcona, who was flying his pennant on the carrier *Veinticinco de Mayo*. Major General Garcia, who was in command of the newly created Malvinas Theatre of Operations, was on board the ex-British Type 42 destroyer *Santisima Trinidad*, which would co-ordinate the landings and act as air traffic control after the airport had been seized. The submarine *Santa Fe* was designated as a special task force and carried a detachment of Tactical Divers.

Task Force 40 was the assault force, broken into a naval and an amphibious division. The Amphibious Force commander was Rear Admiral Gualter Allara, who had recently returned from London as Naval Attaché and was Chief of Fleet Operations. His role was to transport, protect and provide naval gunfire support for the 874-strong Landing Force, which was divided between the *Cabo San Antonio* and the *Almirante Irizar,* was commanded by Carlos Busser and built around the marine battalion landing team of A Company of the 1st and D and E Companies of the 2nd Marine

Infantry Battalions. The latter had recently exercised with the US Marine Corps on UNITAS. The Army was represented by 1st Platoon C Company 25th Infantry Regiment. In support was a Marine 105mm rocket battery, amphibious engineers, a Marine anti-aircraft battery and 1st Amphibious Vehicle Company equipped with LTVP-7 and LARC-5 amphibious tracked vehicles.

The original plan called for the Army platoon to capture Government House. Simultaneously the Amphibious Commando Grouping would seize Moody Brook barracks, ideally without shedding blood. It was vital to Busser's strategy to prevent NP 8901 entering Stanley from Moody Brook barracks or withdrawing into the 'camp' and carrying on a guerrilla campaign. 2nd Marine Infantry would then land at Yorke Bay, seize the airport and occupy Stanley. Casualties on both sides were to be kept to a minimum; the defenders must be made to believe that they were facing overwhelming odds and that resistence was pointless. Once the intervention force had completed its mission, an Air Force team would prepare the airport for the fly-in of the garrison, 25th Infantry Regiment, and the Army platoon would be helicoptered to Goose Green. Major General Garcia would then take command, pending the arrival of Brigadier General Mario Menendez, who had been appointed governor for the duration of the projected negotiations, reckoned to last until December.

Commanded by Lieutenant Colonel Mohammed Seineldin, a fervent patriot and Malvinist with a Lebanese background, 25th Infantry Regiment was usually based at Colonia Sarmiento in the sparsely populated southern province of Chubut and was part of 9th Infantry Brigade of 5th Army Corps. When warned that his regiment was earmarked for deployment to the Falklands, Seineldin renamed it the 25th 'Special' Infantry Regiment although Argentine journalists later christened it the Seineldin Commando Regiment. In Stanley he enlarged it to five companies of about 100 men each by adding D and E Companies. Most of the officers and NCOs were commandos and paratroopers and with a highly trained and motivated training team, he brought the best from his conscripts in a short but tough commando course. The regimental shoulderflash, which was designed by his wife Marta, depicted an armed Argentine soldier standing on the Falklands Islands. Seineldin had raised Halcon 8, the regular cadre for army commandos, and many of the techniques he employed were heavily influenced by unconventional warfare.

It was probably fortunate for the British that as a consequence of the political differences on the Falklands 25th Infantry Regiment remained dug in protecting the approaches to Stanley from the airport. Certainly Seineldin believed he should be allowed to attack 3rd Commando Brigade as it approached Stanley and was highly critical of Brigadier General Oscar Jofre, who commanded the Argentine ground forces in the campiagn, accusing him of 'sinking to zero'.

By 27 March Weinstabl's landing plan had been approved by Garcia and Busser and he ordered 'The Llamada Plan' summoning his marines to barracks. Next morning, the marine battalion landing team filed on board the *Cabo San Antonio* and the *Almirante Irizar,* ostensibly for another exercise. At 12.30 pm the ships weighed anchor and joined the Task Force assembling in the Rio de la Plata estuary. Next day orders were despatched for Task Force 40 to sail and Air Transport Command made its final preparations.

During the day the *Bahia Paraiso* left Leith and vanished into the South Atlantic. Ordered by London to search for her, after three fruitless days *Endurance* found her aimlessly cruising about fifteen miles north-east of Cumberland Bay. In atrocious weather, the two ships played cat and mouse amongst the islands, inlets, coves and icebergs of South Georgia as Barker struggled to maintain contact while Busson and his observer, Sub-Lieutenant Guillermo Guerra, doggedly kept *Endurance* under surveillance. It was important that Barker should not put himself in a position where she could be lost, captured or blockaded. On several occasions he attempted to contact Trombetta but it was obvious the relationship was very cool.

On 23 March the British Naval Attaché in Buenos Aires, Captain Mitchell, had flown to Montevideo to meet the incoming 1982/83 forty-strong NP 8901, which was commanded by Major Mike Norman RM. Norman had expected to be taken to Stanley by *Endurance,* but she was at South Georgia and it looked as though the Royal Marines would be stranded. Mitchell recognized them to be a valuable reinforcement and arrangements were made with the Foreign Office and the BAS for the RRS *John Biscoe* to take them to Stanley. On 29 March Norman's men moved straight into Moody Brook Barracks, while Noott's outgoing detachment was billeted in private accommodation, as was the custom. The use of the research ship gave Argentina the opportunity to claim that she and her sister ship, the *Bransfield,* were engaged in military activities.

Early on 31 March an Argentine newspaper reported the naval and military preparations, from which the British Government deduced that Argentina would invade the Falklands and South Georgia on 2 April and decided that, while she could not accept occupation of British territory, she would not escalate the dispute. Early in the afternoon Barker received orders from HQ Commander-in-Chief Fleet at Northwood to reinforce Britain's sovereignty of South Georgia and to give token protection to the BAS by landing Mills's Ship's Detachment. It was the first time the island had ever been garrisoned and Steve Martin was less than happy. Accountable to Governor Hunt, he now had the military to contend with. A meeting on board *Endurance* reached a compromise – while the present crisis lasted Martin would be in charge, but, if hostilities broke out, Mills would take over and the BAS would conduct themselves as civilians, which meant they were liable for internment.

Initially signals from London ordered Mills to fight to the end, but as the day wore on they became less belligerent and more diplomatically phrased to show the world that if Grytviken was occupied by Argentina, it was done so by force. Barker confirmed that the rules of engagement were to be based on the Yellow Card used by the Security Forces in Northern Ireland. Several types were used by British forces in Northern Ireland and Cyprus including ones dealing with making an arrest, searches and not opening fire until there was no alternative. Soldiers were expected to know the details and abide by them, even in the heat of an incident, and some of those who did not found themselves prosecuted for murder and manslaughter. Fortunately Mills and some of his Royal Marines had completed tours in Ulster and were familiar with the concept, not that they necessarily agreed with the conditions, clearly written by someone inexperienced in the rigours of military internal security.

When the Royal Marines moved into Shackleton House and dumped their stores in Quigley's House, this upset the comfortable routine of the scientists, most of whom had yet to grasp the seriousness of the international confrontation between Great Britain and Argentina. They were sharply reminded of their predicament when they heard Governor Hunt announce on the radio the imminent invasion of the Falklands by Argentina.

The Argentine planners' intention was for Task Force 40 to approach the Falkland Islands from the south and land early on 1 April, but a storm blew throughout the 29th and 30th. The marines on the two transports had an unpleasant time as the heavily overladen ships pitched and yawed violently in the steep seas. Most suffered from sea sickness. Speed was reduced and Garcia and Allara decided to postpone landing for twenty-four hours and to approach from the north. On 1 April Weinstabl broke the news of the invasion to his company commanders and they immediately set to work planning their roles in the operation. Recent air photographs and intelligence revealed that, since NP 8901 had been reinforced by Norman's detachment, the assault beaches and airport were likely to be defended. From the *Santisima Trinidad*, Garcia and Busser sent out new orders. The Amphibious Commandos were to land at Mullet Creek, move north across Stanley Common and simultaneously capture Government House and Moody Brook. The Army platoon was to seize the airport; its deployment to Goose Green was cancelled. Crossing the line of departure was timed for 5.30am on 1 April. During the storm Seineldin, a devout Catholic, had prayed to the Virgin of Rosario to calm the waters for the landings and at the final meeting he persuaded Busser that the operation should be dedicated to the *Virgin del Rosario*. Henceforth the invasion was known as Operation *Rosario*.

After dark Captain Barker, determined to dispense with the attentions of the Argentines, weighed anchor and taking the dangerous route through Merton Passage, kept close to the coast, slipped the cover of the *Bahia Paraiso* and steamed toward the Falklands at best speed into the teeth of a Force 10 gale to give what help he could.

During the day the USA made a concerted attempt to persuade Argentina to step back from open hostilities but it was clear to President Reagan that Galtieri did not want to stop Operation *Rosario*. Governor Hunt then received a signal from the Foreign Office which rather quaintly stated: 'We have apparently reliable information that an Argentine task force could be assembling off Cape Pembroke by dawn tomorrow. You will wish to make your dispositions accordingly.' He was somewhat taken aback for he believed South Georgia would be the centre of tension and had not been told a large amphibious force was at sea bound for the Falklands. He later wryly commented, 'It looks as though the silly buggers mean it'.

2

The Capture of the Falkland Islands and South Georgia

'This is British property. You are not invited.'
Governor Hunt to Admiral Busser after the surrender of the Falkland Islands.

On 1 April Major Norman assumed command of NP 8901 from Gary Noott. It now consisted of three Royal Marine officers, two Royal Navy officers, sixty-six Royal Marines, forty-three of whom had just arrived, and twenty-five looking forward to going home, and nine sailors landed from *Endurance*. Governor Hunt mobilized the Falklands Islands Defence Force but decided not to involve two RAF technicians engaged on classified activities on the islands; indeed to all intents and purposes they remained civilians.

At 11pm Norman briefed the apprehensive naval party at Moody Brook and told them his aim was to buy two weeks' bargaining time in the United Nations. By any standard, 8000 miles from Great Britain, it was a forlorn hope. The recently-arrived Corporal Stefan York, who had been reprimanded by Norman several months earlier, recalled that his manner raised morale, but knew the odds were heavily stacked against them. The concept of operations was to disrupt Argentine attempts to seize the harbour and Stanley Airport. Norman placed Corporal Duff's 5 Section at the airport and ordered that the runway be blocked with obstacles. A GPMG manned by Marines Milne and Wilcox covered the Yorke Bay beaches and had motorcycles for a quick getaway. Corporal Lou Armour's 1 Section was placed at Hookers Point and to his west was Lieutenant Bill Trollope and eight men on the edge of the old airstrip with a Carl Gustav and 66mm. A further kilometre west was 3 Section forming the nucleus for a stronghold. The idea was to delay the Argentine advance and then pepperpot through Stanley to Government House, the seat of government. Corporal Carr's 5 Section was placed on Murrell Heights to cover the southern approaches. In a lonely observation post on Sapper Hill was Marine Mike Berry, also with a motorcycle. Across Stanley Harbour on Navy Point was York's No 6 Section ready to engage enemy vessels breaching the narrows; tucked into a cove was their Gemini. Major Noott was appointed military adviser to the Governor. Norman set up his Tactical Headquarters on Look Out Rocks. The final position for all sections was Government House. The war stores

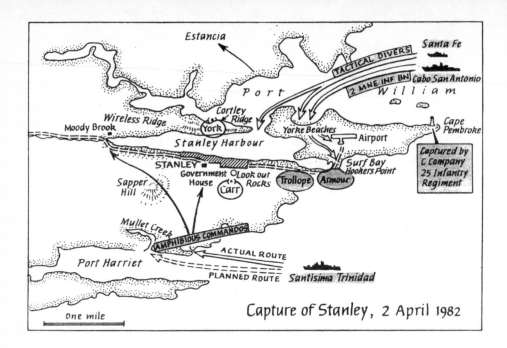

Capture of Stanley, 2 April 1982

were pathetic. The single 81mm mortar tube was cracked and the few rolls of barbed wire were stretched across Yorke Bay beach.

Norman's plan was not markedly different from that of Major Ewen Southby-Tailyour RM, who had commanded NP 8901 from 1977 to 1979. He planned to buy time by blocking both airfields and disrupting landings on Yorke, Pilot and Surf Bays with two four-man sections in prepared bunkers, who would then conduct a fighting withdrawal to Stanley. He opted for three lines of defence, one north-south on the eastern outskirts in the rocks of Hookers Point, the second in the town and the third around Government House, which would be converted into a stronghold. Moody Brook would be abandoned. A fourth section was placed in a covert static position to pass information to the Ministry of Defence and a concealed transmitter room was installed in the attic of Government House. Another section was to be concealed on Cortley Ridge and had a secondary role to move to a hide stocked with pre-dumped supplies overlooking Port Salvador and provide a point of contact for relief forces. In *Reasons in Writing*, Southby-Tailyour says that the civilians had no idea of the Royal Marine deployment, which is probably incorrect. During the counter-intelligence operation after the Argentine surrender, a Falkland Islander said the operational activities of the Royal Marines were well known to the islanders. Whether or not they were well known to them, they were probably well known to the LADE office, the centre of Argentine intelligence operations.

The response by the Falkland Islands Defence Force was disappointing, but the twenty-three men who did report were assigned to a series of observation posts. Former Royal Marine Jim Fairfield was attached to

Government House and the Canadian Bill Curtis, a former air traffic controller, was sent to Stanley Airport to deactivate the directional beacon. Jack Sollis, skipper of the motor coaster *Forrest,* acted as a seaborne radar beacon in Port William and the Cape Pembroke lighthouse keeper Basil Biggs switched off the lamp and watched for shipping from his high vantage point. Patrick Watts kept the radio station open. Meanwhile Chief Secretary Baker, Constable Lamb and the Royal Navy detachment under the command of Colour Sergeant Noone began rounding up Argentines. By 2am on 2 April everyone was in position.

Shortly after 9pm on 1 April, the *Santisima Trinidad* hove-to about 500 metres south of Mullet Creek. The night was calm, there was a light swell and a full moon peeped from scudding clouds. The coast itself was dark apart from the sand glinting on the beaches and the occasional twinkling light. The duty deck watch lowered twenty-one Gemini inflatables. On deck were ninety-two members of the Amphibious Commando Grouping under Lieutenant Commander Guillermo Sanchez-Sabarots.

Lieutenant Schweitzer and a small advance guard first secured the beachhead at Mullet Creek. The main party then pushed off from the grey hull of the gently swaying destroyer, but the current nudged the Geminis north and the outboard engines spluttered to a halt as propellers tangled with long entrails of tough and unforgiving kelp. The commandos whispered curses and cut at the kelp, earnestly hoping they would not be swept out to sea and also would not be detected. On Sapper Hill Marine Berry reported engines being gunned from the south, but at Government House these were interpreted to be helicopters. Schweitzer was unaware that the main party was in difficulties. The commandos extracted themselves from the kelp but some engines then refused to start and others had seized beyond immediate repair. Nevertheless they landed near Lake Point and by 11pm had met Schweitzer's party. Picking up a fenceline, which passed to the west of Sapper Hill, Sanchez-Sabarots' team set off to attack Moody Brook. Lieutenant Commander Pedro Giachino, usually second-in-command of the 1st Marine Infantry Battalion and a volunteer for the mission, skirted Sapper Hill and approached Government House. It was now about 1.30am

At 11pm the *Santa Fe* slowly surfaced off Kidney Island and was reported to Government House by Sollis. Ten Tactical Divers in three Zodiacs motored to the beach east of Yorke Point, crossed to Yorke Bay, checked its beach, nicknamed 'Red Beach', for enemy positions and erected navigation beacons. A small group then motored to the eastern arm of the Port Stanley narrows to watch for British activity in Stanley Harbour. 200 yards across the still dark water was York's section on Cortley Ridge.

By about 5.30am Sanchez-Sabarots was approaching Moody Brook. The going had been hard and it took nearly five hours to cover six miles through territory assumed to be patrolled by the enemy. Some commandos had temporarily lost contact with the column and the lead scout, Lieutenant

19

Bardi, had broken his ankle in a fall and was left behind with an escort. Sanchez-Sabarots's plan was to capture the Royal Marines as they broke out from the barracks. Those who managed to evade capture were to be channelled by the judicious use of MAGs positioned south of Moody Brook along an escape route towards Cortley Hill where they would be unable to reinforce the defence of Government House and could be rounded up. Casualties were to be avoided.

The barracks were ominously quiet, although a light burned in a cabin. No sentries were seen and the night was silent apart from the occasional animal call. Sanchez-Sabarots had expected to hear firing from Government House as some evidence that the main landings had taken place; nevertheless he ordered the attack to begin. Stun and tear gas grenades were hurled into the buildings, but no coughing Royal Marines stumbled out and there was no return fire. The commandos checked the barracks, found nothing and deployed into all-round defence.

Lying on a small hillock south of the House, Giachino split his sixteen men on both sides of Government House. Using night vision aids, the Argentines watched troops moving in and around the buildings and several vehicles parked in the drive. Although the firing at Moody Brook signalled that the Falklands were now under attack, Giachino went ahead with the original plan of entering Government House by a back door and inviting Governor Hunt to surrender.

Hunt admits that he had unwisely given a set of plans of Government House earlier in the year to an Argentine visitor, who claimed to be an architect but it seems that Giachino had not seen them. At about 6.15am, leading four men, he kicked open a back door but they found themselves in the servants' annex, which was empty. Realizing their error, they vaulted a wall into a garden but were seen by Corporals Sellen and Fleet and Marine Dorey covering the annex, who cut the Argentines down at close range. Giachino was badly wounded in the thigh and fell holding a pinless grenade. Lieutenant Quiroga was wounded in the arm. The three survivors dashed into the maid's quarters. Seeing Giachino was wounded, medic Urbina crawled over to tend him but was himself injured by a grenade splinter. Versions of what happened next vary. Both sides agree that the British invited Giachino to throw away the grenade so he could be helped, but he could not do so without the risk of it bouncing back. Since he did not speak any English and none of those inside Government House spoke Spanish, a stalemate developed and the wounded Argentines were left where they were.

When Major Norman at Look Out Rocks heard the firing unexpectedly coming from Moody Brook he drove back to Government House. Realizing that his tiny force would need to face more than one direction, as the Argentines had planned, he decided to centralize at the seat of government and radioed all sections to withdraw to Government House. Chief Secretary Baker had returned, having confined about thirty Argentines, most of whom were employees of *Yacimientos Petroliferos Fiscales*, the Argentine State Oil Company, in a house near Stanley Police Station. Governor Hunt asked Baker to finish the job himself because the naval detachment was required at Government House. As Baker opened the door to leave, a hail of machine-gun fire tore into the brickwork and sent slivers of stone and dust zinging all over the place. Norman, who had only just arrived, ran out to the defensive perimeter shouting, 'Who fired those shots?' Another burst provided the answer and he sensibly retired inside and took up a firing position. Baker joined Hunt underneath the governor's desk. Meanwhile the Royal Marines were steadily exchanging shots with the Argentines.

While the amphibious commandos were approaching their objectives, Sollis and Briggs both reported the *Cabo San Antonio* and its close escort of the destroyer *Hercules* and corvette *Drummond* hove-to in Port William about a mile north-east of Yorke Bay. Reveille for the Embarked Force had been at 4.00am and after breakfast the troops were called by tannoy to the tank deck. An hour later the marines and soldiers sat inside eighteen LVTP-7 and several LARC-5 amtracs while commanders checked their weapons and drivers warmed the engines. The noise was so great in the confines of the tank deck that messages could only be passed by the inter-vehicle radio net. At 6.20am the bow doors opened releasing a cloud of blue exhaust and the amtracs company commander, First Lieutenant Forbice, ordering 'Move now', experienced a surge of patriotism as Argentina set off to recover that which rightly belonged to the nation. Using a red lamp to hold vehicles and then green when the ramp was clear, a naval officer controlled the disembarkation.

The leading wave of four LVTP-7s, carrying Lieutenant Commander Santillan's advance guard, a platoon of First Lieutenant Carlos Arruani's E Company and Second Lieutenant Roberto Reyes' 25th Infantry Regiment platoon, flopped into the sea and slowly motored forward. In the second wave of fourteen amtracs was First Lieutenant Francisco di Paola's D Company, the remainder of E Company and several command LVTPs including Busser's and Weinstabl's amtracs. Busser's LVTP-7's deflector plate, which controlled the flow of water, failed to engage and the amtrac turned in circles until the driver engaged reverse, which pushed the water through both sides and straightened the vehicle's course. And so Busser, planner of the landings, approached the beaches in Argentina's most high-profile campaign in ignominious reverse. Bringing up the rear was a LVTR-7 recovery amtrac and a LARC-5 loaded with ammunition, medical supplies and other essential stores.

Approaching the beach, Santillan picked out the red navigation beacon and ordered the advance guard into an assault formation. At exactly 6.30am, H-Hour, the tracks gripped the sandy shallows of the Falklands, the drivers switched from water propulsion and the amtracs hauled themselves out of the water and lumbered across the beach. Santillan radioed to Weinstabl that there was no sign of the enemy and the upper hatches were ordered to be opened. Fully expecting to be ambushed, he guided the vehicles into a narrow gully and then, reaching a track, turned east to Stanley Airport. The three E Company amtracs took up fire positions to Reyes' infantry, who had disembarked from their LVTP-7 and were fanning out across the runway expecting enemy fire but there was none. The marines dismantled several obstacles while Reyes pushed on to capture the Cape Pembroke lighthouse. Meanwhile D Company had joined Santillan on the road to Stanley. At about 7.15am they passed Hookers Point, still expecting an ambush.

The column trundled past the old airfield and near the Ionospheric Research Station came across several obstacles on the road, including a yellow road repair machine. As the leading amtrac negotiated the obstacles, it was engaged by Trollope's machine-gunner. Marine Gibbs missed with a 66mm but a second Carl Gustav round fired by Marine Brown struck the amtrac a glancing blow on the glacis plate. As the Argentines disembarked into cover, the machine gunner laced the vehicle and when no one appeared, this led the Royal Marines to believe they had killed everyone inside.

Weinstabl ordered Santillan to form a firebase with the Recoilless Rifles and mortars and ordered D Company to assault the enemy. Trollope recognized Weinstabl's intent, and after throwing a purple smoke grenade, pulled his section back into Stanley, leaving the Argentines to deploy the two rifle companies north and south into the town. Woken by the amtrac drivers revving their engines, the shocked townspeople suddenly found themselves occupied. Santillan's advance guard pushed on toward Moody Brook and met Sanchez-Sabarots and his weary commando detachment plodding along the road to Government House.

Busser was anxious. Nothing had been heard from the Amphibious Commando Grouping, although the occasional shot could be heard from Government House. At 7.30am he ordered Lieutenant Commander Barro to send two white anti-submarine warfare Sea Kings to the *Almirante Irizar* to lift ashore A Company, 1st Marine Infantry Battalion and Lieutenant Perez's 105 mm rocket launchers. From his lonely vigil on Sapper Hill, Mike Berry reported this to Government House. Falkland Islanders later also reported 'two large white helicopters' ferrying troops ashore.

Armour and Figg had set up a defensive position outside the Post Office and were joined by Wilcox and Milne. Carr then joined Armour to infiltrate to Government House but it was clear from the invitations to surrender by the Argentines and the colourful responses from Government House that this was a non-starter. The Royal Marines withdrew when they came under fire and returned to the Post Office. In their second attempt Armour's section melted into the shadows of a hedge near the football field and reached Government House. At the Post Office jetty, intending to join York, Carr persuaded Sollis to lower *Forrest's* dinghy into the water but the engine stubbornly refused to fire. Failing to induce Sollis to take his vessel across Stanley Harbour, the Royal Marines went below to await events.

Meanwhile at Government House the Argentine commandos hiding in the maid's bedroom decided to make their move, but were heard by Major Noott who fired several shots into the ceiling. The three Argentines came tumbling down the stairs and surrendered. Governor Hunt had decided that further resistance was pointless and sent for Air Force Lieutenant Colonel Hector Gilobert. Gilobert was well known as the former consul in Stanley and had returned ostensibly to sort out some financial problems at the LADE offices but he was widely believed to be an intelligence officer and the main source of information about Naval Party 8901's deployment. Chief Secretary Baker had not been able to intern him.

Listening to the situation reports from Major Norman, Stefan York decided it was time to leave. After booby-trapping the barrel of the Carl Gustav with phosphorus grenades, he radioed that he was going 'fishing', a cryptic reference to a comment he had earlier made to Norman when asked what he would do if the Argentines invaded. York's section launched their Gemini from Navy Point, and paddling out of the kelp, they started the outboard engine and were heading north when they found themselves apparently being pursued by a destroyer. They made for the shadows of a Polish fishing factory ship and then, keeping inshore, found a small beach, hid the Gemini and melted into the 'camp'. They had only their fighting order. Their packs containing sleeping bags were still at Moody Brook.

Hunt asked Gilobert to negotiate. On the *Santisima Trinidad* Major General Garcia was delighted and passed cease-fire proposals to Busser in Stanley, who suggested meeting the British in front of St Mary's Church. But the white flag he had ordered to be taken had not been packed and several plastic waste disposal bags were used instead. The parley parties walked together to Government House where Busser introduced himself to Hunt, Noott and Norman. Except for the antagonistic attitude of the chief military security officer, Major Patricio Dowling, who was of Irish extraction and definitely did not like the British, the negotiations were all very civil, even though Hunt refused to shake hands with Busser, telling him 'he was an intruder'. There was then the inevitable 'We are stronger than you. I have my duty to do' between the two men. Hunt consulted with the two Royal Marine officers and, realizing that further resistence was quite hopeless, agreed to surrender and 149 years of British colonial rule passed to Argentina and an uncertain future.

Weinstabl reached Government House just as the Royal Marines were surrendering to the Amphibious Commando Grouping. While Noott was escorted to bring the Royal Marines still in Stanley to Government House, British and Argentines went into the garden to attend to the three wounded commandos. Giachino, weak from loss of blood, was gently lifted into an amtrac but died soon afterwards. A eulogy written for him by a lady in Argentina was found on many prisoners during the campaign. The time was

9.20am. The humiliating photograph of captured Royal Marines prone on the road was flashed around the world. Not since Korea at the Imjin River had there been a mass surrender of British forces. An officer told them to get to their feet, apologised and directed them to the football field. A suave Argentine Army officer then strolled over and asked if everyone could be accounted for. A headcount established that Corporal York and four men were missing. The Royal Marines, suffering from the shock of capture, had forgotten not to divulge military information. The officer replied, 'Gracias'.

The Third Geneva Convention requires prisoners of war to give only their number, name, rank and date of birth, the basic data required by the International Committee of the Red Cross to identify captured and retained personnel. Interrogation is allowed provided it does not resort to an assault on the dignity of the prisoner. Since interrogation is an attack on the memory of the prisoner, only naive and poor interrogators use violence. It is of some interest that even after the Falklands campaign and the experiences of NP 8901, practical conduct-after-capture training was still given only to those categorized as 'prone to capture'. Of these, only one RAF and one SAS were captured during the campaign. The rest were apparently not prone to capture and this meant that the vast majority of British prisoners had no idea what to expect or how to behave if captured, except from very occasional theoretical training.

The Navy had done their job and it was now the turn of the Army to garrison the Falklands. Major General Garcia, as Military Governor of the Malvinas, South Georgia and the South Sandwich Islands, and Rear Admiral Allara, were helicoptered ashore and met Busser near Government House. All were euphoric that their forces had achieved their objectives with the minimum loss of life, as they had planned. At 12.15pm, in a short ceremony, the Union flag at Government House was replaced by the Argentine flag and several place names were changed to Spanish, including Stanley, which was renamed Puerto Argentino.

When word arrived that Stanley was secure, the Argentine Air Force's contribution to the intervention, Operation *Aries 82,* began when the first flight, a C-130 and two F-29 Fellowships, took off from Military Air Base Comodoro Rivadavia carrying the remainder of 25th Infantry Regiment and several Air Force specialists. Two hours later the army were taking over from the marines and digging-in around the airport, where, much to the frustration and annoyance of Mohammed Seineldin, most would remain until the war ended. An Air Force AN/TPS-43F surveillance radar was placed near the airport. In accordance with the strategy, Garcia issued orders for the intervention force to withdraw and during the afternoon the returning aircraft flew to Argentina with their own marines, the captured Royal Marine and civilian detainees. Most of NP 8901 later joined the Task Force as J Company 42 Commando to replace M Company, which took part in the recapture of South Georgia.

Although the chance of a British reaction was almost nil, it was nevertheless a tense night punctured with several outbreaks of firing as the jittery conscripts fired at shadows. Somewhere to the north-west York's section reached a remote shepherd's cottage near Estancia owned by a Mrs Watson. New to the Falklands, hindered by the lack of local knowledge, without a radio, cut off from the outside world and concerned about the safety of Mrs Watson if they were captured, York had no alternative but to surrender, and on 4 April he used a kelper's radio to advise the Argentine authorities he wished to do so. The Royal Marines buried their weapons and most of the rations and awaited their fate about which, knowing the reputation of the Argentines, they were not optimistic. Major Dowling and a 181 Military Police Company detachment arrived by helicopter, roughly searched them, tied them with wire and locked them up in Stanley Police station. Dowling later overstepped his authority on several other occasions and was sent back to Argentine in near disgrace in early June.

600 miles to the east, the same gale which had delayed the Argentine invasion was still blowing across South Georgia. At Leith, on hearing the news that the Falklands had been captured, Lieutenant Commander Astiz held a parade, which the French yachtsmen filmed, and raised two Argentine flags in the forty-mile-an-hour wind whipping in from the south. The national anthem was sung and then Astiz declared that with effect from 2 April, 1982, South Georgia would be known as 'Isla San Pedro'. The Argentine strategic intention had been to capture the Dependencies on the same day but the bad weather had precluded the South Georgia operation so Astiz's proclamation was a little premature. There was just one more thing to do – deal with the British at Grytviken.

Keith Mills also heard about the capture of the Falklands on the radio and knew it would only be a matter of time before the Argentines arrived. Following the departure of *Endurance,* he had lost the ability to fly men daily to the Jason Peak OP; nevertheless keen to keep an eye on the Argentines, he sent Corporal Nigel Peters and three Royal Marines by the BAS launch to man it permanently. It was a cold, windswept place and rain and driving sleet often blotted the harbour. Transmissions were kept to a minimum. Mills and Sergeant Leach then planned the defence of Grytviken.

Protected by 100 foot scree cliffs, Mills selected a thirty-foot-high plateau north-west of Shackleton House as his defensive position. As it was still covered in summer tussock grass concealment was not difficult for the four two-man and two three-man trenches covering the approaches from Grytviken and the King Edward Point beach. Corporal Thomsen's five-strong section and a GPMG were placed in front of Shackleton House to enfilade anyone landing on the beach. A two-man LMG section covered the left flank. The assault engineer Marine Daniels, helped by Marines Porter and Church, mined other beaches below the Customs House and several houses were wired with improvised but lethal explosive devices made from

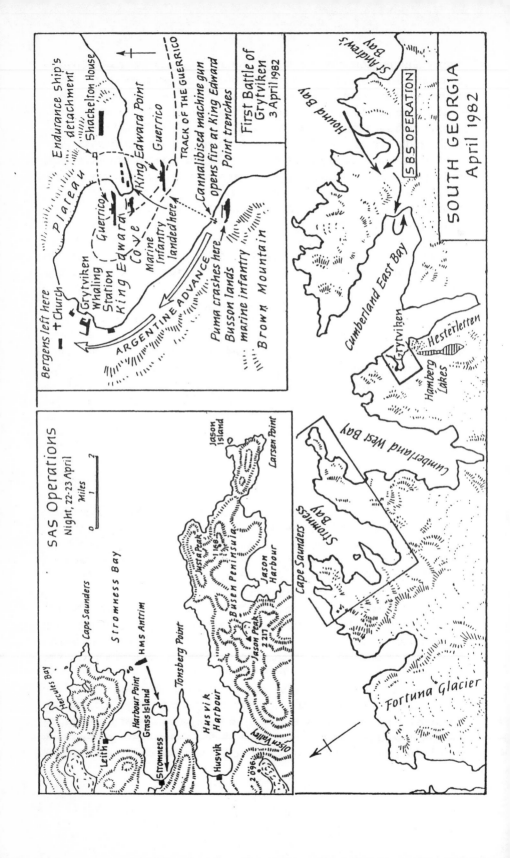

SOUTH GEORGIA
April 1982

St Andrew's Bay

Hound Bay

SBS OPERATION

Cumberland East Bay

Grytviken

Hesterletten

Hamberg Lakes

Cumberland West Bay

Cape Saunders

Stromness Bay

Cape Saunders

Fortuna Glacier

First Battle of Grytviken
3 April 1982

Endurance ship's detachment
Shackleton House
Plateau
King Edward Point
Guerrico
TRACK OF THE GUERRICO
Guerrico
King Edward Cove
Cannalibised machine gun opens fire at King Edward Point trenches
Marine Infantry landed here
Grytviken whaling Station
+ Church
Bergens left here
ARGENTINE ADVANCE
Puma crashes here
Busson lands marine infantry
Brown Mountain

SAS Operations
Night, 22-23 April

Miles
0   1   2

Hercules Bay

Cape Saunders

Stromness Bay

HMS Antrim

Harbour Point
Grass Island
Leith

Tonsberg Point

Stromness

Husvik Harbour

Husvik

Olsen Valley

Busen Peninsula

Justa Peak

Jason Peak
2 217

2 096

Jason Harbour

Jason Island

Larsen Point

empty ammunition tins and bits of metal. The jetty was mined with a command-detonated 45-gallon oil drum filled with a lethal cocktail of petrol, paint and plastic explosive.

Mills planned to hold out until dark, then collect their bergens, more ammunition and rations, which was cached at the whalers' church, withdraw to the 2000-foot Mount Hodges and march north to Maiviken from where they would conduct a guerrilla campaign. With their annual winter training in Norway, the Royal Marines were well suited to winter warfare, which the Argentine's conscripts were not. Steve Martin sent three BAS to join the wildlife photographers Cindy Buxton and Annie Price in St Andrew's Bay.

The Royal Marines were preparing their positions when the *Bahia Paraiso* appeared out of the gloom of a rainstorm and Captain Trombetta radioed Martin that next morning he should stand by for an important message. His brazen tactics were influenced by the loss of surprise after the Argentine victory on the Falklands, the disappearance of *Endurance* and the poor weather. Mills passed this message to Captain Barker and was told: 'The Officer Commanding Royal Marines is not repeat not to take any action which may endanger lives'. This confused Mills for it contravened the Yellow Card rules of engagement to the extent that he was not allowed to open fire; yet, how could he now put up a token resistence?

3rd April dawned bright and calm with a gentle breeze barely disturbing the sea. Sergeant Leach and Steve Martin were debating the feasibility of recovering Peters when, co-incidentally, he radioed that they had photographed a warship enter Stromness Bay and then refuel from the *Bahia Paraiso*. Among Peters' men was Marine McCallion, an Ulsterman who had served an apprenticeship with Harland & Wolff, which had given him an appetite for naval matters. He recognized the ship to be a French Type A69 frigate and was able to give Mills some basic information. Fast, lightly armoured, her twin Exocets and her anti-submarine capability were useless against land targets; nevertheless she carried a useful dual-purpose 100mm semi-automatic gun on the forecastle and a 40mm anti-aircraft gun on her stern. It was the *Guerrico* with Second Lieutenant Luna's marines, who were transferred to the *Bahia Paraiso*.

Trombetta and Astiz finalized the plan. In simple terms, the Alouette would first recce the area and then fly the marines ashore to occupy the BAS accommodation at King Edward Point, followed by the Army Puma flying in more men to occupy Grytviken. The Argentines were unaware that Mills's men were ashore and military resistance was not expected but, if it was encountered, the *Guerrico* would bombard the enemy.

While Leach recovered Peters in a Gemini, *Guerrico's* sudden presence gave added impetus to Mills's preparations. Shortly before 9.30am Lieutenant Busson lifted off from the *Bahia Paraiso* and headed for Grytviken to check the state of the beach a few metres south of the gaol in preparation for the Army Puma landing the marines. He flittered around the area for at least ten minutes, including flying over the position on the plateau, but saw nothing unusual – no troops and no obvious military defences. The Royal Marines remained motionless in their trenches. Satisfied that there were no enemy military ashore, Busson swung away and headed north back to his ship.

At about 10am the *Bahia Paraiso* steamed into Cumberland East Bay and Trombetta called up Steve Martin on the radio: 'Following our successful operation in the Malvinas, your ex-governor has unconditionally surrendered the Falklands and its dependencies. We suggest you adopt a similar course of action to prevent further loss of life. A cease-fire is now in force.' This message contained two blatant items of disinformation. First, Governor Hunt had surrendered the Falklands but not the dependencies. Second, although the UN Security Council had been endeavouring to persuade both sides to agree to a cease-fire, it had been unsuccessful. After conferring with Mills, Martin asked for two hours to consider the implications of the message. He needed to drag the talks out until the afternoon which would buy time for Barker to return. If it came to a battle, the less time spent defending in daylight the better, and an afternoon withdrawal into the mountains would give the Royal Marines a better chance of evasion.

Pretending his low-powered VHF set was faulty, Martin repeated the message on his HF set, hoping that the *Endurance's* radio operators would pick it up, which they did. Breaking radio silence, Barker tried to contact Mills to release him from the rules-of-engagement constraints, but, although virtually every other station in the region heard his efforts, he could not raise Grytviken. When Trombetta radioed that he would be sending marines ashore, Martin told him any such act was illegal and any landings would be met by the military presence on the island. This failed to impress Trombetta and, believing he had the advantage, he lost patience and ordered Martin to assemble everyone on the beach. Although under pressure from Martin not to jeopardize his men uselessly, Mills took over and issued final orders to his men. Martin sent the remaining thirteen scientists to the church to await the outcome of the inevitable battle.

At about 12pm Martin and Mills, both standing outside the radio shack, watched Trombetta bring his ship into Cumberland East Bay and launch Remo Busson for a second time. Commander Alfonso then nosed the *Guerrico* into the bay, her guns trained on Shackleton House. Mills, believing the Argentines were sending a boat to discuss the situation, walked to the jetty accompanied by Daniels and his explosives team. The frigate moved slowly past King Edward Point and went about. Mills's puzzlement at the manoeuvre was distracted by Busson landing seven marines in shallow water at the tip of the point. He waved at the Argentines and pointed to his windproof to indicate there were British troops ashore. The fifth man to jump out of the helicopter tapped his colleague in front on the shoulder and pointed at the Briton. The marine aimed his rifle at Mills, who did a smart about turn and, with Daniels' team, sprinted up the plateau and joined Marine White in his trench. The Alouette left in a swirl of freezing spray and the Argentines dashed for cover into the buildings.

First Lieutenant Alejandro Villagra, the pilot of the Army Puma, took off from the *Bahia Paraiso* with a stick of fifteen marines and, approaching Grytviken from Mount Hodges, was advised by Busson to land his stick further along the beach so they could spread out and link up with the first group. However, the Puma was fitted with skis and Villagra needed somewhere flat to land, but, yawing left and right, could not find anywhere. Mills saw his dilemma and ordered his men to open fire. Virtually every weapon that the Royal Marines could train on the aircraft fired at the troop compartment killing two marines, wounding several others and damaging the hydraulics. Inexplicably, few shots were registered on the cockpit and, in a demonstration of fine airmanship, Villagra and his co-pilot, First Lieutenant Eduardo Leguizamon, coaxed the smoking aircraft away from immediate danger and across the bay where it crashed-landed near the Hummocks and rolled on to its side. Busson's Alouette was slightly damaged in the rear fuselage by the same fusillade and landed close to the smoking Puma to see what help he could give.

Meanwhile the seven marines had broken cover and skirmished toward Shackleton House and Lance Corporal Thomsen's position. At a range of no more than 100 metres Marine Holding opened up with his GPMG and sent the Argentines scuttling into nearby buildings. With a military presence now definitely confirmed to be ashore, Trombetta ordered Alfonso to bombard King Edward Point. *Guerrico* steamed into the bay broadside to the Royal Marines, but, even at maximum depression, most of her 100mm shells smashed into the scree behind the plateau. The deeper Alfonso penetrated King Edward Cove, progressively less ably could he manoeuvre. At a range of no more than about 550 metres, Mills ordered his men to fire at the ship with every available weapon. The target was massive and she staggered under the impact of hundreds of rounds ripping through her thin plates. In an action that would have a significant impact on the battle, Marine David Coombes, normally a steward in *Endurance's* senior rates' mess, fired a 10lb Carl Gustav projectile. The Royal Marines watched it stagger across the white-tipped waves and then, almost on its last legs, smash into the *Guerrico* just above the waterline, sending up a column of white water below the stack amidships. A barely discernible rumble followed from inside.

The frigate reeled under the impact and, below, damage-control parties fought to stop the flow of freezing water rushing in through buckled hull plates. A seaman was killed and several were wounded by flying metal and glass. Pipes and electrical cables were severed, including those serving the traverse of the 100mm gun. Aft, the 40mm was putting useful bursts on to the plateau until the gun crew were cut down by Parsons and Chubb firing accurate bursts with their LMG. The ship moved out of sight behind the BAS buildings, except to Sergeant Leach, who, as she manoeuvred to go about, lay on a table in an upstairs room of Shackleton House and fired fifteen rounds into the bridge, using his sniper rifle and causing consternation as officers and ratings sought shelter from the fusillade.

The *Guerrico* turned through 180 degrees and her stern dropped as she picked up speed to run the gauntlet. Thick black smoke poured from her stack. Coombes and his Number Two, Marine Stonestreet, having already experienced several frustrating misfires, loosed a second projectile which smashed into the hull below the Exocet elevation and launching gear. It is a matter of conjecture whether they could perhaps have turned the tide of history had the projectiles been more reliable. The frigate was again raked from stem to stern, over 1000 strikes later being counted. Corporal Peters was standing head and shoulders out of his trench to have another shot at the ship with a 66mm when he was severely wounded in the arm and shoulder by a rifleman firing from inside the BAS buildings below the plateau.

While the contest between the Royal Marines and *Guerrico* was taking place, Busson's gunner, Petty Officer Gatti, and the Puma loadmaster, Sergeant Jorge Medin, cannibalized a machine gun from the wrecked helicopter and fired across the bay at the Britsh position. Busson was steadily flying the wounded from the Puma to the *Bahia Paraiso* and returned each time with two marines, whom he dropped wherever he could to avoid British fire. In all, Busson flew twenty such sorties and by the time the action was over he had been in the air for three hours; his contribution to the battle was significant. In spite of steady, long-range shooting across the cove, the Royal Marines were unable to stop the Alouette. By this time Luna's marines had advanced to Grytviken and the Royal Marines were in danger of being cut off from making their escape to the mountains.

3,500 yards out to sea, the battered *Guerrico* turned. Her elevation and traverse gear badly damaged, she opened fire with her main armament by training her bows on King Edward Point and four shells in quick succession bracketed the plateau. The situation on the ground had reached a stalemate. The Royal Marines had won a moral victory, shot down a helicopter, damaged another and badly wounded the only enemy warship in the area, but she was still prowling offshore; their strategic position was precarious. Their one casualty badly needed expert attention. On the other hand Mills's men were safe in their defensive positions and had plenty of ammunition. Luna's marines, however, had cut the track to Grytviken. Although *Endurance* was somewhere, she had no troops and was outgunned. During a lull in the shelling, Mills told his men he intended to surrender. The decision was by no means unanimous. Sergeant Leach, a veteran of several of Britain's bushfire wars, suggested they should make for the mountains. Nevertheless he passed the word to cease firing.

The Argentine marines were also cut off from resupply and knew that any attempt to lift them off the beach would be met with devastating fire; they were also low on ammunition. They were thus a little surprised to see a white coat being waved from the plateau and a figure walking down the slope. An Argentine marine left cover and met Lieutenant Mills, who told him that, although his men were well dug in, continued fighting would only result in pointless killing and he was prepared to surrender if the safety of the Royal Marines could be guaranteed. It was, so Mills called his men down the hill, unarmed. The Argentines were astonished to discover that they had been fighting against just twenty-two men and initially suspected a ruse. From the moment of capture the Royal Marines were treated with respect.

Astiz came ashore and, after acknowledging Mills's advice about the mined beach and jetty, invited Daniels to make the areas safe, which is contrary to the terms of the Geneva Convention. Nigel Peters was handed over to an Argentine doctor on the *Bahia Paraiso*, where he received expert treatment and made a good recovery. After a brief search, the Royal Marines, except for Mills, were ferried by landing craft to the transport and accommodated in several noisy cabins below the flight deck and above the engines. All the BAS were accounted for except Steve Martin, but he eventually turned up, having spent two hours sheltering from the fighting in a wet and cold gully dressed only in a shirt and slacks. Shortly before dusk Mills and the BAS were also transferred to the *Bahia Paraiso*. Calling in at Rio Grande, the dead and wounded, including Peters, were taken ashore and then the transport placed herself midway between the mainland and the Falklands as a refuelling point for helicopters en route to Stanley.

Meanwhile *Endurance* had arrived offshore and Barker despatched Ellerbeck to find out what was happening ashore. Settling his Wasp on a ridge overlooking Grytviken, he could offer nothing more than moral support to the Royal Marines and pass information on the engagement back to the ship.

On 13 April the prisoners and detainees were transferred to a large covered swimming pool at Bahia Blanca naval base and placed in the care of Lieutenant Alemmano, who did his best to see to their basic needs. The following day Peters rejoined the detachment with the exciting news that a task force had sailed from the United Kingdom to recover the Falklands and its lost dependencies. By then NP 8901 had been repatriated. On 15 April Mills and Martin agreed to be interviewed by a tribunal of senior naval officers inquiring into the conduct of the Argentine forces on South Georgia. Martin was careful to emphasize the civilian nature of his men. Mills refused to allow the JNCOs to appear before the tribunal but Sergeant Leach stuck only to number, rank, name and date of birth. Various visits were paid to the prisoners and then on the 16th they were taken to an airfield and, after meeting with Stefan York's section, were flown to Uruguay and handed over to British officials for repatriation.

Converted into heroes by the British Government, the Royal Marines were booked into a luxurious hotel in Montevideo and then early on 19 April, they boarded an RAF VC-10 for the long flight to Brize Norton. On board were several Joint Service Interrogation Wing and Intelligence Corps men who debriefed each man from South Georgia, looking for information useful to the Task Force. In the United Kingdom there were yet more debriefings and media interviews for several of the now exhausted Royal Marines. A brief period of leave followed and then Mills was asked if he would return to *Endurance*, which was short of nearly twenty-one crew and desperately needed her Royal Marines. Returning via Ascension Island, they had the satisfaction of guarding Astiz on the RFA *Tidespring*, and then on 25 May Mills's detachment filed on board their ship off Grytviken.

Argentina's euphoria was short-lived. At a debate at the United Nations on 3 April, British condemnation of Argentina's aggression was upheld and Resolution 502 was passed which demanded a withdrawal of Argentinean forces, a cessation of hostilities and a political solution to the differences between the two countries found. The Junta refused to accept the resolution.

3

The Defence of Las Malvinas

'I will give you freedom of action because you will be isolated. Tell me what you need.' Vice Admiral Lombardo to Brigadier General Menendez.

The conundrum faced by Argentina was to answer the question, what would the British do?

Chaos reigned as Whitehall endeavoured to find out if reports of the Argentine invasion were correct and at Westminster politicians carried out damage limitation. Prime Minister Margaret Thatcher acted with characteristic decisiveness when she announced during the famous Saturday morning House of Commons debate, 'A large task force will sail as soon as preparations are complete'.

The outline structure of the Task Force had already emerged. Admiral Sir John Fieldhouse, Commander-in-Chief Fleet, was appointed Commander Combined Task Force 317 (CTF 317) with his headquarters at Northwood. CTF 317 was broken down into several elements. Rear-Admiral 'Sandy' Woodward RN, commanding 1st Flotilla, was appointed to command Combined Task Group (CTG 317.8), the Carrier Task Group, whose role was to ensure the ground forces arrived at their destination in one piece. Many of the ships were already at Gibraltar. The responsibility for the transportation of the troops and the landing plan lay with CTG 317.0, which was commanded by Commodore Michael Clapp RN, in-post Commander Amphibious Warfare at Plymouth. CTG 317.1 was the Landing Group, which was commanded by Brigadier Julian Thompson and consisted of his 3rd Commando Brigade, reinforced by the Spearpoint Battalion, 3rd Battalion Parachute Regiment, and a host of smaller Army and RAF units. Defence cuts had curtailed the Royal Marines' usual winter deployment to Norway; however, his units were very experienced in winter warfare.

After the Ascension Island conference on 17 April, the decision was made to despatch 5th Infantry Brigade, commanded by Brigadier Tony Wilson, and it was designated Combined Task Unit 317.1.2 (CTU 317.1.2) and 3rd Commando Brigade became CTU 317.1.1. Successor to 16th Parachute Brigade and reformed in January 1982, 5th Infantry Brigade was the only 'out of area' formation available, but both its parachute battalions were already with 3rd Commando Brigade. All other formations were committed elsewhere, including 1st Infantry Brigade and Britain's contribution to Allied

Command Europe Mobile Force, which had just returned from deployment in Norway but was heavily committed to the defence of the NATO's northern and southern flanks. Since a divisional structure had emerged, Land Forces Falkland Islands (LFFI) was created and on 20 May Major-General Jeremy Moore RM MC*, in post Major-General Commando Forces in Plymouth, was appointed as its commander. The defence industry also kept a close eye on the situation, ready to react.

The Task Force's greatest problem was to convert at extremely short notice from the defence of NATO and fighting an internal security campaign in Northern Ireland to fighting a conventional war. For some units this was a relatively simple matter but for smaller ones it was a major issue. Critical to the venture was the provision of intelligence but considering the threat that Argentina had posed initially there was remarkable little information available to the Task Force.

The Intelligence Corps, fed on a diet of the Soviet Armed Forces and Irish terrorism and heavily committed to Northern Ireland and NATO, was suddenly required to provide full operational intelligence organizations to support Northwood and LFFI against an enemy in a region about which virtually nothing was known. In spite of the Army's commitment to Belize, there were very few Spanish-speaking linguists and as a consequence, the Task Force was heavily reliant upon Royal Navy and RAF linguists and servicemen with Spanish as a first or second language. Nevertheless the Corps provided HQ LFFI with a full intelligence section, commanded by Captain David Chartres. For the first time ever, the senior theatre intelligence staff officer was from the Corps, Major David Burrell. 5th Infantry Brigade had also a full strength section, but 3rd Commando Brigade had only one in-post SNCO. Its Intelligence Corps section had been chopped in 1972 in response to defence cuts when the Commando Brigade returned from the Far East. It is surprising how many commanders want to fight without knowing much about the enemy. The Corps also provided an imagery analyst on *Hermes*, a signals intelligence unit and an interrogation unit, which arrived after the surrender. Most of the men were drawn from the Corps' depot and training units at Ashford. Brigadier Thompson later praised the 'quality of intelligence assessments from quite early on and through the campaign . . ., the *piéce de résistance* being the identification of positions occupied by the Argentine regiments before we landed, which proved amazingly accurate'.

Although many joining the Task Force were still looking for the Falklands Islands on their maps, the preparations reported in the news reinforced Britain's military intent for all the world to see, including Argentina. The occupied Falkland Islanders were grateful that a government, which for decades had ignored them was suddenly taking an interest in their status but their motivation is discussed elsewhere. In the meantime international politicians, such as US Secretary of State General Al Haig, mediated to identify common ground between Great Britain and Argentina, two countries

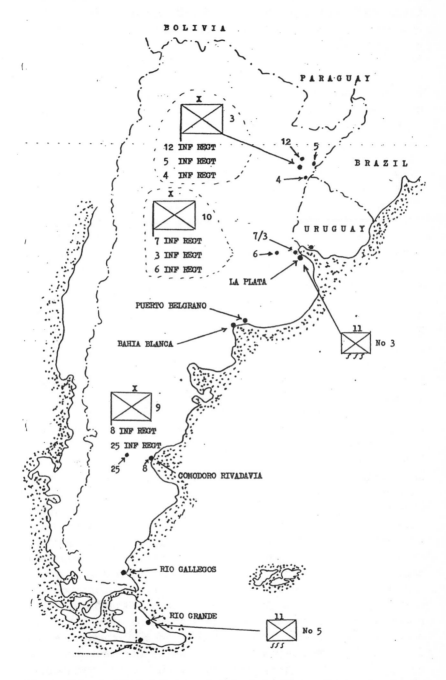

Map used by the HQ 3rd Commando Brigade Intelligence Section showing the
locations of the Argentine units deployed to the Falklands.

35

which historically and diplomatically normally had good relations.

The Junta knew that, unless there was a political settlement, they had a fight on their hands, but there were several options. First, the preferred option of raising the crisis diplomatically and forcing negotiations. Second, call Britain's bluff of military intervention all the way to the wire in the hope that international mediation would prevail. Thirdly, defend the Falklands. The Junta opted for the second and urgent messages cancelling the military withdrawal were sent to Rear Admiral Busser and Brigadier General Daher, whose 9th Infantry Brigade had been earmarked to provide the garrison. But 2nd Marine Infantry Battalion was back in Argentina and Army General Headquarters was therefore ordered to search for a formation to reinforce Daher's men.

The Argentine Army was divided into five corps, with its tactical deployment built around twelve brigades. With their tanks, the 1st and 2nd Armoured Cavalry Brigades were not trained or equipped for operations on the Falklands and the 6th and 8th Mountain and 11th Mechanised Infantry Brigades were facing Chile. 3rd Mechanized Infantry in the north and 7th Jungle Infantry Brigades were not equipped for cold weather operations. Who to send? 4th Airborne Infantry Brigade, which was the National Strategic Reserve, or Brigadier General Oscar Jofre's 10th 'Lieutenant General Nicolas Levalle' Motorised Infantry Brigade at La Plata defending the Atlantic Littoral? On 9 April Jofre was placed on notice to move complete with all assets.

Jofre was fifty-three and had been commissioned into the infantry in December, 1949. In command of 10th Infantry Brigade since December, 1980, he had converted his brigade into a useful infantry formation and was well respected by his conscripts, most of whom had European backgrounds. The formation was named after the Argentine general who laid siege to Montevideo in 1843.

Like other overtly patriotic countries, the Argentine Armed Forces place major emphasis on honour, glory and military tradition. The identities of most formations, units and military bases have an additional nomenclature, for instance 3rd 'General Manuel Belgrano' Infantry Regiment, named after the early 18th Century Argentine soldier and intellectual, and 7th 'Colonel Pedro Conde' Infantry Regiment, commemorating the officer who led the Argentine advance into Chile in 1817. Patriotism and honouring the flag figure strongly in indoctrinating the conscript to understand why he is serving – to protect not only the borders of Argentina but also its cultural, spiritual, political and national way of life – the heart and soul of the nation.

Army and corps level units are prefixed by a number, those under direct command of HQ Army being prefixed from 600, for instance 601 Commando Company and 5th Corps by 181, for instance 181 Intelligence Company.

On 6 April, the first reinforcements arrived when 8th 'General Bernardo

O'Higgins' Infantry Regiment, which was part of Daher's brigade, and several 5th Corps units arrived. The infantry were ferried by helicopter to Fox Bay where they remained until the Argentine surrender. A day later 5th Marine Infantry Battalion deployed straight to Sector Bronze covering Mounts William and Tumbledown and the southern beaches. Organic to 1st Fleet Marine Force and based in Rio Grande in Tierra del Fuego, the battalion was well suited to the cold of the approaching winter.

In his first Land Forces Argentine Occupied Territories Operations Order dated 7 April, Daher calculated that the British had two options. He assumed offensive operations would start 'no sooner than 18 April with the main effort in the Stanley area, secondary efforts in the Fox Bay and Darwin areas and distraction operations in the rest of the islands' By 'distraction' he means Special Forces. Daher believed the sequence of operations would be recces by tactical divers, the delivery of amphibious and heliborne commandos to secure areas of disembarkation, attack key points and secure beaches as a prelude to heliborne assaults by about 500 troops seizing vital ground in preparation for an amphibious assault by two marine battalions. In his second option, Daher suggests that his forces would be subjected to distraction operations, electronic warfare interception and interference and irregulars dislocating the defences. Irregulars he defined as local resistance groups of between eight to twelve local men organized along military lines and lightly equipped with small arms and rocket launchers and with a good knowledge of the ground. They would set up ambush and could act as guides to the distraction forces before amphibious forces arrived.

Daher outlined the concept of operations to ensure the continued presence of Argentine forces, even after the British had landed and give his government a political lever. Fox Bay and Goose Green were designated as strongpoints from which patrols would dominate the ground, but Stanley was to be the castle in the political chess game. He considered that once ashore, the British had fourteen possible approach routes to Stanley from as far afield as Port Harriet and Estancia. San Carlos Water is not mentioned. Indeed it would not be until three days after the San Carlos landings that the Argentines realized that a full-scale assault on Stanley was not part of the British strategy. Daher is complimentary about British abilities, claiming the troops 'have an excellent standard of instruction . . . morale will be good . . . There will be severe restrictions on their logistics caused by the great distance between their probable bases.' Oddly he suggests that a 'high percentage of their personnel are under contract'. The deployment of 1/7th Gurkha Rifles had not yet been announced and he is probably referring to the professional nature of the soldier compared to the conscript nature of the Argentine Armed Forces.

Quite why the Argentines selected 18 April is not clear. Even sailing at full speed, warships of the size capable of landing troops could be offshore about

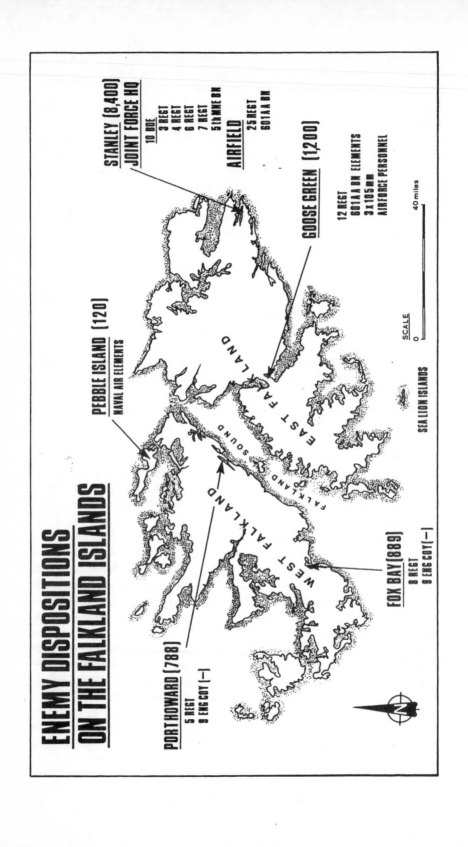

ENEMY DISPOSITIONS
ON THE FALKLAND ISLANDS

STANLEY (8,400)
JOINT FORCE HQ
10 BDE
3 REGT
4 REGT
6 REGT
7 REGT
5 th MNE BN

AIRFIELD
25 REGT
601 AA BN

GOOSE GREEN (1200)
12 REGT
601 AA BN ELEMENTS
3 x 105 mm
AIRFORCE PERSONNEL

PEBBLE ISLAND (120)
NAVAL AIR ELEMENTS

FOX BAY (889)
8 REGT
9 ENG COY (—)

PORT HOWARD (788)
5 REGT
9 ENG COY (—)

EAST FALKLAND

WEST FALKLAND

FALKLAND SOUND

SEA LION ISLANDS

SCALE
0   40 miles

N

three weeks after leaving the United Kingdom but television pictures of the departure of the Task Force showed *Hermes* and *Invincible* laden with Sea Harriers and hardly an amphibious assault ship to be seen.

Two important events also occurred on 7 April. First, Brigadier General Menendez assumed his appointment as Military Governor and the Malvinas Theatre of Operations was absorbed into the South Atlantic Theatre of Operations and therefore within Argentina's sphere of military influence. By nature a conciliator, Menendez had been selected by the Junta because his personality would help him govern the Falklands during the difficult early negotiations with Great Britain. Throughout his tenure he remained convinced that military action was subordinate to diplomacy, even when he found himself military commander after negotiation had failed and he was faced by the British landing at San Carlos. As early as 4 April Vice Admiral Juan Lombardo, then Commander Naval Operations, had told Menendez that he did not want to become involved in any military activity on the Falklands because he, Menendez, would be isolated and only he would know what was needed. Even when a more aggressive military commander was needed after San Carlos, Galtieri did not replace Menendez and the latter subsequently carried much of the blame for the Argentine tactical defeat.

Secondly, Great Britain posted her intention to impose a 200-mile Maritime Exclusion Zone around the Falklands, South Georgia and the South Sandwich Islands on 12 April and threatened to intercept any Argentine warships and auxiliaries found inside the zone. The idea was to hinder the reinforcement of the Falklands.

On 9 April General Headquarters began mustering 100,000 reservists conscripted in *Soldado Clase 62* from the February, 1981, induction. Of a total strength in 1982 of 85,000 men in the Army, 65,000 were conscripts and the annual February induction had barely finished basic training. From 1976 every Argentine male on reaching twenty was expected to be available for military service until aged forty-five. For the first ten years' service affiliated to a front-line unit was expected, with, in the army and air force, one year set aside for basic and trade training. This was extended to two years in the navy and marines. Service could be deferred, for instance to allow for university education. Annual rotation began in February with the conscripts being drafted to the units in which they would serve. Selection was based upon the year in which the conscript was born, thus those born in 1963 were conscripted in February 1982 as *Soldado Clase 63*; some of whom found themselves on active service after just two months' military service. The training cycle ceased in October and the conscripts were progressively released until the following year's recruits were inducted. For the second ten-year period, the soldier is classified as a reservist and is mobilized only in the event of hostilities. For the final five years of military service, he served in the Territorial Guard, a sort of Home Guard.

When Jofre was warned to take his brigade to the Falklands, he ordered

39

the 1982 conscripts to be replaced by reservists. This was done by announcements on the radio, by telegram and by home visits. Having heard and seen the media coverage of the recovery of the Falklands, most were more than willing to serve their country, as the Argentine military philosophy demanded.

Undefeated in any campaign until 1982, the Argentine Army was the backbone of the nation and, unlike in Great Britain, where the Army, until Northern Ireland, was better seen in some far-off colony than heard, soldiers were seen as defenders of the nation. Its motto *'Nacio con el pais en 1810'* (Born with the nation in 1810) reflects its position in the national psyche. At school Argentines are taught that Las Malvinas historically belong to Argentina and consequently *Malvinas es Argentina* is strong in the national psyche as much as *Belice es Guatemala* was fervently believed by the Guatemalans facing the British in Belize several thousand miles to the north in Central America. Many of the captured conscripts were found to have a poem entitled *'Recuperacion'* (literally translated "Recovery"), a homage to Lieutenant Commander Giachino, who was killed in the assault on Government House.

Apart from nearly three centuries of stern Spanish occupation, the only other European powers Argentina had encountered militarily were the British and French. Fresh from snatching the Cape of Good Hope from the Dutch in 1806, Admiral Sir Home Popham landed 1800 men under Brigadier William Beresford near Buenos Aires. He quickly defeated the Spanish and settled into a regime in which the troops behaved almost as badly as the colonists, which was not unusual for the British Army of the period. The people waited for two months and then, when Popham was becalmed in the River Plate estuary, they forced Beresford to surrender. Popham's initiative was welcomed in London as an alternative trade outlet and on 3 February, 1807, Lieutenant General Sir John Whitelocke landed at Montevideo with four infantry regiments. Reinforced by three cavalry and four infantry regiments, he crossed the estuary and advanced on Buenos Aires, but the deeper Whitelocke penetrated the fiercer the resistance grew from the newly-raised 8000-strong militia, whose regiments were based on ethnic origins, in much the same way as some British ones were on regions. Severe street fighting took place in the city and on 5 July Whitelocke was forced to surrender and was cashiered on his return to Britain. Though unsuccessful, the invasion shattered the Spanish administration and the British commercial interests he left behind underpinned the Argentine struggle for independence.

Among the patriots who returned from Europe was Jose de San Martin, who had learned much fighting as an ally of the British in the Peninsular campaign. In 1813 he disbanded the ethnic militia regiments and raised a highly disciplined force based around the Mounted Grenadiers of General San Martin. In 1982, although largely a ceremonial cavalry unit, as the 1st

'General Jose de San Martin' Horse Cavalry Regiment, it sent six MAG machine-gun detachments to the Falklands which were initially attached to 1st 'Los Patricios' Infantry Regiment, the first infantry unit of the Argentine Army. They fought with the 4th Infantry Regiment on Mount Harriet against 42 Commando.

The Spanish colonial army was no match for San Martin's army and in 1817 San Martin with 5000 men crossed the Andes in an epic march and contributed massively to Chilean and Peruvian independence. The next encounter with European forces was in 1843 when two British regiments and 6000 French Foreign Legion supporting Uruguayan independence forced the Argentine General Nicolas Levalle to lift the siege of Montevideo. From 1880 the Army became actively involved in power-broking but very rarely in wars outside Argentina's borders. After the Second World War its strength rose to 145,000 during the Peronist 1950s, but from 1964 remained steady at 85,000, although the size varied according to the number of conscripts who converted to regulars.

In 1973, after seven years of military rule, former dictator Juan Peron was returned as president, but he died the following year and was succeeded by his widow, Isabel. This sparked two years of inter-Peronist faction fighting during which strikes were common and unemployment and inflation rocketed. Into the political void stepped the Monteneros and the rural People's Revolutionary Army. The Monteneros were on the left of the Peronist movement and largely confined their activities to urban areas, particularly in Buenos Aires, financing their operations by kidnapping, extortion and bank raids. The middle-class Trotskyist *Ejercito Revolucionario del Pueblo* (ERP), the People's Revolutionary Army, was established in 1970 and posed the greater threat. It seized control of the jungle-clad mountainous province of Tucuman in 1974 and several Army units were blooded in the counter-insurgency campaign, including the 5th Rural and 4th Airborne Brigades. Their philosophy of direct action provoked a Junta headed by General Jorge Videla into deposing Isabel Peron and he quickly clamped down on civil rights, banned political activity, restricted trades union activities and dismissed most of the judiciary. The Dirty War followed, in which the police, paramilitary and special forces were particularly active. As a result of the excesses of the military, Argentina found herself internationally isolated until President Viola returned the country to global acceptance in the late 1970s.

Conscripts were told from the moment they were inducted that they would be taught military skills to enable them to contribute to the defence of Argentina. National Service was an accepted element of a young man's adulthood nevertheless the young conscripts were not highly regarded in society, a status common in almost every conscript army. Because of the conscript nature of the Argentine Armed Forces, training was necessarily strictly standardized and designed to train recruits with a wide range of education, background and abilities to a common level of basic military skills. An Army training manual set out the requirements expected of every conscript and emphasized that within a month of induction they were to be trained sufficiently well to take over the roles and duties of the outgoing conscripts. In common with every other army, basic training consisted of drill, weapon training, fieldcraft, simple tactics and first aid. Selection for specialist skills was then made, such as unit medical orderly, clerks and drivers. Conditions of service were not arduous and most conscripts served not far from home.

Spanish was the common language and those who had linguistic problems, such as Indians, sometimes found their service extended. The only non-commissioned rank achievable by a conscript was *Dragoneante,* which equates roughly to the US Army Private First Class; there is no equivalent in the British Army. Compared to the British Army, discipline tended to be unsophisticated and slaps and punches by officers and NCOs were not uncommon. There were allegations of field punishments dealt out to unruly 7th Infantry Regiment conscripts on Mount Longdon.

Potential regular NCOs were recruited from schools and conscripts who showed leadership. They then attended about two years' training at the 'Sergeant Cabral' School of NCOs, which was part of the School of Infantry 'Lieutenant-General Pedro Eugenio Aramburu,' located at Campo de Mayo, Buenos Aires. The aim was to produce a leader capable of leading a *grupo,* which is the equivalent of a US squad or British section. To help him, the prospective NCO was issued with an extremely useful *aide memoire* entitled 'Orientation Manual For The Recently Graduated NCO'. The 1981 edition included chapters on the Nation, Country and State, the sanctity of marriage and the family, and introductions to the ideologies of capitalism, communism, socialism, Christianity and liberalism. It then delved into military communications, tactics, vehicle maintenance, a description of all Argentine infantry weapons held at regimental, company and platoon level and military report writing. NCOs had little responsibility except for administration and a duty to care for the physical needs of the conscript. They were not required to train recruits; that was the job of the officer.

Like his colleagues throughout South America, the Argentine officer tends to be Roman Catholic, middle to upper class and with a family history of joining the Armed Forces. Several of the young officers on the Falklands were sons of generals, for instance Lieutenant Luis Martella, who was killed on Two Sisters, and Lieutenant Pasillo, who was captured at Mount Harriet. First Lieutenant Carlos Esteban's father was a former Air Force NCO. The officer took a far greater interest in political affairs than his British equivalent, saw himself as a guardian and defender of the nation, and was encouraged to become involved in the governmental decision-making process, which helped to justify the cause on which he was engaged. Of the eighteen governments, between 1930 and 1982, ten were military governments. The political faction fighting even spilled over to the Falklands when

Oscar Jofre not only had to deal with fighting the British but also to contend with the likes of Lieutenant Colonel Seineldin, the commando Major Aldo Rico and other right-wing officers attempting to undermine his authority. It was perhaps fortunate for the British that the rivalry between Jofre and Seineldin probably resulted in the 25th Infantry Regiment staying bottled up around the airport instead of being in the front line. Several captured Argentine officers regarded the British as no more than mercenaries because they were merely the tools of politicians and equated Northern Ireland with their Dirty War but with one key difference – the Argentine Army knew the political reason for the mobilization of the security forces. The defeat in 1982 seriously damaged their credibility as politico-officers and their ability to become deeply involved in political matters, but this did not prevent Seineldin and Rico leading mutinies in 1987, 1988 and 1990 in protest against their commanders passive response to the jailing of military personnel convicted in civilian courts of torturing and killing civilians in the Dirty War.

In spite of some criticism by the British that the Argentine officer failed to take care of his men, it is important to appreciate that there is a sizeable military, class, cultural and philosophical gap between officer and other rank. The criticism is unfair because British Army standards are being used to benchmark another army's philosophy. In the professional British Armed Forces the regimental philosophy and common experiences in various parts of the world and in Northern Ireland bonded officers and other ranks almost into 'mateship.' There is plenty of evidence during the campaign that, although the concept of *'hermandad'* (brother) between the Argentine officer and other rank was uncommon, the junior officers did their best, as they saw it, to prepare their men for battle and keep them informed. Throughout their occupation of the Falklands, a locally produced briefing note entitled *La Gaceta Argentina* was widely distributed. Following a short editorial, a summary then listed incidents, giving time and date. The British had no such periodical except a short attempt by correspondents with 3rd Commando Brigade to produce an information sheet from the 'The Press Trench.' Only a few were produced and circulation ceased soon after the breakout from San Carlos. Throughout their occupation, Argentine servicemen could send telegrams to their families through open channels. These were accidentally intercepted by *Fearless* at Ascension Island and, since the messages invariably contained military information, were passed to HQ 3rd Commando Brigade, who were then having some difficulty in assessing what was happening on the Falklands.

Potential officers attended a five-year course at the National Army Academy, which is modelled on West Point. Inevitably those who attended this rigorous course bonded for the remainder of their careers and lives although this tended to deter inter-Service co-operation and consequently joint operations, such as the Falklands campaign, tended to be tricky. In much the same way as Soviet officers practised standard tactics, because of the conscript nature of the Red Army, the Argentine officer was also forced to memorize standardized tactics. Discussion and active debate on military philosophy were relatively rare. When the reservists were called up, more officers were required and the fifth-year cadets were commissioned into the Army, several finding themselves on the Falkland Islands and later being accused of brutality when disciplining unruly conscripts. One cadet was killed and four wounded.

Officers selected for field rank attended one of the several technical staff colleges and then had an opportunity to attend a three-year course at the Senior Level War School, which is roughly equivalent to the British Junior Division of the Staff College, where they could earn a degree. Some officers were given the opportunity to attend foreign staff colleges and courses and Argentine officers were regularly seen in the United Kingdom. Officers destined for general rank attended the joint service National War College, some of the delegates coming from the Ministry of Defence and the defence industry. Peculiar to the Army was the *logia* (lodge), a sort of Masonic lodge, which was founded by General San Martin and was designed to further the idea that the Army is the defender of the nation and guardians of tradition

Faith was encouraged in a country rich in Roman Catholicism and each conscript was issued with a small packet, which included a rosary and a prayer attributed to St Francis of Assisi. While the 2 Para padre, David Cooper, made a name for himself as a fighting padre and marksman, Father Piccinalli's sermons dedicated to the Argentine forces on the Falklands, to the Virgin of the Rosary and the Virgin of Lujan helped persuade the Argentine soldier of the religious and historical justification of the war. And in the final hours before surrender Father Fernandez helped to convince defeated 7th Infantry Regiment soldiers to counter-attack. Some veterans believe that Military Air Base Malvinas was kept open throughout the campaign not because of British inability to close it but because Seineldin had buried his rosary beside the runway. During the repatriation phase a group of conscripts asked to take a 3-foot high statue of the Virgin Mary back to Argentina. After a cursory search for contraband, permission was granted.

This conscript South American army, which had not fought a war for 120 years, was about to take on one of the most experienced armies of the age. In 1982 the British Armed Forces were fully professional, tough and well-trained, the minimum length of service being three years. Except for 1968, although even then the British Army of the Rhine remained on twenty-four hours notice to move for six months after the Soviet Union had invaded Czechoslovakia and brought Europe close to war, its national servicemen and professionals had been on continuous active service since 1945. But one wonders if Argentina really appreciated the military strength of the British. When the author Ruben Moro, a Canberra pilot who took part in the campaign, writes 'Although British armed forces had not actually been engaged in a shooting war since the Suez crisis in 1956, Great Britain was nevertheless prepared to meet any contingency arising from its Atlantic Alliance obligations,' he forgets British military operations in Cyprus, Borneo, Aden and Northern Ireland. The British were experienced in amphibious operations and were also thoroughly trained to fight another conscript army on the plains of West Germany. Many garrisons and most campaigns were thousands of miles from Great Britain and, although the logistics of fighting in the South Atlantic did have its problems, isolation was not new to the British forces. Nevertheless fundamental errors were made. Within weeks, some of those who had been down south were in Northern Ireland – back down to earth.

Great Britain has a long military tradition of losing the battles but winning the wars that created an empire, the results of which are still evident through the Commonwealth. Patriotism does not figure highly in modern British regimental philosophy, although it did with their Victorian predecessors. However, in contrast to the Argentine method of commemorating its heroes, the apolitical and servile nature of the British infantry and cavalry is reflected in its unit titles; by servile, I mean servants of the government. Nomenclatures were usually drawn from either those who raised regiments or sponsored them and appear to be haphazard but are based on history and the effects of numerous and usually brutal defence cuts. The Regiment is the backbone of the British Army and though personnel leave for attachments and postings, they invariably return to the regimental family. Even the corps, such as the Royal Engineers and the RAMC, have strong family traditions.

Most of the British had no idea where the Falkland Islands were but when they landed at San Carlos, they found the environment not dissimilar to winter on Dartmoor or at Otterburn and, uncomfortable though it was, they survived without too many non-battle casualties. One problem faced by the officers and NCOs was to persuade their men that this 'exercise' was going to last longer than two weeks. The Argentines found the Falklands uncomfortable and little attempt was made to convince the conscript to use the weather and environment to his advantage. Part of this was because, unlike the British soldier who had exercised in snows of Norway, on the cold plains of north West Germany, in dry American deserts and the jungle of Brunei, the conscripts generally served and exercised near their homes. The British also regarded night as an ally.

The highest tactical formation of both sides was the brigade. The Argentine infantry brigade had a standard organization, irrespective of its role, of three regiments, an artillery group, a logistic battalion, an armoured recce squadron and engineer, communications, transport and medical companies. The formation to which the elements belonged were identifiable by their nomenclature, thus 9th Engineer Company, which was based at Fox Bay, was part of 9th Infantry Brigade. British infantry brigade organization was similar, although 3rd Commando Brigade lacked armoured recce and was reliant upon the Army for artillery and engineers and the Royal Navy for medics and chaplains. 5th Infantry Brigade was in many respects cobbled together and lacked a logistic unit and an artillery regiment until 4th Field Regiment from 7th Field Force in Colchester joined.

The organization of Argentine brigade headquarters was not dissimilar to the British but had an interesting difference. Whereas most staff officers in British headquarters were majors and captains, Argentine headquarters tended to have a higher proportion of majors and lieutenant-colonels. For instance, the 10th Infantry Brigade Chief Intelligence Officer was Lieutenant-Colonel Norbeto Villegas, a career intelligence officer, while his counterpart in 3rd Commando Brigade was Captain Viv Rowe RM, a mountain leader, who had arrived shortly before Christmas, 1981, on a two-year draft.

The average Argentine infantry regiment numbered about 700 men, against the established 650 of a full-strength British battalion, and was organised into three rifle companies, a Command Company, combat support which included a recce platoon, anti-tank platoon, Rasit ground surveillance radar, 120mm Brandt mortar platoon and a logistics company, including the quartermaster and medics. The major difference between the British and Argentine regiments was two 81mm Brandt mortars integrated into Argentine rifle companies whereas in British units, six medium mortars were found in Support Company. The strength of the Argentine support company was about 130.

In 1982 the average Argentine infantry company, which was commanded by a first lieutenant, was divided into a company headquarters and three forty-five-strong rifle platoons, each usually led by a second lieutenant. Platoons were divided into a headquarters, three rifle sections, each of two five-strong fireteams and a support section with two MAG machine guns and about four 3.5" M20 bazookas. Riflemen were equipped with the automatic FAL rifle. Marine companies had a similar order of battle. British infantry platoons consisted of three rifle sections, each section eight-strong with a GPMG, who worked on the classic fire and movement tactic. The 'Arctic' 42 and 45 Commandos, however, had an LMG in addition to a GPMG in their sections, which gave the option of two fireteams per section. British companies are led by majors in the Army and captains in the Royal Marines, which gives a sizeable advantage in experience. There were several occasions when Argentine companies on independent tasks were commanded by a major, often the regimental operations officer.

Critical to the Argentine strategy was to keep open the air route to Military Air Base Stanley and Operation *Aries 82* was extended. On 12 April Vice Admiral Lombardo, the newly appointed Commander South Atlantic Theatre of Operations Command, issued Military Committee Outline Plan 1/82, a lengthy directive detailing the naval and air strategic defence of the Falkland Islands. Reviewing the possible British strategies, he listed four options open to the British from a naval perspective. One, isolate and blockade the islands using submarines and deny the use of the airfield. Two, attempt total or partial recovery by an amphibious or heliborne assault launched from fifty to 250 miles to the east of the objective. i.e. Stanley, supported by amphibious incursions launched from submarines. Three, wear down Argentine forces by using nuclear and attack submarines. And four, since the Beagle Channel conflict was unresolved, Great Britain's response could act as an incentive for Chile to take concurrent action and thereby stretch Argentine resources.

Lombardo recognized that the deployment of Argentine surface units could be restricted by nuclear submarines. To upgrade the Stanley runway for high-performance aircraft would take time and even then it was vulnerable to interdiction by bombing and shelling. The imposition of the Maritime Exclusion Zone on 12 April emphazised the need for an efficient airlift capability and he issued instructions to the newly created Strategic Air Command's Air Transport Command to ensure logistic support for the islands by organizing the Air Bridge, the *Puente Aereo*, and to co-ordinate its operations with the Naval Air Force. There is no doubt the Air Force quickly reached and maintained a high state of operational efficiency throughout the war. Air Transport Command was soon busy flying in reinforcements and equipment using military and civilian transport. During the war 6,712 army, 414 navy and 863 air force personnel and 6,335 tons of army, 200 tons of navy and 1,171 tons of air force equipment were flown from several Atlantic Littoral air bases to Stanley. By contrast the British were almost entirely reliant upon shipping, some already in service but included forty-five 'ships taken up from trade', that is merchant vessels press-ganged into naval service as transports, repair ships, tugs and hospital ships. They moved over 100,000 tons of war stores and equipment, 400,000 tons of fuel and 9,000 men.

To support the military occupation, a forty-strong civil administration team, headed by Air Commodore Carlos Bloomer-Reeve, arrived in Stanley on 6 April. A career Air Force officer, he had been the Argentine Consul in Stanley in 1974/75 and also Under Secretary at the Ministry of Foreign Affairs between 1979 and 1980. Because of his meetings with Nicholas Ridley over the future of the Falklands, Bloomer-Reeve was considered to be the ideal choice to represent the islanders during negotiations with Great Britain and was recalled from the Embassy in Bonn specifically to fill the appointment as Secretary General of the Military Government. Installing himself with the Falkland Islands civil servants in the Secretariat, it was his responsibility to impress on the population the justification of the Argentine cause and reassure them that their lives would not be disrupted. One of his first acts was to ensure the protection of those Falkland Islanders' houses who had been repatriated to be marked with a cross in a circle and the letters "DAP" (Entry Prohibited).

Colonel Estaban Solis, the Chief Civil Affairs Officer at Falklands Operational Theatre, drafted several advisory communiqués signed by Major General Garcia dated 2 April for immediate issue to the population. Communication No 1 reinforced the Argentine claim of sovereignty of the Falklands and, in welcoming the people to Argentina, sought their co-operation. No 2 confirmed that 'colonial and military instructions of the British Government are effectively relieved of their charges' and that General Garcia had been appointed as governor of the Falklands, South Georgia and the South Sandwich Islands. No 3 confined people to their houses until further notice with the threat of arrest if caught outside. Schools, banks, pubs and clubs were ordered to be closed; further instructions would be issued over the radio. Anyone who had a problem should hang a white sheet outside a window, something which the population found abhorrent for it implied surrender. The fourth communication endeavoured to assure the population of their rights – civil, religious, employment and freedom of movement rights. It is interesting that it was issued by a country with a recent appalling human rights record. Solis also issued Executive Edict 1 which laid down that disobedience to the curfew, public order disturbances, insults to national symbols or any action against the Argentine Code of Law could lead to imprisonment. It was a repressive document by any standard, more so when applied to a population used to freedom.

When Brigadier General Menendez arrived, Bloomer-Reeve circulated a communication to all inhabitants of the National Territory of the Falklands, South Georgia and South Sandwich Islands containing an assurance that, although civil rights would be acknowledged, some liberties would be with-held because of the mainland anti-terrorist struggle. Again drafted by Solis, it appealed to the islanders to work with Argentina. Attached to the same document was Edict Number 2 issued by Garcia through Solis, which banned all CB transmissions throughout the occupied territories and threatened from one month to two years' imprisonment if convicted at a court martial. 181 Military Police Company was instructed to enforce this and other edicts issued by the Military Governor.

181 Military Police Company had arrived very soon after the invasion and was based at Stanley Police Station. It appears to have struck a reasonable balance with the local population, even when the Falkland Islanders refused to drive on the right while Argentine military drivers continued to do so. Most of the time the military police were involved in keeping Argentine troops in line. It had a section of large well-fed German Shepherd dogs.

When Great Britain proposed to impose the Maritime Exclusion Zone, the Argentines perceived that the Royal Navy would contact the local popu-lation either by radio or by landing small patrols. At a meeting on 9 April Menendez and his security advisers, Colonel Mendiberri representing the Air Force, Major Dowling the Army and Captain Gaffoglio the Navy, discussed several internal security problems. Orders were issued that anyone in Stanley with a 2-metre band CB radio was to hand it to the Security Warehouse in the Town Hall by 10 April. Those outside Stanley were expected to disconnect their equipment. Owners were meant to receive £200 in compensation.

As the British tightened the siege of the Falklands, on 27 April Bloomer-Reeve advised the people of Stanley that a blackout would be imposed during the hours of darkness and a curfew enforced between 6pm and 6.30am. Only in the event of an air raid would the emergency services be allowed to operate. Shops were to close by 4pm and citizens were advised to restrict their activities. In the event of an emergency, the military police could be summoned.

Resistance to the Argentine occupation was passive nevertheless, with the threat of British landings, the security authorities rounded up several islanders who they thought might decide to take direct action. Gerald Cheek ran the island Falkland Islands Air Service and was one of the Falklands Islands Defence Force who responded to Governor Hunt's mobilization call. Well known for his anti-Argentine views, he was summoned to a meeting at the Civil Affairs department where he refused to continue flying because of the danger of being shot down by Argentine troops. On 27 April, in a scene that must have been reminiscent of the Dirty War, four military police arrived at his house and gave him ten minutes to pack. Cheek bade farewell to his tearful family, was helicoptered to Fox Bay with fourteen other detainees and placed under house arrest with the settlement manager, Richard Cockwell, for the remainder if the war. Two others also arrested were Dr Daniel Haines, formerly of the RAMC, and his wife, also a doctor because, it was alleged, he had tried to send coded answers to questions from the Task Force on his daily radio surgery. Their departure left Dr Alison Bleaney and Mary Elphinstone to look after the medical needs of the people of Stanley.

The only serious confrontation with the Argentine military happened on 1 May when rumours circulated that a full-scale British landing was imminent and a group of anxious civilians sought shelter in a godown. This was reported to Major Dowling, who, fearing it was a resistance group meeting, ordered 181 Military Police Company and 601 Commando Company to throw a cordon around the building with orders to arrest anyone who came out. Negotiations were tense, but it was not until the following morning that the civilians filed out and were immediately arrested. When Bloomer-Reeve learnt what was happening and why the civilians had sought shelter he ordered their immediate release, much to the disgust of Dowling.

Throughout their occupation the Argentines were careful to respect the citizens. In a report to the International Committee of the Red Cross on the day the British landed at San Carlos, they claimed that only five Falklands Islanders had been detained and three crimes by Argentine troops against private property had been dealt with by military tribunals. The Military Government claimed that the civil rights of the population had been rigorously upheld, the only restrictions being forced upon them by the aggression of the Task Force. Indeed, the report claims that British hostile action against Argentine merchant ships en route to the Falklands and supplying outlying settlements was harming the civil population. Attacks on the *Isla de Los Estados, Rio Carcarana* and the *Bahia Buen Suceso* are specifically mentioned. The LADE flights had been suspended when naval bombardments destroyed the aircraft. The report is critical of the decision by 90% of the teachers in Stanley to leave the islands, because they would be seen to be 'collaborating with the supposed enemy', and thereby preventing the continued education of the children. British aggression was said to be preventing bringing in replacement teachers.

The frequent air raids and naval bombardments of Argentine positions on Stanley Common and around the airport were unnerving for people used to the tranquillity of the Falklands. Both sides were careful to avoid civilian casualties and the Argentine civil authorities formed a committee to identify robust houses suitable for air raid shelters. At the end of the campaign, as the Argentines retreated to Stanley, the Military Government issued an instruction that all inhabitants to the west of the Battle Monument were to leave their houses because British shelling made it unsafe to remain. The evacuees were advised to seek shelter in several places, including St Mary's Church and the West Stores. Nevertheless, three people were killed when a British shell hit a house on 12 June.

With equipment deficiencies made up from other units, it is a measure of Jofre's determination and organization that by 11 April the leading element of the 10th Infantry Brigade, 3rd Infantry Regiment, was on its way to the Falklands in an Aerolineas Argentinas Boeing 707. Because his artillery regiment was equipped with US 105mm field guns, which were unsuitable for the Falklands, Jofre was given 3rd Infantry Brigade's 3rd Artillery Group, which had eighteen Italian Oto Melara 105mm Pack Howitzers and was commanded by Lieutenant Colonel Martin Balza. However, the gunners had not previously worked with 10th Infantry Brigade.

Assisted by 181 Intelligence Company, Menendez's Chief Intelligence Officer, Colonel Francisco Cervo, began assessing British intentions. The analysis in Army Group Malvinas Operations Order 1/82 dated 15 April commented upon the long logistic chain, but suggested that the British troops were good, professional and experienced in amphibious warfare. Special Forces would attack the principal maritime and airport embarkation points, followed either by helicopter assault near Mount Longdon or an amphibious assault by at least two Royal Marine commandos in the Stanley sector. Eleven beaches were identified as possible assault beaches, but San Carlos was not yet mentioned. Army Headquarters intelligence assessment often gave detailed organizational and equipment breakdowns of the British order of battle, but some astonishing errors of basic intelligence were made. For instance, it was suggested that the SAS were based in Aldershot and the

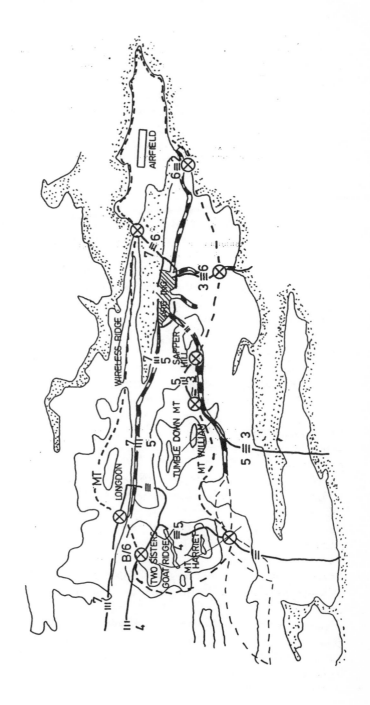

TRACE SHOWING ARGENTINE REGIMENTAL BOUNDARIES
(COPIED FROM A CAPTURED MAP)

decommissioned *Blake* was part of the Task Force and carrying eleven Sea Kings.

With the headquarters of 9th and 10th Infantry Brigades now ashore, Menendez re-organized. In overall command was Malvinas Joint Command. Jofre was appointed Commander Land Forces over Brigadier General Daher and 10th Infantry Brigade assumed responsibility for the defence of Stanley. 9th Infantry Brigade was given responsibility for the rest of the Falklands and ordered to be ready to reinforce Stanley. 181 Communications Company established teleprinter, radio and line networks to link Malvinas Joint Command with the two brigades, as well as operating rear links to Argentina. 602 Electronic Warfare Company had detachments at Stanley and, later, Goose Green.

By 16 April 10th Infantry Brigade was all but complete in defensive positions around Stanley but it would not be until 22 April that its heavy equipment would arrive by ship. Until the later stages of the campaign, like Menendez, Jofre was convinced the main threat would be a landing at Stanley and appears to have ignored the threat from the west. With intelligence assessments predicting that the British Task Force could be off Stanley by 18 April and an expectation of infiltration by Special Forces, Jofre organized his brigade, now known as Army Group Puerto Argentino, to face south, east and north thus:

Sector *Oro* (Gold). 3rd Infantry Regiment covered the southern beaches and possible helicopter landing sites.

Sector *Acero* (Steel). 6th Infantry Regiment covered the approaches from the south-west and south. Its C Company was later assigned to the Reserve and was replaced by A Company 1st 'Los Patricios' Infantry Regiment , which was temporarily designated C Company 6th Infantry. Several snipers later joined 4th Infantry Regiment to support operations on Mount Wall.

Sector *Plata* (Silver). 7th Infantry Regiment on Mount Longdon and Wireless Ridge protected the left flank of the Outer Defence Zone, facing north.

Sector *Cobre* (Copper). Military Air Base, Stanley

Sector *Victoria* (Victory). North-eastern beaches defended by 25th Infantry Regiment.

Sector *Bronce* (Bronze). 5th Marine Infantry Battalion on Mount Tumbledown and Mount William covered the south-west approaches.

Brigadier General Jofre's command included Marines, Navy, Air Force and Coastguard personnel in the Stanley environs, but the political in-fighting between the Services cut across effective command. A document captured on 3 June listed 6,450 Army personnel defending Stanley.

General Galtieri paid a day-long visit to Stanley on 22 April and, after a helicopter recce of the islands, held a long conference at Moody Brook at which it was agreed the British would land at or near Stanley. Menendez said he was short of reserves and asked for another regiment as a permanent heliborne reserve. Galtieri, however, believed there were insufficient troops to occupy the Falklands and this could weaken his negotiation stance. Without consulting the Junta and the chiefs of staff, he sent orders to Major General Garcia that Brigadier General Omar Parada's 3rd Mechanized Infantry Brigade, which was usually deployed along the Uruguayan border in the northern sub-tropical province of Corrientes, should be deployed to the Falklands, much to the astonishment of Menendez. It was part of 2nd Army Corps, so there was representation from three corps, 1st, 2nd and 5th, as well as the Military Institute Command.

When 9th and 10th Brigades left for the Falklands, 3rd Infantry Brigade had joined 11th Mechanised Infantry Brigade in Patagonia to protect the Atlantic Littoral and provide a defence against increasing tension generated by Chile. Parada gave instructions to mobilize his *Soldado Clase 62* reservists but, even so, by the time the troop trains rumbled over the River Colorado, the regiments were still below strength and men were rushed from Buenos Aires to Patagonia. Nevertheless the units were full of new conscripts. To replace 3rd Artillery Group, which had been detached to 10th Infantry Brigade, Parada was allocated 4th Airborne Artillery Group from the National Strategic Reserve with its three batteries of six 105mm Pack Howitzers. On receiving Garcia's orders, Parada's units converged on Puerto Deseado, where most of the equipment was loaded on board four Naval Transport Service merchant ships. Most of 12th 'General Juan Arenales' Infantry Regiment's radios, mortars, vehicles, reserve ammunition, field kitchens and other defence and war stores were on board the *Ciudad de Cordoba*, which hit a rock and returned to port for repairs. The soldiers, travelling in light order, were flown from the Comodoro Rivadavia airhead to Stanley, most arriving between 24 and 29 April.

In a communication with General Herrera at Army Headquarters on 25 April, the day that South Georgia was recaptured, Menendez, while welcoming the reinforcement, which included 101 Air Defence Artillery Group, mentioned that the additions would place a severe strain on his logistics and implied that more helicopters would ease his problems. Herrera told him that the heavy equipment would arrive by ship but would not leave Argentina until it was certain they would arrive safely. Menendez had good reason to be concerned about the ships. The imposition of the Total Exclusion Zone on 1 May proved final, and most of Parada's essential equipment failed to catch up with his brigade, one consequence of which was that 12th Infantry Regiment fought at Goose Green minus most of its heavy equipment.

Herrera mentioned that the Argentine forces on South Georgia, if forced to surrender, had orders to destroy their radios and cypher codes and 'fight to the end.' Almost as an aside, Menendez assured him that Malvinas Joint Command would do the same and re-emphasized his need for commandos 'so that they can become familiar with the islands and its geography in order to be able to operate with the greatest efficiency'.

Now with three brigades, two with full headquarters, Menendez again reorganized his command. He assumed the appointment of Commander Army Group Malvinas and appointed Brigadier General Daher his chief of staff. Parada was assigned to command Army Group Littoral outside Stanley with orders to move his headquarters to Goose Green. His command was:

Sector *Plomo* (Lead). Task Force Mercedes based around HQ, A and C Companies 12th Infantry Regiment at Goose Green.
Naval Air Base Calderon. H Company 3rd Marine Infantry Battalion platoon at Pebble Island.
Mount Wall and Mount Challenger. Task Force Monte Caseros built around HQ, B and C Companies 4th Infantry Regiment.
Mount Kent. Combat Team Solari consisting of B Company 12th Infantry Regiment.
Port Howard. Task Force Reconquest, based around 5th Infantry Regiment at Port Howard. Its commanding officer was traditionally a full Colonel, in 1982 this being Juan Mabragana. 9th Medical Company established a small hospital at Port Howard, one of whose patients would be Flight Lieutenant Jeff Glover, shot down on 21 May by a 601 Commando Company detachment.
Sector *Uranio* (Uranium) – 8th Infantry Regiment at Fox Bay gained from 9th Infantry Brigade.

The wet and cold conditions about to be experienced by Parada's brigade were quite different from the sub-tropical warmth of Corrientes and his troops suffered badly from the lack of acclimatization. Little regard was paid to setting up an efficient logistic chain from Stanley and consequently they lacked appropriate equipment, clothing and training. The least prepared of the three Argentine brigades was deployed to the more distant and desolate parts of the Falklands, but this must be set against the Argentine perception that the British would land at or near Stanley.

The artillery was assembled en masse on Stanley Common under the command of Lieutenant Colonel Balsa at HQ Army Group Malvinas and consisted of B Battery Marine Field Artillery, the four-battery 3rd Artillery Group and three batteries of 4th Airborne Artillery Group. All were equipped with the Italian 105mm Pack Howitzer, which the British 29 Commando Regiment had only exchanged with the 105mm Light Gun, and were therefore very familiar with its capabilities. The additional battery with 3rd Artillery Group was a four-155mm CITEFA howitzer troop from 2nd Artillery Group, (2nd Armoured Cavalry Brigade), and integrated as

D Battery. Firing 20,400 metres with high explosive shells, it was these guns that gave the British such a torrid time before and after the capture of the Outer Defence Zone. On 8 June Army Group Malvinas was advised that an airborne platform had been developed to transport an 8-ton CITEFA and 140 rounds of first-line ammunition in a C-130 and a 101 Artillery Group troop of four howitzers could be expected. This was an unexpected but welcome bonus because the Light Gun counter-battery fire was causing the Pack Howitzer positions on Stanley Common considerable problems. During the night of the 12th two guns were flown in and brought into action. The following night the last two arrived but loading was disrupted by the shelling of the airport and the threat of an air raid but were too late to be of any use and were captured the following day. The gunners also showed considerable ingenuity. 3rd Artillery Group adapted a Rasit ground surveillance radar to support a land-based Exocet which hit *Glamorgan* during the night of 11 June.

Artillery also played a major role in the British campaign. Several months after the end, Brigadier Thompson said:

> The five 105mm Light Gun batteries were perhaps the battle-winning factor in this war. The ability to bring down concentrated, accurate fire crushed the enemy's morale and raised ours. Thanks to training on the passage down, every marine or private soldier learned how to call for fire and correct it; and many did so. Our gunners often brought down fire within fifty metres of our own troops in the attack. We had the utmost confidence in them. Once again artillery proved itself to be the principal man-killing weapon in the land battle. If properly handled, which ours was, it is undeterred by smoke, darkness, snow or fog. It is accurate, almost instantaneous and devastating.

In a frank admission he continues: 'At Darwin/Goose Green, there was not enough artillery and insufficient ammunition because the helicopter was inadequate. The battle was nearly lost as a consequence.' A 42 Commando sergeant put it more simply to the author on 19 June, 1982, while passing a Light Gun battery near Moody Brook: 'They won it for us.' Although the British took three 29 Commando Regiment and two 4th Field Regiment 105mm Light Gun batteries totalling thirty guns and one forward observation and one naval gunfire support battery, he did not know that the British nearly went to war with only the three commando batteries.

Although 4th Field Regiment was earmarked to support 5th Infantry Brigade, it had persistently been prevented from training with it and there was a danger the formation might have deployed without any artillery, had it not been for the intense lobbying of its commanding officer, Lieutenant-Colonel Tony Holt RA. Its 97 Battery was eventually allowed to exercise with 5th Infantry Brigade at Sennybridge; however the brigade was unfamiliar with 4th Field Regiment or indeed with regimental gunnery. The battery was reluctantly given authority to sail with its six Light Guns but further intense pressure by Holt was required to ensure that 29 Battery joined the brigade. This gave a total of twelve guns, six short of the establishment expected of British brigades. On 22 April the composite 41 Battery was formed to provide 3 Para with forward observation parties. Operational difficulties would be experienced when it came to supporting the Scots and Welsh Guards because neither had trained with 4th Field Regiment.

By contrast, the deployment of 29 Commando Regiment was simple and it celebrated exactly twenty years with 3rd Commando Brigade by invading the Falklands on 21 May. Receiving its warning order for deployment on 2 April, within the day its three batteries were ready to move. Thoroughly familiar with the quirks of the Royal Marines, all officers and gunners were commando-trained and highly experienced in operating in hostile environments. Providing naval gunfire support was 148 (Meiktila) Commando Forward Observation Battery, which was one of several artillery units in the British Army with a Special Forces role.

Attached to the Regiment was 12 Air Defence Battery (Shah Shujah's Troop), which was part of 12 Air Defence Regiment. Warned to move on 2 April, their twelve Rapier firing units were in Plymouth two days later ready to load on the LSL *Sir Geraint*, a remarkable feat of organization. Their affiliation to 6th Field Force gave them an invaluable depth of knowledge of infantry warfare. The Falklands terrain, the tactics of the Argentine pilots and the need for visual acquisition at San Carlos forced the gunners to change their methods and fire at the rear of the aircraft as opposed to the front or side. 43 Air Defence Battery, 32nd Guided Weapon Regiment, provided two sections of Blowpipe, which was a welcome addition to the 3rd Commando Brigade Air Defence Troop. The gunners found carrying this cumbersome weapon extremely fatiguing.

Argentine air defence was organized through Air Defence Command and extended its operational cover to include the Falkland Islands, although locally under the command of the Army. With no high-performance fighters to protect the Falklands, it was imperative that as many air defence assets as possible should be deployed. By 6 April Marine, Army and Air Force anti-aircraft and air defence units had been integrated into a single unit working to the Air Defence Information and Control Centre. Marine signallers provided communications. The Marine Anti-Aircraft Battery had landed on 2 April and placed its thirteen Tigercat SAMs and twelve single-barrel 30mm Hispano-Suiza guns around the airport. The Army's 101 and 102 Air Defence Groups brought a total of three 35mm twin-barrelled GDF-002 Oerlikon batteries connected to Skyguard fire control radars, and the Air Force provided a battery of 35mm Oelikons connected to Superfledermaus radars. Two batteries of Air Force Rheinmetall twin-barrelled 20mm guns were also deployed, with one battery moving to Goose Green. At unit level,

Blowpipe and Soviet SAM-7 Strella surface-to-air missiles were widely deployed.

Argentine early warning was provided by the Air Force 2nd Early Warning Group, later renamed Early Warning Group Falklands, which installed a AN/TPS-43F search radar and a TPS-44 surveillance radar on high ground near the airport. With a range of 225 miles, the former was detected on 13 April and was moved, a replica being left in its place. 601 Anti-Aircraft Group brought a Roland surface-to-air missile system, which influenced British air tactics around Stanley.

The terrain ensured that armour played a minor part in the campiagn. The Argentines sent 10th 'Colonel Isidoro Suarez' and 181 Armoured Reconnaisance Cavalry Squadrons, each consisting of twelve-wheeled AML 90s and four jeeps. Largely confined to the roads and firm tracks around Stanley, apart from a minor part in the final hours before the Argentine surrender, they were hardly used, which was perhaps fortunate for the British because their 90mm main armament packed a useful punch. In contrast the British sent two Troops of the Blues and Royals. Each was equipped with two Scorpions mounting the very effective 30mm Rarden and two Scimitars, each with a 75mm cannon. A REME-manned Samson recovery CVR(T) was in support. In spite of their well-known cross-country capability, it was a disturbing measure of the senior commanders' lack of fundamental knowledge about some British equipment that the Blues and Royals were not properly used as an armoured fist until Wireless Ridge. Their fear that the vehicles were unable to go where a person could go was unfounded. Those who had encountered the CVR(T)s in the jungles of Belize and snows of Norway knew that their total ground pressure displacement was lighter than that of a man. On one occasion near Teal Inlet, while working with 3 Para, a Scorpion commander took his vehicle on to very boggy peat in which men were sinking up to their knees and used a kinetic energy tow rope to release a bogged-down tractor.

With the extremely poor roads, paths and tracks, and speed being of the essence to attack a beachhead, Menendez was heavily reliant upon helicopters. 601 Combat Aviation Battalion, which had already seen action in South Georgia, was part of the Infantry and was organized into three elements. The Helicopter Company had a gunship role and was equipped with nine A-109 Hirundos, six Lamas and ten Iroquois. The major troop-carrying capability was provided by A Helicopter Assault Company, flying eight Pumas and two Chinooks, and B Helicopter Assault Company equipped with ten Iroquois. Additional troop heli-lift was also available from the Air Force and Coastguard.

The British troop-carrying capability was provided by 845 and 846 Naval Air Squadrons with Wessex and Sea Kings respectively, who were thoroughly familiar with supporting the Commando Brigade. All but one of the 18 Squadron RAF troop-carrying Chinooks were lost on the *Atlantic Conveyor*.

Several Argentine support units were assembled in single groups. Engineer Group Malvinas consisted of the 9th, 10th, Amphibious Engineers and 601 Engineer Group. Since the amphibious engineers were the only unit to arrive fully equipped, the army sappers were only able to undertake simple tasks such as laying mines and helping to build simple bunkers. By the end of May most defences had been completed but the bombing and shelling would ensure the need for continual repair and maintenance. When they were not engaged on engineer tasks, sappers acted as infantry, which they performed credibly.

It is thought that the Argentines laid about 25,000 mines in about 119 minefields that covered a total of twelve square miles of the Falklands, some of which were laid on beaches, where they were covered by and moved in shifting sands; others sank in the peat, only to rise later and become a threat to man and beast. Origins included Argentina, Spain, Italy, Israel and the USA. In a captured obstacle plan produced by the Amphibious Engineers on 18 April, minefields protect the airfield, Two Sisters and the southern beaches. A captured trace mapped by 601 Engineer Group shows extensive field defences in the sectors occupied by 6th Infantry Regiment and mixed minefields protecting 7th Infantry Regiment on Mount Longdon. In most instances, minefields were wired off and marked by a sign 'Mina', but the wind, bombing and shelling often flattened fences. Instructions were issued by engineer commanders to mark minefields on maps, but these were often lost in the chaos of retreat and withdrawal.

During the Beagle Channel crisis with Chile in 1978, the Argentine logistic organization was severely criticized. With the decision to sit tight in Stanley, the 9th and 10th Logistic Companies were centralized into the Logistic Centre, each supported by unit echelons to collect and distribute supplies, but there was insufficient transport to keep up with the demand, particularly by those units manning the Outer Defence Zone in the hills to the west and Army Group Littoral. Some front-line units suffered from lack of food and fresh water and inadequate ammunition supplies, yet the immense amount of food, ammunition, clothing and equipment found in Stanley godowns indicated a combination of inefficiency, poor routes and British air and naval interdiction on the logistic chain. There is no doubt the destruction of several helicopters after 21 May hampered logistic operations.

Supply to the West Falklands was initially easy, with Fox Bay and Port Howard being supplied by the Naval Transport Service, Falklands Islands Company coasters and helicopters. However, with the imposition of the Maritime Exclusion Zone and attacks on Argentine shipping, the Logistic Centre sought alternative methods, which included heavy drop by a C-130 to Goose Green and Fox Bay on 19 May, the pallets containing, among other items, wellington boots. When supplies ran low, troops resorted to the time-honoured method of requisition. Many British troops were surprised by the quality of some Argentine rations, especially those containing a small bottle of Scotch whisky; how they would have welcomed a small tot in the freezing cold of the mountains. They were a little irked to find that the tins of corned beef were made by a Leeds company!

Apart from the sinking of the *Atlantic Conveyor,* there were few attacks on British maritime or ground logistics and although the demand was great, supplies always got through. 3rd Commando Brigade was well supported by the Commando Logistic Regiment and the LSLs but when 5th Infantry Brigade arrived in early June, it brought only 81 Ordnance Company RAOC and so the Regiment became a divisional asset supporting both brigades, much to Lieutenant Colonel Ivor Hellberg's disappointment. In spite of considerable handling difficulties, stores handled by the commando 'loggies' included 17,000 tons outloaded from the United Kingdom, 1,200 tons of ammunition ferried from Ajax Bay to the 3rd Commando Brigade's forward supply dump at Teal Inlet and 1,000 tons to 5th Infantry Brigade at Fitzroy, as well as 1,590 tons of rations moved and 1,414 tons of fuel. They also provided specialist equipment for the Advanced Forces. Much of the stores were ferried ashore by Mexeflotes operated by 17 Port Regiment RCT and then helicoptered forward to the front-line. The 'loggies' lacked specialist equipment to move containers but the Eager Beaver forklifts proved amazingly adaptable.

An essential element of morale in warfare is the knowledge by the soldier that, if he is wounded, falls ill or is injured, someone will rescue him and hand him over to a doctor for treatment or perhaps to the chaplain for the Last Rites. The soldier's worst nightmare is not so much being wounded but slowly dying on the battlefield with no one coming to his aid. Major Eduardo Carrizo-Salvadores, who commanded the defence of Mount Longdon, is full of praise for 'the stretcher bearers, doctors and nurses who ran into the middle of the explosions in order to save the life of a wounded comrade.' By nurses he means medical orderlies. Carrizo-Salvadores was equally praiseworthy of the signallers repairing telephone lines and mess orderlies delivering food to the platoons under fire. There is some evidence that the Argentine medical system lacked some basic supplies such as drugs and anaesthetics. When Commander Rick Jolly RN, who ran the 'Red and Green Life Machine' at Ajax Bay, inspected the Argentine Field Hospital in the Stanley Community Centre he found a mixture of antiquated operating tables, modern equipment and medical clothing, but useless drugs and antibiotic samples, some of which had been donated by large European pharmaceutical companies.

Argentine medical planning and casualty evacuation procedures were heavily criticized. 9th and 10th Infantry Brigades both brought their medical companies, and surgical teams worked at the King Edward VII Memorial Hospital in Stanley. However, there was no hospital ship, until the repatriation of the prisoners, for the evacuation of the badly wounded, although some were flown out by transport aircraft to mainland hospitals. When West

Falklands surrendered, British medical units dealt with over forty Argentine casualties, some with suppurating wounds over a fortnight old. It was noticeable that when Task Force Mercedes at Goose Green and Army Group Puerto Argentino surrendered, there were very few ambulances – a consequence of the lack of planning. Compared to those captured by the British, Argentine wounded dealt with by their own side fared badly.

By comparison, the wealth of Britain's military experience ensured that medical support was efficient and effective. In the early part of the campaign Royal Navy medical, clinical and dental teams bore the brunt until they were joined by the 16th Field Ambulance and 2nd Field Hospital after the ground campaign began. From first aid at the point of wound or injury to evacuation to Ajax Bay and then on to the hospital ship *Uganda*, the casualty stood an excellent chance of survival. Part of *Canberra* was converted to a high-dependency fifty-bed ward and its No 3 Surgical Support Team dealt with eighty-two British and ninety Argentine casualties. Only three very seriously wounded British died after casualty evacuation from their units on to the *Uganda*.

By mid-April Malvinas Joint Command had evaluated that the absence of Special Forces to deal with incidents outside the main garrisons was a serious handicap and when Galtieri visited on 22 April Menendez pressed his need for a flying column to plug gaps and respond to incidents outside the main garrisons on East and West Falklands. All three Argentine Armed Forces, the Coastguard and the National Gendarmarie each had Special Forces units and there was a large pool available throughout the Armed Forces and in the police.

Communist-inspired terrorism and subversion seeped through Central and South America after Fidel Castro's 1959 invasion of Cuba and, with the USA the mainstay of resistance, it was not long before its military advisers were running counter-insurgency and Ranger courses at the Airborne Infantry School at Cordoba. When the revolutionaries surfaced in Argentina, Special Forces training veered toward internal security operations and the US instructors gave way to the more offensive Israelis and South Africans. In preparation for the 1978 World Football Championships, Major Mohammed Seineldin formed an anti-terrorist unit, Special Team Halcon 8. Consisting of an OC, six subalterns and eight warrant officers and SNCOs, its principal role was to develop unconventional warfare techniques, train potential Special Forces and solve the inherent problem of raising commando units for mobilization. Any of the Halcon 8 cadre could be expected to go operational. It is thought that there were five Halcon 8 with 601 Commando Company on the Falklands but none with 602 Commando Company. It was the first time they were engaged in conventional fighting and after the war a commentator pressed for Argentina to modernize its Special Forces with permanent units and avoid the necessity of committing men without refresher training to a highly specialized form of warfare.

Selection for Argentine Special Forces took place after an individual had either volunteered or had been talent-spotted as suitable for training. The basic selection course lasted three days and included fitness and endurance tests, swimming, military knowledge and IQ. Successful candidates then attended a three-month course at the Commando Wing of the School of Infantry at Campo de Mayo, where comprehensive instruction was given in close-quarter battle, specialist fieldcraft, waterborne activities and urban, rural, jungle, desert and winter warfare. The drop-out rate was high, but those who passed were awarded the prestigious green beret and were either posted to an operational commando unit or back to their parent arm, with the liability of being recalled for Special Forces duty. This was designed to neutralise the political aspirations of officers such as Seineldin, who, in 1989, used 601 Commando Company in an attempt to install a general sympathetic to his politics as Army Commander. An inherent weakness was the lack of bonding, mutual understanding and team spirit although these are countered by the Catholic faith and patriotism. Organization tended to be standard with a headquarters, three sixteen-man Assault Sections commanded by a captain and a Support Section with Blowpipe, Installaza rocket launchers, Brandt 60mm mortars and 7.62mm MAGs. The total strength was typically fifteen officers and forty-nine SNCOs. In contrast, selection into British Special Forces was rigorous and, when a candidate was successful, he tended to remain in Special Forces units for most of his military career, although on occasion he may be posted back to a conventional unit for a tour of duty or to attend a course.

Halcon 8 was not mobilized for the invasion of the Falklands and watched, no doubt green with envy, the Tactical Divers' and Amphibious Commando Grouping's part in the landings. Nevertheless, Major Mario Castagneto, then commanding Halcon 8, prepared 601 Commando Company in case Special Forces was needed and by 10 April it was undergoing a rigorous training programme at the Commando Wing. Shortly after Galtieri returned to Buenos Aires, Argentina received non-aggression guarantees from Chile, and Castagneto was ordered to the Falklands.

During the evening of 24 April, the day Castagneto had planned to get married, he and three officers landed at Stanley and immediately contacted the Special Operations Group, one of two Air Force Special Forces units. Part of 7th Air Brigade based in Moreno, it worked closely with 7th Counter Insurgency Helicopter Squadron, which was equipped with Iroquois and Bell 212s. Its principal roles were air despatch, heavy drop and search and rescue. The other Air Force Special Forces unit was the Combat Control Team, which was part of 1st Air Brigade, a transport formation based at El Palomar. It consisted of about thirty men who prepared dropping zones for the 4th Airborne Brigade. Several times it was thought that this brigade might reinforce the Falklands garrison. Both Air Force Special Forces units arrived soon after the intervention and spent most of their time at Military Air Base

Malvinas at Stanley helping to administer the arrival and rapid departure of aircraft, which they did with efficiency and imagination. The imposition of the Maritime and then Total Exclusion Zone meant that much of the work had to be done at night.

Castagneto discussed Special Forces operations with Jofre and Menendez and they were placed under the operational command of Army Group Malvinas, as the Rapid Reaction Force on thirty minutes' notice, and administered by the Reserve. During the afternoon the advance party visited Lieutenant-Colonel David Comini, commanding 3rd Infantry Regiment, and discussed his defence against amphibious landings.

On 26 April, the day after South Georgia was recaptured by the British, 601 Commando Company left its base at Campo de Mayo and flew to Comodoro Rivadavia. Next day Castagneto accompanied Comini on a helicopter recce north of the Darwin Peninsula and noted the poor going, the many rivers, streams and ponds and abundance of wildlife and sheep, which would aid survival and long patrols. Meanwhile his men arrived in theatre. A recce planned for 28 April was postponed because of poor weather but a number of Kawasaki motorcycles arrived. During the morning of 30 April the company carried out its first operation outside Stanley when 1st Section were helicoptered to Estancia House and found 7.62mm ammunition boxes and some British rations, possibly cached by Corporal York.

By 2 May it was clear to Argentina that unless a political settlement was reached, landings of some sort by the British were likely and so Menendez created a brigade-sized reaction and retaliatory force, 'Z' Reserve, which, because Stanley was considered to be the British objective, was assembled from 3rd Infantry Brigade and placed under command of Omar Parada. In his Preparatory Order for the Reserve, Menendez anticipated armed helicopter incursions, electronic surveillance and naval shelling of defensive positions, principally against Stanley. Task Force Reconquest at Fox Bay was to be ready to land on East Falkland, while Task Force Mercedes at Goose Green was to deploy to Two Sisters, Mount Tumbledown and Wireless Ridge and destroy enemy penetration. Task Force Monte Caseros was to occupy Mount Wall and Mount Challenger to prevent enemy penetration westwards. Combat Team Solari, supported by a Helicopter Company, was to block enemy advances from the north. The strength of the Reserve was enhanced by the two armoured recce cavalry squadrons.

While the reorganization and reinforcement phase was underway, the next question needing to be answered by Menendez was – what will the British do if they decide to land? A document compiled in mid-May suggests the British strategy would be to defeat the Argentine forces, recapture as much of the Stanley peninsula as possible and get Britain into a favourable political bargaining position. This would be achieved by either a high-risk direct assault against a well-defended Stanley sector or a low-risk amphibious assault north east of Stanley with a view to recapturing the town once

1. Argentines loading a trailer on to a landing craft on 2 April.

2. NP 8901 as prisoners outside Government House on 2 April.

3. Four Argentine conscripts stand outside their bunker at Stanley.

4. M Company 42 Commando guard the crew of the *Sante Fe* at Grytviken on 25 April (IWM).

5. Stanley Common. An Argentine army chaplain flanked by two officers stand in front of a bunker dug beneath a lorry. The chaplain has black polythene around his knees to keep him dry when kneeling.

6. Argentine Marine Infantry queue for food, probably on Mount Tumbledown.

Poss TIGERCAT Launcher

Poss Cmd Veh (with whip an

Prob 105mm GUN/HOWITZER

TIGERCAT Launcher

Trench

7. About 20 April. Argentine activity on the Falklands in area of Sapper Hill.

8. Argentine activity on Stanley Common.

VIEW SW

Poss PACK HOWITZER- hy

Area contains either 3 or 6 poss AAA guns

SKYGUARD Radar

Defensive Position

9. HMS *Fearless* off Ascension Island. White strip on the left is English Beach. Green Mountain in backgound.

10. 3 Para practice loading on to a helicopter from *Fearless*. In the left background is *Canberra*.

11. 5 May. A Scimitar of the Blues and Royals at English Beach.

12. Stanley Common. An Argentine conscript stands outside a bunker.

13. Tumbledown. An Argentine Marine Infantry officer poses. He wears a combat waistcoat.

14. 19 May. *Fearless* refuels at sea from *Tidespring*.

15. Gentlemen of the Press at San Carlos. Second left to right Ian Bruce (*Glasgow Herald*), Charles Lawrence (*Sunday Telegraph*), Max Hastings (*London Standard*) and Robert Fox (*BBC Radio*).

16. 21 May. Defence Troop HQ 3rd Commando Brigade and HQ Signal Squadron in the Tank Deck of *Fearless* waiting to go ashore.

sufficient forces were ashore. San Carlos is mentioned as one of three possible landing zones, the others being at Fitzroy and the Port Louis peninsula, which were reckoned to be the most favourable option and could be achieved with minimum losses and thus favourable to British public opinion. The San Carlos option was considered a disadvantage because of the length of time it would take to approach Port Stanley and the possibility that a negotiated cease-fire could be called before the town was recaptured. It was felt that the British would rely heavily upon helicopters.

4

The Second Battle
of Grytviken

4 to 27 April.
See Map Page 26

"It's not exactly as busy as Brighton Front round here, you know."
Allegedly Captain Barker on the excessive secrecy surrounding
Operation *Paraquet*.

On 4 April helicopter pilot Lieutenant Tim Finding RN visited the three BAS
staff and Lucinda Buxton and Anne Price at St Andrew's Bay. *Endurance*
was now the only British naval presence in the region and Barker hid The
Red Plum among icebergs and floes, but next day, low on fuel and stocks,
was ordered to steam north and meet the Task Force.

The British were now blind to Argentine activities and the BAS, contrary
to the scientists' traditional philosophy of apolitical collaboration, found
themselves caught up in a war and field parties quickly formed themselves
into a coast-watching service. Information collated by the ornithologists Paul
Goodall-Copestake and Julian Hector on Bird Island was sent to the BAS
station on Signy Island, 650 miles to the south-west, relayed to the
Bransfield, copied to the Maritime Communication Centre at Portishead and
finally to Cambridge, where it was made available to the Ministry of
Defence. Damien Sanders and Ian Barker, hiding on the slopes of Mount
Hodges, reported on Argentine activity in Cumberland Bay. Tony North set
off from St Andrews Bay to Hound Bay and found no evidence of Argentine
patrolling. Five days later he visited Royal Bay and, after another five days,
returned to Hound Bay but still found no evidence of Argentine activity.
These BAS patrols covered a third of the east coast of South Georgia and
provided valuable intelligence of where the Argentines were not, which was
most of the island.

In Britain there was a political view that South Georgia was secondary to
liberating the Falklands and the Ministry of Defence advised the Cabinet that
its recapture would be relatively easy. As far as the Government was
concerned, Argentina had no legitimate right to South Georgia and therefore
its occupation was regarded as not negotiable. Retaking it would also
demonstrate political resolve and enhance public morale, which, although

not wavering, was becoming a little fed up with the protracted international mediation. Militarily, the island's leeward coast offered sheltered anchorages and a secure forward operating base beyond the range of the Argentine Air Force, from which intelligence-gathering and Advanced Forces raids could be launched against the Falklands, admittedly 600 usually stormy miles to the west. Its recapture would allow the military to plan a relatively safe operation, which the politicians desperately wanted. On HMS *Fearless* Thompson's staff, assisted by Lieutenant Veal, began to plan its recovery.

At about 5pm on 6 April, as Brigadier Thompson was about to join *Fearless* from HQ Commando Forces in Plymouth, Major General Moore told him that Northwood wanted a commando company to remain in Britain for a top secret mission and suggested the composite 45 Commando group on jungle warfare training in Brunei should be brought back. Thompson thought this unwise because they would need to acclimatize and suggested that 42 Commando, who had recently returned from its annual three-month Norwegian winter deployment, would be a better option.

On 7 April Captain Brian Young, commanding the County class destroyer *Antrim* in Gibraltar, was ordered, with quaint naval terminology, 'to proceed with despatch' to Ascension Island. Accompanied by the Type 12 frigate *Plymouth*, commanded by Captain David Pentreath, and the Fleet Oiler *Tidespring*, commanded by Captain Shane Redmond, this small flotilla formed CTG 317.9 for the recapture of South Georgia. The ships crossed the equator on 8 April and were visited by King Neptune and Soviet Long Range Air Force Tupolev-20 Bears flying their regular sorties from Angola to Cuba, now with something tangible to report.

The next day 42 Commando left its barracks at Bickleigh, a few miles north of Plymouth, and embarked on the converted cruise liner *Canberra* in Portsmouth. Captain Chris Nunn's M Company, however, remained behind, concealed in the gymnasium and forbidden to contact their families. Major Guy Sheridan, second-in-command 42 Commando, visited HQ Commando Forces and was told by Moore that although a political solution to the crisis might preclude a landing, he, Sheridan, had been appointed military commander for the recapture of South Georgia. Moore considered the operation to be 'quick, easy and attractive'. Late on the 9th M Company were flown from RAF Brize Norton to Ascension Island where Sheridan met Major Jonathan Thomson, commander SBS, who had been instructed to attach 2 SBS to M Company for the operation, now named Operation *Paraquet*, after the long-tailed parrot. Brigadier Thompson's staff had already christened it Operation *"Paraquat"* after the industrial rat poison. It seemed very appropriate. Sheridan wanted the Mountain and Arctic Warfare Cadre, but was told to expect the SAS Mountain Troop. The Royal Marines embarked on *Tidespring* the following day. Brigadier Thompson and Commodore Clapp were then ordered by Admiral Fieldhouse to be at Ascension Island on 17 April and leaving its convoy, *Fearless* headed south at top speed through the calm, sunny, blue waters off West Africa.

As far as Thompson was concerned, his regular communications with Northwood suggested that the recapture of South Georgia took priority over the liberation of the Falklands. He found this option attractive because it had been several years since 3rd Commando Brigade had practised an amphibious assault with all available assets and resources, and one against a weak enemy would be a useful rehearsal. Thompson now needed to persuade everyone else and gained the support of Clapp, also on *Fearless,* that Operation *Paraquet* was top priority. Their main problem was that the troops and equipment were spread haphazardly throughout the Landing Group and would have to be cross-decked so that the right unit with the right equipment landed on the right beach at the right time. By this time, both men knew M Company was assigned to the operation in addition to Advanced Forces.

When Lieutenant Colonel Michael Rose, CO 22 SAS, heard that the Falklands Islands had been captured and HQ 3rd Commando Brigade was on stand-by for deployment to the South Atlantic, he immediately offered the services of D Squadron, which was commanded by Major Cedric Delves, formerly of the Devon and Dorsets, who had been encouraged to transfer by his adjutant, Captain 'H' Jones. Squadron Headquarters and its four sabre troops, numbering about sixty-six men, and fourteen members of 264 Signal Squadron were briefed at Bradbury Lines, Hereford on 4 April and then, with about 50,000 pounds of palleted equipment, were flown to Ascension Island and embarked on the Royal Fleet Auxiliary *Fort Austin*. With two warships, an experienced winter warfare commando company and a SBS section already assigned to the task, more Advanced Forces seemed a little excessive. It was inevitable that the sheer weight of numbers and influence in favour of the SAS would affect planning. And so it proved.

Information on the Argentines was scarce, but some assumptions could be made from information supplied by Keith Mills and his detachment. The South Georgia garrison was probably no more than a platoon of marines, most of whom were conscripts. Their organization, operating procedures and weapon configuration were not known. Nor was it known if the scrap metal merchants, still assumed to be at Leith, would be conscripted to fight, but, if they were, this would give the Argentines about two platoons. There was no evidence yet to suggest they had interfered with the activities of the BAS field parties or the two women wildlife photographers. The British planners did not know that one of the first decisions made by the Junta was that the defence of South Georgia would be minimal. Air cover could not be provided except from the *Veintecinco de Mayo*, but she had not appeared.

CTG 317.9 arrived at Ascension Island on 10 April and Young was told that his command was to be reinforced by D Squadron. After stowing their mountain of equipment, CTG 317.9, with *Tidespring* carrying two 845 NAS Wessex HU 5 troop-carriers and M Company, left Ascension on the 11th. Two days later the ships overhauled *Fort Austin,* en route to meet

Endurance, and it took all morning to cross-deck Squadron Headquarters, 16 (Mobility) and 18 (Air) Troops to a very crowded *Antrim* and 19 (Mountain) and 17 (Boat) Troops to *Plymouth.* Young then headed south into the white-tipped grey-green South Atlantic swell and the watery sun of a southern hemisphere late summer.

The arrival of D Squadron was not entirely welcome and reports suggest some tension with the Royal Marines. Much of this centred around their differing methods of winter warfare and operational philosophies. Until he was persuaded to share his considerable experience, some SAS doubted Sheridan's expertise as a winter warfare expert and mountaineer. The Royal Marines, like the Army, tend to work in large groups, issue orders and then ask for questions. Not unnaturally, in the SAS, where small teams predominate, there is an independent approach: 'We have a problem, lads, how shall we deal with it?' In any event D Squadron were confident they could handle anything thrown at them. Indeed one SAS veteran of the campaign later claimed that D Squadron alone could have defeated the Argentines on the Falklands. As events would show, this confidence was misplaced.

On 14 April CTG 317.9 had an emotional reunion with *Endurance* and when Captain Barker was invited to join Sheridan's planning group he brought gridded air photographs and a mass of collated information about the topography, meteorology and coastal conditions of South Georgia, literally a few days old. Mountain Troop and 2 SBS cross-decked to the relative comfort of his ship. On the 15th a Kinloss Wing Nimrod, detached to Wideawake airport at Ascension Island, dropped formal operational orders dated 12 April from Admiral Fieldhouse to Captain Young ordering him to reoccupy South Georgia with the minimum loss of life, with 21 April set as the landing date.

In *Antrim's* Admiral's cabin Young's planning group plotted, in great secrecy, the recovery of South Georgia, but Barker found the inter-service tension and the secrecy frustrating and he allegedly commented, 'It's not exactly as busy as Brighton Front round here, you know.' Several options emerged, one of which was to run *Endurance* onto the beach and deliver M Company dry-shod, with *Antrim* and *Plymouth* delivering naval gunfire support. Major Delves, in his role as SAS adviser and squadron commander, was keen to have a say of how best his squadron should be used, as any good commander would do. Sheridan felt Delves was underestimating the operation and environment, but, since no one ever knew what the SAS were doing anyway, he had to assume that the four troops were winter warfare competent. A two-phase plan then emerged with SAS recceing Leith, Stromness and Husvik, while the SBS would recce Grytviken and King Edward Point. If either hit trouble, M Company would land as reinforcements. If all went well, M Company and the Advanced Forces would land together. A Royal Marine operation was fast becoming an Advanced Forces operation and M Company found itself being sidelined.

No one seems to have thought of Captain Trombetta's idea of inviting the enemy to surrender.

Delves then astonished everyone by planning that his twelve-strong Mountain Troop, commanded by Captain John Hamilton, should be dropped by helicopter on the south-east side of the island 20 miles from Stromness Bay and march in. On reaching the objective, the troop would divide into three patrols, one to recce Stromness and Husvik, the second to recce Leith and the third to find helicopter landing sites and beaches. As soon as the strength and dispositions were known, Mountain Troop would regroup and, if able, deal with the enemy in the knowledge that D Squadron could reinforce them. Barker was appalled and explained that the ground was ruthless, even to experienced polar explorers with small sledges. He reckoned it would take at least seven days to reach Stromness and suggested the SAS should land a few miles from Leith and approach from the north-east by Husvik and Stromness. Although one scientist later described the SAS attitude as 'We're the SAS, we can walk on water' Delves conceded that his plan was unwise and then, although he did not know South Georgia or its terrain, insisted the best place to land was on Fortuna Glacier, ten miles to the west of Leith. Dr Richard Law, the BAS director, later advised that this was not a good idea because there were wide crevasses, which would hinder movement. In preparation for their operation Mountain Troop collected stores and equipment available on *Endurance*, including sleeping bags, winter warfare clothing and skis from the Ship's Detachment and Joint Service Expedition stores. The Troop then cross-decked to *Antrim*.

In comparison to the complexities of the SAS proposed operation, the SBS plan was simple – land from *Endurance*'s two Wasps at Hound Bay, cross Cumberland Bay East by Gemini and find an OP overlooking Grytviken.

Back at Ascension Island *Fearless* anchored off Georgetown early on 17 April and Thompson and Clapp had their first full meeting with Major General Jeremy Moore, who advised them not to mention Operation *"Paraquet"*. They then met Sir John Fieldhouse on board *Hermes,* who told them to concentrate on recapturing the Falklands and forget South Georgia. Sheridan was now on his own facing the considerable influence of the SAS.

Concern for her vulnerability to an increasingly active Argentine Navy and Air Force led to *Bransfield* being ordered to leave the South Atlantic the same day. This was a crushing blow to the field parties who had hoped the ship would collect them, particularly as the four BAS on Lyell Glacier were in a pretty poor state, with reduced rations, weak radio batteries and little winter clothing.

To monitor Argentine activity in the area and support the operation, the RAF mounted Maritime Radar Reconnaissance (MRR) operations using Victors based at Wideawake airfield. Early on 20 April Squadron-Leader John Elliot, supported by four tankers, flew the 2000 miles to South Georgia at a height of 43,000 feet and then, dropping to 18,000 feet, carried out a ninety-minute search covering 150,000 square miles. By the time the Victor touched down 14 hours and 45 minutes after taking off it had flown over 7000 miles and established the record for long-range recce under operational conditions. The mission provided valuable information on shipping as well as icebergs and the extent of the pack ice.

Meanwhile Secretary of State Haig had failed to persuade Argentina to evacuate the captured territories and he warned the Junta that Great Britain was expected to take some sort of military action against South Georgia within days. The Cabinet indeed gave final approval for its recapture and operational command was passed to Captain Young, by now well inside the 200-mile South Georgia Maritime Exclusion Zone imposed by Great Britain in early April.

Late on 20 April Young sent *Plymouth* and *Endurance* south-east to the Cumberland Bay area, while *Antrim* and *Tidespring* remained off Stromness Bay. The next day the ice patrol ship moved into St Andrews Bay and Ellerbeck flew ashore to contact the BAS field parties, but found only Peter Stark, Lucinda Buxton and Anne Price, who confirmed they had not seen any Argentines. Totally isolated since the departure of the *Bransfield*, the BAS coast-watching had continued with Tony North and Myles Plant patrolling as far as the Barff Peninsula. Since Stark's great knowledge of South Georgia was desperately needed, he was induced to join Sheridan's planning team on *Endurance* and was replaced by Chief Petty Officer Tommy Scott to offer the ladies some protection. Unfortunately Stark lost an opportunity to brief the SBS, who were about to land, and was led away by an SAS model-maker constructing a facsimile of Grytviken and the BAS base at King Edward Point.

Major Delves still rejected local expert advice and, insisting that Fortuna Glacier was the best option, consulted two Himalayan mountain climbers, both former SAS. Quite why he should seek the views of two Everest veterans in Great Britain who had never been to South Georgia is unclear but it was probably symptomatic of tensions emerging in CTG 317.9 of 'experts with influence' versus local knowledge. Certainly Barker felt that the information provided by the BAS and himself was undervalued. Sheridan, still military commander, could have done with more support.

As dawn broke over the grey heaving mass of the South Atlantic ten miles off Stromness Bay, *Antrim's* flight commander, Lieutenant Commander Ian Stanley, and his crew climbed into the destroyer's anti-submarine warfare Wessex, nicknamed 'Humphrey', and lifted off from the soaking, seesawing flight deck for a preliminary recce of Fortuna Glacier. Although there was driving rain, sleet and a strong wind over the glacier, conditions appeared suitable and Brian Young decided to proceed with the operation. 'Humphrey' joined *Tidespring's* two Wessex and loaded Mountain Troop's heavily-laden troopers, all dressed in nylon winter whites over their combat kit, from *Antrim's* flight deck. With another low front steaming in, Stanley guided the flight to Fortuna Glacier, but the wind rose to 60 knots. The helicopters then ran into thick cloud and rain over the sea and blizzards over the land, forcing Stanley to abort the mission. After lunch the three helicopters again lifted off and, in spite of freezing squalls whipping in from the Antarctic, turbulent winds and whiteout as snow merged with white clouds, Mountain Troop was landed. It was with some relief that Stanley led the helicopters back to the ships.

At about 5.30pm a four-man 2 SBS patrol was inserted by Wasp at Hound Bay, but two more patrols could not be landed because of the rapidly deteriorating weather. Two of the SBS secured the landing site while their colleagues recced the area, during which one of them trod on the tail of a large sleeping elephant seal, which rose up and snarled. They then saw a light in a small hut. Creeping up, one of the SBS knocked and entered to reveal two very startled civilians, who introduced themselves as Tony North and Myles Plant and offered the Royal Marines a welcome cup of tea. The two BAS said they had not seen any Argentines.

As Barker and Stark had predicted, Mountain Troop found the going on Fortuna Glacier extremely bad and they were unable to move as fast as they had calculated. Encounters with crevasses were frequent; a soldier would suddenly drop waist-deep and have to be hauled out by his colleagues. The plan to cross the glacier never materialized. In fact it took nearly five hours to cover about 800 metres. In the rapidly deteriorating conditions, weapons froze and spindrift blocked the GPMG feed trays. Darkness fell and a storm smashed its way through the South Atlantic and struck South Georgia. In winds of 70 knots, the wind-chill factor rose alarmingly and with whiteouts making navigation almost impossible, Hamilton sought sanctuary. Spread over 200 metres, his men sheltered from the ferocity of the wind and discovered what every Royal Marine knew from the Norwegian deployments that individual canvas sheets clipped together to form tents were hopelessly inadequate. Poles shattered in the wind and one entire shelter disappeared into the darkness. Extraction was out of the question until daylight. Hamilton's predicament was serious. Those who opted to sleep in the shelters snuggled into their sleeping bags and dozed against the sides to prevent them collapsing from the weight of snow. Every hour a sentry struggled outside into the howling blizzard to clear snowdrifts from around the tents to prevent them being buried. The soldiers who had lost their tent had no alternative but to shiver fully dressed in sleeping bags in the open. Others sheltered underneath the pulk, which is a small sledge.

At midnight Ellerbeck made one more attempt to insert another SBS patrol but the gale was so strong his Wasp was twice almost blown into the sea. With four inches of snow on his windscreen, he aborted the flight and was literally swept on to *Endurance's* flight deck. The only alternative was to use the Geminis powered by 40-horsepower outboards, which were universally distrusted in the Services. Barker navigated his darkened ship to within

800 yards of the shore and, as the Geminis were lowered over the side, the wind briefly dropped and a winter's moon gave good visibility. Each boat carried six men and their equipment. Thick kelp prevented the SBS approaching the area near the landing site and they were forced to land through heavy breaking surf on the south shore of Hound Bay. Everyone was soaked and frozen. Three of the patrol set off through packs of seals and penguins and made contact with the SBS already ashore. Finding shelter, all twelve men settled down for the night, during which Squadron Leader Seymour carried out a second radar search of the area

For most of the night the ships were battered by a Force 11 gale and Young invited the ship's company on to the bridge in turn to watch great waves bursting down the length of *Antrim*, damaging the upperworks and putting one of the Seacat launchers out of action. Sometimes she was shrouded in freezing spray. The violent motions made it impossible to shove 'Humphrey' into the hangar and it remained on the flight deck tugging and straining at the securing cables. As dawn broke, so did the gale.

On Fortuna Glacier Hamilton and his men repacked the pulks. Although there was some improvement in the weather, the condition of his men was deteriorating quickly. A few hours more and some would be suffering from hypothermia, frostbite and other cold weather injuries, so at about 10am he asked to be extracted. *Antrim's* sick bay was prepared to receive casualties and flight deck crews were briefed on the rescue mission. Although still hindered by snow storms and winds gusting between 70 and 80 knots, at about 10.50am Stanley led the two Wessex and, reaching Antarctic Bay, he instructed them to land on Cape Constance, while he attempted to climb the 1,800 feet up the glacier to the waiting soldiers. Three times he was driven back by dreadful weather but by about 1.30pm the weather had improved and Stanley took the opportunity to return to Fortuna Glacier. Guided by flares from the ground, the Wessex flown by Lieutenant Mike Tidd landed and loaded a stick of six soldiers, including Hamilton. However, soon after it left the ground Tidd lost all visual reference points when the helicopter was suddenly enveloped in a snow squall. Already vulnerable to catastrophic icing, he could not climb clear of the weather and decided to turn back to acquire references but he then noticed his altimeter spinning fast and realized that impact was inevitable. He brought up the nose but the tail hit the ground and the helicopter skidded in a chorus of screeching metal for about fifty yards and then toppled over on its side, slightly injuring Staff Sergeant Phil Curass and Corporal Paul Bunker. The crew and the remainder of the SAS on the glacier were picked up by 'Humphrey' and the remaining Wessex, which had dumped fuel, and they both set off down the mountain. Enveloped by whiteout as he crossed a small ridge over a small fjord, the Wessex pilot, Lieutenant Ian Georgeson, also lost sight of his only point of reference as 'Humphrey' disappeared below him and returned to *Antrim*. Assuming there was the danger of high ground ahead, he landed the Wessex safely but it was pushed broadside by the wind and toppled on its side. Bunker was slightly injured a second time.

Stanley loaded 'Humphrey' with extra blankets and rations for the stranded men, who now numbered seventeen. Accompanied by the needless weight of Delves but joined by the more necessary ship's surgeon and a Medical Assistant, Stanley took off for Fortuna Glacier for a third time, but was twice defeated by the weather. He unloaded the doctor and medic and waited for another window in the weather. Meantime those on the glacier had rigged a survival shelter from the crashed helicopters and retrieved two covered liferafts. The weather improved slightly and, although anxious about 'Humphrey's' luck holding out, Stanley set out across the uninviting sea on his sixth sortie in twenty-four hours. Darkness was creeping fast across the horizon and weather conditions were treacherous when he landed near the two rafts. Although 'Humphrey' was filled with anti-submarine warfare equipment, after a quick conference with Georgeson, Stanley crammed all seventeen on board and the helicopter staggered into the angry sky and, chased by high winds, reached *Antrim*, which was pitching wildly in ferocious seas, shortly before night fell. Instead of hovering to one side and then sliding on to the flight deck, Stanley simply pancaked the helicopter. During the night a third MRR mission was flown.

Meanwhile the SBS had crossed Sorling Valley with the intention of launching the Geminis at the foot of Nordenskjold Glacier but found Cumberland Bay East icebound. A helicopter flew in two Geminis, but one had been damaged and, when severe weather prevented the surviving boat being launched, the crossing was aborted. It would be three days before the SBS could be recovered but their radio communications with *Endurance* would alert the Argentines of a British military presence on South Georgia.

So far Operation *Paraquet* had achieved nothing and the 21 April deadline had been missed. Guy Sheridan was in danger of losing the initiative through no fault of his own because expert local knowledge had been ignored by those who should have known better. Two valuable troop-carrying helicopters had been lost, a day had been wasted recovering Mountain Troop and, since most of its equipment was on Fortuna Glacier, it was ineffective as a fighting unit. While some excuse can be allowed for the failure of the SBS operation, the same cannot be said for the SAS. They thought they knew best; they did not and this potentially compromised the recovery of South Georgia. Lives were also risked to recover them. This was no heroic disaster.

The next night another attempt was made to land the SAS, this time from the sea. Shortly after midnight on 22 April Captain Young gently nosed the battered *Antrim* to a mile east of Grass Island to disembark the fifteen-strong Boat Troop. Commanded by Captain Tim Burls, the patrols were to go ashore in five Geminis, one of which was fitted with a modern 35-horsepower engine loaned from *Antrim*; otherwise all craft were fitted with the unreliable 40-horsepower outboards. It was 3.30am, clear but still rough, when the SAS, dressed in survival suits, scrambled into the Geminis, three to each boat. Within ten minutes three outboards were swamped and Burls decided to go ashore in two tethered convoys, but a gale suddenly erupted from nowhere. Three Geminis made it to Grass Island shortly before dawn but two with flooded outboards were blown into open sea although one coxswain managed to restart an engine and made landfall. *Antrim* then picked up a Mayday call and at 8.10am on 23 April the redoubtable Ian Stanley woke up 'Humphrey' and, after a seven-hour search, found one of the missing Geminis close to Cumberland Bay, eight miles away, almost in sight of the Argentines. The fifth one had disappeared and everyone feared the worst. On Green Island Boat Troop reported little activity in Stromness Bay and shortly before midnight attempted to land near Stromness but the outboards again proved unreliable.

During the morning an Argentine C-130 reported Captain Young's Task Group to Buenos Aires. Young was then advised that an Argentine submarine was believed to be in the area and he ordered CTG 317.9 out of the South Georgia Maritime Exclusion Zone except for *Endurance,* which was to avoid detection. Within hours Captain Barker's luck nearly failed him when the *Santa Fe,* en route from Mar del Plata naval base, came to periscope depth and her captain, Lieutenant Commander Hugo Bircain, locked on to *Endurance* but did not attack. It later transpired that he felt he could not torpedo the defenceless ship, which he knew well. Instead the submarine slipped below the surface and made for Grytviken. On board were eleven technicians and nine 1st Marine Infantry Battalion anti-tank gunners with their Bantam anti-tank missile launchers, commanded by Lieutenant Commander Lagos, sent by Vice Admiral Lombardo in response to a request for reinforcements from Captain Trombetta.

The following morning *Endurance* was hove-to in Hound Bay preparing to recover the SBS when an Argentine Boeing 707 suddenly burst out of the low clouds. The aircraft had been converted for long-range unarmed recce missions and was on the second leg of a triangle to search for the Task Force, which had taken her from Buenos Aires to the Falklands, north to Ascension Island then south to South Georgia before completing the pattern by turning west for the long flight back to Argentina. The Boeing dropped from 40,000 feet and approached the ship twice to within two miles at 3000 feet. The consequence of her appearance was that Argentina was informed that the British Rules of Engagement now permitted the shooting down of any Argentine aircraft. It would be a month before the 707s would again fly recce missions.

The Argentines on South Georgia were now fully aware of the naval activity, although they had been confused by the helicopter activity on 22 April and the failure of the British to appear. An Argentine intelligence assessment on 15 April assumed the SAS and SBS would land before an amphibious assault and Lagos's marines were therefore a welcome reinforcement. By 24 April Argentine intelligence had assessed that an attack on South Georgia was imminent. By about 10pm the *Santa Fe* was off Grytviken and early next morning her passengers were landed and the marines prepared defensive positions.

Boat Troop left Grass Island during the night and even though two engines broke down, succeeded in getting ashore near Stromness and cleared the derelict whaling station. Leaving five men, Burls and three others followed the route taken by Mills and Leach and climbed Harbour Point to look down on Leith. They reported to Delves the generator was switched off at 2am and, apart from a jittery burst of machine-gun fire in the direction of a rockfall, everything was quiet. As dawn crept over the horizon, they saw two marine sections stand-to on a small feature. The SAS plotted each trench, one barely 200 yards from the summit of Harbour Point, a heavy weapons position and a well-constructed headquarters bunker.

Later in the day Captain Young received a powerful reinforcement when the Type 23 frigate *Brilliant*, which was commanded by Captain John Coward, appeared over the horizon. When Admiral Woodward had learnt of the disastrous loss of the two Wessex he ordered Coward to join Task Force 317.9, where her two Lynx would give Young extra versatility. Pounding her way through heavy seas, she refuelled from *Tidespring* and joined *Plymouth* and *Antrim* as they re-entered the South Georgia Maritime Exclusion Zone. The following day, 25 April, reacting to the SBS radio transmissions, the *Santa Fe* carried out a surface standing patrol five miles east of Cumberland East Bay but was discovered by the ubiquitous 'Humphrey' on an anti-submarine patrol covering the approaches to the bay. Seeing a submarine creeping out of the mist about two miles off Barff Point, Ian Stanley carried out a depth-charge attack, the first by the Royal Navy on an enemy submarine since April 1945. By the end of the engagement, in mid-morning, Bircain brought his battle-damaged, smoking and listing submarine alongside the jetty at King Edward Harbour and unloaded a badly wounded steward, who had been supplying the bridge machine gun with ammunition during the attack.

Although the Advanced Forces patrols ashore had provided little intelligence of value, within the hour Captain Young decided to attack South Georgia with the ground forces he had available to him, which consisted of D Squadron, 2 SBS, Sheridan's Tactical Headquarters, an 81mm section, ten Royal Marines from the ship's detachments and NGFO2 and NGFO5 from 148 (Meiktila) Commando Forward Observation Battery, a total of seventy-five men. Most were crammed on board his destroyer. M Company was still 200 miles away on *Tidespring*. Sheridan split the force into three troops. The Royal Marines made up the first troop and were commanded by Captain Chris Nunn. The SBS formed the second troop. The third troop was the remainder of the SAS and was commanded by Major Delves. Sheridan remained military commander. The plan was to fly Nunn's troop, known as the Composite Company Group, to Hesterletten Flats, a grassy patch three miles south of Grytviken. A second assault group from Mobility Troop and 2 SBS would lift off from *Plymouth* and *Endurance* and get itself into a position above the base from which they could bring down covering fire. Naval gunfire support was controlled by Lieutenant Colonel Keith Eve, a highly experienced commando and parachute gunner, while Captain Chris Brown's NGFO5 spotted ashore.

After Young had confirmed that the submarine threat had decreased, Sheridan held his Orders Group and set H-Hour for 1.45pm. At 2.15pm Captain Brown told *Plymouth* to shell Hesterletten and as her shells curved 6000 feet into the air and impacted, Brown's Wasp was approaching the landing site. Stanley in 'Humphrey' was leading the two *Brilliant* Lynx at low level through Merton Passage toward Hesterletten when he was told to abort because he had strayed into the gunline of the bombarding ships. Heaving 'Humphrey' around, he joined the two Lynx orbiting the north end of Cumberland Bay and within five minutes the three helicopters were given clearance to return to Hesterletten. As Stanley later recalled, 'It was very unconventional. This was a commando-style assault force but we had no commando helicopters. Our helicopters consisted of one geriatric ASW Wessex and two of the latest ASW Lynx. None of the pilots were trained for amphibious warfare.' Unloading from 'Humphrey' was slow because the ASW equipment at the door of the helicopter prevented the traditional rush and Mobility and Mountain Troop were obliged to squeeze past one at a time and wait on the ground while loadmaster Petty Officer Fitzgerald handed down their equipment. While the two SAS troops secured the Brown Mountain ridge, Sheridan and the remainder of the Composite Company Group landed.

The 81mm mortar baseplate was set up and Captain Nunn immediately started registering possible targets on Brown Ridge, much to the annoyance of Delves who wanted targets hit along his intended route. Once again the different tactical philosophies of the SAS and conventional forces surfaced. As the ground forces advanced, Captain Brown asked *Antrim* to stand off the entrance of Cumberland East Bay and give close fire support. Remembering what had happened to the *Guerrico,* Young was reluctant, but by 3pm was in position. *Plymouth* also moved up and bombarded the north of King Edward Cove without hitting any buildings. To those ashore and on board it was an impressive if noisy sight. The post-Operation *Paraquet* report later stated: 'Consider NGS effect devastating and surrender indicated before fire plan completed. Demoralisation by NGS absolute.'

Sheridan landed at 3.20pm and, annoyed about the confusion over the use of the mortar, gave orders that 'everyone must sort themselves out and get on with it.' *Antrim* and *Plymouth,* under orders not to shell the BAS accommodation, engaged possible shore targets near the wrecked remains of the Argentine Puma and the track to Grytviken. The assault forces shook out and, screened by the SAS, headed toward the steep slopes of Brown Mountain. Several balaclavas were seen among the tussock grass about 800 yards away and the GPMGs sprayed the area. There was no response and, assuming the enemy to be dead, the SAS covered each other to the spot where they found several bleeding elephant seal bodies. Captain Hamilton and Corporal Davey engaged a suspected enemy position on top of Brown Mountain, which turned out to be a mound of rocks and a whaler's wooden spar masquerading as an antenna.

By 4.30pm the assault force was overlooking The Hummocks; below them was the wrecked Argentine Puma. Sheridan arrived fifteen minutes later and, peeping over the crest, was astonished to see the demoralized defenders displaying white flags on almost every building although the Argentine flag still flew on a flagpole. To demonstrate that future resistance was pointless, he radioed the two warships to show themselves. *Antrim* steamed slowly into Cumberland Bay and Young radioed the Argentines to which the marine signaller replied, 'No shoot! No shoot!' and mentioned a wounded man without legs. More white flags appeared from the main Argentine position at King Edward Point. About fifteen minutes later the defenders filed out of Discovery House and paraded underneath their flag.

Sheridan ordered the advance to halt, but Delves' radio had apparently become defective and he led three men past the crashed Puma, bid an Argentine machine-gun detachment 'Good afternoon' and strolled into Grytviken. During this advance Hugo Bircain advised *Antrim* that the garrison was surrendering and that they had wounded, one seriously. He also mentioned that the helicopter pad and the track from Grytviken were mined. This information was passed to Delves, whose radio miraculously corrected itself. Frustrated at the cavalier advance of Delves, Sheridan left Mountain Troop on Brown Ridge and ordered Nunn's Royal Marines and 2 SBS to follow Delves. He then summoned *Endurance's* Wasp and arrived at King Edward Point a few minutes after Delves and Sergeant Major Gallagher had replaced the Argentine flag with the Union Jack. At 4.05pm Guy Sheridan, CTG 317.9's military commander, accepted the surrender of the Argentines in Cumberland Bay with hardly a shot being fired. Twenty-five minutes later Captain Young radioed London: 'Be pleased to inform Her Majesty that the White Ensign flies alongside the Union Flag at Grytviken'. The wounded Argentine steward, whose foot had already been amputated by the *Santa Fe's* surgeon, was flown for further treatment to *Tidespring*. One British soldier slightly twisted his ankle. After a search for weapons and the improvised devices were defused, Bircain and Lagos both signed the instrument of surrender on *Antrim*. 129 sailors and marines were captured.

The Argentine government were quick to react to the surrender and claimed that South Georgia had been subjected to a naval blockade, followed by an attack on a submarine landing provisions, mail and medical supplies and then the defences had been subjected to a sustained assault by armed helicopters. The small naval force gallantly held out until exhausted. The Argentines seemed to think *Exeter* was involved.

Captain Young still had the Argentines at Leith and authorized Sheridan to use Bircain to persuade Astiz to agree terms. Astiz, however, was truculent and Bircain explained, 'Astiz says he will not surrender. He will fight to the death'. While happy for the scrap metal workers to be interned, he and the remaining marines, all fourteen, would fight. Young ordered Captain Pentreath to take *Plymouth* and *Endurance* with Sheridan and 2 SBS and Mountain, Air and Mobility Troops to Leith and persuade the Argentines to surrender. It was while Barker was discussing with Pentreath what to do when *Antrim's* doctor, Surgeon Lieutenant Neil Munro, took a call from Astiz shortly before 10.45pm offering to surrender. Wary of his opponent, Barker told Astiz to remain where he was, under the guns of two warships, and muster the following morning. While still dark, Pentreath landed the SAS on Harbour Point and then 2 SBS was flown ashore from *Endurance*. Next morning Pentreath and Barker watched as first the workers appeared and then the marines paraded. *Plymouth's* helicopter collected Astiz to sign the Argentine surrender of Leith.

Soon after the surrender the three crew from the missing Gemini strolled in to Leith, much to the relief of their colleagues. Their engine had been swamped by a large wave but they had managed to paddle ashore to a small beach and sheltered in a cave at Cape Saunders, the last landfall before the vast grey mass of the Atlantic Ocean. Although they had lost most of their rations and equipment, they decided not to activate their rescue beacons and to avoid compromising the presence of the British to the enemy, much to their credit.

A hugely disappointed M Company arrived the following day and set about garrisoning South Georgia. 151 naval and marine prisoners were captured and thirty-nine civilians interned. Leith was found to be littered with improvised devices and the prisoners agreed to dismantle them and help mark out minefields, just as the captured Royal Marines had done three weeks earlier. After a night under guard in a warehouse at Grytviken, the Argentines were taken on board *Tidespring*. Astiz was kept separately on *Antrim*.

On 27 April the British moved the *Santa Fe* from its position alongside the only jetty and several Argentine sailors, who were on parole and guarded by Royal Navy seamen with submarine service, agreed to help. On board they were supervised by Royal Marines with instructions to make sure they did not attempt to scuttle the boat. As the submarine moved, it suddenly lurched and under orders from the Argentine commander, Petty Officer Felix Artuso operated a switch which had been listed as forbidden. In spite of being ordered to desist, he ignored warnings and was shot dead by a young sentry. A court of inquiry chaired by Captain Young and attended by Bircain totally exonerated him. The *Santa Fe* was immobilized by explosives and, after slowly flooding, she settled with only her fin showing above the freezing water. Artuso was buried with full naval honours in the cemetery at Grytviken.

On 2 May *Tidespring* left with the prisoners and the recovered BAS personnel and set sail for the warmer waters around Ascension Island from where a Joint Forward Interrogation Team was helicoptered out to join her. Her prisoners were important and the British gathered first-hand information on the enemy. Some of the civilians were also debriefed. The prisoners were flown to Montevideo on 14 May and handed back to Argentina by Uruguay. Because of his suspected involvement in the disappearance of the Swedish girl and French nuns, Astiz was retained by the British at the Royal Military Police barracks in Chichester, where he remained until June 10 when he was repatriated to Argentina.

5

British Offensive and Advanced Forces Operations

1 to 21 May

'Its a fire!' Lieutenant Marega on being told about the explosions on Pebble Island.

While Admiral Woodward's ships were beginning to leave Ascension Island in mid-April, the Landing Group slowly assembled offshore and re-organised, the priority being to ensure men, vehicles, stores and equipment were cross-decked in a logical fashion for an assault landing. Sleepy Wideawake airfield became one of the busiest airports in the world as heli-copters with underslung loads travelled to and from the ships and Vulcan bombers, Victor tankers and VC-10s transports landed at frequent intervals. Dispersal areas developed into the organized chaos of supply dumps. For the troops, day and night landing craft and heliborne assault exercises were held and headquarters practised command and control. Range work and fitness training allowed some to climb Green Mountain from the desolate volcanic landscape at sea-level through African bush of eucalyptus and damp glades of banana and papaya trees to the English market gardens of lettuce, tomatoes and cucumbers, cottages and the island hospital. Higher up were rolling downs, complete with cattle and long, lush grass, fed by moisture blown from Africa and at the top, at the end of a muddy jungle track through bamboo, was a small pool in a cool clearing where passports could be stamped in a small birdhouse. Landing craft ran a ferry service to English Bay with its fine beach, steep shelf and fierce current.

On 24 April the Argentine merchantman *Rio de Plata* was sighted lurking some five miles offshore and a helicopter photographed what appeared to be canoes concealed beneath tarpaulins. The ship had recently been in Lisbon and London suggested that Tactical Divers were on board. When a destroyer picked up a suspected submarine contact, Action Stations was ordered throughout the anchorage and within half an hour ships had scattered to the four points of the compass. Next day a yellow foreign lifejacket was found floating offshore and 45 Commando carried out a cordon and search oper-ation of the island, concentrating on the woods, fields and rain forest of Green Mountain. These incidents prompted Operation *Awkward* in which

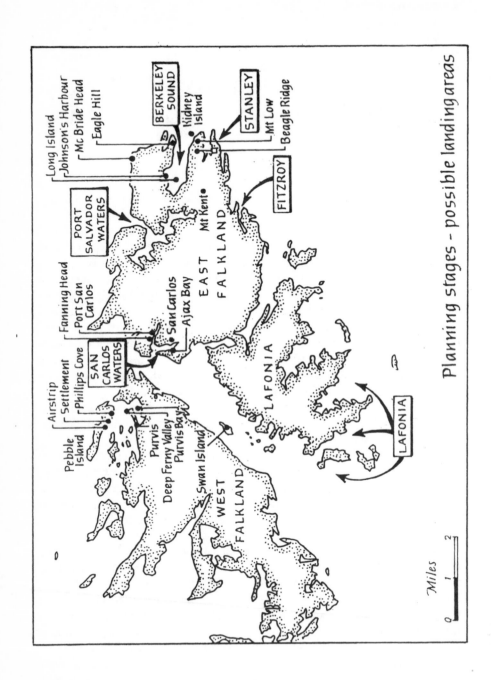

Planning stages – possible landing areas

sentries patrolled the upper decks looking for divers and bored seamen in whalers circled their ship dropping small depth-charges. Divers also regularly inspected the hull. At night the ships left the anchorage. During the day warships carved out a racetrack from English Bay to the beaches off Wideawake and patrolled the horizon.

As the Peruvian Government endeavoured to mediate between Argentina and Great Britain, it was now time to get on with liberating the Falkland Islands. Rear-Admiral Woodward's strategy was to tempt Argentine air and naval forces into the open. British planners initiated the first actions by imposing the Total Exclusion Zone on 30 April but bad weather prevented opening the offensive proper until 1 May.

The offensive was in three stages, the first being an early morning 'Black Buck' raid by a Vulcan bomber operating from Ascension Island on Military Air Base Stanley. Of the twenty-two bombs dropped, only one hit the runway, which was quickly repaired by 601 Engineer Group. The second air phase was low-level raids by Sea Harriers on the Stanley and Goose Green air bases, which inspired the BBC correspondent Brian Hanrahan to announce to the world, 'I counted them all out. I counted them all in,' effectively telling the Argentines that, although 601 Air Defence Group had damaged two Sea Harriers, their air defence had failed. Next time it would not be so easy and Lieutenant Nick Taylor RN was killed attacking Goose Green four days later. Later in the day the third phase began when some of Woodward's Task Force bombarded Military Air Base Malvinas to give the impression of preparatory moves for a landing, which worked, and Army Group Malvinas received several reports of enemy troops. It was on this night the civilians sheltered in a godown. The Argentine Air Force also took the bait and, although four mainland aircraft and two island-based aircraft were lost or damaged, they hit two ships.

The naval bombardment and Harrier harassment of Stanley Common and Military Air Base Malvinas proved particularly demoralizing for the troops. Lieutenant Colonel David Comini's 3rd Infantry Regiment covered the southern beaches in Sector Gold and he recorded that the combination of the psychological pressure of the shelling and bombing, the need to remain alert for landings, the jamming of communications and sixty days in foxholes destroyed the will of his men to fight. 3rd Infantry Regiment was allocated two warehouses in Stanley to rest the men at 200 per day; there was, of course, a huge difference between living in the bunkers compared to the relative safety and comfort of the town. Comini complained of poor and inadequate food, usually a mug of soup and a square meal, but no bread, each day, the difficulty of keeping weapons properly maintained and of the inadequate clothing to protect the soldiers from the wind, cold and rain. 6th Infantry Regiment, on the left flank of 3rd Infantry Regiment, suffered because the 155mms guns were in its sector and a prime target. In spite of the fifty 1000lb, 153 500lb, nine cluster bomb attacks and 1200 naval shells, totalling an estimated 130 tons of high explosive, impacting in their area, most exploding around the airfield, 25th Infantry Regiment and a School of Military Aviation security company defending the north-eastern approaches to Stanley suffered only three killed and eighteen wounded.

The third element of the opening phase of the offensive was to gather intelligence, still at a premium and desperately short on detail. With the help of intelligence organizations in the United Kingdom debriefing the Argentines captured on South Georgia, as well as the repatriated British prisoners-of-war and Falkland Islanders, a picture of life on the islands was beginning to emerge but information on Argentine organization and tactical philosophy was almost zero.

There can be no doubt that the Advanced Forces played a key role in gathering intelligence and were given due credit in the pamphlet *The Falklands Campaign: The Lessons,* presented to Parliament in 1983. Advanced Forces is a term defined in Jane's *Glossary of Naval Terms* as forces used in advance of amphibious landings to recce beaches, clear minefields etc and in the context of this history it will be used to describe SAS, SBS and other Special Forces units. While it is regrettable that much of what happened remains officially shrouded in needless mystery, it is possible to glean part of the story from published sources. There was some opportunity for direct action and both the SBS and SAS were involved in operations which belied their heritage.

The early patrol tasking was selected by Brigadier Thompson and Commodore Clapp after assessing their priorities and needs. Among the early Advanced Forces operations on the Falklands, which began on 1st May, was a G Squadron patrol led Captain Aldwin Wight, formerly of the Welsh Guards, with orders to set up an OP overlooking Stanley and keep a particular eye on Argentine helicopter deployments. It was imperative for the British planners to neutralize them for the Argentines were heavily reliant upon these to move troops and equipment and without them they would be virtually confined to their garrisons, unable to reinforce areas under threat and incapable of deploying the Reserve against the beachhead.

After dark a Sea King lifted off from the Fleet Replenishment Ship *Resource* and, crossing the East Falklands coast, the pilot tucked into the valleys and folds in the ground and dropped down on to the landing site. Door already open, Wight's patrol leapt out and dashed into cover while the loadmaster unloaded their bergens. As the helicopter clattered into the blackness, the patrol moved fast from the area. The signaller carried the radio; its ancillaries, such as batteries, were spread between the patrol. One man took medical supplies, while another carried surveillance telescopes and cameras. Each man carried a 5.56mm Armalite, food, warm clothing, a sleeping bag, and perhaps the odd treat such as curry powder to relieve the monotony of rations, a couple of Mars bars and a book. Movement was usually at night but speed was limited by rock runs, marsh and tussock to little more than about 400 metres an hour.

It took Wight's patrol three nights to reach the target area, Beagle Ridge, where they sited a hide overlooking Military Air Base Malvinas, now a hive of activity. Typically a hide was carved between folds in the ground, lined with a poncho and with chicken wire for a roof, perhaps waterproofed with a lightweight cover, and then lined with turf. The entrance was concealed with a piece of camouflaged netting. The hide, although spartan, had to be reasonably comfortable for it would be the patrol's home for several days. Sometimes food, ammunition and other unnecessary equipment might be cached, although the patrol had to be careful not to tread a route between the two hides. Generally two slept while two observed. Patrols remained hidden during the day and would only emerge at night to stretch stiff legs and do a few exercises.

For twenty-six days, Wight's patrol tracked 601 Army Combat Aviation Battalion. An attempt to bomb it on Mount Kent through the clouds on 19 May failed, but two days later, with the British going ashore at San Carlos, two Harrier GR3s slid over the ridge, passed over the dispersed helicopters and then attacked with cluster bombs and cannon, damaging a Chinook, a Puma and an Iroquois. By the time the Argentines scrambled out of their tents, the Harriers had disappeared into the early morning gloom. The attack effectively grounded the helicopters at a critical time. In the citation for his Military Cross, it stated that Captain Wight had 'produced clear and accurate pictures of enemy activity in the Stanley area, intelligence available from no other means, which proved vital in the planning of the final assault'.

In their original intelligence assessments the Argentines had calculated that distraction forces would appear before the amphibious forces. After the opening of the offensive, Menendez used 601 Commando Company outside Stanley to check out reports of enemy activity. 2nd Section, searching Windmill Island for a suspected enemy radio station, found a British combat jacket and a Gemini. Next night they confiscated the radio of Robin Pitaluga of San Salvador and handed him over to Dowling's military security. 3rd Section embarked in the coastguard cutter *Islas Malvinas* on a coastal patrol from Stanley to McBride Head, but the weather turned unpleasant and the following day the commandos gratefully filed ashore, green and miserable from seasickness.

On 4 May Army Group Malvinas ordered Operation *Margarita* to search Long Island. Pucara and Mentor ground attack aircraft from Pebble Island were first to carry out a detailed recce, followed by an Amphibious Commando Grouping detachment landing from the Coastguard cutter *Las Malvinas*; 601 Commando Company would be inserted by Army helicopters. High-level combat air patrols were to be flown by Mirage IIIs from the mainland. The operation got underway, but when a deep weather front swept in from the south it was cancelled.

During the morning of 9 May Sea Harrier pilots Lieutenant Commander Gordon Batt and Flight Lieutenant Dave Morgan launched from *Hermes* to bomb Military Air Base Malvinas and were permitted by *Coventry* to investigate a surface contact. Breaking low cloud cover, they saw the trawler *Narwal,* which had come to notice several days earlier as tailing the Carrier Group. Batt fired a 30mm burst across her bows, but *Narwal* continued on her course and both Sea Harriers dropped their bombs, Morgan missing, but Batt's penetrated, killing a seaman and coming to rest in the engine without exploding because it had been primed to detonate at height. The trawler continued on her course and both aircraft strafed her, damaging her near the waterline, quite apart from shaking the crew by the ferocity of the 30mm rounds and causing some to abandon ship. The trawler hove-to, wallowing in the gently heaving seas, and Batt and Morgan broke off as two more Harriers arrived on the scene and carried out further attacks on the crippled ship. At noon a Sea King from *Hermes* hovered over the ship and a rope snaked out. Covered by GPMG gunners from two other Sea Kings, an SBS section abseiled down and searched the ship. Of the crew twenty-four were found to be genuine trawlermen but one turned out to be a naval intelligence officer but sufficiently incompetent not to have thrown incriminating documents overboard. The prisoners, including twelve wounded, were winched on to the helicopters and taken to *Invincible.* A prize crew was put aboard the trawler and she was taken in tow by *Glasgow,* bound for South Georgia and technical evaluation. However, she sank in a gale the following day. Her crew were repatriated to Uruguay on 2 June.

While the SAS were busily involved in deep penetration intelligence-gathering patrols, the SBS were also ashore examining possible beaches. Although Major Southby-Tailyour, the extrovert landing craft expert had, during his time commanding NP 8901, circumnavigated the islands and supplied detailed information on the coast, which now needed to be updated. During *Fearless'* voyage to Ascension Island, SBS operations staff had already discussed how they could contribute to HQ 3rd Commando Brigade's intelligence requirements and patrols gathering information on Eagle Hill and Johnson's Harbour in Berkeley Sound, San Salvador Water and San Carlos Water reported little evidence of Argentine activity. Virtually all SBS patrols were landed by helicopter because the relative shallowness of the sea around the Falklands coast was not conducive to launching patrols from submarines. Coastal recce tends to be a little more risky than inland operations and consequently patrols were typically a two-night approach march, three days in the target area and two days return march.

On 25 April the general cargo ship *Rio Carcarana* had breached the Maritime Exclusion Zone and reached Stanley. On 10 May some of her cargo was transferred to the small transport *Isla de Los Estados,* which that afternoon set out to resupply the Argentine garrisons at Fox Bay and Goose

Green. Soon after midnight on 11 May the frigate *Alacrity,* which had been ordered by Woodward to penetrate Falkland Sound from the south, picked up a radar contact off Swan Island, but because the night was misty, her attempts to illuminate the target with starshell proved ineffective. She then opened fire with her 4.5-inch and struck the ship, which blew up in a huge fireball, and disappeared into the night. The Argentine naval authorities in Stanley ignored reports from 5th Infantry Regiment that there had been a huge explosion in Falkland Sound but mounted a search and rescue operation two days later, which found only two survivors, including the captain.

Concerned at the ease of this piratical penetration, Army Headquarters Malvinas instructed Lieutenant Colonel Italo Piaggi, commanding 12th Infantry Regiment at Goose Green, to establish an observation post overlooking the northern approaches to Falkland Sound. He summoned First Lieutenant Carlos Esteban and explained that Army Group were concerned at the ease with which the *Isla de Los Estados* had been sunk. Esteban was the company commander of the 25th Infantry Regiment's C Company and had arrived in Goose Green on 4 April to secure the airstrip. It was his first independent command in a combat zone and, determined to make a success of it, he imposed a strict occupation regime to ensure that the 114 'kelpers' in the settlement complied with the Argentine administration. He was later described by an islander as a 'real soldier'. For the next three weeks Esteban was on his own, linked to Stanley by radio and telephone and the occasional visit by a helicopter.

Meanwhile SBS patrols were checking out the approaches to Ajax Bay and on 12 May a patrol recced Bonners Bay and San Carlos. The following night another patrol, commanded by a sergeant, landed near Port San Carlos and found a beach about a mile west of Sand Bay which fitted the landing requirement almost exactly, steep shelving beaches leading into deep water free of kelp and other obstructions, sheltered from the open sea and with a free exit, in this case a path leading to the settlement. It became *Green Beach One.*

On 13 May, in 12th Infantry Regiment Operation Order 12/82 (Block and Control of San Carlos), Piaggi issued written orders that Esteban was to take a platoon-sized grouping, to be known as *Equipo Combat Guemes* (Combat Team Eagle), to Port San Carlos to control the neck to San Carlos Water, watch for possible landings and report on enemy shipping in Falkland Sound. Esteban selected Second Lieutenant Reyes' 1st Platoon to form the nucleus of his combat team. It will be recalled that Reyes had landed with 2nd Marine Infantry Battalion on 2 April and had captured Pembroke Point lighthouse. From 12th Infantry Regiment, Esteban was given signallers from Command Company, a heavy weapon section and a logistic element, which gave the combat team a strength of sixty men. To help identify ships, he was given a pamphlet of Argentine merchant shipping, which listed the home port, colour of hull and superstructure, tonnage and company insignia. The two Coastguard cutters were also listed.

To prepare for their insertion, a 601 Commando Company patrol was landed on 14 May at Port San Carlos by two 601 Combat Aviation Battalion Puma and two Iroquois helicopters. Finding no evidence of British activity on the San Carlos Water coastal strip, they established an OP on Point 234 on Fanning Head, a tussock-covered feature rising steeply to 768 feet and commanding the narrows into San Carlos Water. But their arrival had been identified by signals intelligence and then confirmed by the SBS sergeant examining beaches near Port San Carlos. The appearance of the commandos led him to believe his patrol had been compromised and in clear, as opposed to code, he requested immediate extraction, which was done the following day. Two Army CH-47s dropped Combat Team Eagle near Port San Carlos and Esteban immediately sent Reyes with a platoon of twenty men, the 81mm mortar and 105mm Recoilless Rifle to occupy Fanning Head while he remained at Port San Carlos with his headquarters, the logistics section and a defence section. For the next week Combat Team Eagle concentrated on manning the observation post and doing some limited patrolling. The Army commandos, meanwhile, were following up reports of a raid on Pebble Island.

Pebble Island lies to the north of West Falkland and is about twenty miles east to west and barely 100 yards wide at its narrowest point, which is near the only settlement. The two principal features are the 237-foot high Marble Mountain Peak at the eastern tip of the island and First Mountain, which, at 227 feet, overlooks the settlement. The terrain is low, particularly to the east where there are several lakes and large ponds. The settlement lies roughly in the centre of the island. In 1982 its approximately twenty-five inhabitants were involved in shepherding the 25,000 sheep. A rough track runs west from the settlement to a croft on the lower southern slopes of Marble Mountain Peak. A jetty on the sheltered south shore is capable of handling the FIC coasters. A Royal Engineers Briefing Map dated April, 1982, lists two airstrips. Strip A15(a) lies to the east of the settlement and has a 650-foot grass runway lying through 130/310 degrees, the state of which depends on the weather. Strip A 14(b) was sited on the sheltered southern beaches of Elephant Bay and was described as 1000 feet of firm beach, but, since it was below the high water mark, it would have to be recced, 'as kelp can cause soft spots.'

Although the Argentine Air Force and Naval Air Command were thoroughly familiar with the location of airstrips throughout the Falklands, on 3 April two S-2A Trackers from the aircraft carrier *Veintecinco de Mayo* were deployed to Stanley Airport and over the next ten days carried out an extensive reconnaissance of the Falklands, including Pebble Island. Both airstrips were considered suitable only for sturdy ground attack aircraft, but the Air Force were unimpressed by the remoteness of Pebble Island and opted to use Goose Green for their Pucara operations. Naval Air Command thought Pebble Island had strategic value and on 24

April Captain Adolpho Gaffolio, the senior naval officer, authorized the formation of Naval Air Station Calderon on Pebble Island. Ground crews were immediately despatched in a Coastguard Skyvan and requisitioned the sheep-shearing shed, the guest house and an unoccupied house as accommodation.

The same day H Company 3rd Marine Infantry Battalion, tasked to protect naval facilities, arrived at Military Air Base Malvinas. Four 1st Naval Air Squadron T-34C Mentor trainers, which had been added to the Naval Air Command order of battle and were commanded by Lieutenant-Commander Batlori, also arrived. Although slow, the Mentor can operate from grass strips and is a steady bomb, rocket and 7.62mm machine-gun weapon platform. It was originally planned that they would join the Pucara 3rd Attack Group at Military Air Base Condor at Goose Green, but as a result of inter-service rivalry and the Navy's complaints at the poor state of the runway, their pilots declined to join the Air Force.

On 26 April H Company was warned for deployment to Pebble Island, but no sooner were orders issued than instructions arrived for Lieutenant Ricardo Marega's 1st Platoon with four 75mm Recoilless Rifles and a MAG group to go to Pebble Island. 2nd Platoon was to remain in Stanley guarding naval facilities and 3rd Platoon and the remainder of the Heavy Weapons Platoon was to protect the fuel dump on Cortley Ridge. The following day 1st Platoon and an amphibious engineer section were taken by the Coastguard Skyvan and Puma to Pebble Island. Marega set up the command post in the schoolhouse, prepared defensive positions and although he insisted settlement life should not be disrupted, next day imposed a curfew between 9.30pm and 7.30am, ordered that generators could only be used between 6.30pm and midnight, commandeered all Land Rovers and confiscated Union flags. The requisitioned FIC coaster *Forrest* arrived two days later bringing the remainder of the heavy equipment and support weapons, ammunition, aviation fuel and an Elta radar. The four Mentors then arrived and Naval Air Station Calderon was declared operational. At first air patrols were ordered to intercept reports of British helicopters inserting the Advanced Forces patrols.

When Military Air Base Condor was raided on 1 May the six Pucara were diverted to Pebble Island, Air Force South and Naval Air Command both agreed to use Pebble Island as an alternative base and Air Force ground crew were flown in. With the start of the shooting war, Marega moved his command post into an underground bunker and ordered overhead protection for weapon pits and trenches. The weather turned nasty and the marines had difficulty in keeping the below-ground defences dry. A 75mm gunpit was resited after it was flooded and the health of marines exposed to the fierce freezing southerly rain caused concern to Marega. The runway then became waterlogged and on 5 May Batlori had no alternative but declare Naval Air Station Calderon closed to fixed-wing operations. This heralded an unhappy time for the pilots, particularly the six Air Force – grounded, separated from their colleagues and relative civilization at Goose Green and now confined to an inhospitable windswept island, but, worst of all, under the command of the Navy. A heavy overnight frost hardened the ground on 7 May and allowed the four Mentors to carry out a patrol to Stanley, much to the disgust of the Pucara pilots.

Argentine activity on Pebble Island was analysed by Major David Burrell's intelligence staff at Northwood in early May and passed to Woodward. By this time the decision to land in San Carlos Water had been firmed up and, since Pebble Island was only nineteen minutes' flying time from the proposed assault beaches, it gave ground attack aircraft plenty of time to stooge around and select their targets. Although Woodward was concerned about the threat, he later admitted that at first he had no idea where the airfield was. On 10 May at a planning meeting on board *Hermes,* he outlined the threat from Pebble Island and asked the SAS liaison officer if he could help. The planners were working on landing sometime between 16 and 25 May and Woodward suggested that it was critical to deal with the airfield by the 15th. The SAS officer said some preparatory work needed to be done including inserting a recce team.

'How do long do you have in mind?' asked Woodward.

'Three weeks.'

'No good.'

'I'm sorry.' Woodward knew that the SAS based their success on meticulous planning but a crisis had developed which needed to be dealt with quickly. 'What about five days?' suggested the Admiral as optimistically as he could. He later recalled that the SAS officer looked at him with incredulity and one of those 'Who does this bloke think we are?' looks.

'I'm sorry, Admiral, that may not be possible. We need three weeks to get it right.'

'I'm afraid it's got to be in five days. It's 15 May or never.' Helicopters were not available after that date in preparation for the landings. By the end of the conference the SAS had agreed to insert a recce patrol of Captain Burls' Boat Troop on the northern coast of West Falkland during the night of the 10/11th and cross the 2000-metre stretch of sea to Pebble Island in Geminis and raid the airfield by 2.30am on 15 May. The stage was set for a traditional SAS raid straight out of the Second World War.

In case they were picked up by radar, the SAS planners rejected helicopter insertion and having lost all confidence in the outboard engines at South Georgia, they also discarded the use of Geminis. Instead they settled for Klepper canoes but, at the time, this was not known to Woodward. The plan was to drop an eight-man patrol and four already assembled canoes at the east end of Purvis Bay on the night of 10 May, paddle around to Deep Ferney Valley and find a lay-up position from which to watch Pebble Island before crossing.

Because of bad weather, it was not until dusk on 11 May that the patrol was landed by Sea King but Burls' intention to paddle to Deep Ferney Valley had to be cancelled because it was far too rough to launch the Kleppers. By the time they had dismantled their canoes and manpacked them to Deep Ferney Valley, a bone-wearying task which took two journeys, it was nearly daylight and they concealed themselves in the valley but were not in position to observe Pebble Island. By now the patrol was a day behind schedule. Next night they found an OP from which they observed the east end of the island in preparation for crossing that night to Phillips Cove. The only enemy they saw was a Chinook helicopter, probably from 601 Combat Aviation Battalion, which flew at low level over them and went to Pebble Island to deliver supplies. As newcomers to the Falklands soon find out, the vicious winter squalls of the day invariably give way to an almost serene evening calm and shortly after midnight the eight canoeists set out across a near flat sea, keeping well to the south of the swift tidal race between Pebble Island and the mainland. Burls established a small beachhead and then with four men set off to recce the settlement and the airfield to the west. The remaining four men dismantled and hid the canoes. Difficulty was already being experienced with communications, a problem that was to persist all day, which was resolved when two men from the recce patrol set up a radio relay on some high ground while Burls and a colleague pressed on over the flat and featureless ground.

Peering over a crest above the settlement, the two SAS saw an operational airfield with eleven aircraft neatly dispersed around the runway. It was almost too good to be true and, covering each other, they cached their bergens and carried out a close recce, plotting the positions of the garrison. The ground was so flat they crawled virtually everywhere and, when they had finished, had to leave their bergens behind. Poor signals continued to frustrate communications between the patrol and then the Royal Signal operators on *Hermes* picked up 'Squadron attack tonight. Landing site Phillips Cove. 11 aircraft. Real. No further information. Confirm ETA.' Major Delves could hardly believe his luck and after sending the message 'ETA Squadron 22.30 hrs' instructed Captain Hamilton to raid Pebble Island.

Woodward detached *Hermes,* the destroyer *Glamorgan* and the frigate *Broadsword* from the Carrier Group to steam at best speed for Pebble Island. Delves' plan was for Mountain and Mobility Troops to raid the airfield, while Captain West's Air Troop cleared the settlement of Argentines. With Captain Chris Brown's NGFO5, forty-five men were available. Shortly before midnight the heavily-laden soldiers filed across the darkened, gently swaying flight deck to four Sea Kings, but the combination of their weight and the fuel load was too much and forty-five precious minutes were spent burning off the fuel. At last the helicopters rose, slipped to one side, dipped their noses and at low level clattered into the darkness.

At 12.45am on 14 May, an hour behind schedule, Boat Troop at Phillips

Cove heard the helicopters, noses up as they swung in, dropping to the ground, doors open, troops out and then away. Hamilton was briefed by Burls and then the three troops set off in small groups, some guided by Burls' canoeists, across the featureless landscape. Most of the men were carrying between 200 and 400 rounds of GPMG ammunition, two mortar bombs and their usual operational equipment. Mountain Troop carried most of the explosive. The mortar and a small protection team were dropped off on the high ground and as the men passed, they dropped off their bombs. If a contemporary account by a participant is to be believed, when some of Mobility Troop did not make this RV because they had no guides, Hamilton abandoned the idea of clearing the settlement and planned for Air and Mountain Troops to attack the airstrip. The assault group pushed on 4000 metres to the forward RV, which was manned by Captain West and Sergeant Major Gallagher, at the eastern end of the runway. Hamilton spread Air Troop right and Mountain Troop left, lying in the damp tussock grass until H-Hour, now timed for 2.15am.

Guided by Chris Brown, bang on time *Glamorgan* dropped high explosive on to the western edge of the runway, the expected direction from which the Argentines would launch a counter-attack, while illumination rounds lit up the airstrip. Lieutenant Marega ordered stand-to and everyone sheltered in their trenches. The SAS mortarmen also fired illumination, but every time a bomb left the tube the recoil drove the baseplate deep into the soft ground and they lost trajectory and elevation. An eerie glow wobbled over the runway as parachute flares gently floated to the ground. Hamilton ordered the two troops to open fire. Covered by Air Troop, Mountain Troop in pairs systematically placed charges on the aircraft, vandalized equipment and ripped out wiring, but found dealing with the Pucaras difficult because of their height. Nevertheless aircraft began to burn, ammunition exploded and a loose rocket ignited fuel spilling across the runway. Corporal Davey of Mountain Troop was wounded in the leg by flying shrapnel and, after being given first aid by his patrol commander, Staff Sergeant Phil Curass, he hobbled back to the forward RV for further treatment.

An Argentine marine recorded: 'There was a heavy bombardment which was probably the softening up for a major amphibious assault on the airfield. Fires were seen burning at the far end of the runway. A patrol then reported that fuel had caught fire and two aircraft were on fire.' It seems as if Lieutenant Marega didn't realize that he was faced with a raid and despatched a fire-fighting party to deal with the burning aircraft. When the SAS saw them running out with their extinguishers, they opened fire and the Argentines, not unnaturally, beat a hasty retreat into cover from where they opened desultory fire in the general direction of the eastern end of the runway. Now knowing the airstrip was being attacked, just as Trooper Armstrong was putting explosive on the last aircraft Marega ordered the blowing of a charge half-way along the runway. The combination of the charge and explosions from an ammunition dump blew over several of the SAS, one of whom, Corporal Bunker, suffered concussion. He had also been injured when the helicopter crashed on Fortuna Glacier. The SAS withdrew under desultory fire from the marines, who were still slightly puzzled as to what was happening.

By 2.45am, now fifteen minutes behind schedule, the troops assembled at the forward rendezvous where everyone was accounted for. The raiding party collected the mortar crew, moved as fast as their two casualties would allow and were back to Phillips Cove by 5.30am and back on board *Hermes* just as a sliver of dawn fractured the dark horizon. The naval medical assistants quickly whisked the two casualties away for treatment, one of them recalling that 'we were looked after admirably'. The ships sped as quickly as they could from the area.

Ashore, Marega ordered his men to remain in their positions and to expect an enemy attack at first light. He recalled: 'When none came, a patrol was despatched to clear the area. They found live and spent 7.62mm and 5.56mm rounds, confirming the enemy had indeed landed. While I requested an air recce of the island, which was refused, Air Force and Coastguard personnel checked the damage. While we were warned to receive reinforcements, the Air Force were told to prepare to evacuate Pebble Island.'

In military terms, the raid was a total success. Of the six Pucara, one suffered serious damage to its engine and wing roots, three suffered minor engine and wing damage, another had shrapnel and blast damage, while the sixth could still fly. One Mentor was totally destroyed, another was badly damaged, the third had suffered minor damage to its engine and the fourth was pitted with small arms fire. The Coastguard Skyvan was totally destroyed. It also removed part of the threat to the landings, although another still existed – Goose Green.

The following midday a 601 Combat Aviation Battalion CH-47 carrying fifty Army commandos made a pass over the smoking wrecks and settled down on the runway. As the commandos trooped down the ramp a stampede of Air Force and Coastguard pilots and ground crew made what one witness described as 'an undignified rush' to the helicopter. For the settlement, the consequences of the raid were serious. The Argentines were convinced that the islanders were implicated and a marine and commando patrol carried out a house-to-house search, but found only an illegal transceiver, which was sent to Stanley for technical evaluation. The settlers were then detained in the house of Griff Evans, the settlement manager, where they remained for the next month. Conditions were difficult and anyone who needed to leave had to ask permission. On one night they were told to extinguish the Rayburn cooker because it was feared that the glow would act as a beacon for British ships prowling offshore. When the Argentines cut down the CB antenna, Nobby Clarke rigged up a clandestine one so that everyone was kept abreast of the news.

Not unexpectedly the garrison was jittery the next night and there were several false alarms as the marines fired wildly at shadows. The next morning Marega sent a patrol on to First Mount to observe approaches to the settlement and on 17 May an eight-man commando patrol carried out an extensive heliborne sweep of the island but found nothing of interest. The next day they returned to Stanley, leaving the marines and the remainder of the Air Force to garrison the island. Life then developed into a mixture of boredom, occasional excitement as British aircraft bombed the now useless runway and hopes that they would be evacuated. On 28 May a Twin Otter evacuated several sick and wounded Air Force personnel, including a shot-down pilot, and on 1 June two Naval Air Command Sea Kings, specially adapted with additional fuel tanks, flew non-stop from Comodoro Rivadavia and evacuated several naval personnel but none of the marines. It was probably these two aircraft that were spotted by a Harrier pilot flying over the airstrip and reported to an SBS patrol, who happened to be on the island looking for a suspected land-based Exocet.

Meanwhile Major Ian Crooks, second-in-command of 22 SAS, assembled B Squadron on Ascension Island for deep penetration raids to attack the Argentine Air and Naval Air Forces in southern Argentina. According to some sources, principal targets are thought to have been Super Etendards operating from Military Air Base Rio Grande, which had sunk HMS *Sheffield,* and the Hotel Santa Cruz, which was the accommodation of the Mirage, Skyhawk and KC-130 tanker pilots at the Rio Gallegos Military Air Base, and had become a centre of intelligence intrigue and a security nightmare for Argentine counter-intelligence officers. The area was well-known for its British and Chilean sympathies.

The plan was to land two Hercules at night and then, according to one participant, 'Go in with a big brass neck, like the Israelis at Entebbe.' and shoot up the dispersal areas with a troop of 'Pink Panther' heavily-armed Land Rovers. The plan does seem a trifle ambitious considering that the Hercules would have to fly virtually the length of the Argentine Atlantic seaboard against an air force on a war footing supported by sophisticated radar on the coast and on the Falklands.

During the night of 19/20 May an 846 NAS Sea King piloted by Lieutenant Richard Hutchings lifted off from HMS *Invincible* and dropped an SAS recce team near Rio Grande. However, poor weather prevented Hutchings from ditching the helicopter, as he had been instructed to do to preserve the security of the operation, and he landed on a beach near Agua Fresco, about eleven miles from Punta Arenas, and burnt it. Several days later he and his two crewmen gave themselves up to the Chilean authorities. When the SAS recce heard about the destruction of the helicopter, they aborted their mission and made for Chile. 11th Mountain Infantry Brigade raised a twenty-strong commando unit and, with counter-intelligence officers, began searching for the infiltrators. The Argentine press then ran a story of several British commandos being captured, which effectively compromised Argentine operations. Nevertheless on 4 June two backpackers were detained acting under suspicious circumstances as they were about to cross the border near a small mining village. One managed to escape but his colleague, who was carrying a New Zealand passport, was captured and gave contradictory stories. He was about to be delivered to a special inter- rogation centre in Buenos Aires when the senior officer in the area, Brigadier General Guerrero, ordered his release, possibly under diplomatic pressure. SAS interest in the mainland airfields continued almost to the conclusion of the war.

Meanwhile the SBS were now concentrating their efforts in San Carlos Water. A patrol covering Ajax Bay experienced a major fright when a heli- copter hovered over their hide, the rotor down-draught disturbing the turf and chicken wire and almost exposing the occupants. Fortunately the aircrew were too involved in some other task to look below them and, after the helicopter disappeared, the patrol could do little except lie very still until dark and then repair the damage. The patrol commander considered a crash exfiltration, but, when there was no follow-up, he remained where he was. Another patrol had the disconcerting experience of a helicopter landing close by so the pilot could relieve himself.

In readiness to lay on naval gunfire during the landings, on 16 May Captain Willie McCracken and NGFO2 were landed from *Alacrity* in a Gemini in Ajax Bay. After caching some food and ammunition, they set off for Sussex Mountain. Tail-end Charlie was Bombardier 'Jacko' Jackson and, having the distinct impression that they were being followed, he signalled to the others to take cover. Everyone adopted all-round defence on the wet grass and, straining into the darkness, a figure appeared over the ridge from which they had just come. Then another and another, all in single file, all mumbling and it wasn't in English. When the file grew into a large group, McCracken, fearing they had been compromised, signalled to his men to prepare to fire. Still mumbling to each other, the figures neared the anxious patrol and then one of them waddled up to the prone gunners, gently squawking. The patrol relaxed as the platoon of penguins passed.

On 17 May an SBS team went ashore from *Brilliant* at Middle Bay, north of Fanning Head, and confirmed that only Combat Team Eagle had occu- pied the hill. By the 18th San Carlos Water had been confirmed for the landings and, to preserve their security and avoid drawing attention to the area, all patrols were withdrawn, leaving only the one covering Ajax Bay

Meanwhile G Squadron scouted West Falklands and monitored possible Argentine reaction at Port Howard and Fox Bay, as well as confirming areas where there were no enemy. In a decision that would have far-reaching consequences for Menendez's ability to react to the San Carlos landings, Brigadier General Parada was given 1st and 2nd Sections of 601 Commando

Company to help 5th and 8th Infantry Regiments clear enemy strongly believed to be operating on West Falklands. Arriving on 20 May, the commandos patrolled Purvis and White Geese settlements with nothing to report. In Stanley 3rd Section patrolled Mount Low but found no evidence of British landings.

6

The Landings in San Carlos Water and the Defence of the Beachhead

21 May to 3 June

'Ah! Good morning, Mr Miller!' Major Collet to Alan Miller at Port San Carlos after landing.

Several hundred miles to the north CTG 317.0 was ploughing through the grey South Atlantic. During the lunchbreak of 13 May, *Fearless's* wardroom was arranged so that Brigadier Thompson could give his orders for Operation *Sutton*, the first stage of the repossession of the Falklands. Delegates were checked by his Intelligence Section against an attendance list and directed to their seats, major unit commanding officers in armchairs in the front, key small unit commanders in the next row and the remainder filling up. There was a keen sense of anticipation – this was the first set of orders for an opposed landing on enemy-held territory since Suez and the years of exercising in Norwegian snows, on West German plains and Belizean jungles were about to be put to the test.

At 2pm Thompson strode up to the dais: 'Good afternoon, gentlemen. Orders,' and then sat down. Major Southby-Tailyour gave a terrain brief and was then followed by Captain Rowe, Thompson's Intelligence Officer, with the current intelligence picture. In West Falklands was 9th Infantry Brigade with two infantry regiments at Port Howard and Fox Bay, although one was reported to be in a poor state with reports of sickness, malnutrition and a collapse in morale. On East Falklands outside Stanley was 3rd Infantry Brigade with a large garrison at Goose Green. Stanley was defended by 10th Infantry Brigade. A helicopter base was believed to be on Mount Kent and a strategic reserve of unknown composition thought to be somewhere around Darwin. Air intelligence was less clear with several fundamental questions to be resolved, such as whether the mainland-based Skyhawks and Mirages could reach the Falkland Islands, carry out their mission and return without refuelling. The indications were that they could not. Stanley Airport was assumed to be non-operational for these aircraft; therefore a considerable threat was reduced. Helicopter availability

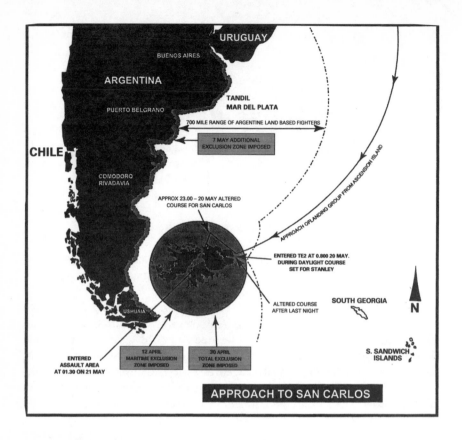

gave the Argentines a battalion-sized lift capability with gunship escort.

The Chief of Staff, Major John Chester, gave a precise briefing on the friendly forces available to support the landings and then Thompson stepped up to the dais: 'Mission. To land at Port San Carlos, San Carlos and Ajax Bay to establish a beachhead for mounting offensive operations leading to the recapture of the Falkland Islands'. He repeated the sentence and continued: 'Design for battle. A silent night attack by landing craft with the object of securing all high ground by first light'. Addressing each commanding officer by name, Thompson told the briefing that the amphibious assault would be led by the Royal Marines, as befits their role:

First wave
40 Commando from *Canberra* to land on *Blue Beach* at San Carlos.
45 Commando from *Stromness* to land on *Red Beach* at Ajax Bay.

Second wave
2 Para from *Norland* to pass through 45 Commando and secure Sussex Mountain.

3 Para from *Canberra* to land at *Green Beach* and secure Port San Carlos.

Floating Reserve
42 Commando on *Canberra*.

Diversions
D Squadron to fly ashore from *Intrepid* and convince Task Force Mercedes they were being attacked by a regiment – 'noise, firepower but no close engagement'.
Glamorgan to be active in Berkeley Sound and keep Army Group Stanley occupied.

Tasks were then allocated to the supporting arms and services. Chester added flesh to the bones by giving detailed orders for the landing and subsequent operations and added that, although the Commando Brigade would wait for 5th Infantry Brigade, if the opportunity for exploitation arose, the beach-head would be breached and an advance made on Stanley. Two officers from Commodore Amphibious Warfare then outlined the landing plan using complex overhead slides to show landing craft arrangements. One delegate later commented: 'Although I am sure they understood it, I had the general impression no one had a clue what they were talking about'. The logistic plan was then explained by Major Gerry Wells-Cole, the Deputy Chief of Staff after which Thompson reminded his officers that, in the event of an opposed landing, the killed and wounded were to be left, otherwise the impetus of the assault would be lost. It was this comment that to many thrust home the reality of the situation. The enemy would be firing live rounds, not blanks. So detailed were the orders that there were no questions and he concluded 'May I remind you that this will be no picnic. Good luck and stay flexible'. The orders group, which had lasted nearly two hours, broke up in a hubbub of conversation – the one thing not shared was the date and time of D-Day.

The sudden mention of '*EC Guemes*' at Port San Carlos in signals from Northwood the next day was greeted with alarm by HQ 3rd Commando Brigade. Had the enemy identified the assault beaches? Were they strengthening the defences? The Intelligence Section assumed the worst – an unidentified unit, possibly an advanced guard to an unknown organization had planted itself in the area where the landings were to be made. The obvious assumption until further information became available was that 12th Infantry Regiment at Goose Green was somehow involved. Only time would tell but hopes had been high that the anchorage was unoccupied. Now all eyes in the United Kingdom and on the ships were concentrated on Stanley and Argentina for evidence of the area being strengthened. A member of Thompson's intelligence staff recalls:

'The immediate concern was that no one knew what the initials "EC" stood for in the signals until Captain Rod Bell solved the problem "That's easy. EC stands for

97

Equipo Combate which translates into Combat Team". Bell had been raised in Costa Rica and Spanish-American was his first language. Half the problem was solved; we assumed there was a company strength unit on Fanning Head. Shortly afterwards we received another report that the EC Guemes patrol base was at Port San Carlos. Another assumption could now be made that the unit probably had infantry support weapons to control the neck of San Carlos Water.'

400 yards to the east of Fanning Head is Partridge Valley through which runs a stream to the sea and about nine kilometres also to the east is Port San Carlos. There is no defined track between the two and although the ground is relatively level, the going is bad. It was now vital to find out discreetly the strength of the enemy, where they were and what they were doing. A strong force could jeopardise the entire landing.

SBS operations to screen San Carlos Water were resurrected but there were no helicopters because they had disappeared over the horizon when *Hermes* left the area after the Pebble Island raid and so the Brigade was entirely reliant upon Northwood and the SBS operations, particularly the Ajax Bay patrol, for information. It soon became obvious that Combat Team Eagle was not an advance guard and because even a small unit could disrupt landings, as Keith Mills had done, Julian Thompson issued orders for Advanced Forces to destroy the enemy on Fanning Head. 3 Para would deal with the patrol base at Port San Carlos after landing.

In the assault ships the units were finalizing their preparations for the landings after the orders had been issued when during the evening of 18 May, a signal arrived on Thompson's desk from Northwood expressing concern that since *Canberra* was the transport for three major units (40 and 42 Commando and 3 Para) during the landings, they were to be dispersed. If she was hit, the casualty lists would inevitably be high which would jeopardise the success of the assault. Although Thompson rather glosses over the issue in his book *No Picnic*, there was intense frustration at having to change the plan at this late stage, quite apart from the difficulties of cross-decking troops by landing craft almost under the noses of the Argentines in mid-South Atlantic in broad daylight. Overnight Thompson and the Amphibious Warfare staff reorganized the assault:

First wave
2 Para to land from *Norland* in *Intrepid* landing craft on the shingled *Blue Beach* 2 and move into positions on Sussex Mountain to deal with any moves from Goose Green.
40 Commando to land from *Fearless* on *Blue Beach*.

Second Wave
45 Commando would then go ashore from *Stromness* on the sandy *Red Beach One* at Ajax Bay and secure the refrigeration plant.

3 Para would land from *Intrepid* on *Green Beach One* at Sandy Bay.

Floating Reserve
42 Commando to go ashore from *Canberra*.

Fanning Head
3 SBS to deal with the 'Fanning Head Mob'.

Diversions
D Squadron to occupy Task Force Mercedes.
Glamorgan to be active in Berkeley Sound.

The first wave now included paras and some Royal Marines were unhappy that their traditional amphibious first-ashore role had been usurped by the ubiquitous Parachute Regiment.

Next day dawned grey but mercifully calm, which in the South Atlantic meant a long choppy swell, and landing craft transferred 3 Para to *Intrepid* and 40 Commando to *Fearless* from the *Canberra*. The men lowered themselves by rope from a side door into landing craft that were about three feet below one second, fifteen seconds later. A fully-loaded Royal Marine fell into the sea and was hauled soaking wet, shaken but nevertheless thankful that he had not been crushed. Tragedy struck in the late afternoon when a Sea King on its last lift transferring twenty-seven men from D and G Squadrons from *Hermes* to *Intrepid* smashed into the sea and quickly sank, killing eighteen SAS, the only RAF fatality of the war and a Royal Marine loadmaster. It was the greatest loss the Regiment was to suffer since 1944.

An Army NCO on *Fearless* describes conditions:

'With 1400 troops on board, life promised to be uncomfortable. Several 40 Commando SNCOs were stretched out in the Mess. I checked my kit for the final time, stowing my seaman's bag with clothing I would not need in a corner of the Tank Deck. There were no more reports of enemy activity in the San Carlos area. Everything seemed quiet as we awaited political approval to enter the TEZ and then at 22.14 hours Captain Larken announced an alteration of course. Action Stations was broadcast. No undressing for bed now and no reasonable meals in prospect, just Action Messing of a bread roll and a mug of soup; galley cookers were extinguished just as they had been in Nelson's time. Our Mess was deserted of its Navy members, all of whom had closed up, and a First Aid party headed by the Ship's Paymaster prepared the space for the reception of casualties. Those of Embarked Force not at work carried out their final preparations and turned in.'

With political verification to proceed with the landings received from Northwood, Brigadier Thompson ordered Captain Samuelson, his Operations Officer, to signal the Brigade giving the D-Day as Friday 21 May and H-Hour, the time the landing craft grounded, as 3.30am local time with all objectives secured within six hours of landing. Recipients were asked to acknowledge. That night the Landing Group began its approach to the San Carlos assault beaches. The Army NCO goes on:

20 May (D-1) broke with grey skies and the prospect of bad weather. The wind droned and whistled through the rigging and stanchions. Our convoy was grouped in a close air defence formation with warships, LPDs, LSLs and merchant ships pushing through the deep waves. Ahead, *Canberra* nonchalantly cast aside the seas while *Fearless* lurched, bows lifting high and then crashing down, throwing aside great sheets of water, the buried stern straining to lift the bows bit deep into the next waves. "Goffers" [waves] smashed into the bridge and the Oerlikon gunners on the bridge wings sheltered as salt water poured into scuppers and streamed aft. Watchkeepers in foul-weather gear scanned the distant horizons. Bright signal lamps flashed from distant ships shrouded in mist; it would have reminded Atlantic convoy veterans of their youth.

Breakfast was an unappetising mug of meat and beans with a roll, hardly meriting the wait in the queue. There was no obvious enemy reaction to our proximity to the Falkland Islands. Would we get away with it? There was nothing to do except monitor enemy activity. Radio silence had been imposed anyway and dissemination of information was impossible. FTV showed 'Saturday Night Fever'. I dozed on my bunk. Lunch was bread and soup, another unappetising gruel, and I was getting hungry. It would be good to eat compo rations when we were ashore. Another film "Pelham 1-2-3" and then an hour of Benny Hill, which raised spirits. As dusk swept over the horizon, the convoy shook into an anti-submarine formation. All enemy submarines had been accounted for except one, which was said to be in the TEZ. Night fell and the gale blew itself out. Nothing further to report in the office, so I returned to my refuge, my bunk, and went to sleep.

When Samuelson became concerned that *Norland* had not replied to his signal, it emerged that the ship's literalizer, the equipment which deciphers code, had broken. Signal lamp would take hours and be liable to mistakes and so the signal was passed to *Broadsword* by gun-line and she pulled away, turbines whining. As the frigate approached *Norland*, bows pushing away great white swathes of briny, *Norland* flashed: 'Do you know something we do not?' *Broadsword's* yeoman brusquely replied: 'Yes, stand by for line!' There was a sharp crack, the long line snaked over to the pitching transport and the signal was passed. It was immediately taken to Lieutenant-Colonel 'H' Jones, who told his officers that 2 Para had four hours to occupy Sussex Mountain and prepare defensive positions for a possible counter-attack from Goose Green.

On board *Fearless,* Advanced Forces tasked 3 SBS, Captain Hugh McManners' NGFO 1, both on *Antrim*, and two 3rd Commando Brigade Air Squadron Gazelles helicopters to deal with Combat Team Eagle. Captain Rod Bell was to accompany the patrol. Based on the limited information available, the plan was for the SBS to go ashore shortly before the landings

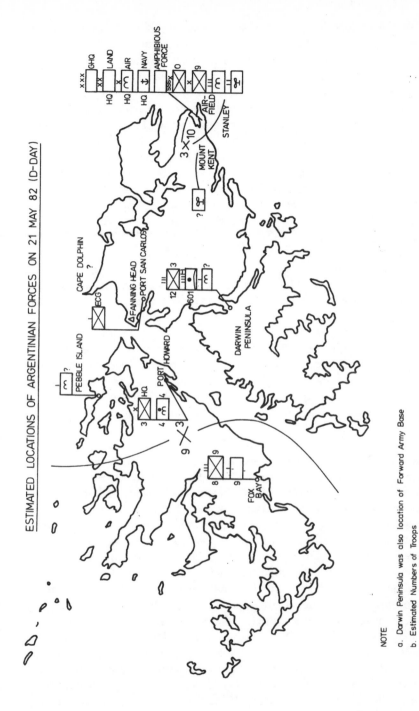

ESTIMATED LOCATIONS OF ARGENTINIAN FORCES ON 21 MAY 82 (D-DAY)

NOTE

a. Darwin Peninsula was also location of Forward Army Base

b. Estimated Numbers of Troops

a. Stanley — 8400   Port San Carlos — 40   Fox Bay — 890

b. Darwin Peninsula — 1200   Pebble Island — 120   Port Howard–200

101

and invite the Argentines to surrender, which should establish their willingness to fight.

Just after midnight on 21 May the Landing Group crept toward the narrows guarding San Carlos Water. The most recent intelligence about the Port San Carlos sector was passed to 3 SBS and *Antrim* launched the heroic 'Humphrey', which had been fitted with a thermal image camera. Hugh McManners wrote: 'The sweep along Fanning Head showed clusters of bright glow worms in pairs and in about fifteen. There were several of these groups to the north of the Head and a group actually at the top of the feature. We had found our heavy weapons company.' The SBS were briefed from the video tape and reminded that their aim was to ensure the ships could enter the narrows with safety and if necessary the Argentine combat team, now nicknamed 'The Fanning Head Mob', was to be destroyed. Captain Bell found a battery-driven loudspeaker.

While the SBS were completing their preparations, the first-wave assault companies filed into their landing craft. Great was the relief that the Landing Group had arrived without loss after such a long voyage and the only tension was that to be expected by troops about to land on occupied shores. But the carefully laid plan carefully calculated by the Amphibious Warfare staff immediately went awry when *Fearless'* ballast pump mechanism, which controlled water levels on the tank deck, failed, leaving 40 Commando's LCUs high and dry on steel. Captain Larken ordered the dock gate to be lowered and the sea poured in. 'Retract the LCUs' and the four LCUs slowly went astern into the darkness of Falkland Sound. A slight swell was running in the clear, cool and starlit night, silent except for the gently throbbing engines of the ships.

Within eleven minutes of *Intrepid* anchoring her four *Tango* LCUs set off to find *Norland* but had trouble in doing so and with radio silence in force, Colour-Sergeant Davies on *Tango One* was forced to identify each ship with a shielded signal lamp. Eventually he found *Norland* and, while the other three LCUs slowly orbited, he went alongside but there were no mooring points and he had to manoeuvre the landing craft constantly to keep it alongside. 2 Para found the business of loading without rehearsal from the dark cramped interior of a merchant ship, weighed down with radios, Carl Gustavs, helmet, belts of ammunition and bergen, ten feet down a wobbly rope ladder into a landing craft continually being manoeuvred in the slight swell an altogether different prospect from filing into the wide bellies of Hercules transports on well-lighted airfields. Companies became mixed up and one soldier fell badly breaking his pelvis. The confusion produced inevitable inter-Service rivalry and Major Ryan, of Headquarters Company, later accused the Royal Marines landing craft crews of being 'ill-disciplined and noisy, shouting, lights'. Southby-Tailyour, ever the gentleman, gave 2 Para and *Norland* great credit for the manner in which they achieved the complexities of loading.

The leading assault companies were meant to cross the Line of Departure at 1.45am but with the *Norland* embarkation problems, Brigadier Thompson slipped the schedule by an hour on the premise that it was more important to assault in formation than keep to a timetable and land piecemeal to be picked off by the defenders. As the last LCU, *Tango Four*, coxswained by Sergeant Garwood, motored alongside *Norland* to collect the remainder of 2 Para's first wave, Southby-Tailyour found an anxious Lieutenant-Colonel Jones on *Tango One* and commented that if they left without *Tango Four* and steamed at full speed, they would only be about forty minutes behind H-Hour. Jones was quick to reply, 'Let's go!'

Southby-Tailyour told Garwood to follow at best speed and then assembling the seven LCUs and eight LCVPs into a column, ordered them to switch off their navigation lights and, sixty-five minutes behind schedule, crossed into San Carlos Water. At full speed, he hugged the shadows of the shoreline for the five-mile approach to the assault beaches. *Plymouth* was in San Carlos Water ready to provide naval gunfire support at a moment's notice from NGFO 2. Above them the fighting around Fanning Head had developed and shells were swishing overhead.

At about 1am 3 SBS assembled on the gently heaving flight deck of *Antrim* and it soon became obvious the patrol commander's plan was flawed. As had happened prior to the Pebble Island raid, the Sea King could not lift off because of the weight of equipment and after the fatal ditching of the Sea King, no one was prepared to take chances. A slightly chaotic reorganization took place during which it was calculated that four lifts would be needed. The landing site was about ten minutes flying time from the ship and 1500 metres north-west of Finally Rocks and 3000 metres south east of Fanning Head. Eventually the thirty-five strong patrol was assembled about 2500 metres from the Argentine position. Heaving their bergens on their backs and slinging the belted ammunition wherever they could, the SBS shook out into single file and immediately began to stumble over the lumpy tufts of tussock grass and large weed-like plants. There were frequent stops as scouts scanned the ground ahead. The timetable began to slip.

Above the sweating Royal Marines, Second-Lieutenant Reyes was woken by a sentry who reported hearing helicopters going to and from the west. Reyes assumed they were landing troops and although no targets were clearly identified in the darkness, ordered the Recoilless Rifle to be fired into the narrows but there was no reaction. He reported the activity to Esteban and then dozed beside the radio.

By about 2.15am 3 SBS were still 1000 yards short of Fanning Head and since *Antrim* was on station, Hugh McManners radioed for ranging shots but none came. For the first but not the only time during the campaign a ship's 4.5" main armament hit a snag at a critical time. The 60mm mortar team plastered the objective with about twenty rounds to no great effect except to lighten their loads and further alert the Argentines. By 2.30am

Antrim had cleared the fault and she bracketed Fanning Head. Calling for fire for effect, McManners ordered twenty airbursts, which destroyed the Recoiless Rifle and caused some casualties. The bombardment was followed by sporadic shelling every minute to persuade the Argentines to concentrate more on survival and be less aware of the close proximity of British troops, who were now on a ridge from which they could observe Fanning Head. The Argentines were also gently nudged by the creeping barrage straight into the killing zone and this had the desired effect. In between the shelling, Reyes pulled his men into the lee of Fanning Head, and failing to contact Esteban, then decided to evacuate the OP.

McManners was gazing through his thermal imager when he was astonished to see figures coming over the ridge and moving into Partridge Valley; others seemed to be digging in on top of Fanning Head. The SBS formed an extended line with the GPMGs placed on the flanks, while the mortar and a small defence party covered the rear. Everyone opened fire, lacing the hillside, and then ceased fire. It was now time to invite the Argentines to surrender. A GPMG fired a burst of tracer over their heads and Captain Rod Bell coughed, cleared his throat and spoke into the microphone. The loudspeaker emitted a feeble, comical splutter. He twiddled the knobs but it still refused to work. Although the wind was in the wrong direction, he then shouted at the Argentines to surrender and four men sat down. A larger party, led by Reyes, sneaked off in the darkness back to their positions on Fanning Head and opened up with a MAG, confounding the theory that the Argentines would not fight. Keen to persuade them to surrender, Bell and a few SBS set off to find them, but without success. McManners called for more shelling and another group of four Argentines, exposed half-way up the hill, waved a white cloth, which signalled the end of the action. Two more surrendered and four wounded were found by the SBS, who after having their wounds treated, were evacuated later in the day.

Most of Reyes' platoon had escaped, but those who were not captured within days spent the next three weeks in the San Carlos area. Reyes and a small group were captured by a 40 Commando patrol on 8 June, suffering from trench feet, frostbite and hunger although they had survived on cormorants and sheep.

Meanwhile forty men from D Squadron were helicoptered to about two miles north-east of the Darwin Peninsula. Each man carried about eighty pounds of equipment, principally weapons and ammunition, and, marching in the darkness across the rough terrain, found a position on high ground north of Camilla Creek and proceeded to shoot up First Lieutenant Morales' Recce Platoon. The frigate *Ardent* was meant to support the diversion but the naval gunfire support team ashore could not give corrections because their codes were invalid. Morales radioed Piaggi that he was under fire from a strong force, which was exactly what D Squadron wanted the Argentines to believe.

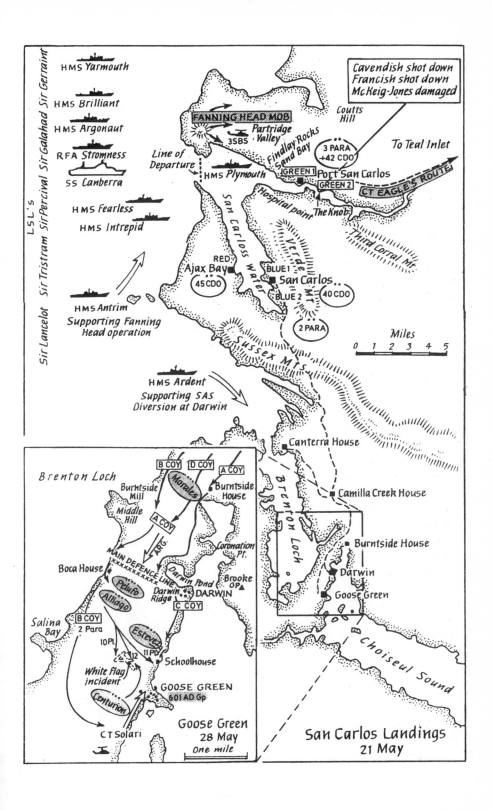

LSL's Sir Lancelot Sir Tristram Sir Percival Sir Galahad Sir Geraint

HMS Yarmouth
HMS Brilliant
HMS Argonaut
RFA Stromness
SS Canberra

HMS Fearless
HMS Intrepid

HMS Antrim
Supporting Fanning
Head operation

Line of
Departure

FANNING HEAD MOB

Partridge
Valley
3 SBS

HMS Plymouth

Findlay Rocks
Sand Bay

Coutts
Hill

Cavendish shot down
Francish shot down
McKeig-Jones damaged

To Teal Inlet

GREEN 1 Port San Carlos
GREEN 2

3 PARA
+42 CDO

CT EAGLE'S ROUTE

Hospital point
The Knob

Third Corral Mt.

San Carloss water
Verde Mt.

RED
Ajax Bay
45 CDO

BLUE 1
San Carlos
BLUE 2

40 CDO

2 PARA

Miles
0 1 2 3 4 5

Sussex Mts.

HMS Ardent
Supporting SAS
Diversion at Darwin

Canterra House

Camilla Creek House

Brenton Loch

Burntside House

Darwin

Goose Green

Choiseul Sound

Goose Green inset:

Brenton Loch

B COY D COY A COY
Burntside
Mill
Manaia
Burntside
House
Middle
Hill
A COY

MAIN DEFENCE LINE
xxxxxxxxxxxx
ARG.

Boca House

Coronation
Pt.

Darwin
Pond
Darwin Brooke
Ridge OP
DARWIN

Pelud
Albago

C COY

B COY
2 Para

Estivoza

Salina
Bay

10 Pl.
12
11 Pl.
Schoolhouse

White Flag
incident

GOOSE GREEN
601 AO Gp

Centurion

CT Solari

Goose Green
28 May
One mile

San Carlos Landings
21 May

Piaggi then advised Brigadier General Parada that he was under attack but was advised to stay where he was because there was no intelligence to suggest that a landing on Darwin was imminent. Shortly before dawn, the SAS broke contact and began the long march to Sussex Mountain.

Nearing San Carlos, Major Southby-Tailyour searched Bonners Bay for the flimsy wooden jetty below the settlement. Inside 2 Para's open landing craft, for those not used to them, life was uncomfortable – cramped and with nowhere to sit except on your bergen. 'H' Jones encouraged his men to push forward to the front, which dipped the bows into the swell and water slopped over the gunwales. Light spray floated across the welldeck. Some paras loaded their weapons and there was an negligent discharge from a Sterling, the bullet bruising a soldier's foot, which did little to soothe the nerves of the anxious paras.

Approaching *Blue Beach Two,* Southby-Tailyour ordered the 40 Commando landing craft to heave-to while he guided 2 Para to *Blue Beach One. Intrepid's* landing craft moved into line abreast and with his night goggles Southby-Tailyour searched for the tiny red spot indicating the beach centre marked by 3 SBS. Nothing. He had arranged other signals – Alpha in morse – *Beach safe*; Bravo – *Be careful*; Charlie – *Enemy on beach* and no light meant *Cock up or enemy on beach.* Nothing but darkness. Southby-Tailyour was in a quandary, because he implicitly trusted the SBS. Returning to the small bridge, he found 'H' Jones had issued 'Prepare to beach' and told him, that although the SBS had not been seen neither had any enemy, therefore he intended to land. Colour Sergeant Davies lowered the ramp and as it crunched on to the stony beach about five metres offshore, he ordered B Company 'Troops Out!' No one moved, and after a slight delay a para officer shouted 'Paras! Go!' to which someone in the well-deck cynically replied, 'This is supposed to be an invasion.' At 4.30am local time the airborne 2 Para splashed up the beach, much to the irritation of the Royal Marines. As they waded ashore they heard from the darkness 'Who the hell are you?'

'2 Para. Who are you?' replied Major John Crosland, the company commander.

'3 SBS. We thought you were coming on the 24th.'

'Par for the course,' replied Crosland, already thoroughly dissatisfied with the arrangements. As the LCUs backed off the beaches Sergeant Garwood arrived, having motored at full speed from *Norland.* Since 2 Para had landed in some confusion, the move off the beach in order of march foundered and Jones broke radio silence and encouraged his company commanders to sort the battalion out. Eventually C Company led off and, in a long snake, began the eight-kilometre 'tab' up the 900 foot-high Sussex Mountain. A section of 43 Battery, 32nd Guided Weapons Regiment RA, carrying the cumbersome and unwieldy Blowpipe missiles, accompanied the column.

With 2 Para safely ashore, 40 Commando landed on *Blue Beach Two* a

SAN CARLOS — SKETCH

(Compiled from maps, chart, air phots and sketch by
Patrick Burnsten.)

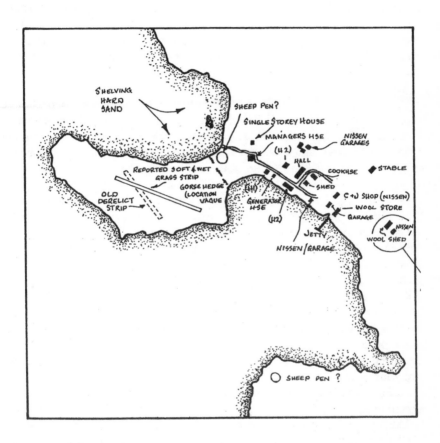

(H1) SINGLE STOREY HOUSE
(H2) Two " "

San Carlos – sketch. An important intelligence source was several Falkland Islanders repatriated to Great Britain. Most were debriefed by Intelligence Corps and the information was then sent to HQ 3rd Commando Brigade. This map was used by 40 Commando.

few minutes later. A Company cleared White Rincon and then dug in on the western slopes of Verde Ridge. B Company cleared Little Rincon and joined A Company. C Company cleared San Carlos settlement, hoisted the Union Jack and dug in south of the settlement.

Communications between the *Fearless* Amphibious Operations Room and other shipborne units were not working well, which was not unusual. The operations staff were not aware of the *Norland* delay nor indeed the success of getting ashore at the *Blue Beaches,* although the fighting on Fanning Head could be clearly heard. At about 5.30am, two hours behind schedule, the landing craft collected 45 Commando from *Stromness*. The coxswains were reasonably familiar with the approach to *Red Beach* at Ajax Bay and landed the Commando who then cleared the derelict refrigeration plant and 'yomped' up the northern slopes of Sussex Mountain in depth to join 2 Para.

There were delays loading 3 Para on *Intrepid* but, as dawn flushed out the darkness, the landing craft left the relative warmth of the dock for the chill of early morning. Two LCUs carried Scorpions and Scimitars from 4th Troop, the Blues and Royals to soften up any opposition, otherwise most of the battalion was jammed into four LCVPs. Southby-Tailyour accompanied 3 Para to the unexplored *Green Beaches*. Wary of mines, he navigated straight to *Green Beach One* and, as the landing craft fanned into their assault formation for the final approach, unlucky *Foxtrot Four*, skippered by Colour Sergeant Brian Johnston, grounded in about three feet of water twenty yards short of the beach. Johnston and his crew of three Royal Marines and two Royal Navy were later killed when their landing craft was sunk by Argentine aircraft in Choiseul Sound on 8th June. He was awarded the Queens Gallantry Medal for rescuing survivors from *Antelope*.

Southby-Tailyour, seeing the beach had been secured by a SBS patrol and believing it nonsense to ask men to wade ashore at the beginning of a winter campaign, ordered the LCUs to stand off and signalled the four LCVPs to crossdeck the companies from the grounded LCU. The other LCUs found a dry landing across a stony beach about 500 yards to the west. Inevitably the grounding induced the inherent rivalry between the red-bereted infantry and green-bereted landing craft crews to erupt, not all entirely polite. Southby-Tailyour collected the Advanced Forces and returned to the ships, some of which were now beginning to filter through the narrows into San Carlos Water. A clear dawn had sprung from the east and all was peaceful.

Hearing the shelling but not the small arms fire from Fanning Head, First Lieutenant Esteban attempted to contact Reyes for nearly three hours without success. No runner appeared and there was no sign of retreating Argentines. Fearing the worst and having no idea what was happening, he ordered Grey Alert at 6.30am and, as dawn crept over the hills to the east, he deployed observers to overlook the still but misty surface of San Carlos Water. All seemed quiet until, at about 7.10am, sentries reported that a large white ship and three warships could be seen outside the narrows. Climbing on to high ground, Esteban saw three more warships in Falkland Sound and ten minutes later a landing craft was seen leaving the side of the white ship. As the early morning mist dispersed, he saw more landing craft full of troops 'travelling in all directions' and radioed Lieutenant Colonel Piaggi that landings had been made and requested an air attack.

In Port San Carlos the settlement manager, Alan Miller, had heard the shelling of Fanning Head. As dawn broke, he climbed a hill and was astonished to see *Canberra* in the distance and landing craft slowly approaching beaches west of Sand Bay. Miller, his son and a friend alerted the settlement and running down to Sand Bay waving a white handkerchief, they were totally surprised when a Parachute Regiment officer stood up from behind a gorse bush and bade him, 'Ah! Good morning, Mr Miller!' The officer was Major David Collet of A Company. Much of his information about Port San Carlos had come from Mrs Miller, who was in UK, and had been filtered to Brigade Intelligence who prepared hand-drawn maps and details of personalities for 3 Para. Miller warned Collett that the Combat Team Eagle was at the eastern end of Port San Carlos.

At 7.30am Esteban's men reported troops identified as Royal Marines, in fact 3 Para, advancing from the west toward Port San Carlos. Esteban concluded that resistance was futile but decided not to break contact. Confirming the landings to Piaggi, he closed down his rear link so that essential items could be collected and withdrew his forty-two men to high ground east of the settlement to avoid being cut off.

In response to Esteban's request for air support, four Falklands Pucara Squadron aircraft, based at Goose Green, were briefed to search for reports of helicopters putting troops ashore at Port San Carlos. Captain Jorge Benitez and Lieutenant Brest, his wingman, and Major Carlos Tomba and Lieutenant Juan Micheloud were on the runway when *Ardent,* twelve miles offshore in Grantham Sound and still supporting the SAS diversion, opened fire, twenty rounds hitting the runway. Of the first pair, only Jorge Benitez managed to take off and he searched for British activity around Bombilla Hill. Finding nothing, he moved his search pattern west, saw ships in San Carlos Water and then noticed a column of troops, 2 Para, moving up from the beaches. Benitez lined up to attack but his Pucara staggered as it was hit by a Stinger missile fired by a D Squadron Air Troop SNCO. His engine was struck by a second missile, but he managed to climb before he lost control, ejected and watched his aircraft smash into the ground near Flat Shanty. He floated downwards and walked to Goose Green.

The Stinger had been brought to the South Atlantic by a group of SAS recalled from training in the USA. One of them, Staff Sergeant O'Connor, formerly Welsh Guards, had made himself proficient with the system and it was intended he should train other SAS. However he perished when his Sea King ploughed into the sea, taking with him the training manuals. The kill on the Pucara was more luck than judgement. The same soldier fired several more missiles at Argentine aircraft and missed each time.

Meanwhile Tomba and Micheloud failed to find any British helicopters and, searching for opportunity targets in Port San Carlos, were shot at by a 43 Battery Blowpipe. Returning to Goose Green, they were directed on to a patrol directing accurate naval gunfire on to the runway but were jumped by three Sea Harriers and Carlos Tomba was shot down. Micheloud found cover in cloud.

At 8am two C Flight 3rd Commando Brigade Air Squadron Gazelles lifted from the *Sir Galahad* to recce locations for the T Battery 12th Air Defence Regiment Rapier sites. The aircraft cleared two positions and then split up on the second phase of their mission to escort and protect Sea Kings bringing stores ashore. At about 8.40am Sergeants Andrew Evans and Edward Candlish, both Royal Marines, rendezvoused with Lieutenant Ray Harper RN lifting off from *Canberra* with an underslung load of mortar bombs and carrying a T Battery recce party. Harper flew toward Hospital Point and then on towards Port San Carlos.

On the ground, Esteban, believing he was about to be encircled by heliborne troops, ordered his men to fire at the helicopters; in his hand-written report of his actions at Port San Carlos, he reported the Gazelles to be Sea Lynxes. Realizing he had overshot the leading elements of 3 Para, Harper dropped his load, banked and warned Evans that he had unexpectedly come under ground fire. Esteban then came under fire from 3 Para's leading platoons, who had reached the area of the Community Centre. He then claims that a Gazelle approached his position at a height of about forty feet and loosed six rockets at his men before it banked to follow the Sea King. Concentrated fire was brought to bear on the helicopter, hitting the rotor and gear box and crippling it. Mortally wounded, Evans ditched the Gazelle about fifty yards from the jetty but because its floatation gear had been removed to make the payload lighter for a GPMG mount, it began to sink. Both sergeants managed to untangle themselves from the wreckage and surfaced, Candlish then inflated the lifejacket of the barely conscious Evans. Ashore, Esteban ordered a cease fire, but it does seem some troops either failed to hear or ignored the order. Under fire and wounded, Candlish dragged Evans downstream about 500 yards to Port San Carlos and hauled him up a steeply shelving beach to a group of "kelpers", who took them to the settlement bunkhouse where the cook, Thora Alazia, and the schoolteacher, Suzanne McCormick, tended the wounds of Sergeant Evans but he died soon afterwards.

The incident spread like wildfire throughout the ships and it was feared that the conflict would develop into a nasty affair. Perhaps the enemy were going to revert to the brutality of the Dirty War, but, as events turned out, this was an isolated incident of young and inexperienced conscripts caught up in the maelstrom and confusion of battle. Nevertheless they justifiably shot at the helicopters, which had made themselves vulnerable, another example of the inexperience of combat. As one Argentine sergeant later said, 'What is the difference in shooting men struggling in the water to being under naval gunfire and cluster bombs while struggling to survive on the ground?' Whatever the sentiments of this soldier, both sides generally stuck to the Laws of Armed Conflict.

The scene of the short action was marked by a thin wisp of smoke, which provided an aiming point for 3 Para's mortars. Daniel Esteban moved east to The Knob to avoid the barrage, but, to his astonishment, another Gazelle appeared near their position. Crewed by Lieutenant Ken Francis and Lance Corporal Brett Griffin, both Royal Marines, it was also working with a Sea King. Francis's radio was not functioning properly – he could receive but not send – and picked up orders to recce The Knob. Arriving at about 8.45am, he overflew Cameron Point at very low level and then as the helicopter banked to pass over Port San Carlos, it was struck on the starboard side by ground fire from Combat Team Eagle. The helicopter smashed into the ground upside down near Clam Creek very near the Argentine position, killing both crew instantly as the force of the impact disintegrated the forward fuselage. Esteban later reported that his men had come under fire from its inboard GPMG and they had brought it down as it manoeuvred to fire its rockets.

Shortly after these incidents a 1st Attack Squadron MB-339 Aermacchi piloted by Navy Lieutenant Guillermo Crippa took off from Port Stanley on a triangular patrol to Port San Carlos, south to Darwin Peninsula and then back to Stanley to check unconfirmed reports of landings being reported by Task Force Mercedes. Morning glare and rising mist forced him to approach from the north and, passing over Jersey Point from Foul Bay, he saw ships in Falkland Sound. Dropping to 500 feet, he made a low level approach to find out what has happening and was about to attack a Gazelle, which he identified as a Lynx, when he noticed the frigate *Argonaut*. Crippa carried out a rushed rocket and 30mm cannon attack, which caused some damage to the forward Seacat deck and wounded two sailors, one of whom lost an eye. Under fire from rail-mounted GPMGs and a Blowpipe on *Canberra*, a Seacat missile from *Intrepid* and *Plymouth's* 4.5in main armament, Crippa banked and flew up the Port San Carlos valley, coolly counted the ships and returned to Port Stanley to make his report, his aircraft slightly damaged. For this sortie he was awarded Argentina's highest award for gallantry.

3 Para were determined to clear the Port San Carlos vicinity quickly. 79 Commando Battery, in positions near San Carlos, fired the first fire mission of the war and Mortar Platoon peppered the area around The Knob. The Blues and Royals were not let loose in the mistaken belief that their CVR(T)s could not be driven on soft peat. The enemy would not have got far. Lieutenant Esteban ordered another shift to the east and yet another Gazelle, this time flown by Captain Robin Makeig-Jones RA with Corporal Roy Fleming RM appeared in front of Combat Team Eagle. Believing it was about

111

to direct naval gunfire on to their positions, he ordered sustained fire which caused the helicopter to veer away with superficial damage on to the Sir Galahad.

This was the first use for several years by the British of helicopters in a conventional war scenario and the losses brought about a hurried change in policy. Esteban had already recognized that the helicopters tended to be exposed for a sufficient period to allow small arms to be directed at them. Air artillery observation and armed offensive action was largely abandoned in favour of casualty evacuation, communications and moving light loads over secured ground.

The destruction of the two helicopters had not paralysed his men, as Esteban thought it might, and, full of confidence, Combat Team Eagle slipped away under intermittent mortar and small arms fire. Apart from those missing after Fanning Head, the unit had suffered no casualties, although their problems were only just beginning as they struck out east toward Douglas, which they reached four days later. They were helicoptered back to Stanley, but within the week most were captured at Goose Green.

A and C Companies 3 Para were tasked to clear the area of Combat Team Eagle, which resulted in the first "blue on blue" of the war between British units when A Company opened fire and called down a fire mission on a group of figures. They were in fact C Company who also thought the figures in front of them were Argentines, opened fire and asked for artillery support. Mistakes at Battalion Headquarters and by the gunners ensued and, in addition to the firefight that had developed, mortars shelled the battlefield. Two Scimitars then appeared and opened fire on C Company and then a helicopter called in to evacuate two severely wounded paras was damaged. At Battalion Headquarters Lieutenant Colonel Hew Pike realized that two of his companies were firing on each other and ordered cease-fire.

The actions at Port San Carlos and Fanning Head were the only ground forces clash on 21 May but during the six hours of daylight the Argentine Air Force launched eleven raids. These tended to be piecemeal, of two to four aircraft coming in low and fast from the west using the ground to shield their approach and giving the ships and air defences precious few seconds to react. Nevertheless, the defences were sufficiently strong to prevent the aircraft from doing serious damage to the Landing Group. Five Daggers, five Skyhawks and two Pucara were shot down at the cost of three pilots, in addition to the Puma and Chinook destroyed on Mount Kent. By the end of the day the British were established ashore but Ardent had been sunk and Andromeda and Brilliant damaged. Had the Argentines used 'big wing' tactics, it is possible they would have overwhelmed the Falkland Sound defences and could have got at the ground forces. By the end of the day, twenty-four Royal Navy and three Royal Marines had been killed but Secretary of State for Defence John Nott was able to report: 'Seven weeks after the Argentine aggression, British troops are tonight firmly established back on the Falkland Islands'.

Caught by surprise, the Argentines were in a quandary. By chance Junta member Lami Dozo was visiting Air Force HQ at Comodoro Rivadavia when reports of the landings filtered through and he talked to some of the pilots who had flown against the beachhead. Returning to Buenos Aires, he convinced his colleagues that, while the British were still re-organizing and to prevent them consolidating, thereby delaying the arrival of 5th Infantry Brigade, the beachhead should be attacked as soon as possible. But in spite of Guillermo Crippa's courageous flight over the San Carlos Water, Menendez's senior intelligence officer, Colonel Cervo, was convinced that only part of 3rd Commando Brigade had landed and 5th Infantry Brigade was therefore available to land anywhere else, including the Stanley beaches. Menendez also expressed this opinion to the Junta and refused to send forces to attack the beachhead. In any event, the British had crippled his helicopter lift capability. There was nothing Army Group Malvinas could do except wait and see. For the next ten days San Carlos Water was the scene of courageous flying and at times desperate defence by ships protecting the beachhead, but the British gained the upper hand and the beaches became the logistic funnel through which men and supplies were fed into the advance on Stanley. When the Argentines did react, it was too late and too weak.

It had long been suspected that the Argentines were overlooking San Carlos Water anchorage, but it was not until 25 May that the evidence emerged. Lieutenant Commander Dante Camiletti had arrived in Stanley with the Amphibious Support Force and when Brigadier General Daher resurrected Operation *Cameleon*, a plan to neutralize British air defences thought to be north of Mount Usborne, he immediately volunteered when the Marines were asked to supply personnel. Camiletti was allocated ten marines. Shortly after dawn on 23 May two Army Iroquois helicopters landed his patrol on Chata Hill and after lying up all day expecting to see British patrols, that night they reached Bombilla Hill and spent another fruitless day observing. They then set off for Cerro Montevideo still searching for the British. As they crossed the Rio San Carlos a Harrier flew over while they were in midstream and everyone frantically sought cover expecting it to return. A small patrol led by a sergeant returned with news that he had seen helicopters with underslung loads and Camiletti dispersed his men around the beachhead and installed himself on Mount Verde, reporting the activity below him until he was captured hiding underneath a rock by a member of 40 Commando on a 'shovel patrol'. On the same day two more of the Fanning Head Mob were captured.

Further suspicions that there were still Argentines in the hills around the anchorage bore fruit on 30 May when a Sea King landed near HQ 3rd Commando Brigade and out tumbled three very bedraggled but armed Argentines. The loadmaster dropped a small bag of belongings on to the ground and waved as the helicopter lifted off. No capture report – nothing. It turned out the three were from the School of Military Aviation who had been manning a radar beacon on Verde Mountain. They had run out of rations and tried to surrender to passing British patrols but without success. Unfortunately the helicopter crew could not be found so that the Argentines' radar post could be inspected.

Meanwhile Brigadier Thompson was under pressure to do something about the Argentine garrison at Goose Green.

7

Goose Green

'Hit the enemy really hard and they will fold.' "H" Jones to 2 Para
See Map p. 105

The settlement of Goose Green lies at the neck of Lafonia. In 1982 there were 127 settlers, most of whom were involved in sheep farming. A deep-water jetty in Darwin Harbour serviced the FIC coasters. About five miles to the north along a track is the tiny settlement of Darwin with about twenty-five settlers. Both settlements are serviced by a school and an airstrip. The 1982 RE Briefing Map lists the 400 yard Darwin airstrip as having a slight slope to the west otherwise it is 'good, fairly firm.'

Because of its highly classified nature, some information was withheld from Thompson's intelligence staff and they experienced difficulty calculating the Argentine order of battle and projected strengths. Equally, the rules about handling this information, mostly from signals intelligence sources, meant that it could not be released. This dilemma was resolved at a chance meeting in the Chief Petty Officers' mess when the Electronic Warfare senior rate, who had just arrived from UK, met two NCOs of the intelligence staff. The previous night his team had intercepted a communications link between Stanley and Argentina transmitting welfare messages which always included name, number, rank, unit and location of the sender. The next day the Chief arrived at the Chapel, where the Intelligence Section was based, and astonished the NCOs with the quality and quantity of information. Its authenticity was proven beyond doubt and within days HQ 3rd Commando Brigade had an accurate picture of the layout and organization of Army Group Falklands. This source became vital to their collation and often provided collateral to the official highly classified information. It was astonishing that the Argentines should have run this link without some security.

12th 'General Arenales' Infantry Regiment, commanded by Lieutenant Colonel Italo Piaggi, had been ferried by helicopter to Goose Green on 28 April. Numbering 643 all ranks and usually based in the northern subtropical province of Corrientes as part of 3rd Infantry Brigade, not only were its soldiers unfamiliar with the penetrating wind and freezing rain of a South Atlantic winter but its move to the Falklands had been confused and unsettling. After 10th Infantry Brigade moved to the Falklands, 12th Infantry Regiment was rushed by rail and lorry to strengthen the border with Chile. En route, a police car overtook the convoy and gave Piaggi new orders to join 3rd Infantry Brigade's move to the Falklands from Puerto Deseado. He was horrified. He had been in command only since March and over 50% of the regiment were the February, 1982, intake of conscripts, not even half-trained. He had collected some reservists from Patagonia on the move south. Five of his platoon commanders had only recently graduated from the National Army Academy and hardly knew their men. On 24 April 12th Infantry Regiment flew from Comodoro Rivadavia to the Falklands in light fighting order.

The regiment was deployed first to Two Sisters and Mount Harriet, in depth to 7th Infantry Regiment on Mount Longdon and Wireless Ridge. Piaggi's adjutant, Captain Eduardo Corsiglia, and First Lieutenant Ignacio Gorriti's B "La Florida" Company, renamed Combat Team Solari, joined the Reserve on Mount Kent as air cavalry. When it became apparent that the British were determined to recover their lost territories either by political means or, if that failed, by military action, Brigadier General Parada sent 12th Infantry Regiment to Goose Green with three missions. First, to provide a reserve battle group, known as Task Force Mercedes, to reinforce Army Group Puerto Argentino; secondly, to occupy Goose Green, and thirdly, to defend Military Air Base Condor. Wing Commander Wilson Pedrozo was appointed garrison commander, although Piaggi was responsible for tactical developments.

Piaggi assumed a position of all-round defence, with First Lieutenant Jorge Manresa's A Company establishing the main defence along a gorse hedge across the isthmus from Darwin Hill to the remains of Boca House. The company was understrength with some of 1st and 2nd and all 3rd Platoons still on Mount Kent. Second Lieutenant Morales' Recce Platoon patrolled as far north as Camilla Creek, sometimes using a corral south of Burntside House as his base. First Lieutenant Ramon Fernandez's C Company covered the approaches from Lafonia. To replace B Company and in reserve in Goose Green, a composite company was assembled from Headquarters Company and placed under command of Second Lieutenant Ernesto Peluffo, one of the fifth year officer-cadets commissioned from the National Army Academy. An 8th Infantry Regiment platoon, commanded by Second Lieutenant Guillermo Aliaga, another April graduate, covered Salinas Beach and Carlos Esteban's C Company 25th Infantry Regiment remained at the Schoolhouse.

Piaggi had graduated from the National Army Academy in 1957 and was experienced in jungle and mountain warfare. With a reputation for leading from the front, he believed that his personal presence affected morale and inspired his men. Generous in commendation, he was also unsparing in criticism; he had to be in a conscript army. But under command Piaggi now had units from three separate regiments from two brigades from different corps, none of whom had ever worked together and rated in quality from good – Esteban's company – to uncertain – Pelufo's platoon. On paper he had a full regiment, but was weak in infantry of quality and experience. The 12th Infantry Regiment chaplain, Father Mora, wrote, 'The conscripts of 25th Infantry wanted to fight and cover themselves in glory. The conscripts of 12th Infantry Regiment fought because they were told to do so. This did not make them any less brave. On the whole they remained admirably calm.'

9th Engineer Company laid minefields south of the ruins of Boca House, covering Salinas Beach, the north end of the airfield and on both sides of the inlet north of the Schoolhouse, and another was laid between Middle Hill and Coronation Ridge. To compensate for the loss of his vehicles, Piaggi received four Mercedes jeeps fitted with radios, but he had no field artillery, although Captain Braghini's Army 601 Air Defence Group 35mm section could be used in the ground role, and instead of fourteen Recoilless Rifles, he had one and that was with Manresa's company. Of ten 81mm mortars, eight were on the *Ciudad de Cordoba* and the one 120mm mortar he had was damaged. The absence of B Company meant that he was fourteen MAG machine guns short.

On 29 April twelve Pucara of the 3rd Attack Group, renamed Pucara Squadron Falklands, arrived from Stanley and several civilian and non-operational aircraft were dispersed around the airstrip to deceive British air photo readers. 1 May was a day of increased Britsh air activity. Shortly after daybreak in what turned out to be a fortuitous move, Pedrozo ordered the four CH-47s to be parked in Goose Green. During the morning three 800 NAS Sea Harriers launched from *Hermes* bombed the airstrip, destroying a Pucara and damaging two on the ground. Three patrolling Pucaras were diverted to Naval Air Base Elephant on Pebble Island where they remained until damaged by the SAS a fortnight later. The raid caught the defenders by total surprise and for several hours chaos and confusion reigned as the Air Force struggled to restore order amidst exploding ammunition and burning aircraft and equipment. Seven Air Force were killed and fourteen wounded and Pedrozo was forced to declare the base non-operational. Braghini was censured for the unsatisfactory state of the air defence. For the settlers the attack proved unfortunate and using the excuse of ensuring their safety, Pedrozo confined them to the community centre for the next twenty-nine days.

At mid-afternoon on 4 May Braghini's gunners, alerted by the early warning radar at Stanley to three aircraft approaching Goose Green up Choiseul Sound, shot down Lieutenant Taylor's Sea Harrier, which exploded in a huge fireball, smashed into Calf Park, careered across the Darwin track and came to a standstill near the eastern perimeter of the airfield.

At Brigadier Thompson's Orders Group for *Operation Sutton* on 13 May, his Intelligence Officer, Captain Rowe, had confirmed the existence of a large

117

Argentine garrison at Goose Green. Available at Port Howard were about 1000 troops of the 5th Infantry Regiment and 900 8th Infantry Regiment at Fox Bay although there was doubt about their combat efficiency. Crucial intelligence about Argentine tactical deployments in the field, command and control, and organization was still missing and would remain so throughout the campaign. On the same day, as we have seen, Piaggi ordered Combat Team Eagle to establish a blocking position at San Carlos. Its unexpected appearance and the possibility that the Argentines might move on to Sussex Mountain as soon as the landings were spotted induced Thompson to order the SAS to organize a diversion at Goose Green and move 2 Para up the landing order.

As soon as Menendez appreciated the strength of the British landings, he knew that Goose Green was vulnerable, if only as a benign cancer to be removed, but, although convinced that the main assault would be directed at Stanley, Army Headquarters refused to reinforce the garrison with part of the Strategic Reserve, except for a weak artillery Pack Howitzer troop.

On 21 May, ordered by Parada to send four guns to Task Force Mercedes and attach the remaining two guns to C Battery 3rd Artillery Group, Lieutenant Colonel Carlos Quevedo, commanding 4th Airborne Artillery Group, decided that they should be detached from First Lieutenant Carlos Chanampa's A Battery. He had already visited the Darwin Peninsula at the end of April and plotted possible targets. With some difficulty, two howitzers and 1000 rounds of ammunition were stowed on the Coastguard cutter *Rio Iguazu*, commanded by Captain Gopcevich, but it was not until after dawn on the 22nd that she finally got underway. Gopcevich hugged the coast, but at about 11am the cutter was seen in Chioseul Sound by two patrolling Sea Harriers and, during the fierce exchange, was forced to beach his damaged cutter at Buttons Bay. A Malvinas Helicopter Squadron Bell-212 from Goose Green collected the survivors and delivered a working party who recovered the guns, although one was badly damaged. The remaining two guns and a jeep were flown by helicopter to Goose Green.

On 12 May Major General Moore, still a week away, had issued a directive to Thompson, which read:

> You are to secure a bridgehead on East Falklands, into which reinforcements can be landed, in which an airstrip can be established and from which operations to repossess the Falklands can be achieved. You are to push forward from the bridgehead area, so far as the maintenance of security allows, to gain information, to establish moral and physical domination over the enemy and to forward the ultimate objective of repossession. You will retain operational control of all forces in the Falklands until I establish my Headquarters in the area. It is my intention to do this, aboard *Fearless*, as early as practicable after the landing. I expect this to be approximately on D+7. It is then my intention to land 5th Infantry Brigade into the beachhead and to develop operations for the complete repossession of the Falklands Islands.

Moore does not mention a full-scale attack, but suggests that the beachhead was to be secured for 5th Infantry Brigade, information gathered and the enemy dominated. Task Force Mercedes clearly presented a threat to the beachhead and when Brigadier Thompson visited 2 Para on 22 May he ordered Lieutenant Colonel Jones to prepare a plan to raid Darwin Peninsula to keep the Argentines off balance and inflict as much damage as possible on the garrison. So began a week of debate, order, counter-order and near disorder as those in comfortable offices in distant London and Northwood sought to control events in the muddy and cold trenches around San Carlos Water. Thompson endeavoured to keep his brigade focused on his principal objective – capture Stanley and finish the war. Anything to do with the Darwin Peninsula was a side-show unless the Argentines showed signs of stirring and so far Task Force Mercedes seemed content to remain behind its defences.

Within twenty-four hours Thompson was under severe pressure to do something, in spite of the worsening logistical problem caused by the air raids. He rejected a demonstration on West Falklands and a series of raids along the coast because they involved the complexities of amphibious operations and there were few, if any, enemy around Douglas and Teal Inlet. If there was to be a raid, Goose Green was a logical target. The following day Thompson issued 2 Para with a warning order to raid the Darwin Peninsula and assigned Jones three Light Guns from 8 Commando Battery ('Black Eight'). Jones immediately flew to San Carlos where he and his intelligence officer, Captain Alan Coulson, were given the latest intelligence. They also received an assessment from G Squadron, largely based on Corporal Trevor Brookes' observations, which had suggested there was probably only one infantry company. Task Force Mercedes had apparently vanished. Inserted in early May on the eastern shores of Darwin Harbour and under constant threat from enemy aircraft and ground patrols, Brookes and three colleagues watched Goose Green for sixteen days. There is no doubt he contributed to the intelligence picture, for which he was awarded a well-earned Military Medal, but the information was limited to what he could see. Collateral gathered during the diversionary raid strengthened the SAS belief there was one company defending Goose Green.

Controversy about how much 2 Para did know about Goose Green will doubtless be debated for years. Information was available in HQ 3rd Commando Brigade from early May. However an unhealthy competition had developed between the long-term, mundane and steady growth of intelligence by Brigade HQ and the exciting but relatively short-term information gained by the SAS. A member of Brigade HQ recalls: 'I was already aware that the SAS had made a questionable assessment of the enemy strength at Goose Green, but if 2 Para chose to believe the SAS, the deeper they penetrated toward Goose Green, the more unknown they would face. The intelligence gained from the sergeant was the most

119

recent available.' In the event, the former probably proved more accurate.

Intelligence at any level relies on information-gathering from a variety of sources, which is all then thrown into the assessment pot from which an analysis can be made. Brigadier Thompson employed a system of unit liaison officers, who were specifically instructed to report to his Intelligence Section before they entered his Command Post and before they returned to their units. While 2 Para's post-operation report is highly critical of 3rd Commando Brigade's passage of information and the lack of intelligence at this moment of the campaign, there was actually very little to report. Air imagery interpretation was limited because the aircraft either flew too high or too low and strategic information from high-level sources was not widely available because of its protective caveat. There were no prisoners and patrols found no evidence of the enemy.

Another problem was lack of training. On exercises, where war is practised, the group least catered for were the intelligence staff, usually because there was no enemy. Consequently opportunities to convert information from photographs, patrols, prisoners, documents and neighbouring units into intelligence were infrequent. Intelligence officers rarely had the opportunity to deliver the intelligence picture and those listening were often not familiar with the correct way of handling the detail given at these briefings. In spite of the major role played by intelligence in Northern Ireland and the acceptance that it was vital to know about the enemy, surprisingly in the Falklands campaign there were suspicions about the accuracy and credibility of intelligence. While HQ LFFI and 5th Infantry Brigade both had Intelligence Corps-manned sections, 3rd Commando Brigade were seriously deficient. When Major Julian Thompson arrived as Brigade Major in January 1972, he found the Intelligence Corps section had been disbanded as a consequence of defence cuts. In 1982 there was just one Intelligence Corps SNCO and the remainder were Royal Marines, but, since Intelligence was not a specialist qualification, their learning curve was steep. Most Commando Intelligence staff had attended a Regimental Officers' and NCOs' Intelligence Course, but, strangely the same course was not open to the Brigade Intelligence Section. Of all the brigades, 3rd Commando Brigade was the weakest in its ability to analyse enemy intentions and yet it was about to fight a battle against an enemy about whom no one in Whitehall knew much, let alone anyone at San Carlos.

Patrolling is a valuable method of data acquisition, but, because of SAS interest in Goose Green, it was discouraged and therefore information from OPs, prisoners and patrols was simply not forthcoming, a not uncommon feature of the campaign. In their post-Op Corporate report 2 Para wrote: 'The activities of the SAS were particularly frustrating. SAS operations both before Darwin/Goose Green and Wireless Ridge inhibited the Battalion's own patrolling activities and yet no proper debriefing of the SAS patrols was ever made available to the Battalion.' Strong words indeed from a battalion with traditionally close links with the SAS, but by no means isolated sentiments. The consequence was that 2 Para was heavily reliant upon information supplied to them from sources and agencies they did not necessarily trust.

Air imagery is an important element of the intelligence collection process, although the evidence can be faked, as the Argentines managed to do by giving the impression that the runway at Stanley Airport had a bomb crater in the middle, when in fact it was fit enough to take C-130s, nevertheless a picture is worth a thousand words. Shortly before *Fearless* left Ascension Island, HQ 3rd Commando Brigade received air photographs of Goose Green which showed three CH-47 helicopters nestling in the settlement and nine aircraft dispersed on the airstrip. Some assessments were made. Fixed- and rotor wing aircraft require ground crews, who need to be protected and, since it was not then known that Army gunners had shot down Taylor's aircraft, the assessment was that Goose Green was predominantly an Air Force garrison of about 300. Information then began to emerge from the Electronic Warfare CPO that 12th Infantry Regiment had arrived in late April, which suggested that Goose Green was developing into a major Army garrison and Air Force base.

Prisoners are valuable sources of information. Most will have been in touch with their colleagues very recently and the act of capture by foreign soldiers speaking a strange language makes them particularly vulnerable. When the Task Force left the United Kingdom it was seriously short of Spanish linguists. The Commando Brigade, for instance, was reliant upon an RAF Flight Sergeant and the piratical Gibraltarian Lance Corporal Ivor Garcia, a Royal Marine who had spent seventeen years as a driver, his abilities as a natural Spanish speaker dormant until the Falklands campaign, when he was in sudden demand, much to his astonishment. By the time the Commando Brigade landed at San Carlos, several other linguists had been identified, including the ubiquitous Captain Rod Bell. 5th Infantry Brigade had similar problems.

During the afternoon of 22 May 3 Para captured a Combat Team Eagle sergeant above their positions at Port San Carlos, who turned out to be from 25th Infantry Regiment and had spent several weeks at Goose Green. Mindful that any information on the nearest enemy unit was important, he was handed over to Thompson's intelligence staff. The sergeant confirmed that Goose Green was strongly defended by 12th Infantry Regiment but the soldiers were suffering so badly from the weather that stand-to was rarely practised. He mentioned a company of Air Force cadets, which was new information. In the event of an attack, C Company 25th Infantry Regiment would gather on the eastern beaches and outflank the enemy by a sheltered approach along the beach. Useful tactical intelligence had now become available. It is of some interest that, in spite of the importance of this prisoner, the only authors to mention him are by Robert McGowan and Jeremy Hands in *Don't Cry For Me, Sergeant Major.*

Documents are also useful sources, provided there is the expertise and time to translate them. During the search of Combat Team Eagle's headquarters in Port San Carlos a radio net diagram showed Task Force Mercedes to consist of three rifle companies, a recce platoon and support and logistic elements. This helped to confirm 3rd Commando Brigade's long-held belief of at least an infantry regiment at Goose Green.

Over the next two days Jones presented his plans to Brigade HQ. Using helicopters to lift 2 Para was rejected because of the shortage of aircraft, although he was offered four Sea Kings to fly in the Light Guns. A night amphibious landing in Brenton Loch was also rejected on the grounds that precise navigation would necessitate the use of radar and could compromise the operation if picked up by enemy counter-measures. An escort of warships would also be required, but they were tied up screening the beachhead against the Argentine air raids. The third and final option of walking the 15 miles, as the crow flies, to Goose Green was accepted although the difficulties of the going were only just being realized. C (Patrol) Company operating near Cantera House reported a strong Argentine company and a troop carrier. Lieutenant Jim Barry, Royal Signals, commanding D Company's 12 Platoon, was lifted by helicopter to within two miles of the building to investigate but it took four hours of navigating across virtually featureless 'bad' going before the house was attacked and found to be empty.

In much the same way as Thompson was indirectly having to deal with meddlesome politicians, Brigadier General Menendez was also having his problems. By the 24th Argentine Intelligence finally concluded that a landing by 5th Infantry Brigade near Stanley was remote and the San Carlos beachhead was the main effort. The Joint Operations Centre was established at Comodoro Rivadavia under the operational command of Major General Garcia and for the first time in the war the activities of the three armed forces were grouped into a single headquarters. All information to and from subordinate theatre commands, including Army Group Malvinas, passed through the new headquarters. Influenced by Vice Admiral Lombardo, the Joint Chiefs of Staff decided that, although an attack on Goose Green was likely, the best option was to leave the beachhead alone and instead attack Admiral Woodward's ships and the logistic link from Ascension Island. Consequently the National Strategic Reserve was not mobilized although 2nd Airborne Infantry Regiment remained on stand-by at Menendez's request. The failure to attack the ground forces was, arguably, a serious blunder. The only raid, on Ajax Bay on 27 May, proved costly to 45 Commando, which lost all its Milan posts and missiles.

With 5th Infantry Brigade estimated to arrive sometime between the 28 and 30 May, the Joint Operations Centre suggested to Menendez that, since the Navy and Air Force had already made their sacrifices, it was now time for the Army to show its commitment by destroying the San Carlos beachhead. The problem for Menendez was that he was in no position to counter-attack. Indeed as opposed to 'Z' Reserve coming to the rescue of Army Group Malvinas, it was the Reserve who were now in the front line and needed the support of Army Group Malvinas. But the Air Force had lost air superiority. The strategically important destruction of the 601 Combat Aviation Battalion hide on Mount Kent and the loss of helicopters rescuing two stranded 601 Commando Company sections on West Falklands severely constrained his ability to move troops. His men would have to walk, but they were not used to marching long distances over rough terrain and then be ready to fight against an enemy well dug-in and supported by artillery, naval gunfire and close air support a few minutes' flying time away. Deploying 5th and 8th Infantry Regiments from West Falklands was discounted because shipping was likely to be intercepted by the Royal Navy. Menendez argued that if he had to use Army Group Malvinas to deal with the San Carlos beachhead, the defences of Stanley would be vulnerable to a landing and therefore the opportunity of drawing the British to the negotiation table would be lost. He proposed to increase patrols against the beachhead, which were already underway, mount Special Forces operations behind the British, threaten the beachhead with 12th Infantry Regiment and reinforce Stanley and Goose Green with the National Strategic Reserve. But the Air Force were prepared only to fly troops to Stanley, from where they could then be helicoptered to Goose Green.

Lieutenant Colonel Jones briefed his company commanders during the afternoon of the 24 May, telling them that Goose Green would be raided early on the 26th. After last light Major Phil Neame's D Company descended Sussex Mountain, collected 12 Platoon and was about half-way to the Camilla Creek House to secure the start line when he received a message from Jones that the operation had been cancelled. With his eyes firmly on the investment of Stanley as the key objective, Brigadier Thompson, when presented with an opportunity to seize Mount Kent in a *coup de main*, switched helicopters tasked to fly in 'Black Eight' to Camilla Creek House to insert D Squadron recce patrols as a prelude to inserting 42 Commando and a battery of six guns. Chinook helicopters were expected from the *Atlantic Conveyor* during the night and it was envisaged that the entire Brigade would then break out by helicopter. Without the guns, the Darwin Peninsula option was a non-starter. Not renowned for his patience, Jones fumed that an opportunity he had 'waited for nearly twenty years had been cancelled by a f......... marine'. He, of course, was not dealing with London's political impatience of the inactivity in the beachhead, as Thompson daily was, and was determined to attack Goose Green. D Company about-turned and trudged back up the path to Sussex Mountains, leaving 12 Platoon at Cantera House. That evening Brigadier Thompson learnt that the *Atlantic*

Conveyor had been sunk and it now seemed that the Commando Brigade would have to walk to Stanley.

Keeping to his original timetable of attacking on 26 May, next day Jones arranged for helicopters to be at the 2 Para LZ at 6am to lift D Company to Camilla Creek House but he was told that only one aircraft was available, and then none. The raid was off, yet again, which did little to soothe his impatience. 12 Platoon was recalled and by the time they reached the Sussex Mountains they were cold, short of rations, hungry and tired.

Thompson still favoured waiting for 5th Infantry Brigade and in another fractious satellite link, told Northwood that SAS recce patrols had been inserted on to Mount Kent, but he was not in favour of committing 42 Commando until more helicopters were available. The weather was also too poor to lift the guns to support the proposed raid on Goose Green and so 2 Para's operation was off. In his book *Goose Green* Adkin emphasizes that Thompson's military superiors were under intense pressure from armchair politicians and he was told, 'You don't need recces for Mount Kent and you don't need guns to assault Goose Green.' No one who had passed the rigorous Staff College course could make such a ridiculous remark and it left Thompson seething that a comfortable headquarters 8000 miles to the north was directing tactical military operations. It was clear that further debate with Northwood was career-limiting and, in his own words, 'I was given a direct order to attack Goose Green, so I sent 2 Para against it.' Northwood also told Thompson to break out of the beachhead, which was in direct contravention of the orders issued to him by Major General Moore. For those at San Carlos their futures were in the hands of militarily inexperienced politicians who would later say that the 'dead gave their lives'.

Lieutenant Colonel Jones was delighted to be told by Thompson that the Goose Green raid was on. An updated intelligence summary indicated that there were at least 1000 Argentines capable of defending the isthmus, but judging by their inaction against the beachhead, they did not seem to have an offensive capability. A more detailed intelligence briefing being given to Captain Coulson at Brigade HQ was interrupted by Jones, in a hurry to meet with his helicopter at "Busbee", the San Carlos landing site.

Jones urged 2 Para to move by last light, which was a great relief to soldiers thoroughly fed up with the inactive days they had spent on the windswept hill. Wet feet in freezing waterlogged trenches had already caused twelve men to be evacuated with trench foot. Resentment at the Argentine Air Force beating up the anchorage, the inactivity on the ground and the lack of information had led to a lowering of morale and operational mistakes, which in turn led to several near 'blue on blue' incidents and did little to heighten confidence. Having already trudged the route, D Company led 2 Para, equipped in fighting order, down Sussex Mountains. Patrol Company would fight as a weak rifle company and Support Company took just two 81mm mortars, the Milans and several GPMG (SF). The start was chaotic as the battalion 'snake' tabbed at an unrealistically fast pace, more suited to the sandy paths of Aldershot. Those with heavy loads fared badly and it was only after a soldier in A Company collapsed that the initial eagerness and classic stop-go, stop-go march changed into a more practical pace for fighting a war.

In support was *Arrow* in Brenton Loch, on call through Captain Kevin Arnold's NGFO 4, and the three 'Black Eight' Light Guns, each with 320 shells, who were to be flown to Camilla Creek House during the night of 27 May. With the lack of artillery locating equipment, the gunners were reliant upon Mark 1 eyeball reports. The 32nd Guided Weapon Regiment Blowpipe detachments had found working with the Parachute Regiment almost beyond their capabilities and were joined by a Royal Marine Air Defence Troop detachment. When Recce Troop 59 Independent Commando Squadron RE had been warned for the operation, Lieutenant Clive Livingstone RE scrounged an LCU to recover kit from the *Sir Lancelot*, which had been evacuated after being hit by a bomb which failed to explode. The sappers, who had not slept for nearly thirty-six hours, joined the battalion as they disappeared into the night. The Medical Officer, Captain Hughes RAMC, received support from Captain Wagon RAMC, who usually worked with the Field Surgical Teams at Ajax Bay. Given fifteen minutes notice to move, he crammed medical equipment into a bergen and arrived on Sussex Mountain shortly before 2 Para left.

Oddly, Thompson did not allocate the Blues and Royals to 2 Para. Although his Brigade had exercised with the 16th/5th Lancers on Salisbury Plain in 1981, the Royal Marines rarely operated with armour and were not familiar with CVR(T)s, their quick-firing cannon and their ground pressure capabilities, but there were several Army in his headquarters to whom he could have turned for advice. The Blues and Royals would have been invaluable in close support.

During the day Menendez instructed Parada to move his headquarters to Goose Green and take command of operations against the beachhead, however he never arrived because the CH-47 duty flight commander refused to accept Menendez's orders as they had not been ratified by the local Air Force headquarters. It later emerged that, although Menendez was in overall command of operations on the Falklands, naval and air force headquarters frequently refused to implement his orders until they had been ratified by their own headquarters. Parada therefore instructed Piaggi: 'Task Force Mercedes will reorganize its defensive positions and will execute harassing fire against the most advanced enemy effectives, starting from this moment, in the assigned zone, to deny access to the isthmus of Darwin and contribute its fire to the development of the principal operation. The operation will consist of preparing positions around Darwin for an echelon defending the first line, and occupying them and from there putting forward advanced

125

combat and scouting forces, as security detachment, supporting the principal operations with harassing fire against Bodie Peak-Cantera Mount-Mount Usborne.'

In other words, Menendez's agreed strategy with the Joint Operations Centre of launching 12th Infantry Regiment at the beachhead had been cancelled in preference to preparing positions to defend the Darwin Peninsula and an advance to contact north, supported by artillery fire, to meet the British, as opposed to waiting for them – sound tactics for experienced troops, but Piaggi's men were anything but experienced and he opposed the strategy. Although Manresa had developed a strong defensive position across the isthmus with interlocking arcs of fire covering the minefields and supported by C Company 25th Infantry Regiment, who regularly practised counter-attacks and plugging gaps, his company was moved forward to Coronation Ridge and replaced by Ernesto Peluffo's composite platoon. He expressed concern to Piaggi that his half-trained company were leaving the security of their defensive position. The redeployment unsettled the conscripts, who set about digging in. During the night Chanampa's guns registered on to targets identified by him during his April recce and from the map. Most were astride 2 Para's route, which brought some discomfort to the paras on the wrong end of the shelling. The Argentine method of air and artillery interdiction was to nominate several features on a map as a marker and call for corrections.

Shortly before dawn on 27 May D Company secured Camilla Creek House and, with movement kept to an absolute minimum, 2 Para crammed themselves into the one house and ten outbuildings, with Battalion Headquarters jammed into a coalshed, but at least warmth was generated. Still desperately short of information about the Argentine forward positions, Jones sent two Recce Platoon patrols to look for the Argentine guns. Corporal 'Taff' Evans, accompanied by a forward air control party under command of Captain Peter Ketley, installed his patrol on a small feature north of Camilla Creek and, as the early mist cleared, saw, 300 yards to the south, Morales' Recce Platoon having breakfast from a field kitchen trailer. From high ground several hundred yards to the north-east, Lieutenant Chris Connor reported Darwin Hill to be unoccupied. At about 9am Ketley was summoned back to Battalion to report on the enemy, but his arrival did little to soothe the impatience of Jones who had just requested an air strike on six targets. Ketley was ordered to rejoin Evans forthwith.

Meanwhile events were unfolding in London which would have a direct bearing on events at Goose Green. When the Signals Platoon tuned into the 10am BBC World Service news, the listeners heard, 'A parachute battalion is poised and ready to assault Darwin and Goose Green'. There was stunned silence as the enormity of this major breach of security sunk in. No one owned up, or ever will, to the blunder but it seems unlikely that it was released by Northwood or the Ministry of Defence. There had also been intense media speculation by armchair generals about attacking Goose Green but the information was too accurate to be speculative. A logical explanation is that it must have been leaked, for the sake of political expediency, to a journalist by someone close to the War Cabinet, someone who was impatient with the apparent lack of activity by 3,000 British servicemen in the San Carlos beachhead facing 14,000 Argentines on the Falklands and was prepared to commit 450 men against an estimated 1,100 enemy. The motive can only have been to force Thompson into fighting a battle he did not believe necessary. Not only was the essential element of surprise lost but 2 Para were committed to battle without the three-to-one advantage. 'H' Jones was furious and ordered his battalion to disperse.

At about 10.30am Morales' sentries saw movement near where Connor's patrol was operating and sprayed the area with machine gun fire. To cover his own withdrawal, Evans called for indirect artillery support, but this was rejected; A Company would help instead. He was then told that an air strike was on its way and not long afterwards, two Harriers appeared over his position. Squadron-Leader Bob Iveson and his wingman, Flight-Lieutenant Mark Hare, approached Darwin Peninsula from the north-east and headed over the isthmus, expecting to be guided by Captain Ketley, but there was silence. They pressed on with their mission and met with considerable small arms ground fire from Manresa's men. They made a second pass over the Argentine position, dropped their cluster bombs, which gave Evans time to withdraw covered by his GPMG gunner, Private Theale. The Harriers made a third run, but Braghini's 35mm Oerlikons inflicted terminal damage on Iveson's aircraft. With his tail in bits and the engine seizing, Iveson baled out and, making his way to Paragon House, was picked up three days later by 3rd Commando Brigade Air Squadron. Meanwhile Jones had called an Orders Group for 11am, but, since the Battalion was now well spread out, several key participants did not receive the message and his patience wore even thinner.

Piaggi and Parada both half-believed the BBC breach to be a hoax because they sensibly believed that no one in their right mind would broadcast an attack to the whole world. Morales then reported that his forward section had opened fire on enemy patrols. Ordered by Piaggi to investigate suspected British activity north of Camilla Creek House, Morales and three soldiers drove a commandeered blue Land Rover north along the track to San Carlos. About a mile from the house Morales stopped to look and listen. 150 yards up the track the despondent Peter Ketley and his party were plodding along to rejoin Corporal Evans when they saw the Land Rover. To Morales' astonishment there was the crackling of automatic fire and everyone dived out of the Land Rover and a short firefight developed. An Argentine sergeant ran back to the vehicle to reach the radio, but two rounds through the windscreen at short range shattered his illusions. Ketley, now much happier, met Evans and between them they escorted the prisoners, one of whom was wounded, to Camilla Creek House. Both patrols were back by 2.30pm.

One problem faced by the Brigade Intelligence staffs was the credibility of prisoner information gathered by units questioning prisoners with inexpert interpreters without knowing what information was required. Morales and the unwounded prisoners were questioned by Captain Coulson with the assistance of Captain Bell, an inexpert questioner helped by an expert linguist but inexpert interpreter. Arguably 2 Para were given insufficient Spanish linguists to deal with prisoners captured before and during the battle and were denied a valuable intelligence asset. The four prisoners failed to reach San Carlos before the battle.

At 3pm, as the light was fading fast, Lieutenant Colonel Jones at last held his Orders Group. There was still much to do, not the least of which was planning and battle preparation down to section level. Lieutenant John Thurman RN, who knew the area well, described the ground and then soon after Coulson began the crucial intelligence briefing, Jones' impatience got the better of him and he stopped Coulson before he had finished. Consequently the companies went into battle without all the intelligence available to them, a fundamental error of judgement. Giving his plan, Jones told the group that the raid had developed into an all-out 'six-phase night/day silent/noisy battalion attack':

Phase one – Support Company to establish a machine gun, mortar and Milan fire-support base at the western end of Camilla Creek. Patrol Company would secure the start line at the junction of Camilla Creek and Ceritos Arroyo and then become Battalion reserve.

Phase two – At 2am A Company would attack the right flank of 12th Infantry Regiment toward Darwin Hill, while B Company attacked the left flank around the derelict foundations of Boca House.

Phase three – At 3am A Company would attack Coronation Point while D Company would deal with an identified platoon position on high ground 1000 metres north of Boca House.

Phase four – At 4am B Company would attack Boca House.

Phase five – At 5am A Company would exploit to Darwin while Patrol Company pushed through B and D Companies to clear the airfield.

Phase six – By 6am A Company were expected to take Darwin while B Company dealt with 25th Infantry Regiment at the schoolhouse. Patrol Company would then move into a blocking position south of Goose Green while D Company liberated the settlement.

The fourteen hours of darkness were to be used to cover the 6500 yards to Goose Green, nine hours of which were for battle preparation and the move through the start line, leaving five hours to advance against an enemy in depth over unknown ground – an optimistic calculation to defeat a regiment about which little was known. Naval gunfire support and artillery was on call, but only when the enemy were obviously aware of the attack. Jones concluded his Orders: 'All previous evidence suggests that if the enemy is hit hard, he will crumble.' Quite how he reached this conclusion is unclear but no intelligence assessment had yet concluded that the Argentines were a pushover. British analyses continually downgraded the quality of the Argentines, and still do, although the efficiency of their April invasion seems to have been quickly forgotten. There was then no evidence to suggest they would fold quickly.

Time was short and some company, platoon and section orders groups lacked detail. At 10pm Patrol Company and the 59 Commando Squadron RE troop began clearing the route to the start line, which included the sappers wading waist-deep in freezing water to check three bridges for obstacles. By 1am the route was secure and Support Company went firm north-west of Camilla Creek and Recce Platoon had secured the start line along a fence, but about 400 metres north of the correct fence. Long columns of paras plodded along sodden tracks in pitch darkness buffeted by a freezing wind whipping across the moors. The approach had been exhausting and many, after two sleepless nights, were tired.

To the south Manresa's despondent men huddled in their trenches. They knew from the BBC that paras were on their way to Goose Green. They were desperately short of heavy weapons and many were ill from poor water, poor food and the cold. Their quilted jackets, scarves, gloves and woollen underclothes were insufficient to keep out the biting Antarctic wind. The logistic chain from Stanley had failed and on 10 May Piaggi gave the companies permission to butcher sheep, which were in abundance. On 19 May morale had been raised when a C-130 flying from the mainland parachuted in eight tons of canned food.

The Battle of Goose Green

At 1.45am on 28 May *Arrow* opened fire. A Company's assault on Burntside House was delayed because it could not be found and it wasn't until about 2.35am that it began its deliberate attack opposed only by a 12th Infantry Regiment recce patrol in the corral, who fired a few shots in the general direction of the paras and then rejoined their platoon. The silent attack quickly became an extremely noisy one. Inside the house, Mr and Mrs Morrison, his mother and a friend lay on the floor as bullets smashed windows, sieved the walls, dislodged the roof and sparked a fire. The paras then splashed across Burntside Stream and went firm in the corral.

At about 3am, on time, Major Crosland's B Company, with Tac HQ and D Company following, crossed Low Pass. *Arrow* was asked to illuminate the objective, Burntside Hill, but her main armament jammed and Captain Ash, the forward observation officer, arranged for 'Black Eight' to open fire. 6 Platoon bumped into positions held by Manresa's inexperienced and frightened conscripts and in the darkness the fighting became confused with some Argentines trying to surrender while others resisted. Manresa lost touch with Piaggi when his Mercedes was grenaded and the radio wrecked.

The pressure was too much for the inexperienced conscripts, and as the paras dealt with each trench, resistance crumbled. Accurate shelling by Chanampa's guns added to the chaos and 5 Platoon, clearing abandoned trenches, was held up by two stubborn Argentines in a trench. It was about 4.30am and still dark when Manresa ordered the remnants of his weak company to withdraw and, amid the crack and flash of grenades, the swirling mists of phosphorous and the staccato hammer of automatic fire, they broke contact, leaving behind both 81mm mortars and the Recoilless Rifle and gathered around Lieutenant Horacio Munoz-Cabrera's platoon in depth on Coronation Ridge. Many of his men were from the warlike Guarani Indian clan but had been badly shaken by the fighting, nevertheless Manresa and his NCOs managed to calm the conscripts down and directed them back to the main defence line. With less than half of his men accounted for, Manresa had bought valuable time and 2 Para was well behind schedule. Several Argentines were later found still huddled in their sleeping bags in the bottom of their trenches, clearly terrified by the violence of the night fighting. Piaggi later declared great admiration for the manner in which Manresa's men had handled themselves.

On 2 Para's right flank, D Company missed the start line and coming upon a track they thought led to Goose Green, believing they were still bringing up the rear and with no instructions from Jones, sat down to rest. Unfortunately Tac HQ appeared out of the darkness from behind them and Jones, annoyed that his reserve company was in front of him, stomped off down the track and immediately came under fire from Coronation Hill. He returned to D Company and instructed Neame to deal with the enemy. But Neame had no real idea where the enemy were or what his position was in relation to A and B Companies and, with Jones breathing down his neck, he ordered an advance to contact. It was now about 4am and Jones needed to push on quickly if he was going to reach Goose Green within the four hours he had given himself. He still had 4 miles to go, every inch held by the enemy.

Fully alerted to the British advance, Munoz-Cabrera was ordered by Piaggi to hold Coronation Hill, but when D Company approached, some of his men ran. The remainder, mainly Guarani Indians, defended their penetration vigorously and, in Neame's words, 'embarrassed' the paras when two .50 Brownings raked D Company's right flank at short range, killing two of 10

Platoon approaching a dry stream bed. But 11 Platoon were unable to engage in case they hit 10 Platoon. Slightly above them, the Argentines were uncertain. The British had suddenly disappeared. Firing slackened, although mortar bombs were still smacking into the ground. In the darkness, noise and confusion of a night battle, command and control are difficult and it is often the individual who discovers the solution. A para had the idea of throwing a fragmentation grenade, followed by a phosphorous. Others caught on and 10 and 11 Platoon worked together to attack the machine guns. As they reached them, another position in depth opened up at short range and Lance Corporal Gary Bingley and his GPMG gunner, Private Barry Grayling, charged the position. Grayling was wounded in the hip and, although the machine gun was silenced, the Argentine gunner's last rounds hit Bingley in the head and he was killed instantly. The fight with Munoz-Cabrara had been vicious and cost D Company three dead and two wounded and overshoots landing on B Company, a few hundred yards to the west, had caused a minor disagreement between Crosland and Neame. With his right flank now reasonably secure, Jones ordered A Company to advance. It was about 4.30am. Advancing quickly, Major Dair Farrar-Hockley found Coronation Point clear of enemy and, seeking permission to advance on to Darwin Hill before first light broke, was told to wait until the CO arrived.

Meanwhile Brigadier General Parada promised Piaggi support as soon as it was light and the weather permitted, but kept pressing him to counter-attack, as he would do throughout the day. Piaggi felt that if he could hold the main defence line he stood a reasonable chance of victory and pushed Guillermo Aliagi's 8th Infantry Regiment platoon on to Boca Hill from where he would have a good view north to Boca House. He also ordered Second Lieutenant Nestor Estevez to take his 1st Platoon, C Company, 25th Infantry Regiment from the Schoolhouse on to Darwin Ridges, as they had often practised. There Estevez and Pelufo agreed that it was more important to defend than counter-attack. Estevez spread his platoon west on to Darwin Ridge from where he could support Pelufo and guard any approaches around Darwin Pond. Survivors of Manresa's shattered company had also withdrawn and one estimate suggests 200 defenders occupied at least twenty-five trenches, bunkers and shell scrapes. Pedrozo also took the opportunity of a break in the weather to evacuate the Army Bell 212 helicopters. The CH-47s had left three days before.

Lieutenant Colonel Jones' philosophy of tight control induced a delay, which would prove fatal to A Company. Leading his Tac HQ across the dark battlefield, he eventually found Farrar-Hockley and authorized him to seize Darwin Hill. 3 Platoon took up a fire position north-east of Darwin Pond near the bridge, a move which irritated Jones because first light was not far off. At about 7.00am A Company advanced, Second Lieutenant Mark Coe's 2 Platoon leading. Ahead was a thin fence and 150 metres beyond it and to the east the 100-foot-high Darwin Hill and to the west Darwin Ridge. A re-entrant led on to Darwin Ridge and a gorse-filled gully led on to the eastern slopes, which Farrar-Hockley selected as the route on to Darwin Hill. Although trenches and tents had been identified by Brookes' SAS patrol, Chris Connor had correctly suggested Darwin Hill was not occupied in strength.

Rain was falling and dawn was creeping over a very grey horizon. Visibility was poor and in the gloom Estevez' men suspected the figures they saw approaching them might be A Company survivors. Corporal Tom Camp's section were in the gorse when three figures appeared on the spur and there was a brief conversation, which neither side understood, until one of the figures shouted in Spanish. Camp's men opened fire and headed up the gully, followed by Corporal Dave Hardman's section, but the defenders, alerted that the approaching column were not Argentines, opened fire. Corporal Steve Adam's section rushed toward the re-entrant and straight into the heart of the Argentine position and were driven off by very heavy fire, which wounded two men, one of whom would not be recovered for four hours. He then joined Camp in the gorse. Company HQ and most of 1 Platoon made it to the gorse, but the rest were strung out in the open back to Darwin Pond and north of the fence. They began a firefight with Pelufo's men and were eventually forced to seek cover on a Darwin Pond beach. A Company was split in half. It was about 7.45am.

At about the same time B Company, moving down Middle Hill toward Boca House across ground very similar to Salisbury Plain, long rolling grass slopes devoid of any real cover, came under fire from Aliaga's men on Boca Hill. 4 and 6 Platoons dashed for the gorse line but 5 Platoon was caught in the open and struggled back up the bare slopes of Middle Hill, taking casualties all the time. A firefight developed and when ammunition ran short, Private Stephen Illingworth was shot dead retrieving some abandoned webbing full of ammunition. Every time a move was attempted Aliaga's and Pelufo's platoons brought fire down on B Company. Captain Ash attempted to bring down artillery fire but found it difficult to correct. 2 Para had been halted.

Eight miles to the rear, 'Black Eight' was having great difficulty. The high demand for missions meant that the recoiling guns frequently had to be resighted, which took about fifteen minutes. One gun developed a buffer oil leak, which was cured with rifle-cleaning oil. Empty shell cases littering the netted gunpits had to be removed to give the gunners room in which to serve their guns and contributed to fatigue amongst the detachments, most of whom had not slept or rested for thirty-six hours. The troop were to fire 900 shells, roughly one round every minute. First Lieutenant Chanampa also had his difficulties. A gun with a broken wheel had been repaired by the battery armourer but a fourth gun, damaged in Choiseul Sound, was almost beyond repair. With 12th Infantry Regiment falling back and his gun positions under mortar fire, he changed his positions several times and always into unprepared sites. The one jeep he had was invaluable in moving the guns and ammunition, complete moves often being achieved in about fifteen minutes.

The foul weather which prevented Harrier operations did not hinder the Pucaras. At about 8am three appeared over Camilla Creek and, although buffeted by the wind and rain, carried out a low-level rocket attack. Lieutenants Cimbra and Arganaraz then approached the 'Black Eight' gun line but were engaged by a 32nd Guided Weapons Regiment Blowpipe, which missed but was enough to put Cimbra off his approach. A missile launched at Arganaraz also missed and exploded on the ground, flinging the Pucara upside down, but it righted itself. All three aircraft returned to Stanley.

Farrar-Hockley's immediate problem of several trenches on the eastern slopes of the spur was dealt with by a small group of soldiers using 66mm, grenades and a GPMG mounted on the back of Private Robert Pain to gain some elevation. The fighting developed into a series of unco-ordinated individual and group attempts to break the Argentine hold on Darwin Ridge. A left-flank attack led by Lieutenant Coe up the gorse gully on to the spur was defeated by heavy fire from Estevez's platoon. Farrar-Hockley grouped six GPMGs under the command of Sergeant Barrett as a temporary fire base to dominate Argentine positions on Darwin Ridge, but could only keep them fed with ammunition for about an hour. North of Darwin Pond, 3 Platoon, giving support, came under heavy mortar fire. A request for a Harrier strike was refused because of fog at sea. Success was going to be slow, about the last thing 'H' wanted.

The defenders of the main defence line resisted with tenacity. Manresa and his Company Sergeant Major, Juan Coelho, were everywhere, encouraging the remnants of A Company. In anticipation of a Skyhawk ground attack support, Coelho laid out strips of white sheets as markers. Even when he was badly wounded in the head, Ernesto Pelufo's platoon resisted. It seems that the young platoon commanders inspired the frightened and lukewarm conscripts. When Estevez was mortally wounded while adjusting artillery fire, his radio operator, Private Fabrizio Carrascul, continued to direct the guns until he too was killed. Thereafter Chanampa's targets tended to be speculative, based on his personal knowledge and from the map, which probably explains why 2 Para appeared not to be particularly disturbed by artillery in the early phases of the battle. Estevez was posthumously awarded Argentina's highest gallantry award.

At 9am Piaggi reported to Menendez that the British attack had been halted and optimism prevailed in Stanley that victory might be possible. This was a critical period, during which 2 Para were most vulnerable. Had plans to helicopter Combat Team Solari from Mount Kent straight on to Darwin Ridge, supported by a strong counter-attack by Fernandez's C Company and C Company 25th Infantry Regiment, materialized, 2 Para would probably have been forced to withdraw. However, poor weather and inexperience ruled and the opportunity went begging.

Under a grassy bank at Darwin Pond, Jones was impatient to find out what was holding up the advance and he and his Tac HQ dashed across the open to join Farrar-Hockley in the gorse. It was about 8.30am. To some, the appearance of the CO was a bad omen; he had been 'killed' too often on exercise. 'H' issued orders to attack a position assaulted without success an hour earlier, but it was a forlorn hope and cost the lives of Captains Wood and Dent and Corporal Hardman. But help was available for A Company. When Neame radioed to Farrar-Hockley that he could outflank the main defence line by slipping on to the western beach although Aliagi's platoon on Boca Hill would have to be dealt with, Jones replied, 'Don't tell me how to run my battle.' It was the sort of comment expected on exercise where lessons are learnt at no human cost. Major Crosland also suggested that if the Boca Hill position could be taken, B Company could roll up the enemy from the west. Captain John Young, before he was severely wounded on Middle Hill, suggested bringing up Milan Platoon on to Middle Hill to shoot at the main defence line. Patrol Company's second-in-command, Lieutenant Peter Kennedy, assembled at least twelve GPMGs on the eastern slopes of Coronation Ridge and asked A Company to nominate targets, but Jones told him, 'Get off the radio. I'm trying to run a battle.' Had Jones become too involved in the fight for Darwin Hill and lost the big picture of how best to use all 2 Para to solve the problem?

As always, Jones led by personal example and, shouting, 'Come on, A Company, get your skirts off! Follow me!', without telling anyone or looking to see who was following, he set off up the gully that Corporal Adams had attacked, followed by Sergeant Barry Norman, his close escort, presumably to get behind the Argentines. Attacking the position held by Corporal Osvaldo Olmos' *grupo,* he was badly wounded on the right-hand slope of the re-entrant about six feet short of the trench. Jones's operator, Sergeant Blackburn, immediately radioed 'Sunray's down'. At HQ 3rd Commando Brigade there was disbelief. It was about 10.30am.

Soon after this small action A Company began to unlock the defences of the main defence line. Company Sergeant Major Colin Price missed a bunker with a 66mm, but Corporal Dave Abols hit another and then, when the paras began to seep on to the ridge, white flags appeared at about 1.10pm and Farrar-Hockley ordered cease-fire. The critical battle for Darwin Ridge was over. 2 Para had lost three officers and three other ranks killed and eleven wounded. Of the ninety-two Argentines involved, eighteen were killed, six from 25th Infantry Regiment, and thirty-nine wounded, over fifty percent casualties. Collecting Guy Wallis' 3 Platoon, Patrol Company moved through A Company.

When Major Chris Keeble at Battalion HQ heard the message 'Sunray's down' he took command of 2 Para and, assessing that the best opportunity

134

of success lay with B Company, immediately passed temporary command to John Crosland. To a great extent Keeble's tactical philosophy had been shaped after a two-year staff posting to the *Bundeswehr*, which allowed commanders on the spot to act within reasonably loose parameters. About half an hour later he led Tac 2, laden with extra ammunition, south toward the front line but had to scramble for cover as two Pucaras roared overhead.

In response to requests for casevac helicopters, two 3rd Commando Brigade Air Squadron Gazelles and two Scouts were made available to 2 Para to fly in ammunition and return to Ajax Bay with casualties. After being briefed at Camilla Creek House, Captain Jeff Niblett RM led the Scouts forward to the RAP. Meanwhile a second sortie of two Pucaras took off from Stanley to support Task Force Mercedes and shortly before 11am they arrived over Camilla Creek House and saw the two Scouts. Lieutenant Miguel Gimenez, on his second mission of the day, singled out Lieutenant Richard Nunn RM's Scout and, in spite of its frantic manoeuvring, shot it down, killing the pilot and severely wounding the observer, Sergeant Belcher. Returning to Stanley, the Pucaras became separated in the mist and Gimenez vanished. His wrecked aircraft was found in 1986. Nunn's brother, Chris, had commanded M Company 42 Commando in the recapture of South Georgia.

Between them Crosland and Neame organized the outflanking of the main defence line. Leaving B Company to deal with Boca House and with 10 Platoon, all the company GPMGs and Support Company in a firebase on Middle Hill, Neame led 11 and 12 Platoons on to the beach. Although bombarded by Milan, the Argentines responded by mortaring the firebase, but when two more Milans struck Aliaga's position, white flags began to appear and Jim Barry's 12 Platoon led D Company on an anxious approach across open ground to the hill. When Corporal Spencer detonated an anti-tank mine, which knocked over several paras, the firebase gunners opened up on Boca Hill and another Milan slammed into Aliaga's position. 12 Platoon were dangerously exposed, advancing across open ground against an enemy position which was showing white flags but were now under fire. Neame frantically radioed for everyone to stop firing. Fortunately the Argentine will to fight had been broken and 12 Platoon moved on to Boca Hill to find that twelve Argentines had been killed in the bombardment. Fifteen prisoners were taken, most of them terribly injured by the Milans, including Aliaga, badly wounded in the head. The survivors withdrew towards Goose Green.

At about the same time, at Stanley Racecourse, First Lieutenant Esteban was cramming about eighty men from the remainder of A Company and the survivors of Combat Team Eagle into an Army Puma and six Iroquois. Warned to move to Goose Green earlier in the day, he had waited until 11am before final orders arrived. Escorted by two Hirundo gunships, the flight arrived at a landing site several hundred yards south of Goose Green and

Esteban, Piaggi's most experienced officer, led his men into the shrinking perimeter. Reporting to Piaggi, he was told to hand over the A Company reinforcements to Second Lieutenant Vasquez, and organize the defence of Goose Green with Air Force personnel converted into infantry. Esteban took no further part in the fighting.

All that now stood between the British and Goose Green was Vasquez's recently-arrived 3rd Platoon, which had moved up to defend the Schoolhouse and Second Lieutenant Gomez Centurion's 3rd Platoon, C Company, 25th Infantry Regiment, which moved up to plug the gap to the right of the School of Military Aviation security company holding the high ground around the airstrip flagpole. Lieutenant Fernandez was still southwest of Goose Green covering the approaches from Lafonia. The lack of radios was impeding Piaggi's ability to control the tactical battle although Parada was still encouraging him to counter-attack.

Leaving A Company on Darwin Ridge, Keeble reorganized 2 Para. Instead of sending Crosland and Neame on a wide right-flanking march to approach Goose Green from the west and surround the remainder of the Argentine defence, D Company was sent across the battlefield to seize the airfield. Meanwhile the sight of Patrol Company and 3 Platoon advancing down the lower slopes of Darwin Hill, making for Darwin, was a tempting target for the Air Force 1st AA Group 20mm gunners and Army mortar and machine-gun crews and they opened fire, killing one man and wounding eleven, including Major Hugh Jenner, the company commander. The British had been caught flat-footed advancing without adequate support across open ground against an active enemy. Support Company was brought up to suppress the Argentine fire, but the range was excessive. It was now about 2.30pm.

Neame detached 10 Platoon to examine what appeared to be a command bunker on the edge of the airfield. Weak from casualties and with Corporal Owen's section rounding up prisoners, it was fortunate that the resistance met from School of Military Aviation cadets and Air Force Rh 202 gunners was frail, and the positions were quickly cleared. Suddenly the paras began to receive fire from the Machine Gun Platoon behind them and waving their red berets managed to get the fire lifted, but it had been a 'blue on blue'. Neame had hoped to avoid the Schoolhouse, a known strongpoint, but before he could advance to Goose Green he had to deal with it because it threatened his left flank. But his company was split, with 10 Platoon at the airfield, while Barry's 12 Platoon had run into some mines and, after their experience at Boca Hill, were nervous. Neame had only Waddington's 11 Platoon, but as he was about to attack he learnt that Barry and two soldiers had been killed arranging a surrender near the airfield flagpole – the so-called white flag incident, the circumstances of which remain shrouded in mystery.

It is known that Barry was leading 12 Platoon up a track toward Goose Green when they thought they saw a white cloth being waved near the airstrip flagpole and seemed to believe that some Argentines wanted to surrender. Informing Company Headquarters, Barry was told to wait for further instructions, but the message appears not to have reached him as he then led Corporal Paul Sullivan's section forward to the white cloths about 100 yards away. As Barry and his radio operator, Private Knight, approached, some Argentines stood up with their weapons above their heads, while Sullivan deployed his GPMG team to cover them. It seems that Barry invited Second Lieutenant Centurion to surrender, who refused and apparently told Barry, 'Son of a bitch! You have got two minutes to return to your lines before I open fire. Get out!' As Barry was turning to leave, there was a burst of sustained fire, probably from the Machine Gun Platoon on Darwin Hill, unaware of this very local truce and seeing only Argentines in the open. The Argentines in the trenches immediately opened up at point-blank range and Barry was killed. Sullivan's section gave covering fire, but he and Lance Corporal Smith were also killed in the general confusion. Another soldier was badly wounded.

11 Platoon then attacked the Schoolhouse complex by firing four 66mm at a shed, but only one hit. As the platoon manoeuvred to attack the school itself, Waddington led a small group along the southern foreshore of the inlet and met the Patrol Platoon commander, Captain Paul Farrar, and Company Sergeant Major Greenhalgh leading a small group across the bridge. Thereafter the two companies intermingled. Attacking a building, Waddington swears he pulled the pin, but, for some inexplicable reason, the normally reliable grenade failed to detonate. Patrol Company cleared an outhouse and set fire to the double-storey building with grenades. As soon as the attack began, Vasquez evacuated the building and withdrew, covered by accurate fire from Braghini's two 35mm Oerlikons, which prevented further British exploitation to Goose Green. Waddington spent fifteen minutes sheltering in a pool of icy water while Captain Farrar was pinned down in a shell-scrape by a very accurate marksman.

At about the same time, having crossed the bridge, Peter Kennedy and a Patrol Platoon section moving along the track to Goose Green fired at some figures about 150 metres ahead. They turned out to be 12 Platoon, still in some disarray after the 'white flag' incident but firmly under the control of Sergeant Meredith. Kennedy told the sergeant he needed a section to capture the airfield and, joined by Privates Sheepwash and Slough, Kennedy skirmished past an exploding ammunition dump, cleared a bunker, noted some napalm canisters and then, as they crested the hill near the flagpole, saw Goose Green about 500 yards away. Finding no one in support, Kennedy withdrew to find that Keeble had ordered Patrol and D Companies to go firm. B Company, meanwhile, advanced several hundred yards east of Boca Hill, captured some of the School of Military Aviation Company and went firm about 500 yards west of Goose Green.

During the afternoon three Pucaras flew into Stanley from Argentina and two were immediately prepared for a sortie against identified mortar positions at Goose Green. Two quicker Navy MB-339 Aeromacchis were also assigned to the mission. Shortly after 2.30pm the two Aeromacchis flew north across the smoking battlefield and attacked D Company, strung out along the track to the settlement, with rockets and cannon. Everyone dived for cover except for Marine Strange of 3rd Commando Brigade Air Defence Troop. He shot down Sub Lieutenant Daniel Miguel, who died as his aircraft ploughed into the ground near B Company. Hoping that the wind would screen the sound of their engines, the two remaining Pucaras approached from the north-west and once again D Company found themselves on the receiving end of an attack, this time napalm dropped by First Lieutenant Micheloud. No one was hurt but everyone was alert and Micheloud's wingman, Lieutenant Cruzado, ran into massive ground fire which smashed his controls. He ejected but was shot at as he floated to the ground, while his aircraft reared up and cartwheeled into the ground near B Company. Cruzado was taken prisoner and next day was taken to HQ 3rd Commando Brigade.

Three Harriers, which had been on call on board *Hermes* since 2pm, then arrived over the battlefield and, guided by Captain Arnold, attacked the 35mm Oerlikons on the promontory. Cluster bombs dropped by the first two aircraft missed and fell into the sea, which erupted into a seething mass of water. The third Harrier scored several hits with two-inch rockets around the Argentine position, damaging some of the guns' controls. Although still within Piaggi's defensive perimeter, the gunners abandoned the guns and left the Argentines dangerously exposed and without air defence.

By the late afternoon, Brigadier General Menendez had begun to realize that the situation at Goose Green was very serious and arrangements were made to release Combat Team Solari from the Reserve to reinforce Task Force Mercedes. An Army Puma, six Iroquois and a CH-47 were sent to Mount Kent to collect the first stick of 100 men, commanded by Captain Corsiglia. Just as the helicopters were taking off First Lieutenant Ignacio Gorriti, the B Company commander, received a message from Parada cancelling the move but it was too late. Left behind was Second Lieutenant Mosterin's platoon. En route, the flight encountered Micheloud's sputtering Pucara staggering back to Stanley. Shortly before dusk, the helicopters landed south of Goose Green. It remains a matter of speculation whether the fresh Argentines had sufficient night-fighting skills, but to B Company, low on ammunition, cold, hungry and tired, they posed a major threat and Crosland pulled back on to high ground in a defensive posture. Lieutenant Weighall called for a fire mission, which was so accurate that the first shells exploded on the landing site. Corsiglia sent a patrol to Goose Green and waited on a beach. Two NCOs sent by Piaggi appeared out of the gloom and explained that the British had virtually surrounded Goose Green. The patrol then returned with orders for Combat Team Solari to make their way into the settlement and act as the reserve company.

Night fell over the battlefield, now silent except for the clatter of British helicopters collecting casualties and moving up supplies. Although Piaggi still had considerable war material and was confident he could withstand a siege, the chances of relief were slim. Army Group Malvinas considered evacuating the garrison by sea and encouraged Piaggi to abandon Goose Green, make for Lafonia across the Bodie Creek bridge and wait for the commando-trained Major Oscar Jaimet and B Company 6th Infantry Brigade from the Reserve. But even Menendez realized that resistance was futile and authorized Pedrozo and Piaggi to decide the best course of action. At about 5.30pm Parada told Piaggi, 'It's up to you,' reminding him that continued resistence should not lead to unnecessary loss of military and civilian lives. Major Alberto Frontera, Piaggi's second-in-command, reckoned that he could hold out against the 600 or so believed to be surrounding Goose Green. There is some evidence that the Argentine interception of radio communications before and during the battle led them to believe they were facing a brigade and were hopelessly outnumbered. Certainly one officer under interrogation believed the attacking force to be about 800. Equally, the British believed they were up against a far bigger fighting force than was actually directly engaged, which was a total of eleven platoons from three regiments. Piaggi later recalled, 'The battle had turned into a sniping contest. They could sit well out of range of our soldiers' fire and, if they wanted to, raze the settlement. I knew that there was no longer any chance of reinforcements in the form of 6th Regiment's B Company and so I suggested to Wing Commander Wilson Pedrozo that he talk to the British. He agreed reluctantly.' Shortly after midnight one of Piaggi's officers used Eric Goss's CB to contact Alan Miller at Port San Carlos to arrange a cease-fire. In return, Keeble sent in two prisoners with terms for Piaggi and the ultimatum if they returned by 8.30am this would signal surrender had been accepted.

Major Keeble decided that he could persuade the enemy to surrender and planned a massive all-arms firepower demonstration on call from HQ 3rd Commando Brigade, if needed. Thompson placed J Company 42 Commando on immediate stand-by to reinforce 2 Para. The two Argentine NCOs arrived back at his HQ well before the deadline with the news that Pedrozo and Piaggi wanted to discuss terms. It was the Argentine Army's National Day and usually a time for celebration, but for 12th Infantry Regiment 29 May would always be remembered as the day it capitulated. Agreement for a full unconditional surrender was reached and Pedrozo, as the senior officer, held a short parade of Air Force, Coastguard and Navy prisoners who then laid down their weapons. After burning the regimental flag, Piaggi then led out about 800 anxious soldiers who assembled in front of their astonished captors. They were then allowed to collect their belongings, but a few frustrated and angry soldiers smashed and looted property.

The battle cost 2 Para sixteen killed, half of them from D Company, and thirty-three wounded. A Royal Marine pilot and a commando sapper were also killed. Of the about 300 who took part in the fighting, Task Force Mercedes lost 145 killed and wounded, with 12th Infantry Regiment losing thirty-one killed, 25th Infantry twelve killed, five from 8th Infantry, two from 1st AA Group, four Air Force and one Navy pilot. They were buried on Darwin Hill. About 1007 were taken prisoner. Not since October, 1975, had the Argentine Army suffered such a loss when 19th Infantry Regiment lost twelve killed to an attack by 500 ERP in Tucaman province.

That evening Wing Commander Pedrozo and Lieutenant Colonel Piaggi were helicoptered to San Carlos and met by Brigadier Thompson. Although Piaggi was immensely proud of Task Force Mercedes and later said it 'would have fought until the last man if Parada had demanded it', at the time he was bitter and angry with his superiors and felt he had been sacrificed. His men had fought a battle with insufficient combat support and had forced 2 Para to fight a long battle by night and day, longer than any other Argentine commander would do. His men were not the tough Germans, hardy Middle Eastern tribesmen or clever Irish republican terrorists previously met by 2 Para, but were barely trained, unused to the climate and had few heavy weapons. Piaggi confounded Jones's theory 'Hit them really hard and they will fold', but he was forced to resign his commission. For the second time during the week Argentine troops had stood their ground and it was only when resistance was seen to be futile that withdrawal and surrender were contemplated.

A major problem for 3rd Commando Brigade was dealing with the prisoners, but since the idea of capturing large numbers of Soviets in a Central European war was inconceivable; it had never been rehearsed. The plan was to select some for interrogation while the remainder would be placed on the *Sir Percivale*. Lance Corporal Garcia, the Gibraltarian driver whose second language was Spanish, became a key figure in the process.

The loss of the prisoner-of-war camp and Chinook helicopters on the *Atlantic Conveyor* added to the difficulties of evacuating the prisoners from Goose Green although the settlement's sheep-shearing godown offered some protection. The remaining helicopters were needed to support 3rd Commando Brigade's breakout, which meant the prisoners were a secondary priority. An idea of marching them from Goose Green was rejected. The weather was now much colder and sharp frosts covered the landscape. In the meantime the Argentines helped to clear up the battlefield. In a tragic accident, four 12th Infantry Regiment conscripts were moving artillery shells from the area of the schoolhouse when there was a massive explosion. A British medical orderly hauled two men from the inferno but a third was horribly wounded and could not be reached; he was shot to relieve him of his agony. The fourth man lost both legs and was rushed to Ajax Bay but died on the operating table. Two days after the surrender Private Ruiz was found still alive in a waterlogged trench but very severely wounded. Evacuated to Ajax Bay, he was nursed back to health.

By 30 May a screening centre, Hotel Galtieri, had been set up in the San Carlos manager's farmyard. Sergeant 'Buster' Brown and Defence Troop, 3rd Commando Brigade Headquarters and Signal Squadron provided a guard force. For the next week selected prisoners were questioned about Argentine tactical philosophies, organization, weapon systems and the situation in Stanley. Inevitably the prisoners were a mixed bag and included an Air Force warrant officer. Immaculately turned out, swarthy and moustachioed, he said he usually worked at Air Base Comodoro Rivadavia despatching troops to Stanley. He had been busily checking a C-130 load when the ramp shut and the aircraft took off, much to his distress. He ended up at Goose Green running the field post office. A session with a gunner was interrupted when two members of Defence Troop entered to check the blackout of a window in the ceiling. Piling two chairs on each other, one of the Royal Marines climbed this precarious contraption, but unfortunately it wobbled, collapsed and crashed to the floor. Unperturbed, the pair then propped a ladder but broke the first few steps. It was the perfect but unintentional 'Incompetent Approach' to interrogation.

In the middle of dealing with the Goose Green prisoners, five 602 Commando Company, who had been captured at Top Malo House, arrived, as did several others rounded up by patrols. The Junta were slow to admit defeat, but when the news was broadcast, Venezuela and Guatemala offered to send airborne units to 'smash the British in the Falklands'. The US encouraged Argentina to consider a four-part solution to the war. But for Brigadier Thompson, now that the tricky and pointless battle of Goose Green was over, all concentration was centred on the breakout from San Carlos and the advance to Stanley.

8

Breakout

'There's nowt for it but bimble out there to find out ourselves.' Sergeant
Millard, Intelligence Sergeant 42 Commando, on the lack of information

'We'll have to bloody well walk,' was Lieutenant Colonel Whitehead's
response on being told about the sinking of the *Atlantic Conveyor*. While 2
Para were engaged at Goose Green, 45 Commando broke out of the beachhead and 'yomped' to Douglas while 3 Para set out on the long 'tab' to Teal
Inlet. In front, Advanced Forces scouted with a few men from D Squadron
22 SAS already on Mount Kent. Thompson regarded its occupation as critical to the battle for Stanley and issued orders for it to be seized by 42
Commando in a *coup de main* the following night, the 29th May. Lieutenant
Colonel Nick Vaux selected K Company to lead the attack.

A feature of uneven ridges and valleys, Mount Kent was also seen by the
Argentines to be key to the defence of Stanley but it had been abandoned
the previous day when Combat Team Solari had reinforced the doomed
Goose Green garrison. If the company had still been on the feature,
the British would have had another difficult battle to win but unaware to the
Argentines, the remainder of D Squadron occupied the feature.

What the British did not know was that Menendez was throwing a Special
Forces screen across 3rd Commando Brigade's front to gain intelligence and
raid its logistic chain as it advanced. So far the cream of the Argentine Army
had been ineffective. Two green-bereted 601 Commando Company sections
sent to Port Howard had been cut off for several days after the landings,
which meant that Menendez was in no position to harass the British beachhead, and Lieutenant Commander Camiletti had been captured by 40
Commando, as we have seen, and so he asked Major General Garcia to send
another Special Forces company.

Major Aldo Rico, second-in-command of the 22nd Mountain Infantry
Regiment and another fervent Malvinist, had already reasoned that, with one
Special Forces unit committed to the defence of the Falklands, another
should be raised to defend the Atlantic Littoral and provide battle casualty
replacements. This was accepted by Army Headquarters and on 21 May,

142

Rico was withdrawn from a mobilization exercise on the Chilean border and ordered to Campo de Mayo to command the new unit, 602 Commando Company. Brought up to a strength of fifty all ranks by four cavalry warrant officer Blowpipe instructors and two medics, few were physically fit for active service after several years in line units.

After the San Carlos landings, Major Castagneto, who commanded 601 Commando Company, and Brigadier General Daher, Menendez's Chief of Staff, had devised Operation *Cameleon,* the first of several Special Forces operations, to neutralize a suspected British air defence position north of Mount Usborne using 601 Commando Company and the Air Force's Special Operations Group but Daher felt that, with two commando sections stranded on West Falklands, success could not be guaranteed and cancelled the operation.

The two sections were frustrated at their inability to react to the British landings and a plan was drawn up to recover them. In the mid-afternoon of 22 May three 601 Combat Aviation Battalion Pumas and a Hirundo gunship lifted off from Stanley for Goose Green, but with Sea Harriers lurking in the area, the garrison was on 'red alert.' The helicopters crossed Falkland Sound and, using the natural contours, flew up the coast toward Port Howard until a ship was seen dead ahead in the gloom, but not wanting to risk it being British, the flight returned to Goose Green. In fact, the ship was the abandoned *Rio Carcarana* which had been run aground in Port King after being attacked by Harriers on 16 May. Next morning the helicopters made landfall at Shag Cove, but were seen by Flight Lieutenants Dave Morgan and John Leeming flying a combat air patrol over Falkland Sound. Morgan dived among the scattering helicopters and shot down a Puma, which crashed and exploded as 120mm mortar ammunition detonated. A Hirundo hiding in a ravine was strafed and the second Puma, its rotors glinting silver against the green tussock, was destroyed by Morgan. The third Puma escaped damage and, after recovering the aircrew from the smoking wrecks and a shot-down Dagger pilot, pressed on to Port Howard. On 24 May 2nd Section 601 Commando Company loaded on to the surviving Puma and returned to Moody Brook in a nerve-wracking flight. This was the second disaster in two days for 601 Combat Aviation Battalion and the loss of more valuable troop-carrying and escort helicopters severely limited Menendez's ability to counter the British landings. 1st Section remained on West Falklands and four days from the end of the war intercepted a Mountain Troop patrol directing naval gunfire on to Port Howard, killed Captain Hamilton and captured his radio operator, Sergeant Fosenka.

With the return of 2nd Section, Daher resurrected Operation *Cameleon* and shortly after dark on the 23rd a four-man patrol cached ammunition and supplies on Mount Simon. The next day Daher personally saw other patrols off and warned them that, because of the helicopter attrition rate, extraction could be difficult. As Castagneto noted when he first arrived, the commandos

143

found the going difficult and one patrol covered just two miles in daylight. The weather also turned nasty and on 25 May the wet and weary patrols were extracted by a Malvinas Helicopter Squadron CH-47. All reported considerable evidence of British helicopter activity but no troops. Planning immediately began for a Special Forces operation to re-occupy Mount Kent during the night of 29 May.

Menendez urgently needed 602 Commando Company and on 26 May their training was terminated. Next day, after being flown in a C-130 at low level to the blacked-out and shell-damaged Military Air Base Malvinas, they joined 601 Commando Company. Some SNCOs, in particular, later perceived 602 Commando Company to be an ad hoc unit flown to the Falklands because Menendez had greater faith in Special Forces than infantry. Some later questioned the company's leadership and the viability of a successful mission. Under the stress of operations, these views manifested themselves on several occasions and may have influenced tactical decisions.

On 28 May, while Task Force Mercedes was desperately defending Goose Green, Menendez assembled all Special Forces, irrespective of their Service loyalty, into a single formation under his direct command – the Special Forces Group – and issued orders for Operation *Autoimpuesta,* a plan to plant a north-south screen to strike at the British logistic line of communication and to capture British soldiers, which, it was felt, would boost morale. 601 Commando Company was to set up an OP on Mount Estancia. Menendez entrusted the capture of Mount Kent to Captain Andres Ferrero's twelve-strong 3rd Assault Section, 602 Commando Company and Major Jose Spadaro's sixty-five maroon-bereted 601 National Gendarmerie Special Forces Squadron, a total of seventy-seven men. Major Jaimet's B Company 3rd Infantry Regiment would then be flown in as the garrison. Since the Falklands was now part of Argentina, the National Gendarmerie, who patrolled her borders, provided a detachment on the islands. The remaining two assault sections were to occupy Mount Simon and Bluff Cove Peak. The Air Force Special Operations Group were meant to reinforce Mount Estancia on the 31st and then occupy Smoko Mount but, because the Argentines believed they had sunk *Invincible* the day before, they were redeployed to guard the TPS-43 radar against an expected attack by the SAS. There were already several prepositioned radars manned by cadets and NCO instructors from the School of Military Aviation around San Carlos but contact had been lost with most of these.

Lieutenant Horacio Losito, of 1st Assault Section, 602 Commando Company, later recalled the preparations:

At 21.00 Captain Jose Verseci returned with the Orders for the mission. Normally we followed a strict planning sequence but this was aborted for several reasons and had to be adapted to the reality of the situation and not the text-book style.

144

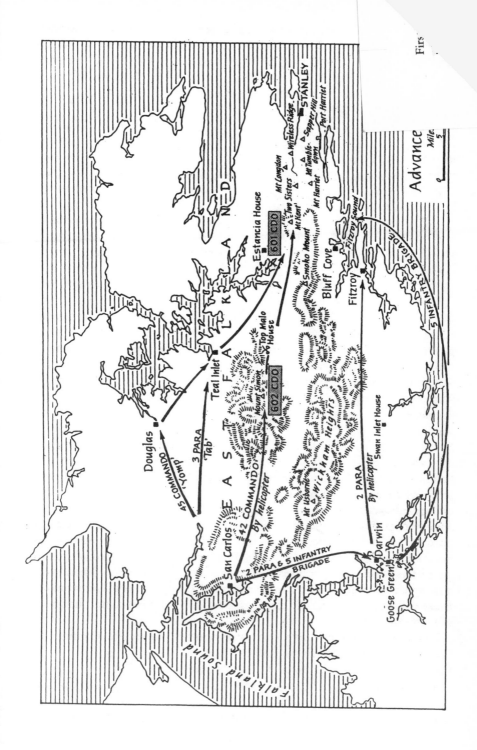

First

Advance

Miles

5

Falkland Sound

San Carlos

Douglas

45 COMMANDO 'Yomp'

3 PARA 'Tab'

Teal Inlet

42 COMMANDO By helicopter

Mount Simon

Top Malo House

Wickham Heights

Mt Usborne

2 PARA & 5 INFANTRY BRIGADE

Goose Green

Darwin

Swan Inlet House

2 PARA By helicopter

5 INFANTRY BRIGADE

Fitzroy

Fitzroy Sound

Bluff Cove

Smoko Mount

Estancia House

40 CDO

45 CDO

Mt Kent

Two Sisters

Mt Longdon

A Wireless Ridge

STANLEY

Mt Tumble- down

Sapper Hill

Mt Harriet

Port Harriet

E A S T   F A L K L A N D

, the very short period between drawing up the plan and the start of the oper- ,ion, at 06.00 the following day. Secondly, the nature of the mission, our speciality being combat missions rather than the recce we were now being asked to do. This confused us. Thirdly, the great quantity of equipment we had to prepare, some of which had only recently arrived in Stanley. One fundamental observation is that in peacetime one should practise planning, in detail, so that in hostilities when the enemy creates the unknown factor and when the physical and psychological conditions are different, the sequence can be greatly reduced.

Nevertheless the operation was detailed, in particular the first phase of getting close to the objective and subsequent operation on Mount Simon. The later phases were badly planned. In all commando operations, withdrawal is fundamental but generally less attention is paid to it than the offensive phase. An important feature of planning is to bring people back for future operations.

It should also be remembered we had been in Stanley for just three days, had done some short recces of the defences and were still familiarizing ourselves with the situation. We knew nothing about the area to the west and had no knowledge of the threat or the enemy's ability to intercept or jam our radios. Intelligence was scarce but no one was at fault; it simply wasn't available.

Without realizing it, Losito neatly highlights the operational impracticality of the Argentine method of raising ad hoc Special Forces for operations. On 29 May, after being given the latest intelligence, the Special Forces Group linked up with 601 Combat Aviation Battalion at Moody Brook and the Racecourse and shortly before dusk 602 Commando Company were flown out. But a front of rain and thick wet mist then covered Stanley and Lieutenant Colonel Juan Scarpa, the senior Army helicopter pilot, cancelled the remainder of the fly-out until 8am the next day. The most recently arrived Special Forces unit thus found itself in the field isolated in unfamiliar terri- tory and with very little of relief or reinforcement until the next day.

Verseci's section was dropped near Top Malo House, which is about seven kilometres from Mount Simon, and, believing it would give his patrol a better chance of success, Verseci split it into two groups. The commandos noted the harshness of the terrain, the difficulty of crossing rivers and the wide rock runs, nevertheless they made good time and by 1pm came together near the summit. An observation post was slotted underneath a large rock and a patrol base of one- and two-man sangars was dotted just below the summit. The weather deteriorated into freezing squalls and high winds whipping in from the south nevertheless they saw British helicopters with underslung loads, including the 18 Squadron Chinook, sole survivor of the sinking of the *Atlantic Conveyor*. They may have been witnessing the aborted insertion of K Company on to Mount Kent and attempts were made to radio this in- formation to HQ Special Forces Group. However the antenna was found to be faulty and, although they could receive, they were not able to transmit.

Meanwhile throughout 29 May 42 Commando had buzzed with antici- pation, but by midday Lieutenant Colonel Vaux had heard nothing about the helicopters until he waved down a Sea King, whose pilot told him he had been tasked only for the morning. A Chinook RAF pilot, exhausted after forty-eight hours of flying, offered to fly in the guns if the Sea Kings would take the troops but they wouldn't and a disagreement developed, with Vaux blaming HQ 3rd Commando Brigade for the failure to produce aircraft. At the time he didn't seem to appreciate the tension in Thompson's Command Post as the staff wrestled with limited resources, all the while being pulled in three directions, to the south by Goose Green, to the east by the SAS operation on Mount Kent and to the north by the departure of 45 Commando and 3 Para. An observer describes the tension:

It was a cold afternoon when a lieutenant commander entered and told Major Chester that the insertion of K Company was not possible because most of the pilots were over their allocated daily flying hours. Major Chester was furious. 'The operation has been planned for weeks. My men are working twenty-fours hours a day and will continue to do so until we win this war. Go back, get those helicopters loaded and fly to Mount Kent. We simply cannot cancel everything because of some peacetime regulation!' The naval officer was utterly crestfallen at being so publicly addressed, picked up his helmet and left without saying a word. There was momentary silence, 'Carry on, gentleman,' and Chester was back to his normal cool, calm and collective self. There wasn't much sympathy with the unfortunate officer. We were fighting an enemy superior in strength who had just proved they would fight and therefore every move to keep them off balance was essential.

On Mount Kent D Squadron, thinly spread out, received no warning of Operation *Autoimpuesta* and were totally unprepared for the sound, at about 6am, of helicopters approaching from the east, in fact a Puma and four Huey helicopters bringing in twenty-nine commandos consisting of Captain Eduardo Villaruel's five-strong HQ Section and Captain Tomas Fernandez' 2nd and Captain Ferrero's 3rd Assault Sections, both twelve-strong. In the wintry darkness the helicopters became separated and Fernandez landed near Bluff Cove Peak and was detected by Sergeant Stone's Mountain and Arctic Warfare Cadre patrol on Bull Hill. But the Argentines were unaware the fly-out of the remainder of the Special Forces Group had been cancelled.

Ferrero's section landed on the eastern slopes of Mount Kent and were soon engaged in a confusing close-quarter night battle with Boat Troop of exploding grenades, sudden firefights at close range and the abrupt scuttle of boots over rocks. Ferrero, First Lieutenant Francisco Maqueda and First Sergeant Arturo Oviedo used the cover of a blizzard and, covered by rifle grenades, infiltrated the SAS defences and forced the British, with two badly wounded, higher up Mount Kent. Meanwhile, according to his patrol report, Villaruel had also landed on Mount Kent and, avoiding contact, withdrew to high ground north of the hill. At Advanced Forces, the repercussions of abandoning Mount Kent and regrouping at Estancia were discussed but Thompson, keen that he should have the feature, told Major Delves that it

147

was critical to hold it and put him in command of all forces in the area.

Meanwhile K Company, Tac HQ and four 81mm mortars approached Mount Kent in Sea Kings but heavy snow showers, 'white-out', approaching darkness and extremely poor visibility prevented landing and the pilots groped their way back to San Carlos, frequently landing to pinpoint their location, and deposited the Royal Marines, thoroughly relieved to be back, on terra firma. The fighting on Mount Kent continued for most of the night but by daybreak Ferrero, without any sign of Major Spadaro, had abandoned Mount Kent and headed for Mount Estancia.

After dawn on the 30th Captain Fernandez set off for Mount Kent but at about 11am, headed for high ground after losing two men killed by heavy fire from the east. Meanwhile Villaruel saw a five-man patrol, possibly SAS, heading for Estancia and then soon afterwards two survivors of Ferrero's patrol appeared out of the gloom, thoroughly relieved to be back amongst friends. Using the mist and rain as cover, he then moved higher up Bluff Cove Mountain. In mid-morning four Army helicopters were seen collecting troops from Mount Wall and Sergeant Luis Luna returned with a helicopter and the news that they were supporting the deployment of 4th Infantry Regiment on to Two Sisters and Mount Harriet. The pilot was given a map reference to pass to Major Rico for when he deployed into the field. Shortly afterwards two Harriers screamed overhead and attacked the helicopters, but they managed to avoid destruction. Mid-afternoon four Royal Marines, probably the Mountain and Arctic Warfare Cadre, passed and Villaruel asked HQ Special Forces Group to send out a radio and a 120mm mortar.

The fly-out of Captain Jorge Emeterio's Gendarmerie was delayed because of Harrier patrols and it was not until shortly before 11am that the Puma took off but near Murrell Bridge, it crashed, killing six and injuring eight. At least four helicopters were flying 4th Infantry Regiment from Mount Wall to Mount Kent and it is possible the Puma may have been brought down by Argentine ground fire but more likely it hit the ground avoiding rockets from the two Harriers which had passed over Villaruel's position. During the afternoon Villaruel was joined by Ferrero.

Believing Ferrero and Villaruel were still in the area, Fernandez set off for Mount Kent after dark but was ambushed on its lower slopes. But help for the SAS was on its way. Although startled by the shooting as Fernandez's section clashed with the SAS, K Company were finally landed on the lower western slopes and it did not take long for the LS to be totally secured for the fly-in of the Light Guns by the Chinook. By first light the leading elements of 42 Commando were firm on Mount Kent. About eighteen kilometres to the east they could see Stanley. Fernandez's section spent the night extricating themselves from the ambush and although two more SAS were wounded, he lost Sergeant Alfredo Flores taken prisoner and flown straight to Ajax Bay with the SAS casualties. Any information gained from interrogation never reached HQ 3rd Commando. Over the next two nights 42 Commando, 2nd

Troop 59 Independent Commando Squadron RE and all 7 Commando Battery, joined K Company. L Company and the sappers were immediately pushed on to Mount Challenger and an observation post, *Tara,* which was named after one of Vaux's daughters, was established on Mount Wall. By this time, Vaux knew that his next objective was Mount Harriet.

Operation *Autoimpuesta,* so far, was not going well and with the British now occupying Mount Kent, Major Rico was given command of Special Forces operations. He cancelled the deployment of 601 Commando Company and instructed Major Castagneto to rescue 602 Commando, who were to assemble on Mount Estancia.

Meanwhile, with no sign of 601 Commando Company, Villaruel, Fernandez and Ferrero set off for Stanley at midday. During the morning Castagneto had led a column of motorcycles and requisitioned Land Rovers toward Mount Estancia but west of Two Sisters it was mortared by 42 Commando and lost one man wounded. Abandoning the Land Rovers, Castagneto and seven men reached the northern slopes of Mount Kent but came under mortar fire at about 10pm. He withdrew but was forced to leave a wounded commando behind. The motor-cycles were recovered the following day and the wounded commando was brought in by an officer two days later who had stayed behind to help him.

On Mount Simon Verseci had listened with anguish at Fernandez' desperate efforts to escape the trap. The clash worried him for the intelligence update had suggested there was definitely no enemy between Mount Simon and Stanley. Anxious about being cut off and unable to transmit, he decided to link up with a 601 Combat Engineer Battalion company known to be at Fitzroy bridge. A suggestion to insert the two cavalry warrant officers and their Blowpipes into the British helicopter corridor was rejected in favour of avoiding all contact. Shortly before midday Verseci abandoned the inhospitable summit and headed south across the soaking, misty 'camp', but the combination of freezing penetrating drizzle, low damp clouds, heavy loads and fatigue soon began to take its toll among the unacclimatized commandos. Navigation was difficult and before long most were oblivious to the enemy threat and intent only on their own survival. By 3pm the patrol had covered three miles and was on the banks of the Arroyo Malo, a stream swollen with the early winter rain and an altogether uninviting proposition to cross on a dark winter's evening. Another snowstorm swept across the moorland and, there being no alternative, the commandos plunged waist-deep into the icy water and emerged the other side thoroughly fed up. Verseci took the advice of two Antarctic veterans and decided not to shelter in the open near the original LS but to press on to a group of buildings marked on his map as Top Malo House. The prospect of a night out of the constant wind boosted morale and loads were all of a sudden much lighter.

It was nearly dark when the Argentines saw Top Malo House, a small complex of an abandoned two-storey timber building, an outhouse and a privy overlooking a small corral. The house itself had been built on a small plateau, which sloped away to the Mullow Stream, which spilled into the Arroyo Malo. One section cleared the immediate area and, finding no signs of the British, the Argentines moved into the welcome shelter of the house.

But Verseci's section had been seen by Lieutenant Fraser Haddow's Mountain and Arctic Warfare Cadre four-man patrol, which just happened to be in the area. A small Royal Marine organization skilled in mountain and winter warfare, the Cadre was ideal for medium-range reconnaissance and flank protection. When the Falklands war broke out, its strength was larger than normal because the lengthy Grade Two Mountain Leader course was nearing its end and, with the urgent need for specialist troops, the final exercise for the students was the war. During his tenure as Commander 3rd Commando Brigade, Brigadier Thompson used the Cadre as the Brigade Recce Troop and when he was preparing to break out of San Carlos, he had sent them on ahead as a light infantry screen. Captain Rod Boswell, who commanded the Cadre, was still spreading the patrols across the Brigade's intended line of march when Haddow's report was received.

Believing that his patrol had been compromised and the Argentines were there to neutralize him, Haddow waited to see what would happen. When nothing did, it dawned on him that he had not been spotted and he asked for support but with most of the Harriers engaged in other operations and, with night approaching, close air support was refused. At Brigade HQ strenuous efforts were then made to find a unit that could help Haddow, but everyone was involved in the break-out, except for 40 Commando, fretting at being left behind to protect the BMA. The only unit available was the Cadre and Boswell tried to direct other patrols to meet Haddow, but atmospheric conditions that night made high frequency radio transmissions impossible for the one and only time during the war. Eventually he gathered nineteen men from his reserves, Stone's patrol, which had just returned, and his own headquarters. These he split into a seven-man fire support group and a twelve-man assault group. The frustrations of the night were further aggravated next morning when the first helicopter to arrive at 'Busbee' was not for him. At about 8.30am a Wessex arrived and Boswell's men were flown fast and low to the LS, 1200 yards from Top Malo House. Picking up a fence line, Boswell led the patrol on to a crest overlooking the house and ordered 'Fix bayonets!'

Inside the house most of the Argentine commandos were preparing a leisurely breakfast when the helicopter was heard. Ours or theirs? And then Lieutenant Ernesto Espinosa, on watch with the MAG on the upper floor, reported that it did not have the Argentine yellow recognition stripe on the tail and must be British. Seconds later he shouted, 'Here they come!' and there was a frantic rush for weapons and equipment as the commandos took

150

up positions to defend the house. Outside another snow flurry swept across the moorland.

On the high ground above Mullow Stream Boswell reasoned that, since there was no movement inside the house, surprise had been achieved. He fired a green mini flare, the signal to begin the attack, and three 66mm smashed into the timber house, which began to crumble around those inside. Corporal Groves, armed with a L42 sniper rifle, shot an Argentine who appeared at an upper window. This was probably Espinosa, who was wounded early in the fighting. Another 66mm volley ripped into the building and was the signal for the assault group to advance.

The impact of the rockets momentarily paralysed the Argentines but they quickly organized themselves and returned fire. The house was now alight and Verseci realized he must abandon it, but he had three wounded, First Lieutenant Humberto Martinez, First Sergeant Juan Helguero and First Sergeant Humberto Medina, injured after being pinned beneath debris from a smashed wall. First Sergeant Miguel Castillo jumped downstairs, which left Espinosa upstairs giving covering fire with the MAG until he was killed by a M79 grenade. Verseci decided that the best option was to shelter in Mullow Stream and, as he gathered his men by the front door ready to rush out, a grenade exploded outside knocking over most of those inside and wounding Lieutenant Losito in the head. Recovering, the Argentines flung open the door, broke out, took up positions and returned fire, slightly wounding Corporal 'Mac' McClean in the hand when a round hit the 66mm tube he was about to fire.

Boswell adjusted the fire support group to fire on to the Argentines and ordered the assault group to advance in skirmish order, as had been practised so often and which he had briefed the previous night, with two teams of four leapfrogging each other. But, to his utter astonishment, the carefully thought-out plan was totally ignored and all eleven Royal Marines rose and, yelling and screaming, charged down the slope, leaving their commander momentarily behind. Keen to lead from the front, Boswell sprinted after them. One section angled toward the burning house and the dazed Lieutenant Luis Brun, who was firing his pistol, was wounded a second time. He tried to throw a grenade but was too weak from loss of blood. The wounded Horacio Losito continues:

The enemy were now about fifteen metres away. They were without any protection, as they thought they were not going to meet any resistance, believing us to be dead or wounded, but they had not reckoned with the covering fire from inside the house. I made for the stream, as did almost everyone else. The ground was totally devoid of cover and our only protection was our own tactics. So we ran a few yards, threw ourselves on the ground and returned fire. Sergeant Sbert joined Captain Verseci and First Lieutenant Gatti giving covering fire from the fence but he was killed rescuing the wounded Lieutenant Helguero, hit yet again by a grenade splinter.

The fighting became chaotic, both sides exchanging shots at close range. The momentum of the Cadre charge was lost when it seemed that no one knew where the enemy were and there was a short pause. A group of Argentines broke cover from the corral and headed toward the fence and there was another burst of furious firing from both sides. The Cadre shook out and began to advance toward the fence. Losito recalls:

> The British passed the house and came toward us in a classic assault, straight out of the schoolbooks, shouting and firing according to their tactical philosophy. I crossed a fence between the house and stream and tumbled into the stream, dazed and bleeding badly. My intention was to cross, but there was total confusion, shots, explosions, shouting and I was then hit in the thigh and fell into the ditch. My head wound was bleeding profusely and I wondered if an artery had been cut. I could hardly see, but remained calm amidst the firing and shouting. I tried to tie a tourniquet around my leg, but since the enemy were close, I did not have the time and, wriggling on my back, returned fire but with little success.

When the British reached the corral, one section moved left and the other right. One of Sergeant Doyle's ammunition pouches was hit by tracer, which detonated some rounds, severely wounding him in the arm and shoulder. A third group of four Cadre moved to the back of the house to deal with a group of Argentines in dead ground who were disrupting the efforts of the fire support team and had wounded Groves in the chest as he was adjusting his position. In the bed of the stream the Argentines were reasonably well organized, albeit damp and soggy. Black smoke was swirling across the battlefield and both sides found it difficult to work out from where the fire was coming. Sergeant Stone broke cover to draw enemy fire but was quickly cut down and severely wounded in the stomach.

Meanwhile the British foursome on the left flank moved around Top Malo House, forced the Argentines in the dead ground to withdraw and prepared to roll up the commandos in the stream. On the right a section had occupied a small knoll from the river bed and began to call on the Argentines to surrender. But the fighting continued, one Argentine being hit five times by 5.56mm Armalite rounds but still on his feet, while Stone had been incapacitated by a single 7.62mm FAL round. The Argentines were in a quandary and some began to surrender, while others fought on. Losito was having his own problems:

> The British came at us from three directions. I fired as if I were on the ranges, correcting the sight, firing, correcting, firing, re-adjusting and holding my breath as I squeezed the trigger. I believe I hit someone. But I was losing blood and getting weaker, without noticing it. I surfaced through the haze to find myself next to a colleague telling me not to fire any more as we were completely surrounded.
> The end was very dangerous. It is not easy to surrender when one carried the responsibility of my commando beret and the success of the mission. The outcome

for a commando is victory or death and I continued firing. To my right two British came towards me and because I was drowsy, I didn't realize at first they were shooting; it sounded like rain on sand. I swung round to fire but having no strength, slowly collapsed into the ditch, oblivious of the water. One of them [*possibly Corporal 'Mac' MacGregor]* pointed his rifle at me and, thinking he was going to shoot, I entrusted myself to God. However he lowered his weapon, dragged me out of the ditch, took away my FAL and said, 'No problem; it's war.' He then tied a tourniquet on my leg with his scarf. He asked if I had any medicine and, when I told him my kit was in the house, he took out a morphine capsule from his inside pocket and injected my leg. One or two Argentines were still resisting further down the stream and we were in danger of being caught in crossfire.

The calls to surrender became more urgent and it was then that the survivors of 1st Section 602 Commando now realized the hopelessness of the situation and gave up. The fight had lasted about fifteen minutes. While the wounded, four British and six Argentines, were treated, the remaining five prisoners were searched and, in one of those moments of camaraderie between enemies who have experienced the same violence, Boswell mentioned to Captain Verseci, 'Never in a house!' The Royal Marines checked the burning house, peat shed and corral for survivors. Corporal MacGregor checked the privy and called upon anyone inside to come out and receiving no answer, he fired a burst through the door. Much to his, and everyone else's, astonishment the timber building exploded in a massive blue flame as the gases ignited and showered everyone with splinters. It seemed a suitably amusing end to the battle. Within the hour the wounded were flown to Ajax Bay and the prisoners were taken by a 45 Commando Troop first to Teal Inlet and then, by Sergeant Bob Dilley, the Intelligence Sergeant, on to 'Hotel Galtieri' at San Carlos. The two dead Argentines, Lieutenant Espinosa and Sergeant Sbert, were both awarded Argentina's highest medal for gallantry.

The virtual destruction of 602 Commando Company signalled the end of Operation *Autoimpuesta* and Army Group Puerto Argentino was now virtually blind to the British advance. Of the 170 commandos earmarked for the operation, about fifty made it into the field and of these, thirty-two men had been killed, wounded or were still missing. One man had been taken prisoner but no British had been captured.

With more pressing matters to resolve, namely the defence of Stanley, Brigadier General Daher handed over command of the Special Forces Group to Major Rico. Although commandos would take part in the patrol battles before the British attack on the Outer Defence Zone, they were not used in its defence, where their experience would have most probably bolstered the two infantry regiments holding the line and given the attackers a stiffer test than they faced. Menendez missed an opportunity not only to make the British pay for their advance on Stanley but also to buy time to force them

153

to the negotiating table. Plans were drawn up to use the coaster *Monsunen* to insert a commando patrol base behind British lines at Fitzroy, but, with the rapidity of the British advance and the ever-present threat that it may be cut off by landings, the scheme was rejected. 601 Commando Company protected the operational helicopter base of 601 Combat Aviation Battalion at the Racecourse against the threat of raids and the Gendarmerie assisted 181 Military Police Company with security operations in and around the Stanley sector.

Ahead of 3rd Commando Brigade on the night of 2 June there was a 'blue on blue' between the SAS and SBS in the Long Island area. What happened is still speculation. Reports suggest that a four-man SBS patrol encroached into an area dominated by the SAS and were challenged. The front three stood still but the Tail End Charlie took cover. The SAS machine gunner then opened fire killing Sergeant 'Kiwi' Hunt. While the SAS would later claim that Hunt had allowed himself to be ambushed, the judgement of the machine gunner must be questioned. Another version is that the SBS patrol had seen the SAS and split into two pairs. The leading pair, which included Hunt, moved forward to investigate and immediately after being challenged were cut down at close range. A brief firefight developed until both sides realised it was a 'blue on blue'. The incident inevitably deepened the rivalry between the SAS and SBS. Had the SBS been a large Argentine patrol, the SAS had effectively compromised themselves at a considerable distance from other British patrols where stealth might have been the preferred option. The effectiveness of the ambush must be also questioned in that only one 'enemy' was killed as opposed to all four.

Until 24 May, Menendez remained convinced that the British would land at or near Stanley but when he realised San Carlos was the primary beach-head, he hurriedly re-organised Army Group Puerto Argentino to face west. 7th Infantry Regiment, which was commanded by Lieutenant Colonel Omar Gimenez and was based at La Tablada in Buenos Aires province, had arrived in light order on the 14 April as part of the 10th Infantry Brigade deployment. Packs and other equipment followed several days later. It was deployed to Sector 'Silver', which covered Mount Longdon, Wireless Ridge and Moody Brook barracks.

On 17 April, the day *Fearless* reached Ascension Island, Gimenez gave Major Carlos Carrizo-Salvadores, his operations officer, B Company and ordered him to defend Sector Silver Two on Mount Longdon, on the extreme left flank of Army Group Stanley. Accompanied by six men from Command Company, he was flown up by Army helicopter and was met by Captain Eduardo Lopez, the company commander, who had arrived earlier in the day with a small logistic detachment. Next day the two officers carried out a detailed recce of the feature and based their defence on the British attack coming from the north. Second Lieutenant Juan Baldini's 1st Platoon was placed on the western slopes covering the approaches from the Murrell

River. Baldini was later heavily criticized by veterans for being indifferent and selfish toward his men although this seems to have come from several petulant soldiers who failed to appreciate his efforts to keep them alive in difficult conditions. In any event Baldini was awarded a posthumous medal for gallantry during the battle for Mount Longdon and the parade square at 7th Infantry Regiment is named after him. First Sergeant Raul Gonzalez's 2nd Platoon covered the northern slopes and Second Lieutenant Enrique Neirotti's 3rd Platoon occupied the eastern sector. Lieutenant Hugo Quiroga's 1st Platoon, 10th Engineer Company, were on the southern slopes in depth. Sector Headquarters was in the centre.

Contemporary accounts on the life of Argentine soldiers during their occupation are few although *Los Chicos De La Guerra* (Children of the War) and Bramley's *Two Sides Of Hell* give an insight into life on Mount Longdon, notwithstanding personal observations by soldiers from both sides.

Carrizo-Salvadores' 287 men settled on the exposed mountain but found digging-in difficult. Trenches often filled with water, so most of the Argentines burrowed among the rocks and built bunkers and sangars with rocks or peat, with interlocking fire zones. Bunkers generally accommodated two men and were about a metre deep, topped by a tent and corrugated iron metal sheet covered with peat, stones and rocks for camouflage. Shelves were cut to store ammunition and cigarettes. The soldiers felt comfortable in their bunkers – out of the way of meddlesome officers and NCOs and safe from bombardment. Sappers laid minefields on all likely approach routes and the Rasit ground surveillance radar with Baldini scanned the ground. Little patrolling was carried out by the infantry. Weapon oil and cleaning kits were a rarity and weapons quickly rusted. Weapon-testing appears not to have been carried out, which led to some soldiers having little confidence that their weapons would work when the time came. Ammunition came up in wooden boxes and had clearly been in store for years, but at least the wood could be used for campfires. The British were later to comment on the filthy state of the prisoners, little realizing that some cooking was done over wood and peat fires, the oily grime settling on uniforms and creating a layer of weather-proofing.

Hygiene, a critical indicator of living in the field, was difficult and most water came from the ice-covered ponds. Private Barreto, part of a Browning M2 .50 machine-gun team, claimed he washed just four times in sixty-six days. Mealtimes are one of the few times soldiers in the field can socialize. Cooking was done centrally from wheeled field kitchens towed onto their positions, but the food tended to be poor or even inadequate and some soldiers reverted to raiding the stores, risking arrest by the military police or field punishment, or shopping in Stanley. From 1 June, 4th Infantry Regiment were given permission by their commanding officer, Lieutenant-Colonel Diego Soria, to use their US "C" ration packs, which helped to raise morale and keep the soldiers fit. Harsh southerly winds and freezing rain drained the energy and morale of the soldiers; life was hardly idyllic and conditions sapped their will to fight. About the only comfort was the occasional parcel, often containing gloves, scarves and sweaters knitted by well-wishers and letters from schools and pen pals addressed to *Al Soldado Argentino*. Mount Longdon suffered little enemy interference except for a brief bombardment from three ships during the evening of 1 May.

Major General Moore wanted to assault the outer defences by 6 June, but Brigadier Thompson reckoned he would not be ready until the 8th. One of his major problems was the lack of intelligence. Air photographs were not available and prisoners captured at Goose Green knew nothing. As Sergeant Millard, Intelligence Sergeant 42 Commando, said, 'There's nowt for it but bimble out there to find out ourselves'. A Royal Marine officer commented that patrols were finding it difficult to snatch a prisoner because it was a skill rarely exercised in peace. In spite of several clashes, not one prisoner reached the two Brigade Headquarters, and Intelligence Sections were thus reliant upon information from patrols and OPs to plot positions and guess routes and assembly areas. In any event killing the enemy seemed more important. Interestingly, Argentine patrols, tasked to capture prisoners, also found the reality of doing so difficult.

In the north, 3 Para had set up a base three kilometres west of Estancia by 31 May and captured several survivors from Combat Team Eagle, still on the run from Port San Carlos and most in a pitiful state. Next day Estancia was liberated in a swift operation and A Company crossed the Murrell River and secured Mount Estancia, which dominated the area. To dominate the valley south to Mount Kent, B Company occupied the southern slopes of Mount Vernet, while C Company climbed to the summit and saw Stanley in the distance. The Blues and Royals accompanied them, but a Combat Engineer Tractor, which should have also gone, suffered gearbox problems so preventing it from helping the troops to dig in.

By intensive patrolling, 3 Para seized the initiative from 7th Infantry Regiment. While the twelve four-man patrols of Patrols Platoon searched for enemy positions, rifle company fighting patrols, probing Mount Longdon, often clashed with Argentine engineers laying minefields. The Royal Engineers spent four days exploring and clearing routes from Estancia to the Murrell Bridge and Mount Longdon. Most patrols developed into close-target recces of obstacles and minefields and the bridge was regularly checked for demolition. All information was fed to Captain Giles Orpen-Smellie, the Intelligence Officer, who assessed that Mount Longdon was held by one and a half companies of 7th Infantry Regiment and elements of 601 Commando Company all equating to a battalion-sized organization. His assessment was a little pessimistic, for Mount Longdon was held, and always had been, by B Company. In support was artillery firing from the general area of Moody Brook.

Located between 1st and 2nd Platoons, Sergeant Nista, Major Carrizo-Salvadores' Rasit operator, first picked up enemy movement on the night of 4 June when movement was detected about 4000 yards to the north-west and it wasn't sheep but probably a 3 Para patrol which brought back several mines for technical examination. Sergeant Gonzales' platoon stood to while Carrizo-Salvadores telephoned Lieutenant Colonel Gimenez for a 155mm fire mission. The following day a 601 Commando Company found evidence of British patrolling. Although it was obvious the British were approaching from the west, Menendez still feared an amphibious assault in the Stanley area and during the night 3/4 June all units were placed on alert for an amphibious landing. 601 National Gendarmerie Special Forces Squadron and 181 Military Police Company with their dogs patrolled Stanley for signs of internal unrest. The two Army commando companies stood by ready to react to alerts.

The neutralization of the Special Forces Group denied Malvinas Joint Command eyes and ears north of Mount Kent, the direction from which 3rd Commando Brigade was now advancing. An Argentine intelligence assessment suggested that the main British thrust would be along the Goose Green-Stanley axis on a three-battalion front, the most northerly being on Mount Kent with a secondary thrust believed to be coming from Green Patch. Army Group Puerto Argentino therefore realigned its defence to face west. Carrizo-Salvadores' sector simply did a smart left turn. 1st Platoon remained covering the approaches from the Murrell River and was given a Recoilless Rifle, which Baldini placed on his left flank. In the centre he had a Cobra and an 81mm mortar, and on both flanks, a .50 Browning manned by the Marine Infantry Anti-Aircraft Battalion. First Sergeant Gonzalez' 2nd Platoon was moved to cover the north slopes, the right front flank of the Outer Defence Zone, but had no additional support weapons. Neirotti's 3rd Platoon exchanged places with the 10th Engineer Company platoon and was strengthened with an 81mm mortar, a .50 Browning and, on the left flank, a Recoilless Rifle. Carrizo-Salvadores placed his CP, the company 81mm mortars and his logistic detachment in the centre of Mount Longdon. In effect he switched his defence from north to west by placing the infantry platoons in the front line and keeping the engineers in depth.

In the centre 45 Commando filed into Teal Inlet on 1 June. By now Whitehead knew his next objective would be the distinctive twin peaks of Two Sisters, which, together with Mount Harriet and Goat Ridge, formed a formidable barrier to Stanley. The western peak is about 920 feet high, while the eastern one is a few metres smaller. 300 yards to the south-west across a saddle is a 1700-yard long string of three rocky spinebacks, lying east to west. The going is mainly rock runs, although the approaches tend to be boggy. With Menendez' defences originally facing north, Two Sisters was not included in the defence of Stanley. However, he now had to face west and, with the unexpected arrival of Parada's brigade, he could now afford to defend the summits and pulled 4th Infantry Regiment back from Mounts Challenger and Wall.

4th Infantry Regiment was normally based in the warm northern town of Corrientes and, like its sister, 12th Infantry Regiment, its deployment to the Falklands had been turbulent. It first reinforced 11th Mechanized Infantry Brigade defending the Atlantic Maritime Littoral and then on 27 April arrived at Stanley by air minus most of its heavy equipment left on board the *Ciudad de Cordoba*. Lieutenant Colonel Soria made every effort to replace the 1982 conscripts with reservists and volunteers, but, by the time the regiment landed, a substantial proportion had only been in the Army since February. 1st and 2nd Platoons A Company were immediately sent to Mount Low while 3rd Platoon guarded Government House. The remaining companies were assigned as Task Force Monte Caseros and deployed to Mount Wall and Mount Kent, ready to react to the expected British landings at Stanley. Digging in these rocky outcrops also proved very difficult and poor logistics and the hostile weather soon affected the morale and health of soldiers more used to the warmth of northern Argentina.

Command of Two Sisters, known to the Argentines as Dos Hermanas, was entrusted to Major Ricardo Cordon, Soria's operations officer, with the bulk of the defenders drawn from Captain Maxpegan's C Company. Cordon divided his 170-strong command into two elements. On the south-west group of rocks he placed Second Lieutenant Marcelo Llambias-Pravaz' 3rd Platoon on the extreme west with Lieutenant Luis Martella and two Mortar Platoon 81mm mortars in the centre. Later reinforced by 1st Platoon A Company, he placed them in a roving role north-east of 3rd Platoon. On Two Sisters itself Second Lieutenants Miguel Mosquera's 1st and Jorge Perez-Grandi's 2nd Platoons built bunkers on the western rock crags, while Cordon put his CP on the eastern peak but his Rasit was defective. The 10th Engineer and the Amphibious Engineer Companies provided much-needed sapper and infantry support.

Major Jaimet's B Company 6th Infantry Regiment was moved to plug the gap in the low ground between Mount Longdon and Two Sisters, two platoons astride the Stanley/Estancia track and the third in depth near the eastern summit of Two Sisters, for which the company also had responsibility. This company was undetected by British patrols. 6th 'General Juan Viamonte' Mechanized Infantry Regiment was commanded by Lieutenant Colonel Jorge Halperin and was a component of 10th Infantry Brigade. Normally based in the Mercedes area of Buenos Aires, it had been flown to the Falklands Islands on 14 April and was immediately assigned to Sector Steel defending the southern coast. B Company was detached to the Reserve and in its place Halperin received, first, a detachment from 181st Military Police Company, and then, when A Company 1st 'Los Patricios' Infantry Regiment arrived, it joined as C Company, releasing the military police to their normal duties.

158

Condor Troop, 59 Commando Squadron RE, who usually operated with 45 Commando, were comfortably settled into a cowshed at Teal Inlet when the Troop Commander, Captain Dunstone, warned Sergeant Sam Halkett that he, the three section commanders and four sappers were to join a Recce Troop patrol led by Lieutenant Chris Fox, the Troop commander, to gather information on minefields and positions on Two Sisters. The patrol was meant to be flown forward to Bluff Cove and establish a patrol base. However, fog closed in and they set out on foot out in light order and passing Fisherman's Cottage, a distance of about nine miles, the weather improved sufficiently for a Wessex to pick up the patrol and its equipment and drop them just below Bluff Cove Peak. Halkett's men were establishing a small defensive position when 155mm shells landed about 100 yards, which suggests they had been seen by an artillery observation post on Two Sisters. Fox then moved to 42 Commando's Headquarters Company where the patrol bivouacked in miserably damp conditions.

At last light on 5 June, Fox followed a line of telegraph poles and frequently stopped and by about 7pm the patrol reached the Murrell Bridge and, to their surprise, found it intact though shell craters littered its approaches, suggesting it had been registered by Argentines artillery. The patrol crossed the river and, because communications were breaking up, Fox left a rebroadcast station on a small hill. About 2500 yards to the south were the distinctive shapes of Two Sisters, clear in the bright moonlight, and their objective, the positions held by Jorge Perez-Grandi's 2nd Platoon.

Halkett suggested to Fox that Recce should lead until they found a minefield. Halkett recalls, 'Thankfully he agreed (lemon)'! The going worsened and the patrol waded through squelchy marsh grass. After about 800 yards, the lead scout found a low wire and, after a quick inspection, Halkett believed they had found a minefield but about 350 yards away a group of Argentines sat around a campfire. With Fox and a Royal Marine giving close protection, he and Corporal Fairbairn crawled into the minefield and, using time-honoured mine-clearing techniques and crawling no closer than 150 yards to the enemy, they prodded at the ground making several penetrations but did not find any mines. Using the 42 Commando net, Fox called for a fire mission, but when he could not provide authentication to identify his callsign, 42 Commando refused to relay the message to the gunners, much to his frustration. Halkett called forward Sappers Jones and Dallas, and, line abreast, all four prodded and lifted turf, but still found no mines, although Dallas cut a sample of an electric cable for evaluation. The patrol returned to the rebroadcast station where Fox again attempted to call a fire mission on the enemy, again without success. He then led a small patrol to see if an approach to Two Sisters could be made from the west. An hour later the entire patrol was plodding back to Bluff Cove Peak and arrived tired, hungry and wet just as daybreak was creeping over the horizon, They had covered about fifteen miles in sixteen hours.

159

Next night Sam Halkett and a small team of Royal Engineers again accompanied another patrol commanded by Fox. Concealing themselves in a rocky outcrop at the western end of Two Sisters, they ambushed an engineer patrol escorted by Llambias-Pravaz's 3rd Platoon moving down from the feature intent on using the misty drizzle to lay a minefield on the southern approaches to the feature. The Argentines covered their withdrawal with artillery fire but lost an infantryman and two amphibious engineers, Privates Ramon Ordonez and Victor Olavarria. Fox was shot through the hand. Soon after this incident an unidentified Amphibious Engineer NCO contacted Halkett and asked for a short truce to recover the bodies. He agreed, which earned him the nickname 'Uncle Sam' from the Argentines, and their respect.

A patrol led by Lieutenant Jonathan Shaw found documents in an abandoned command post on Mount Kent, which included an operations order referring to 12th Infantry Regiment's role in the Reserve to help Army Group Puerto Argentino and a document listing the strength of the units in Stanley. A map sparked some interesting debate because it showed several numbered circles but no one knew what they meant until after HQ 3rd Commando Brigade had been attacked on Bluff Cove Peak by four Skyhawks on 12 June when a meaningless intercepted message from a pilot was passed to the Intelligence Section from Y(EW)Troop RM for evaluation: 'Ninety-three now, ninety-three now!' Several captured maps provided the answer. The Argentines had been sold 1:50,000 maps identical to those used by the British except there were no grid lines. Their method was to select several features, such as hills, streams and settlements and number them. Ninety-three was Bluff Cove Peak.

The weather turned vicious with rain, sleet, and snow, and, at times hurricane force winds creating a windchill factor that sometimes dropped to –30C degrees.

The Commando Logistic Regiment had become a divisional asset supporting both brigades. Supplies were moved forward by LSL to the Brigade Maintenance Areas and then by helicopter to unit echelons. Landing craft or Rigid Raiders supplied isolated units. The calls on helicopter tasking were severe and this often meant that the issue of urgently needed supplies to the units was delayed. The helicopter support taken for granted on exercises failed to live up to expectations. The loss of the Chinooks on the *Atlantic Conveyor* added to the logistic problem. In preparation for the attack on Stanley every man was issued with two days' supply of rations and ammunition, every vehicle fuelled to overflow and every gun and mortar supplied with 500 rounds, with a further 500 in reserve.

HQ 3rd Commando Brigade made intensive efforts to ensure that supplies of ammunition, rations, mail and water reached the troops. The majority was shipped in by LSL to its forward Brigade Maintenance Area at Teal Inlet, and then, after sorting by the B Echelons, was flown to the units. It was inevitable in the chaos and confusion of war that the logistic system sometimes broke down and 3 Para, nearer to civilians than the two

Commandos, became adept at solving their supply problems by seeking the co-operation of locals with tractors and Land Rovers. When K Company were withdrawn from the exposed summit of Mount Kent, 42 Commando's Quartermaster, Captain Dennis Sparks, flew their bergens in and it was like Christmas all over again as the troops dug deep looking for dry socks, dry underwear, warm clothing and chocolate bars tucked into side pockets. Some Royal Marines had hung on to their Arctic sleeping bags, but many in both brigades had the standard temperate sleeping bag and, although a welcome change to the blankets and greatcoats of their predecessors, were inadequate, and most suffered from rigorous use. 3 Para estimated that at least ten sleeping bags had broken zips, which defeated warmth retention; the waterproof underside was useless. To compound the shelter problem, ponchos could not be used in the treeless terrain of the Falklands. Captain Ian Gardiner, who commanded Z Company 45 Commando, later wrote:

The last citadel of a man's morale is his sleeping bag! The comfort and resource it offers is amazing. On occasions when one is being shelled, or hears bombing, it is an instinctive reaction to wriggle deeper into one's "green slug". When all else failed, when the world was at its glummest, even if the bags had failed to turn up, one was always vaguely comforted by the prospect of climbing into a dry bag eventually. On one occasion early in the campaign, I awoke at 5am to find myself and my bag soaked through. After mentally weeping for an hour or so, I perceived the rain was becoming less persistent. "Aha," I thought, "if it stops, I could get up and stamp around and start getting things dry" As the rain faded so my spirits gathered. The rain stopped. I waited for ten minutes, just enjoying not getting any wetter. The rains started again! I pulled the wretched sodden bag over my head and smoked a cigarette. But one hardened.

The inadequacy of some clothing and equipment, about which the British troops had been complaining for years, became evident. The Sterling magazine often fell out. The ankle-length DMS boots and cloth puttees failed to keep feet dry and nylon-based socks did little to prevent blisters or to ensure that feet were warm. The 3 Para RAP in a private house at Estancia was soon dealing with cases of trench foot and nasty blisters from the long march across broken ground, all avoidable non-battle casualties. Physical and mental resilience, fitness and personal organization in the field were a vital survival factor. Gardiner continues:

Colder and more bitter nights followed and it was not the last time our citadels were breached, but we refined our methods of living in this inhospitable place to such a degree that by the end, we were like wild animals and almost preferred it outdoors. We could have lived in the wilds indefinitely on what we carried in our fighting order. Never let it be said that we had come to the end of our endurance by the time we reached Stanley or that the weather would have beaten us. We could have gone on for ever.

Veterans of both sides will sympathize with Gardiner's sentiments.

In the south Lieutenant Colonel Nick Vaux had been advised by Brigadier Thompson that his next objective would be Mount Harriet and Goat Ridge, which he, Vaux, had christened *"Zoya"* after his wife and *"Katrina"* after a daughter. The former rises from 300 feet along the track to Stanley to 850 feet at its highest point in under 600 yards, which runs east to west, and is principally crags and rock. 1200 yards directly north across an open boggy saddle, lies the 2000-yard long Goat Ridge, which rises to 600 feet. A shepherd's track connects Murrell Bridge to Two Sisters through Mount Harriet and then to Mount Tumbledown and Stanley. Another track connects Mount Challenger to Mount Harriet.

Placing his CP and with the regimental aid post in the middle of Mount Harriet, Lieutenant Colonel Soria sent Second Lieutenant Oscar Silva north with his 2nd Platoon, A Company, to defend Goat Ridge and divided Mount Harriet between B and Command Companies with the inter-company boundary running north-south through the centre of the position. First Lieutenant Carlos Arroyo's B Company defended the western end of the position with Second Lieutenant Eugenio Bruny's 2nd Platoon on the left and Lautaro Jimenez-Corvalen's 3rd Platoon on the right. In depth to them was the HQ 3rd Infantry Brigade Defence Platoon, commanded by Second Lieutenant Pablo Oliva, and Support Platoon. In depth to B Company was First Lieutenant Garcia's Command Company with Second Lieutenant Emilio Samyn's 1st Cavalry Regiment platoon on the southern slopes of Mount Harriet and to its left Recce Platoon. Protecting Second Lieutenant Mario Juarez's 81mm Mortar Platoon, dug-in below the eastern summit, was Second Lieutenant Mosterins's 12th Infantry Regiment platoon from Combat Team Solari. Amphibious engineers laid minefields south and west around Mount Wall, south-east to the Stanley road and around Mount Harriet. On call to 4th Infantry Regiment was 3rd Artillery Group.

On 3 June, while Jofre was visiting Soria on Mount Harriet, reports were received that a strong 4th Infantry Regiment fighting patrol seeking pris-oners had captured a British observation post on Mount Wall. Lieutenant Chris Mawhood's Recce Troop had been manning the post on Mount Wall, which was nicknamed 'Tara' by Vaux after another daughter, when they first came under heavy mortar fire and then were attacked by infantry. The situation became so critical that the British forward air controller with Mawhood prudently destroyed his laser rangefinder with a well-aimed bullet before withdrawing. Within twenty-four hours Lieutenant Tony Hornby's Troop had recaptured the observation post. The rangefinder was found by a 602 Commando Company patrol when it attacked the obser-vation post on the night of 5 June but recovered by the British after the battle for Mount Harriet but not before its capture was blazoned across news-papers in Argentina.

Vaux was relieved to be told the Brigade operation would take place at night. Quickly deciding not to commit 42 Commando along the track which led direct from Mount Kent to Mount Harriet, his patrols searched for a wide right-flanking approach from the west, the direction from which the Argentines least expected to be the axis of attack. By this time, Vaux's unit had not had a ration resupply for five days. On 3 June an L Company patrol checking a bridge across a culvert ran into a minefield before they had crossed the Stanley-Fitzroy road and it took seven hours to evacuate the seriously wounded 15-stone rugby player Marine Mark Curtis. The next night assault engineers cleared a path through this minefield and on 5 June Sergeant Nev Weston led an L Company fighting patrol south of the road but it also ran into a minefield and Marine Kevin Patterson was badly wounded. With Weston was Sergeant Tom Collins and three men from K Company, who were to carry out a deep penetration patrol south of the road. While Patterson was being casevaced by helicopter, Collins told Vaux he was happy to continue. It was a critical decision and Collins led the patrol to the western end of Mount Harriet, but was spotted by an Argentine patrol. Both sides sought cover and Collins slipped into a small peat pond of freezing mucky water followed by the others who leapt on top of him. A stand-off developed during which Collins asked Lance Corporal Steve Sparkes 'How's your bottle?' (Slang for courage). When Sparkes replied 'It went pop hours ago', it reduced the entire patrol into fits of uncontrollable giggles. After about an hour, the Argentines' withdrawal along the road was carefully plotted by Collins. They may have been from Captain Fernandez's 2nd Assault Section, 602 Commando Company, who were then helping O Company, 5th Marine Infantry Battalion, to dominate the area from its position at Pony's Pass. Nevertheless it was this patrol that convinced Vaux to persist in seeking a route on to Mount Harriet from the south-east.

By 6 June Julian Thompson believed that he had sufficient intelligence to mount an attack on the Outer Defence Zone on the 9th. Before moving his headquarters from Teal Inlet on to the slopes of Mount Kent, he sought assurance from Major General Moore that 5th Infantry Brigade would be ready to continue the attack into the heart of the Argentine defences. But Brigadier Tony Wilson, as we shall see, was experiencing all sorts of frustrations, largely caused by the lack of shipping.

During the night Captain Ruben Figueroa's 2nd Assault Section, supported by Captain Jorge San Emeterio and four Gendarmerie, investigated reports from Major Jaimet of enemy activity around Murrell Bridge. While the recce party were looking for an ambush site, the patrol came under machine-gun fire from north of the bridge and, counter-attacking, found only flattened grass, warm empty cartridge cases and a radio set with some signals instructions. They remained in the area for the remainder of the day calling down 155m shelling on suspected enemy activity. Shortly after dark

Figueroa handed over to Captain Jorge Jandula's 3rd Assault Section and Captain Eduardo Santos' Gendarmerie section and led his weary but elated men back to Stanley. This was 601 Commando's last operation outside Stanley and the Blowpipe teams were placed under command of the integrated air defence organization.

On 8 June, at a conference held on *Fearless* between Thompson, Wilson and Brigadier Waters, General Moore's deputy, the discussion focused on a divisional plan to attack the Outer Defence Zone on a narrow front on Mount Harriet from the south along the Fitzroy-Stanley track. Intelligence indicated this was the direction expected by the Argentines. Thompson argued that the advance to Stanley was nothing like fighting a manoeuvre battle in north-west Germany, with which the Army was thoroughly familiar but the Royal Marines were not. It would be a deliberate and slow infantry assault and he suggested that if the attack was to be on a narrow front, to support the second phase against Mount Longdon and the Inner Defence Zone (Mount Tumbledown, Mount William and Wireless Ridge), artillery and supplies would need to be moved on to the plain north of Mount Kent. Since this was in full view of Mount Longdon, it was critical to capture it and Two Sisters in Phase One. The meeting broke up when news of the disastrous attacks on the *Sir Galahad* and *Sir Tristram* reached the conference room. Next day Moore visited Thompson and confirmed that the drive into the Stanley defences would be a three-phase operation:

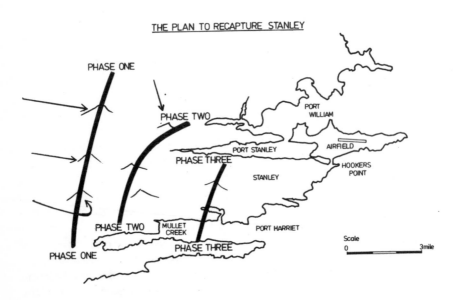

THE PLAN TO RECAPTURE STANLEY

Phase One
3rd Commando Brigade assault on the Outer Defence Zone.
3 Para would seize Mount Longdon.
45 Commando would attack Two Sisters and then exploit to Mount Tumbledown.
42 Commando, supported by the Welsh Guards and two companies of 40 Commando, to replace the losses suffered at Port Pleasant, would attack Mount Harriet and then be prepared to support 45 Commando.

Phase Two
5th Infantry Brigade attack the south Inner Defence Zone
The Scots Guards and 1/7th Gurkha Rifles to attack Mount Tumbledown and Mount William.
3rd Commando Brigade attack north Inner Defence Zone.
2 Para attack Wireless Ridge.

Phase Three
5th Infantry Brigade
Seize Sapper Hill.
3rd Commando Brigade
Seize positions south of Stanley and capture the town. The Commando Brigade intelligence staff had already prepared information for fighting in Stanley.

3rd Commando Brigade's assault was delayed by the disaster to the two LSLs and it was now important to keep the enemy guessing but there were still no specific orders to take prisoners. Lieutenant David Stewart of 45 Commando was ordered by Ian Gardiner to take his Troop and 'cause casualties and harass the enemy'. Accompanying him was Corporal Wilkie's Recce Troop section, assault engineers and a forward observation party commanded by Corporal Engleson of 'Black Eight'. Shortly before the patrol departed, several men dropped out suffering from acute stomach cramps caused by poor water. Sterilizing tablets were in short supply. Stewart did not know that his patrol would take him into a sector reinforced by a Special Forces group commanded by Major Rico consisting of 602 Commando Company and National Gendarmerie with orders to take prisoners.
    In brilliant moonlight the Troop crossed the moorland between Mount Kent and Mount Challenger. In the distance Mount Harriet was being bombarded. At about 4am they forded the Murrell River and approached the positions held by Second-Lieutenant Llambias-Prava's 3rd Platoon. To support 7 and the Recce Sections moving up the slope, Stewart sent 9 Section up a stream bed while he remained in reserve with 8 Section. When the Argentines opened fire, Wilkie called for illumination and, as the flare burst,

attacked a machine gun. Leaving Recce to reorganize, 7 and 9 Sections pushed on up the hill and engaged a small group of Argentine National Gendarmerie moving down the left flank toward Troop HQ. Stewart strengthened his left flank with 8 Section but was forced back into cover after coming under heavy machine-gun fire from high on Two Sisters. Deciding to withdraw, Stewart instructed Corporal Engleson to shell the Argentine positions. However, Gendarmerie manning a machine gun put down fire across the intended line of withdrawal. Until this had been silenced no one was going anywhere and so Troop Sergeant Jolly and Marine Marshall neutralized the enemy with well-directed bursts of fire. Matters worsened when rifle grenades dropped behind them. Fortunately for Stewart, Argentine artillery was slow to respond and when 'Black Eight' shelled the Argentines cutting off his line of withdrawal, Stewart first gathered his Troop in a hollow and then withdrew down the slopes and into cover. There were no casualties but everyone was low on ammunition. Stewart and his weary but elated Troop reached 45 Commando shortly after dawn. In his intelligence debrief, he claimed seven enemy killed. The same night a 45 Commando fighting patrol made a navigational error and attacked what it thought to be an Argentine position but was in fact Mortar Troop on Mount Kent. Four Royal Marines were killed in this 'blue on blue'. Major Rico would later commend the professional conduct of Stewart's Troop.

Vaux was now even more convinced that attacking along the Goat Ridge – Mount Challenger track was impractical. A K Company fighting patrol used the cover of harassing Second Lieutenant Jimenez-Corvalan's platoon to smuggle two M&AW Cadre patrols into a lie-up position on Goat Ridge. The two patrols penetrated the Argentine positions and established an observation post about thirty yards from the Two Sisters-Mount Harriet-Mount Tumbledown sheep track and plotted Argentine activity and dispositions in dead ground to the British. The next night the eight men crept off the ridge and reported their findings to 42 and 45 Commandos. Meanwhile Tom Collins and Lieutenant Colin Beadon, the Milan Troop Commander, felt their way across the bare moorland south of Mount Harriet and found positions from which the Milans could fire down on to the Stanley road. Collins also found a fence which would do as a start line.

Sergeant Pettinger and Private Absolon led a 3 Para rifle platoon close to Mount Longdon in a dress rehearsal for the planned attack but were picked up by Sergeant Nista's Rasit. Carrizo-Salvadores ordered stand-to of his sector and opened fire on the two nearest contacts while artillery shelled the furthest contact, some 3500 yards away.

With battle now joined, Major General Garcia was keen to reinforce Army Group Malvinas and on 5 June instructed Menendez to plan a counter-offensive. He proposed to drop the Amphibious Commando Grouping, the 4th Airborne Brigade and the newly-formed 603 Commando Company on to Wickham Heights. On paper the proposal was formidable – on high ground

166

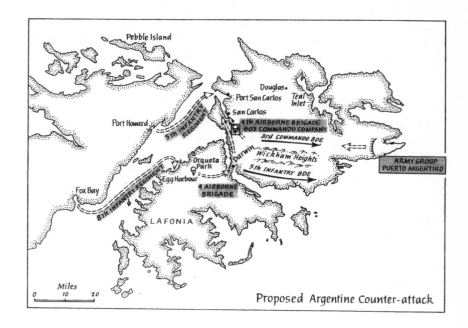

on the flanks of both British brigades. However 4th Airborne was without its artillery, which was already deployed to the Falklands with 3rd Infantry Brigade. Menendez, having suffered serious helicopter losses, was without air superiorty. On 8 June Brigadier General Daher flew to Buenos Aires and two days later met with the Joint Operations Group to discuss the counter-offensive, named Operation *Buzon* (translated as *Mailbox)*. He implied that the situation was not as bad as perceived, claiming that the troops were healthy, which generally they were, morale was high and there were suf-ficient stores to last until 23 June. He did not admit that the logistic chain had collapsed under British pressure but emphasized there were problems in acquiring intelligence. As for the offensive, Daher put forward three co-ordinated phases:

Phase 1.
The beachhead and main supply base at San Carlos should be attacked from Port Howard by 5th Infantry Regiment reinforced by elements of 4th Airborne Brigade. In all options 603 Commando Company was to harass the enemy lines of communications and logistic centres.

Phase 2
Task Force Reconquest to attack Darwin from Fox Bay. A captured docu-ment gives the aim 'Reconquest Task Force will attack and consolidate Darwin and will continue to attack north and west'. The operation was envisaged to be in three phases:

167

a. Either an amphibious landing at Egg Harbour and Cutter Cove or a heliborne assault to capture Orqueta Park, which seemed a little optimistic at this stage of the campaign.
b. Reorganization to secure the beach- or airheads.
c. Op *Tucuman,* the attack on Darwin, followed by all-round defence and preparation of a DZ for 4th Airborne Brigade and delivery of the Amphibious Commandos for an advance on San Carlos. Darwin and San Carlos were relatively weakly held by rifle units, San Carlos by elements of 40 Commando and there is no doubt they were vulnerable.

Phase 3.
Army Group Stanley to counter-attack the British facing the Outer Defence Zone.

President Galtieri was unconvinced about the ability of the air force to gain and hold sufficient air superiority to transport an entire brigade. Rear Admiral Busser detected flaws in the amphibious plan, not the least of which was the lack of assault shipping. The two available ships, *Bahia Buen Suceso* and *Monsunen,* could ferry in one lift nearly 1800 infantry, but they lacked any experience in amphibious warfare techniques and the men would have to be taken ashore in ships' boats, Gallipoli-style, which would lengthen the time the Navy and Air Force flying from the mainland needed to retain local superiority. Busser noted that the intense British bombardment of Military Air Base Stanley had yet to close the runway and therefore there was no guarantee that shelling Darwin and San Carlos would be any more successful.

In Phase 2 it would be vital for the Air Force to achieve air superiority, if only temporarily, not only to allow Naval Transport Service and requisitioned shipping to ferry the two regiments across Falkland Sound but also to give close support for 4th Airborne Brigade flying from the mainland. It was also critical for the Navy to control the neck of San Carlos Water.

With poor weather closing in and after due consideration, the plan was rejected and Daher was told to tell Menendez that he had enough troops to fight to the end and was not to surrender. Any counter-attacks should be from within its own resources. In the event Daher took off for Stanley two days later but his aircraft was unable to land and he returned to Argentina. Although staring defeat in the face, the Junta was still striving for a negotiated settlement. In believing that Menendez could hold out for at least ten days and since the Air Bridge was still open, the Joint Operations Group authorized the continued piecemeal reinforcement of Army Group Falklands with the despatch of 2nd Airborne Infantry Regiment. The weather and the speed of the British advance prevented its full deployment and only a platoon arrived in time to join 7th Infantry Regiment on Wireless Ridge.

It is difficult to gauge whether Operation *Mailbox* was a serious option or

merely a forlorn hope by the beleaguered Junta staring international humiliation in the face. The Argentines had not taken advantage of several
opportunities to disrupt the British ground forces. The Air Force left them
alone in the beachhead except for the raid on Ajax Bay. The fear of the British
landing at or near Stanley meant that Army Group Puerto Argentino
remained confined in Fortress Stanley. The response to the San Carlos landings had been left to the newly-arrived and inexperienced 3rd Infantry
Brigade. 12th Infantry Regiment had battled at Goose Green minus heavy
weapons and 42 Commando's occupation of Mount Kent had been opposed
only by a commando unit. The Special Forces Group operations had been
remarkably ineffective considering the number of troops committed. When
5th Infantry Brigade found themselves in disarray at Port Pleasant after the
attacks on the two LSLs, there was no response from Army Group Stanley
or the brigade-strength Reserve. Only Diego Soria sought permission to
attack the decimated Welsh Guards and that was rejected.

On 10 June Moore issued confirmatory orders for Phase One and
Thompson relayed them to his brigade for a night attack on 11 June. Vaux
was unhappy that his start line was to be secured by the Welsh Guards, not
that he doubted their ability, but because he had not operated with them
before and undoubtedly there would be liaison, command and control difficulties. As darkness fell 3rd Commando Brigade stirred and 1500
commandos and paras left their trenches and silently prowled across the crisp
moorland. Behind them gunners stood by their guns, medics prepared their
instruments and HQ staff waited for the first contact with the enemy. The
night was very cold and clear, with an early frost. A full moon scudding
between clouds silhouetted the mountains and threw long shadows across
the crisp grass.

9

The Battle for the Outer Defence Zone

Mount Longdon, Two Sisters and Mount Harriet
11 and 12 June

'If we had a company up here, we would have died of old age before it was captured.' Lieutenant Colonel Whitehead after the capture of Two Sisters.

3 Para, accompanied by 9 Para RE recce teams and guided by D Company, left their company hides along predetermined routes to their forming-up place. Lieutenant Colonel Pike's plan was simple – a silent attack until contact was made and exploitation dependent on the strength and resistance of the enemy: A Company was to seize the ridge *Wing Forward,* north-east of the western summit, which was defended by First Sergeant Gonzalez' 2nd Platoon, while B Company was to clear the northern slopes of a suspected company position, in fact Lieutenant Baldini's platoon, and capture the two summits *Fly Half* and *Full Back.* A and C Companies were held for exploitation to Wireless Ridge. On priority call to the battalion was *Avenger* and 79 Commando Battery, whose six Light Guns were each allocated 500 rounds. The sogginess of the terrain meant that gun detachments usually had to dig their guns out after twenty rounds and readjust.

Each company had a GPMG fire support group, which were formed from Wombat Platoon, whose anti-tank weapons were still afloat. Support Company also provided two fire bases. The Manpack Group was led by Major Dennison, who usually commanded Support Company, and consisted of six GPMG(SF) and an LMG manned by Drums Platoon, five Milan posts each with three missiles, eighteen stretcher-bearers from the Army Catering Corps, REME, RAPC, RCT and Mess staff, who doubled up as ammunition porters, each man carrying the not inconsiderable weight of 600 link ammunition and the primary battalion-manned RAP, which also provided an additional medic to each rifle company. Two journalists tagged along at the end. The Vehicle Group consisted of the six 81mm mortars, one Milan post, the secondary RAMC-manned RAP, a 9 Para RE section, a 32nd Guided Weapon Regiment Blowpipe section and five BVs, three requisitioned tractors and trailers and four civilian Land Rovers.

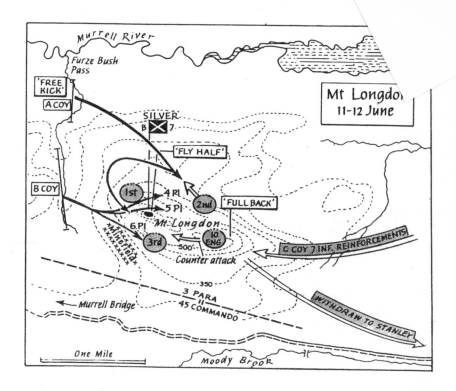

During the approach the Manpack Group sliced through B Company and half of 5 and all 6 Platoons became separated for about half an hour. There was then a delay in crossing the Murrell Bridge, which was also being used by 45 Commando for its attack on Two Sisters. After about four hours B Company were approaching *Free Kick* and, to make up for lost time to cross at H-Hour at 8.01pm, Major Mike Argue ordered his guides to approach the objective from the west as opposed to the northwest.

On Mount Longdon an Argentine 81mm mortarman dropped an illumination round down the tube and, soaring about 800 feet into the darkness, it burst into a bright light which spread across the surrounding moorland and drifted earthwards in an eerie glow. The defending platoon commanders had nothing to report which was unusual after the intense activity of the previous week. Nevertheless Major Carrizo-Salvadores ordered extra vigilance because he was certain 3 Para would attack during the night and because of the patrol activity, he believed it was likely to come from the west. Nevertheless, in spite of his suspicions, he ordered Sergeant Nista to switch off the Rasit in case British electronic warfare detected it. It was a serious misjudgement and probably lost him the battle. To pass the time, Carrizo-Salvadores and some of his men listened to Pope John celebrating Mass

..: the Basilica of Lujan. Periodically flares soared into the night and drifted in the breeze. At 8.15pm 3 Para, bayonets fixed, crossed *Free Kick*.

Covered by the Manpack Group, B Company, 4 and 5 Platoons up, had about 800 yards to go before it reached the lower western slopes of Mount Longdon below Baldini's position. Lieutenant Jonathan Shaw's 6 Platoon veered to the south-east to clear the southern slopes of *Fly Half* of Lieutenant Neirotti's platoon. The moon silhouetted the dark, jagged peaks of Mount Longdon and Argue advised the platoons to seek cover in the long shadows thrown across the moorland. By 9.15pm the company had advanced about 500 yards and the two leading platoons shook out into an assault formation. The ground began to slope upwards and 5 Platoon found themselves with room to manoeuvre among the crags. Below them Lieutenant Ian Bickerdike's 4 Platoon was unexpectedly channelled into rocks, which caused some bunching.

At about 9.30pm the silence of the night was shattered by a mine ripping into the legs of Corporal Ian Milne, a 4 Platoon section commander. The Rasit defence section opened fire and, as the attack developed, Baldini's platoon fought hard. At the request of Carrizo-Salvadores, Brigadier General Jofre ordered 3rd Infantry Regiment to assist and Captain Ruben Zunino's A Company was ordered to move by lorry to Mount Longdon under the command of Major Guillermo Berazay, the regimental operations officer.

Lieutenant Colonel Pike had 79 Commando Battery ready 'at my command' and the first rounds were soon falling on to the Argentine positions. Below *Fly Half* Corporal Oscar Carrizo's section was overrun by 6 Platoon but, resistance stiffened as Corporals Geronimo Diaz and Gustavo Pedemonte's infantry sections and Corporal Domingo Lamas's marine machine gunners defended their bunkers. The paras' traditional élan and speed were soon outwitted by the reality of battle and Argue ordered artillery support and rounds were soon bursting on the Argentine positions. Carrizo lost an eye and was later captured. When Lieutenant Neirotti and his platoon sergeant were both badly wounded, Captain Lopez took over 3rd Platoon and gave Shaw's men a torrid time, especially when they missed a large bunker in the darkness and had to turn around and deal with it. The deeper the paras penetrated 3rd Section's defences, the more difficult the advance became, even when they moved into open ground, losing four men almost immediately. 6 Platoon then strayed into the crossfire of a .50 Browning firing on 5 Platoon and stopped. With *Full Back* about 700 yards to the east, Shaw set about recovering his wounded. He had lost twelve dead and wounded.

Squeezed into narrow rock runs, 5 Platoon, taunted by Argentines shouting American jargon and rolling grenades down the slopes into what became known as Grenade Alley, were showered by rock splinters and shrapnel. 7th Infantry Regiment was recruited from Buenos Aires, where

172

many of the conscripts saw American films and adopted American obscene phrases – 'son of a bitch', etc. Section formation broke up as the paras sought cover, and then, as individuals and small groups, they battled up the slopes, forcing their way between Baldini's platoon and Lama's marine machine gunners. A .50 Browning pinning down Corporal Len Carver's section was dealt with by four paras storming the position. The swearing and the finding of dead and wounded marine infantry machine-gunners dressed in camouflaged fatigues at first led 3 Para to believe that they had faced mercenaries from the US. This was thoroughly investigated by those screening the repatriated prisoners but only Argentine nationals were found.

4 Platoon, moving north around *Fly Half*, drove into Baldini's right flank and began to seep into 2nd Platoon. A troublesome machine gun was silenced by Sergeant Ian McKay with 66mm and small arms fire, but another one opened up further up the mountain. With his field telephone link from Baldini cut by the shelling, Carrizo-Salvadores used the machine gunners' line and learnt that Baldini's situation was very serious but that he was organizing a counter-attack. Shortly afterwards Baldini was killed manning a machine gun and Corporal Rios took over, until he was also killed. Baldini was later stripped of his boots by paras. At about midnight Carrizo-Salvadores launched Quiroga's forty-five strong 1st Platoon 10th Engineer Company in a counter-attack along the spine of the ridge to relieve the pressure on 1st Platoon, which allowed the platoon sergeant, Rolando Spizuocco, to send the survivors back to the main defence line near the command post. He rescued several wounded men under fire.

Meanwhile A Company had crossed *Free Kick* into dead ground. They heard the mine shatter the silence of the night and increased their pace as they came under fire from Sergeant Gonzalez' 2nd Platoon. On the left Second Lieutenant John Kearton's 1 Platoon, in the cover of a peat trench, engaged the Argentines but had to be careful not to hit B Company attacking *Fly Half*. Second Lieutenant Ian Moore's 2 Platoon, on the right, sheltered under a low peat bank. Carrizo-Salvadores organized a fire mission in support of Gonzales from 4th Airborne Artillery Group and the 155mm howitzers of D Battery 3rd Artillery Group. In between fire missions in support of 4th and 7th Infantry Regiments, the batteries shelled at long-range identified enemy artillery positions, including a battery reported 1300 yards north of Bluff Cove Peak.

Pounded by the 105mm howitzers, A Company was held up and Lieutenant Colonel Pike had no alternative but to order Major Collett, commanding A Company, to move around to the west of Mount Longdon, pass through B Company and seize *Full Back*. As it passed close to where Ian Milne was being tended, three soldiers from 2 Platoon helping to lift him into a BV were wounded by another mine.

Although under severe pressure, the Argentines were holding. The panting,

173

sweating B Company saw the rock ridges giving way to moorland and 550 yards to the east *Full Back* silhouetted against the moon. Ahead of them was Carrizo-Salvadores' main position. Marine machine gunners in a well-defended reverse slope position raked the paras as they crested the ridge. At 3rd Commando Brigade Headquarters Brigadier Thompson was concerned because it seemed 3 Para had been brought to a virtual standstill and, since the narrowness of the ridge did not allow for reinforcements, one consideration was to bring the battalion off the ridge. Messages then arrived indicating that the battalion was on the move again.

Every move by Bickerdike's 4 Platoon had drawn withering fire from a .50 machine gun on the slopes defended by Gonzales' 2nd Platoon, the rounds striking the rocks in a mass of sparks and ricochetting into the night. Others thudded into the turf. B Company was dangerously close to defeat. The machine gun must be silenced if the momentum was to be maintained, however it was tucked into a substantial sangar and was protected by several riflemen. Bickerdike dashed forward from a shallow depression to recce the enemy position but was quickly wounded in the thigh by a burst which threw him backwards. His radio operator, Private Cullen, was shot in the mouth by the same burst but refused evacuation and continued to man his radio. Bickerdike called, 'Sergeant McKay! It's your platoon now!'

Sergeant McKay and Corporal Ian Bailey, commanding the left-hand section of 5 Platoon, agreed that they must cross to the next cover, which was a short thirty-five metres, but miles under fire. McKay shouted for covering fire and then he, Bailey and Privates Burt, Jones and McLarnon broke cover. First Sergeant Gonzalez' men opened fire, killing Burt and wounding Jones, but the three survivors grenaded a position and moved on. Bailey tumbled over, shot in the hip, and McLarnon dived for cover. Bailey later described McKay 'going on to the next position but there was no one else with him. The last I saw of him, he was going on running towards the remaining positions in that group.' A short time later the troublesome .50 Browning ceased firing. McKay's sole attack weakened the Argentine defence and he was awarded a posthumous Victoria Cross for this act of gallantry, which turned the tide in favour of 3 Para.

Major Argue, close behind 5 Platoon, having heard that 4 Platoon had lost both its senior commanders, sent Sergeant Des Fuller forward to take command. Fuller found Bickerdike where he had fallen and was able to glean enough information to mount an attack. With Corporal McLauglin's section providing fire support, he led 4 Platoon in a series of aggressive attacks and overran several sangars, but at the cost of five wounded. When machine-gun fire halted the platoon, Fuller provided fire support for McLaughlin attacking the gun until his section was halted by grenades being rolled down the hill. The Argentines were confident and on more than one occasion, after a position had been silenced, out of the darkness the paras

174

17. 22 May. Combat Team Eagle NCO escorted by 3 Para Regimental Police sergeant at Port San Carlos.

18. 22 May. An unusual sight! Two officers of 3rd Commando Brigade HQ and Signal Squadron dig their trench at San Carlos.

19. About 23 May. Marine Russell Craig, Defence Troop HQ 3rd Commando Brigade, manning a GPMG (SF) at San Carlos. Craig later became a "star" in the the BBC film about the M & AW Cadre *Behind The Lines.*

20. Capture of Lieutenant-Commander Cameletti by 40 Commando at San Carlos. The Royal Marine in the beret is Lieutenant Gibson, Intelligence Officer.

21. The Pucara pilot shot down at Goose Green on 29 May is interrogated at San Carlos.

22. Intelligence Section, HQ 3rd Commando Brigade at Teal Inlet on 2 June. From left to right Corporal Brian Dodd, Marine 'Taffy' Evans digging, Marine Ken Loftus, Marine 'Sid' Sidall and Colour Sergeant Neil Smith. Note the rocky ground.

23. Defensive position at Teal Inlet.

24. 11 June. Thompson, Moore and Wilson confer at HQ 3rd Commando Brigade on Mount Kent.

25. 14 June. Abandoned 105mm Pack Howitzer, probably by 4th Airborne
    Artillery Group.

26. 14 June. Argentine infantry file past one of the 155mm CITEFA howitzers
    landed at Stanley during the last night.

27. Special Category prisoners outside the BAS offices, Stanley, on 15 June.

28. Outside the FIC offices, paras supervise prisoners clearing up Stanley.

29. The jetty at Stanley. In foreground 160 Provost Coy RMP search prisoners.

30. Stanley, 17 June. Major Roberto Berazy and Lieutenant-Colonel David Comini, 3rd Infantry Regiment, after selection as Special Category prisoners.

31. Three School of Military Aviation prisoners being searched at San Carlos. This gr
spent three days trying to be captured by passing British patrols until a helicopter
finally picked them up.

32. The Intelligence Section, 3 Commando Brigade, on 15 June.

would hear, 'Hey! Amigo!' followed by a machine-gun burst ripping into the rocks and turf.

At about 2am Major Dennison and the Manpack Group joined 6 Platoon and the stretcher-bearers began to evacuate casualties from the primary RAP. B Company Sergeant Major Weekes was already organizing the collection of the wounded and evacuated Bickerdike and Cullen, whom he found still engaging the enemy. Colour Sergeant Brian Faulkner had established the primary RAP in Grenade Alley and, within fifteen minutes of the first contact, Captain Burgess, the Regimental Medical Officer, was treating the first casualties, his priorities being resuscitation and preparing them for evacuation. One stretcher-bearer later recalled, 'I didn't have enough guys because there were so many casualties it meant a number of trips. I remember taking one young lad out. I'll never forget him. He was alive when I carried him but he died in my arms. It was his eighteenth birthday.' During the night the medics dealt with forty-eight British and five Argentines, twenty of whom were evacuated before first light. One soldier died undergoing treatment. The lack of natural protection from the shelling and mortar fire made life difficult, and twice, when counter-attacks threatened, Faulkner deployed anyone fit enough to defend the RAP. On another occasion he led an attack to an area where he knew there were casualties. For his gallantry he was awarded the Distinguished Conduct Medal. The wounded were evacuated to the RAMC-manned RAP by BV, which could take two stretchers or seven walking wounded, a mile west of the Murrell Bridge, whence they were flown first to Teal Inlet and then on to the field hospital at Ajax Bay by 3rd Commando Brigade Air Squadron helicopters. Most were transferred to the *Uganda*. 3 Para would later comment on the inadequacy of the plastic lightweight stretcher but favourably on the high standard of first aid administered under difficult conditions. The Argentines had no such medical support and many of the wounded were recovered by the British, including Lance-Corporal Colemil shot in the leg as he tried to slip through B Company's lines.

By 1.30am Major Carrizo-Salvadores knew that the situation on Mount Longdon was very serious. He had not heard from Baldini and Gonzales for some time and feared the worst. The British had seized the western summit and, although a counter-attack by the engineers helped relieve the pressure, he was gradually being prised off Mount Longdon. Direct contact with Lieutenant Colonel Gimenez on Wireless Ridge had been lost, but he was still in touch with Army Group Puerto Argentino through whom he relayed messages. When he asked for reinforcements, he heard Gimenez being instructed to send a sniper section to Mount Longdon. At about 3am, soon after his men had been pushed off *Fly Half*, Carrizo-Salvadores was astonished when First Lieutenant Raul Castaneda, who commanded 2nd Platoon C Company on Wireless Ridge, burst into his CP. Mainly reservists from the same suburb of Buenos Aires, his soldiers knew each other well and most had night vision goggles. Carrizo-Salvadores briefed him and, after giving him three soldiers from Command Platoon as guides, he sent Castaneda to join First Sergeant Gonzales and counter-attack from the north. Castaneda's platoon soon gained a reputation for reckless courage and not only held up 3 Para on several occasions in hand-to-hand fighting but also gave Carrizo-Salvadores valuable time to organize an orderly withdrawal. When the platoon's radio operator was killed, Private Leonardo Rondi dodged enemy groups to deliver messages to Castaneda's sections and, in a tussle with a para, won a red beret and an SLR, which he later gave to Carrizo-Salvadores.

B Company had taken a beating. While 6 Platoon was still biting deep into Neirotti's platoon, Major Argue withdrew the battered 4 and 5 Platoons and formed them into a single unit under command of Lieutenant Mark Cox. Lieutenant Colonel Pike then arrived to help reorganize the attack and instructed Captain McCracken to arrange for 79 Commando Battery and *Avenger* to bombard Gonzales' platoon. *Avenger* left the gun line at 2.45am after firing 150 rounds. The area was still under heavy Argentine shelling and Captain Orpen-Smellie was wounded in the arm. Arriving at the RAP, he found the six-strong medical team working hard and, shoving his arm in his jacket, returned to Tac HQ.

Using a sheep track, Cox attacked under cover of McCracken's shifting barrage but had hardly advanced thirty yards when they were challenged and then a volley cut into the platoon. The Argentines had simply sheltered in their robust sangars and emerged when the shelling shifted. Cox and his radio operator took cover in a dip, but could not see the enemy. Those at Company HQ saw muzzle flashes and McCracken hit a sangar with a 66mm to mark it. Cox was still unsure of the enemy position and, ordering his rear section to throw grenades at the sangar, he and his radio operator broke cover to a spot from where they could see it. There was no more firing from the Argentine position, although groaning could be heard.

Confident that the nearest Argentine positions had been overwhelmed, Cox's platoon advanced but then came under fire from Carrizo-Salvadores' defences. Disappointed that the enemy were still not finished, he moved on to the spine to outflank the enemy, however, Neirotti's men were alert and wounded three paras. By now B Company had suffered over 50% casualties and Pike decided it should go firm and allow A Company to continue the attack. He ordered Dennison's Manpack Group to re-assemble as a single firebase ready to support the advance.

Major Collett moved A Company on to the northern slopes. Two GPMG (SF)s from the company support group covered the ridge and 79 Commando Battery shelled positions held by Corporal Lamas' marine machine gunners and Sergeant Pedro Lopez's 120mm mortar platoon. As virtually every British soldier knew, and upon which 3 Para would comment in their post-Operation *Corporate* report, the '58 pattern webbing fighting order was awkward and difficult to fight in, particularly when picks or shovels are attached. Second-Lieutenants Kearton and Moore told their men to take off their webbing and stuff ammunition, grenades and dressings into their pockets. Both officers had noted that the arcs of fire of the two machine guns which had held up B Company did not meet, leaving a narrow gap between some rocks through which they intended to advance.

Learning from B Company's experiences, A Company systematically cleared each Argentine position before advancing. When a section was halted, someone took cover behind a rock and either lit a cigarette or shone a torch to mark his position and shouted corrections. Positions reinforced with turf were then ripped apart by the machine guns, which allowed pairs of paras to crawl up, lob a grenade and then shoot and bayonet the occupants. Inevitably progress was slow, but by the time 1 Platoon was on the ridge there was evidence of the Argentines beginning to abandon their positions. Major Carrizo-Salvadores abandoned his CP when a Milan missile smashed into some nearby rocks. 2 Platoon then joined 1 Platoon and the advance quickened to such an extent that McCracken's supporting barrage was stopped. The Argentine platoons rigorously defended *Full Back*, but were gradually weeded from their positions, and 3 Platoon passed through to seize the eastern extremity of Mount Longdon against considerable resistance. The wounded Corporal Manuel Medina of Castaneda's platoon took over a Recoilless Rifle detachment and fired along the ridge at Support Company killing three paras, including Private Heddicker, who took the full force of the round, and wounding three others. 2 Platoon took about an hour to clear eight positions at the cost of Private Coady, who took a sudden interest to see the effect of his grenade and was injured in the face and shoulders when it exploded.

At about 5am Carrizo-Salvadores knew the end was near, but refused instructions from Brigadier General Jofre to abandon Mount Longdon after he had cancelled an order to move another C Company platoon onto the feature. B Company and the marine machine-gunners had retired in good order and he felt confident enough to plan a counter-attack to rescue the fifty of his men taken prisoner. Earlier in the battle he had considered negotiating a truce to recover his wounded. But by 6.30am Jofre finally convinced him and his optimistic platoons to evacuate Mount Longdon and help defend Stanley. B Company assembled at the eastern summit and of the 287 men he began the battle with, only seventy-eight were mustered, many of them sappers. Calling for machine-gun and mortar fire from Sergeant Lucero's machine-gunners and Major Jaimet's infantry on Mount Tumbledown, he broke contact and led his battered company into Stanley. In addition to the fifty taken prisoner, the Argentines lost thirty-one killed and at least 120 wounded.

Several minutes later A Company captured *Full Back* and a few

Argentines, including the wounded marine Private Colombo, still firing his .50 Browning and refusing orders to withdraw. 3 Platoon re-organized ready to receive a counter-attack from Wireless Ridge but daybreak brought a damp heavy mist and the first shells. Captain Burns' 2 Troop 9 Para RE cleared the trenches, sangars and bunkers of booby traps, made safe several Cobra missiles and dealt with other items left behind by Carrizo-Salvadores' men. They also collected several wounded of both sides and helped guard the prisoners of war. Sergeant McKay was found in a marine machine-gun bunker which had given 4 and 5 Platoons such a difficult time. Mount Longdon had fallen after ten hours of severe fighting which cost 3 Para seventeen killed, most in B Company.

Eleven years after the war Corporal Carrizo claimed that he was shot after surrendering. This rather goes against a photograph taken by a *Daily Express* photographer which shows paras working hard on the wounded Argentine. Considered unreliable by some colleagues, Carrizo is widely believed to have given himself a self-inflicted wound nevertheless. A former Parachute Regiment officer also claimed that he had seen a British soldier march a wounded Argentine to a grave and shoot him. Other reports alleged that the ears of killed Argentines had been collected by a British soldier. It is of some interest that none of these allegations were aired immediately after the Argentine surrender, indeed several 7th Infantry Regiment interviewed by Daniel Kon for his book on 10th Infantry Brigade *Los Chicos de la Guerra* commented upon their humane treatment after capture. Nevertheless the British Government considered them serious enough to initiate a Scotland Yard investigation, which was inconclusive. Significantly the Argentine authorities distanced themselves from Carrizo's allegations, including Brigadier General Jofre and Major Carrizo-Salvadores.

Mindful of the need to keep casualties low, Lieutenant Colonel Whitehead chose a simple two-phase right straight jab and left hook attack on Two Sisters. X Company was to seize the western peak, known as *Long Toenail,* from the west and, two hours later or when ordered, Y and Z Company from Murrell Bridge, nicknamed *Pub Garden,* would assault the eastern peak, called *Summer Days,* from the north-west. The entire Commando would then regroup and assault Mount Tumbledown. The attack would be silent until engaged. In direct support was 'Black Eight' and *Glamorgan.* To replace the Milan firings posts destroyed in the air raid on Ajax Bay, Milan Troop 40 Commando joined X Company and 45 Commando's troop was converted to a heavy weapons troop. Captain Dunstone RE divided his commando sapper sections among the companies.

At 5pm Captain Gardiner's X Company set off in the moonlight along a six-kilometre route cleared by Recce Troop, but it rapidly became apparent that it was inappropriate for the Milan Troop, carrying heavy firing posts

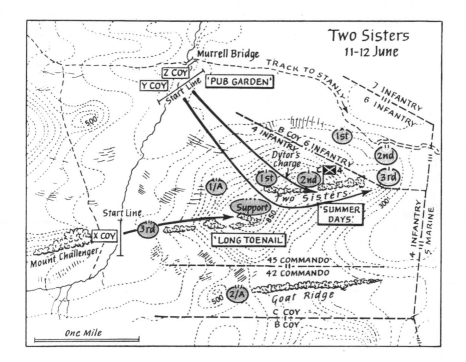

Two Sisters
11-12 June

Murrell Bridge
TRACK TO STANLEY
Z COY
Y COY
'PUB GARDEN'
Start Line
7 INFANTRY
6 INFANTRY
500'
B COY
4 INFANTRY 6 INFANTRY
1st
Dytor's charge
C 4
2nd
1/A
1st
2nd
3rd
Two Sisters
Start Line
Support
'SUMMER DAYS'
300'
850'
4 INFANTRY
5 MARINE
X COY
3rd
'LONG TOENAIL'
Mount Challenger
45 COMMANDO
42 COMMANDO
500'
2/A
Goat Ridge
C COY
B COY
One Mile

and forty missiles, each weighing thirty pounds. One man was knocked unconscious when he fell over a cliff, but he was revived and carried on, if a little blearily. Gardiner had estimated that the approach to his start line would take three hours, but it was not until 11.30pm that his weary company reached the forming-up place, two and a half hours behind schedule. Feeling there was no alternative but to break radio silence, Gardiner advised Whitehead that he was late and was calmly told, 'Carry on as planned. I will do nothing until I hear from you'. Gardiner was greatly relieved and told his troop commanders to forget the frustrations of the approach, make their final preparations and let him know when they were ready. Ten minutes later they were.

Y and Z Company and Tac HQ had moved from north of Mount Kent into an assembly area during the morning and at about 5pm they also began the six kilometre march to their forming-up place. Shortly before 9pm the long column reached the start line south of the Murrell Bridge, which had been secured by Burns' 2 Troop RE, diverted from supporting 3 Para.

At 11.15pm X Company splashed across the chilly Murrell River. All was silent apart from the occasional clinking of equipment and
was the fighting on Mount Longdon and some 155mm sh
Murrell Bridge. Lieutenant Kelly led his 1 Troop and th

179

support group, crossed the open ground, reached the base of Two Sisters and halted to allow Lieutenant Stewart's 3 Troop to pass through and take up the advance. Still encountering no opposition, Stewart advanced toward *Long Toenail*, but at 11.30pm, after advancing about 600 yards up the ridge, came under heavy machine-gun fire from Second Lieutenant Llambias-Pravaz's thirty-strong 3rd Platoon.

Llambias-Pravaz was one of the April 1982 graduates from the National Army Academy and now commanded a platoon weakened by casualties and sickness but he had taught his men discipline, patriotism and courage. With fixed bayonets and supported by Corporal Mario Pacheco's 10th Engineer Company section on *Summer Days*, they taunted the Royal Marines with Guarani war-cries and beat off efforts to close with them. Gardiner pulled 3 Troop back so that 'Black Eight' and Mortar Troop could saturate the position, but the gunners were on another mission and Mortar Troop were delayed because the baseplates were sinking into the soft turf after firing a few rounds. Milan Troop fired missiles at Llambias-Pravaz's men and Lieutenant Chris Caroe's 2 Troop advanced against stiff opposition from Lieutenant Martella's Support Platoon on *Long Toenail*. Among the boulders, the Royal Marines used fighting-in-built-up-area techniques and clawed their way to *Long Toenail*, only to be forced off by a defensive fire mission from 3rd Artillery Group. However, they groped their way back and dealt with the machine-gunners covering the retreating Argentines.

At about the same time, *Glamorgan* and *Yarmouth* were preparing to leave the gunline, leaving *Avenger* to support 3 Para. *Glamorgan* was about seventeen miles offshore and taking a short cut across the shore-based Exocet limit line when the radar picked up a signature of the same size and speed of a 155mm shell. *Glamorgan* took no evasive action until *Avenger*, ten miles to the north, reported the signature was a land-based Exocet. Within *Glamorgan's* main armament range, a Seacat missile passed close to the Exocet, which skipped on to the flight deck and skidded into the hangar. Burning fuel from the Wessex flooded through a hole into the galley and a fireball thundered into the gas turbine room. The fires were brought under control, but nine men were killed and fourteen others injured, mostly chefs and helicopter maintenance crews.

Keen to fight while darkness lasted, Whitehead decided that if an advance to Mount Tumbledown was to be achieved, it was vital for Y and Z Companies to begin their attack without waiting for X Company to secure *Long Toenail*. Adjusting his timings, he instructed Major Davis' Y and Captain Michael Cole's Z Companies to advance on *Summer Days*, clear in the moonlight against scudding clouds. Shortly after X Company crossed its start line, an Argentine defensive fire mission pounded the ground they were about to cross. They were within 400 yards of the summit when Lieutenant Clive Dytor's 8 Troop located several bunkers held by Perez-Grandi's 2nd

180

Platoon in bunkers about 400 yards up the slopes and in a whispered discussion on the radio with Cole on how best to tackle the opposition, Dytor rejected Whitehead's idea of standing up and advancing, citing the risk of high casualties.

When it became obvious that the fighting around Long Toenail was more than a patrol, Major Cordon alerted his command. A flare fired by 2nd Platoon fizzled and bounced along the ground, still alight. In the glow, Perez-Grandi's men were startled to see British lying on the slopes and a firefight developed, with little movement from either side. Most of the Argentine fire cracked over the heads of the Royal Marines sheltering behind rocks firing a few rounds in the general direction of the enemy, later admitting that the Argentine cover was good and they didn't think their fire was that effective. However, stalemate stopped when the 3rd Artillery Group and Major Jaimet's 120mm mortars began to range on to the western summit causing casualties in Second Lieutenant Paul Mansell's 7 Troop. A mortar round also landed in the middle of 9 Troop, wounding two section commanders and killing a commando sapper. Marine 'Blue' Nowak was killed by machine gun fire from Perez-Grandi's platoon and forever will be remembered by the small blue square in the corner of the Company flag. The hollow in which they had been taking shelter became a forward RAP. Y Company also suffered from the mortar fire. In spite of the discomfort of the shelling Whitehead ordered both companies to stay where they were and organized artillery fire on Long Toenail.

3rd Artillery Group continued to pound the western edge of Summer Days and mortar rounds fell behind Z Company. Dytor, of 8 Troop, realized that staying was achieving nothing and withdrawal was out of the question. Leaping between 7 and 8 Troops, he shouted, 'Forward everybody!' Some Royal Marines thought he was crazy and one swore at him to get his head down, but his three section commanders yelled, 'Move now!' and the Company skirmished up the slope shouting the company battle cry 'Zulu! Zulu!' and ran into stiff resistance, 7 Troop from Perez-Grandi's platoon and 8 Troop encountering Second Lieutenant Mosquera's 1st Platoon. 45 Commando's Mortar Troop bombed the rear of Summer Days and crept back onto the summit, killing several Argentines. For nearly an hour the Argentines weathered the bombardment but the conscripts were unable to prevent 8 Troop seizing the high ground. Mosquera was severely wounded. Although supported by Martella's machine guns on Long Toenail, the battered Argentine platoons recoiled in front of the Royal Marines. Dytor was ordered by Whitehead to seize Summer Days' southern slopes and 8 Troop advanced with a captured .50 Browning, although few Royal Marines knew how to use it, and cleared several positions held by Mosquera's battered platoon, but were pulled up by B Company 6th Infantry Regiment pasting the crest.

Y Company, unable to advance without becoming involved in Z

Company's battle, were shelled losing two troop commanders wounded. Whitehead ordered Davis to break contact and move south along the southern slopes until he was alongside Z Company and Tac HQ. A Carl Gustav projectile engaging a troublesome .50 Browning post swished uncomfortably close over the head of Whitehead, who was up with Dytor. Y Company then advanced across the saddle between the two peaks against fierce opposition but as they were spilling on to the southern slopes leading to *Summer Days*, the Royal Marines came under heavy fire from Cordon's headquarters and from Jaimet's 6th Infantry Regiment company, one of whose conscript .50 machine-gunners, Private Oscar Poltronieri, was overrun several times but each time made his way back to his platoon. Whitehead instructed the fired-up Dytor to go firm and, to avoid a 'blue on blue' in the darkness, instructed Captain Cole to seize *Summer Days*. Wary of a wire-controlled mine, X Company crossed the slopes and when 4 Troop reached *Summer Days* went firm to repel the expected counter-attack. To the south, X Company had pushed Llambias-Pravaz' platoon and Corporal Pacheco's sappers off *Long Toenail* by about 2.45am.

The Argentines lost several wounded, including Perez-Grandi hit by shrapnel and Private Luis Mendez who died of his wounds in Argentina. 45 Commando's Mortar Troop caused havoc among Cordon's reserve, Second Lieutenant Juan Nazer's 1st Platoon A Company, and the shaken conscripts began to disappear into the darkness. When Cordon was captured in his CP the defence of Two Sisters disintegrated. With the telephone lines to the CP in shreds, Llambias-Pravaz, now cut off from Two Sisters, led his men to join M Company 5th Marine Infantry Battalion on Sapper Hill.

Second Lieutenant Aldo Franco, with his 3rd Platoon B Company 6th Infantry Regiment, commanded the rearguard and fell back to an alternative position on the eastern slopes known as *Cambio*. When he reached *Summer Days,* Captain Davis sent Corporal Siddall and Bombardier Holt 350 yards on to the lower eastern slopes to deal with a suspected mortar position. Leaving Siddall's section to cover them, the NCOs found a place from which to observe the Argentines and then attacked killing one and capturing three, one of whom was wounded, all from Major Berazey 6th Infantry Regiment company group.

So ended the battle for Two Sisters, two and a half hours after 45 Commando crossed its start lines and was essentially won by Clive Dytor's crazy charge, for which he was awarded the Military Cross. Three Royal Marines were killed and also one Royal Engineer. Ten Argentines were killed, fifty were wounded and fifty-four taken prisoner, none of whom reached 3rd Commando Brigade Headquarters.

45 Commando reorganized and at 4.30am, with only about two hours of daylight left, Whitehead radioed Brigadier Thompson that he was preparing to exploit to Mount Tumbledown, but, much to his frustration, was ordered to remain where he was because a 3000-yard advance in daylight

across open ground against a well-prepared position about which little w̄ known was too risky. The guns were also low on ammunition, 'Black Eight' having fired 1500 rounds during the night and, critically, 42 Commando had yet to secure Mount Harriet. Tired after the exhilaration of the battle and with their sleeping bags and equipment still at Bluff Cove, Whitehead gave his men permission to scavenge the Argentine positions and soon little shelters sprouted across Two Sisters against the snow that was now falling. Sleeping bags and boots were prized as were the Argentine ration packs with their cigarettes and, with luck, a tot of Scotch whisky.

Captain Dunstone's commando sappers checked the Argentine positions for booby traps and traced the various cables that littered the hilltop. Most were telephones. The Royal Marines were astonished by the ease with which Two Sisters had been captured and indeed Major Cordon was later heavily criticized for his lack of aggression and retired from the army. As Whitehead remarked when daylight exposed the near invincibility of Two Sisters, 'If we had a Company up here, we would have died of old age before it was captured' nevertheless the Argentines, many who had been conscripted in February, had fought hard. Dawn broke and 45 Commando, like 3 Para, soon began to suffer from the long-range shelling.

Lieutenant-Colonel Vaux's plan to capture Mount Harriet was audacious and widely regarded as an example of a classic modern night attack. While Major Mike Norman's J Company, who were formally NP 8901, created a diversion on Wall Mountain, the remaining two companies of 42 Commando would make a wide march south across the Stanley-Fitzroy track and right hook Mount Harriet from the area of Pony Pass. K Company was to seize the eastern summit and once secure L Company would then take the western summit, *Zoya*, and exploit to Goat Ridge ready to support 45 Commando's attack on Mount Tumbledown. On call was 7 Commando Battery and *Yarmouth*. In support was Captain Hicks' 2 Troop 59 Commando Squadron RE.

During the day Mortar and 10 Troops set up the diversion on Wall Mountain. At 4.15pm, after last light, Captain Peter Babbington's K Company left Mount Challenger and, after dumping their bergens at the assembly area, were led by 9 Troop through the minefield, across the Stanley-Fitzroy track, south around a lake to the forming-up place north of the road. Two Milan posts covered the Stanley track in case the Argentines counter-attacked with Panhards. Milan Troop found the going difficult and by the time they reached their position, the schedule had slipped. At about 5.30pm Captain David Wheen's L Company moved off, twice stopping when mortar illumination rounds rose high into the night and slowly drifted down. There was a moment's anxiety when there was an negligent discharge. As planned, 7 Commando Battery pounded the ridge, which wounded at least twenty-five defenders. At about 6.30pm the composite thirty-five-strong Porter Troop formed from Headquarters Company left with the GPMG (SF)

183

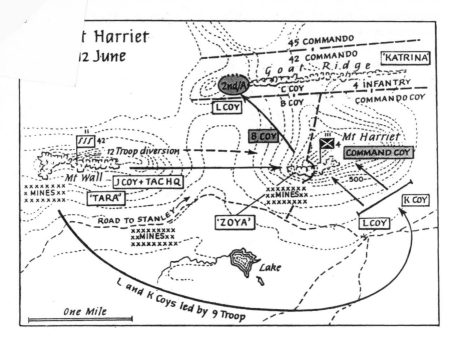

t Harriet
l2 June

45 COMMANDO
42 COMMANDO
'KATRINA'
Goat Ridge
2nd/A
C COY
4 INFANTRY
L COY
B COY
COMMANDO COY
B COY
III
Mt Harriet
III 42
COMMAND COY
12 Troop diversion
4
Mt Wall
J COY + TAC HQ
500
xxxxxxxx
x MINES xx
'TARA'
xxxxxxx
xxMINESxx
K COY
xxxxxxxx
xxxxxxx
ROAD TO STANLEY
'ZOYA'
L COY
xxxxxxxxx
xxMINESxx
xxxxxxxxx
Lake
L and K Coys led by 9 Troop
One Mile

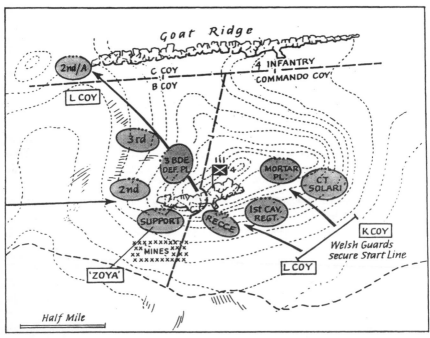

Goat Ridge
2nd/A
C COY
4 INFANTRY
B COY
COMMANDO COY
L COY
3rd
3 BDE
DEF. PL.
III
MORTAR
4
PL.
CT
SOLARI
2nd
1st CAV.
REGT.
SUPPORT
"C.C."
K COY
xxxxxxxxxx
Welsh Guards
xxx
Secure Start Line
xx MINES xxx
xxxxxxxxxx
L COY
'ZOYA'
Half Mile

184

tripods and sights and 10,000 rounds of ammunition ready for immediate use once Mount Harriet had been captured.

9 Troop had trouble finding the Welsh Guards Recce Platoon, which had been tasked to secure the start line, until they were spotted several hundred yards on the wrong side of the fence marking the start line. At 10pm, just as Vaux released K Company, Wheen radioed that his company had strayed off the route and, although exceedingly wary of minefields, were confident of reaching the forming-up place on time. About half an hour later he was ready. To the north, the fight for Mount Longdon was underway. On Mount Wall 10 Platoon began its deception of a phoney patrol clash and were laced by Argentine machine-gunners on Mount Harriet. Mortar Troop illuminated *Zoya* and Milan Troop loosed several of the leisurely, lurching and twisting missiles on to their targets.

K Company moved undetected into the shadows of Mount Harriet and covered about 700 metres in thirty minutes, with Babbington whispering progress reports into his radio. The Royal Marines infiltrated deep into Command Company's position at the eastern end of Mount Harriet without being detected until a Mortar Platoon sentry, Corporal Mario Cortez, heard rustling in the frozen grass but thought it might be an Argentine Special Forces patrol until he realized his error and fired a shot. Because it was difficult to pinpoint enemy positions, the Royal Marines adopted fighting in built-up area tactics and, working in pairs or half sections stormed the trenches, bunkers and sangars with grenades, 66mm missiles and bayonet but it took nearly forty-five minutes of stiff fighting before the lower eastern positions were overrun. 1 Troop overran Second Lieutenant Mario Juarez's Mortar Platoon, denying Lieutenant Colonel Soria valuable support and severely wounded the platoon commander. 2 Troop quickly dealt with Mosterin's 12th Infantry Regiment platoon and the 4th Infantry Regiment Recce Platoon on Mount Harriet's eastern slopes. Confused and overwhelmed by the sheer momentum of the night attack, the inexperienced conscripts began to surrender until rallied by First Lieutenant Jorge Echeverria, Soria's Intelligence officer, until he was badly wounded.

Although dealing with prisoners was already becoming a problem, Babbington called Lieutenant Heathcote's 3 Troop forward but 1 Troop then reported stiffening resistance from machine-gun positions held by the 1st Cavalry Regiment platoon, commanded by Second Lieutenant Samyn. Bunkered in rocks, they took it in turns to shoot at the Royal Marines until Corporal Steve Newlands, working with Corporals Mick Eccles and 'Sharkey' Ward, silenced the position but was badly wounded in doing so; all three were awarded the Military Medal. Although 3rd Artillery Group were accurately shelling Mount Harriet, using Soria's CP, which had been set on fire by a phosphorous grenade, as a marker, Babbington felt sufficiently secure to move his Tac HQ onto the position. K Company pressed on, captured the Argentine RAP post and reached *Zoya*.

Vaux then released L Company. Wheen's plan was to approach from the south-east, capture the western end of Mount Harriet and advance on Goat Ridge. Within 150-yards of crossing the start line they ran into a deluge of fire from Second Lieutenant Oliva's HQ 3rd Infantry Brigade Defence Platoon defending the central southern slopes. Wheen's suppressive fire came very close to K Company advancing toward the western summit until both company commanders resolved the problem and a potentially disastrous 'blue on blue' was avoided. 7 Commando Battery accurately shelled the Argentine positions and helped L Company to overrun Oliva's position, but they then clashed with Second Lieutenant Bruny's 2nd Platoon hurrying to reinforce the Defence Platoon. The fighting raged to and fro along the ridge. Corporal Jose Gonzales was wounded in the eye but carried on directing his section and Private Orlando Aylan, in a position just below the eastern summit, held up the Royal Marines with accurate shooting until killed by a Carl Gustav fired at short range. It took L Company nearly six hours to advance 600 metres.

Shortly before his CP was overrun Soria joined First-Lieutenant Arroyo on the western summit to organize a counter-attack, but, seeing 4th Infantry Regiment was cut off from Stanley, agreed that it was folly to commit in-experienced conscripts to such a suicidal venture. He ordered his men to make their way to Tumbledown, but only Second Lieutenants Silva's platoon on Goat Ridge and Jimenez-Corvalan's 3rd Platoon on the northern slopes of Mount Harriet avoided capture. Soria was captured soon after-wards.

There was still fighting when Vaux led his Tac HQ across an uncleared route direct from Mount Wall to Mount Harriet at about 6am. J Company passed through and took up defensive positions to repel the expected counter-attack from Mount Tumbledown. Meanwhile L Company advanced quickly across open ground to seize Goat Ridge but came under fire from Silva's platoon in its western crags. 5 Troop withdrew to allow a fire mission to pound the rocks and then 4 Troop continued the advance and captured the objective. Mount Harriet had been captured and over 300 Argentines surrendered. Two Royal Marines were killed and twenty-eight wounded. The Argentines lost five 4th Infantry Regiment, one 1st Cavalry Regiment private, three HQ 3rd Brigade Defence Platoon and one sapper killed and about fifty-three wounded. The rest of the defenders, including Soria, were captured.

As the morning mist cleared, Argentine artillery shelled the lost peaks, resulting in 42 Commando losing seven Royal Marines wounded, including Marine Steve Chubb, who had been captured at South Georgia in April. Captain Rodrigo Soloaga's 10th Armoured Recce Squadron directed artillery fire on to Mount Longdon and a 3rd Artillery Group officer spotted from a helicopter, causing 3 Para to lose six killed and seven men wounded, including Corporal Denzil Connick, who lost both legs. He would later be instrumental in forming the South Atlantic Medal Association, which is open to those awarded the medal, to immediate next-of-kin and to Falkland Islanders, and whose motto is 'From The Sea, Freedom', epitomizing the aim of the campaign.

Although Captain Burns regrouped his para engineers out of the killing ground, he lost an NCO killed and a sapper wounded by a mortar bomb fired from Wireless Ridge. More serious for the Argentine gunners was that by the end of 12 June most of the 155mm ammunition had been used up.

At about midday 3rd Artillery Group came under intense counter-battery fire with shells landing close to C Battery. First-Lieutenant Jorge Cerezo, who commanded C Battery 4th Airborne Artillery Group in gun positions near Moody Brook, recalled:

I had five Oto Melara in a circle to provide 360 degree fire support. Each gun had sixty rounds and at the battery ammunition point 500 metres away was a further 2000 rounds. The enemy artillery fire on our front line was continuous and caused numerous casualties which demoralized the troops. The attrition rate was so severe the CO ordered the FOOs to be changed every two days. Every time I was given a fire mission, the British shelled our position, but their inaccuracy sometimes permitted us to service the guns, load and fire. When the situation became untenable, everyone took cover in shelters until the enemy ceased fire. Saint Barbara protected us and prevented major losses. An enemy shell destroyed a B Battery shelter but no one was hurt just shaken up. On another occasion a detachment had loaded a gun and were forced to take cover when they saw it fire. It had been set off by a direct hit. Two soldiers in the Command Post were killed by naval gunfire and a B Battery gunner was mortally wounded by counter-battery fire.

The guns sank in the muddy waterlogged gunpits and recoil problems began to develop. Lieutenant Colonel Balza ordered the guns to be removed from their emplacements.

St Barbara is the patron saint of gunners. The chapel at the Citadel in Plymouth, home to 29 Commando Regiment, is dedicated to her and the Royal Artillery had a yacht named after her.

For the British Phase 1 was complete and they now overlooked Stanley. The night's fighting had again shown that the Argentines were prepared to fight. 7th Infantry Regiment had given 3 Para a hard time, largely because they were thoroughly familiar with Mount Longdon and had good defences. The inexperienced conscripts of the 4th Infantry Regiment had already lost eight killed and forty wounded in the skirmishes west of the Outer Defence Zone but fought hard; nevertheless 42 and 45 Commando found their attacks were a little easier, made even more so by good patrolling.

Brigadier-General Jofre was appalled by the loss of the Outer Defence

Zone and severely criticized Ricardo Cordon for losing Two Sisters. To bolster wavering units, he threatened to shell any unit considering withdrawal. Menendez signalled the Joint Operations Centre: 'We need immediate support from the mainland to bombard defined targets. The National Reserve must do all that is possible to prevent the fall of Stanley.' Later in the day the fifty-strong 2nd Airborne Infantry Regiment platoon flew in and joined 7th Infantry Regiment on Wireless Ridge. 603 Commando Company and the Amphibious Commando Grouping remained on short notice to move to the Falklands.

10

The Battle for the Inner Defence Zone

Tumbledown, Wireless Ridge and Cortley Hill
13 and 14 June
'*Aye, sir. I'm f........ with you!*' Unknown Scots Guardsman to Major
Kiszely.

Tumbledown Mount had been occupied by 5th Marine Infantry Battalion
since 6 April. Led by Commander Hugo Robacio and numbering about 650
men, mostly conscripts, some with two years' service, the battalion was
based at Rio Grande in the southerly province of Tierra del Fuego. Captain
Ricardo Cionchi's M Company was on Mount William, with Captain
Eduardo Villarraza's N and Captain Ricardo Quiroga's O Companies on
Tumbledown. On call was B Battery Marine Field Artillery Battalion.
Battalion HQ and the Amphibious Engineer Company were co-located to
the north about 300 yards west of Felton Stream.

Tumbledown stretches about 2000 yards east to west and is 800 yards east
of Goat Ridge. It rises sharply from the south through peat and crags to 800
feet at its centre summit. About 700 yards east of the centre is the eastern
summit at 750 feet. In between the saddle dips to 700 feet. The ground itself
is peat, rocks and crags. Tumbledown Mount and Mount William are the
gateway to Stanley. Capture them and Stanley is invested.

Robacio was reasonably certain that the British would attack along the
Stanley-Darwin track, and the events along the road to Goose Green after 6
June seemed to bear this out. He instructed Captain Quiroga to move O
Company into a blocking position between Mount William and Pony's Pass
leaving N Company to defend Tumbledown. Sub Lieutenant Daniel
Vasquez's twenty-six strong composite 4th Platoon on the centre summit
dominated approaches from the west. On the northern slopes Robacio posted
First Sergeant Jorge Lucero's 3rd Platoon and on the saddle between
Tumbledown and Mount William was Second Lieutenant Marcelo
Oruezabala's 2nd Platoon with Second Lieutenant Carlos Bianchi's 1st
Platoon on Mount William. Sub Lieutenant Mino's 5th Amphibious Engineer
Platoon moved into defensive positions on the south-western slopes of the
feature in rocks above and behind Vasquez. The marines coped well with the
hostile conditions; nevertheless showers, rest and recuperation were rare.

189

On 31 May 2 Para, still at Goose Green, passed under command of its parent formation, 5th Infantry Brigade, then coming ashore at San Carlos with 1/7th Gurkha Rifles, 2nd Scots Guards and the Welsh Guards. The day before, for the first time, Major-General Moore had taken full command of the LFFI in the field. During the long voyage south on the *Queen Elizabeth*, communications to and from his *ad hoc* headquarters were unreliable.

Both Guards battalions were on public duties when their commanding officers, Lieutenant Colonels Mike Scott and John Ricketts respectively, ordered their guardsmen to discard their red tunics and bearskins for combat uniforms and steel helmets and join 5th Infantry Brigade for immediate deployment to the South Atlantic. An exercise at Sennybridge shook them down and they then embarked to the comfort of *Queen Elizabeth II* for the long voyage south. Both units had equipment shortages with some guardsmen being issued with blue civilian bergens painted green to replace the virtually useless '57 pattern large pack. To convert the battalions into a wartime establishment, some reorganization was required and Major the Hon Richard Bethell MBE, who was commanding the Scots Guards Headquarters Company, after an absence from the battalion of about twelve years with the SAS, was told to form a Recce Platoon from the Drums Platoon and volunteers.

The contrast for two battalions sent from public duty to the hostility of winter warfare against an enemy firing live bullets could not have been greater. It still needs to be explained why combat-ready units, such as those with 7th Field Force in Colchester, were not selected. This does not detract from the good performance of both battalions, although on occasion they could have listened to those with greater experience, especially at Port Pleasant.

With a strong Argentine army at Stanley, it was important for Brigadier Tony Wilson, who commanded 5th Infantry Brigade, to keep level with 3rd Commando Brigade's breakout so that the enemy could not use the Stanley/Goose Green track to attack the Royal Marines' right flank, but his ability to move quickly was severely limited by the loss of the Chinooks on the *Atlantic Conveyor*. With 2 Para on Wickham Heights protecting his left flank, he planned to march the thirty-five miles on the track from Goose Green to Fitzroy, but there were no harbours or beaches to support the advance and consequently the troops would have to carry the heavy equipment and this quickly proved unrealistic, in spite of Admiral Woodward's protestations. 5th Infantry Brigade was also still sorting itself out after the long voyage and much of the equipment was still at San Carlos, including the Brigade Headquarters communications.

2 Para resolved the problem when they discovered that a telephone from Swan Inlet House to Fitzroy might still be working; this could be used to find out if the Argentines were at Fitzroy. Initially Wilson was sceptical about the scheme, but on 2 June he told Major Keeble, 'Do it'. 6 Platoon was

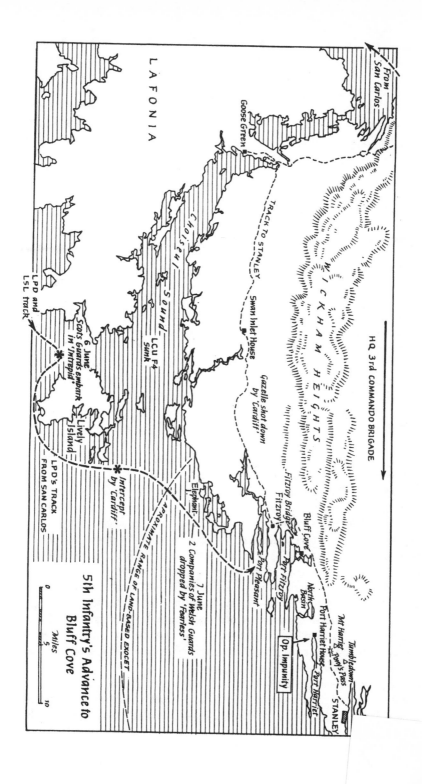

From San Carlos

LAFONIA

HQ 3rd COMMANDO BRIGADE

Goose Green

TRACK TO STANLEY

Swan Inlet House

Gazelle shot down
by 'Cardiff'

W I C K H A M   H E I G H T S

Fitzroy Bridge
Fitzroy

Bluff Cove

North
Basin

Mt Harriet
Goat's Pass

Tumbledown

Port Harriet House
Port Harriet

STANLEY

Op. Impunity

Choiseul   Sound

LCU F4
Sunk

6 June
Scots Guards embark
in 'Intrepid'

Lively
Island

Elephant

7 June
2 Companies of Welsh Guards
dropped by 'Fearless'

Port Pleasant

Port Fitzroy

APPROXIMATE RANGE OF LAND-BASED EXOCET

Intercept
by 'Cardiff'

LPD and
LSL track

LPD's TRACK
FROM SAN CARLOS

5th Infantry's Advance to
Bluff Cove

0   5   10
Miles

helicoptered to Swan Inlet House from where Major Crosland telephoned Fitzroy and established from the 'kelpers' that there were no Argentines in the area. Wilson saw an opportunity and, with his agreement, Keeble commandeered the only Chinook, which was still moving the brigade from San Carlos, loaded it with eighty men, double its capacity, and with six 656 Squadron AAC Scouts, flew Tac HQ, A and B Companies and a mortar detachment to Fitzroy. An observer with a M&AW Cadre patrol over-looking the settlement saw the Chinook and, not expecting it to be friendly, radioed 7 Commando Battery on Mount Kent, just eight miles to the north, for a fire mission. Fortunately the patrol commander recognized the heli-copter to be the sole survivor from the *Atlantic Conveyor* and cancelled the order. Next day the remainder of the battalion was flown in.

While these moves were underway Lieutenant Colonel David Chaundler arrived from the United Kingdom and took command of 2 Para. Parachuted into the sea to join the Carrier Battle Group, taking over the mantle from the charismatic Jones and the eventual victor at Goose Green, Keeble, was not without its difficulties.

The speed of the move caught Moore by surprise, but, with 2 Para so far forward and without support, which meant that 5th Infantry Brigade was off balance, he had to quickly re-allocate resources to Wilson. Also Moore was keen to attack Stanley on 6 June and on the 4th asked Commodore Clapp to get Wilson as far forward as possible. As we shall see events conspired against total success.

Clapp's initial plan to move the two Guards battalions on *Intrepid* and the Brigade logistics in *Sir Tristram* as far as Bluff Cove was scuppered next day when he received instructions from Admiral Fieldhouse at Northwood that no LPDs were to leave San Carlos in daylight because they carried the same political weight as an aircraft-carrier and were too risky to lose. Ultimately the role of LPDs is to land troops in the right place at the right time ready to fight and someone somewhere had forgotten that to win wars risks are essen-tial. Shortly after *Intrepid* left San Carlos during the evening of 5 June, her captain confirmed this to Major Southby-Tailyour, who was helping Clapp plan the move, '*Intrepid* is not politically allowed further east than Lively Island. The risk to an LPD is too great' Clapp and Southby-Tailyour then devised a plan to transport the Scots Guards in *Intrepid* as far as Lively Island and embark the 600 men into the ship's four LCUs for the voyage to Fitzroy. The LCUs would remain in Port Pleasant next day and meet with *Fearless* bringing the Welsh Guards and other units the following night. Southby-Tailyour, who was by now very anxious about the LCU operation, was told by *Intrepid's* captain that the only ships he would see will be enemy. He was also not supplied with the ship recognition signal.

Meanwhile 5th Infantry Brigade's communications had broken down, largely because the signallers had been given insufficient time to prepare for the move to Fitzroy after the Chinook had been hijacked and equipment was still arriving from San Carlos. To add to their problems, a Scout carrying the Brigade's signals officer, Major Forge, was shot down by *Cardiff* while flying south of Wickham Heights along a flight path *presumed* to be used by Argentine C-130s.

At 8.30pm *Intrepid* sailed and, on reaching Lively Island in deceptively good weather at about 2.30am next morning, the troops filed on to the open landing craft, a new experience for many of the guardsmen. The failure of Admiral Woodward to brief the details of the operation to his captains nearly ended in a disastrous 'blue on blue' when *Cardiff*, already keyed up after shooting down an unidentified aircraft, but in fact the Scout suddenly had a surface radar contact and fired starshells. There was alarm in the LCUs as the powerful Type 42 destroyer loomed out of the darkness to investigate and then disappeared without the courtesy of identifying herself. The weather then turned appalling, swathes of ice cold sea frequently burst over the open sides drenching the soldiers, many of whom were sea-sick. At first light, after a nerve-wracking six hours in open landing craft, the soaking guardsmen saw the welcome sight of Bluff Cove and were guided into defensive positions by 2 Para, but by that time they were in no state to fight.

The Scots Guards quickly sorted themselves and on 7 June Recce Platoon, operating from Port Harriet House, began Operation *Impunity* with orders to destroy two Pack Howitzers positions and a radar which Brigade Headquarters believed to be in the area, but nothing was found. Next day Sergeant Noble's G Squadron patrol, earmarked to operate at Seal Point to identify Argentine guns on Stanley Common, agreed to join the platoon and set off in two Land Rovers driven by Tim Dobbyn and Mike Mackay, who both lived at Bluff Cove. With only about 600 yards to go, Dobbyn's vehicle hit a mine and everyone dismounted only to find that they were in the middle of a minefield. Withdrawal was nerve-wracking, but the damaged Land Rover was repaired and the group returned to Bluff Cove. Meanwhile Sergeant Allum, the Recce Platoon sergeant, was gathering useful intelligence, in particular that the Argentines were well prepared to meet any attack along the Stanley-Darwin track.

With Bluff Cove in danger of becoming overcrowded as 5th Infantry Brigade assembled, but without seeking Moore's authority, Brigadier Wilson ordered 2 Para to concentrate at Fitzroy in strength. Southby-Tailyour agreed that, since Fitzroy bridge was still demolished and the battalion was faced with a long march around Port Fitzroy, they could use *Intrepid's* LCUs to ferry the battalion across Bluff Cove creek but no more. Meanwhile other 5th Infantry Brigade assets on the *Sir Tristram* arrived at Port Pleasant shortly before dawn on 8 June. After dark the previous evening, *Fearless* with the Welsh Guards on board, sailed as far as Elephant Island but *Intrepid's* LCUs failed to make the rendezvous, apparently because of poor weather. Captain Jeremy Larkin, her captain, loaded two of his LCUs with about half the Welsh Guards to carry on to Bluff Cove. By now there were six valuable LCUs well forward and when Larken returned to San Carlos, it was felt they would be more than sufficient to unload *Sir Galahad,* which had spare capacity on board for the remainder of the Welsh Guards to be cross-decked to the LSL. *Sir Galahad* arrived at Port Pleasant about 7.30am.

Southby-Tailyour was curious why *Intrepid's* LCUs had not made the rendezvous and learnt, to his astonishment, that this had been achieved by a Parachute Regiment officer apparently brandishing a pistol to persuade the LCU coxswains to ferry 2 Para to Bluff Cove, which was against Southby-Tailyour's direct orders. The landing craft then became storm-bound and missed the rendezvous.

Wilson's communications problems were further compounded when a *Fearless* LCU, *Foxtrot Four,* while returning from Goose Green with some 5th Infantry Brigade Headquarters and Signal Squadron radio Land Rovers, was sunk in broad daylight in Choiseul Sound by a 5 Group Skyhawk piloted by Ensign Vasquez on an anti-shipping sortie.

The arrival of the two transports had been seen, probably from Mount Harriet, and five 5 Group Skyhawks, commanded by First Lieutenant Cachon, flew from Rio Gallegos and approaching Fitzroy settled down into a low-level bombing run. The rest of what happened at Port Pleasant is history, but a Ministry of Defence press release the previous day stating that the Argentine Air Force was beaten seemed a little premature.

The move of 5th Infantry Brigade had been a near-disaster and much of the blame could be levelled at Northwood, who disallowed the LPDs to be used in their truly amphibious role – to land troops in the right place at the right time ready to fight. After six hours in open landing craft in the middle of a South Atlantic storm, the Scots Guards were anything but ready for military operations. Considering there was a low enemy threat between Goose Green and Fitzroy, 'Exocetitis' (the fear of Exocets) had irrationally taken hold among some Royal Navy commanders, even those at Northwood. And, as we have seen, the failure of Woodward nearly ended in a 'blue on blue', which would have cost the lives of many soldiers. And 2 Para's threat to the LCU coxswains beggars belief and had an impact on the Welsh Guards beyond their imagination. As far as the Pleasant Cove disaster is concerned, one does have to question why Woodward allowed two lightly-armed logistic ships to enter the cove without adequate close air defence from a warship or combat air patrol.

In his *Amphibious Assault Falklands,* Michael Clapp criticizes 5th Infantry Brigade for their performance. He forgets it was a newly restructured brigade with a long airborne tradition, but untrained in amphibious operations, and rushed to war with little preparation with three major units with whom it had not operated. Rather unkindly, some of its more energetic officers had dubbed Wilson's headquarters the 'Wait Out, Brigade', which, in British military communications, means 'I will return your call in due course'.

194

Wilson had exploited an opportunity to advance, even if it caught him un-balanced for a short time and, with Clapp's help, he nearly pulled it off. The risk was worth it. But now disasters had been thrust upon its brigadier and he duly carried the can for Northwood's interference and retired early.

On 9 June Brigadier Wilson briefed his officers that 5th Infantry Brigade must be ready to support the 3rd Commando Brigade attack on the Outer Defence Zone on the night of 11/12th, with the Scots Guards, reinforced by the fourth Gurkha company, providing right-flank protection for the Royal Marines. At the same time 1/7th Gurkhas were to patrol aggressively against Tumbledown and Mount William in the hope that the defenders would surrender. If the two features did not fall, both battalions were to mount a co-ordinated daylight attack on Tumbledown from the south-west at first light on the 12th, the Gurkhas seizing Mount William; the Welsh Guards would then advance on Sapper Hill. Major Bethell remarked to Lieutenant Colonel Scott the plan would not work and went to bed. Next morning he was light-heartedly accused by Scott of causing him a sleepless night, but Bethell insisted that battalions had not rehearsed such a complex operation, and if they ran into a minefield, breaching would take time and both battal-ions could therefore hit the objective piecemeal. Scott then told Bethell he wanted a diversion.

In preparation for the next phase, Lieutenant Colonel Scott sent a heli-copter to recover Captain Scott, the Recce Platoon commander, from Port Harriet House, which effectively compromised Operation *Impunity*. With indications that the Soria's 4th Infantry Regiment were preparing to deal with the British presence, Recce Platoon withdrew toward North Basin but were mortared and came under small arms fire from Mount Harriet, which caused three casualties, including Allum. These were evacuated by helicopter and Captain Scott returned to guide the remainder through a minefield to be met by 3rd Troop Blues and Royals. The Argentines later claimed they had defeated a Welsh Guards attack.

The Blues and Royals had been switched from 3rd Commando Brigade to 5th Infantry Brigade to take advantage of the better going in the south. Leaving Estancia, the two Troops crossed the central range of hills and arrived at Bluff Cove six hours later, instead of the expected thirty-six hours, which again discredited the sceptics who did not believe the CVR(T)s could handle difficult terrain. 2 Para passed back under command of 3rd Commando Brigade for the attack on Wireless Ridge.

12 June dawned bright but cold. During the night, as we have seen, 3rd Commando Brigade had destroyed 4th Infantry Regiment and severely damaged 7th Infantry Regiment but were unable to exploit to Tumbledown. Brigadier Wilson was under intense pressure to follow through as planned and, according to Major Chris Davies, who commanded 9 Para Squadron RE, was keen to do so. Davies and Lieutenant Colonel Tony Holt pleaded with him to resist the urgency because the guns needed to be brought forward

and the objective softened up before sending in the infantry. Davies recalls: 'It would have been madness to expect the Scots Guards and Gurkhas to go virtually from line of march into a complex night attack over completely new ground.' Thompson was sympathetic and, before Moore joined them at his headquarters on Mount Kent, suggested to Wilson that he apply for a twenty-four hour delay. Moore agreed; nevertheless the decision was greeted with some irritation at 3rd Commando Brigade, which was further incensed when its HQ was attacked by 5 Group Skyhawks during the afternoon and forced to carry out a crash move while preparing for 2 Para's attack on Wireless Ridge.

Moore also agreed to Thompson's suggestion the Scots Guards should attack Tumbledown at night from Goat Ridge, with 42 Commando securing their start line. Patrolling against Tumbledown was out of the question, but Scott managed to fly his company commanders and key officers to observe Tumbledown from Goat Ridge and Mount Harriet. Richard Bethell found the diversion Scott was seeking, a small Argentine position west of Pony's Pass.

Early on 13 June Sea Kings lifted the Scots Guards on to Goat Ridge where the guardsmen carried out their battle preparations amid intermittent shelling, losing one man wounded. Precious little Intelligence had arrived from documents or the 400 prisoners being processed at Fitzroy and thus both 2 Para and the Scots Guards had little information on the Inner Defence Zone. With H-Hour set for 9pm, Scott issued his confirmatory orders at 2pm for a four-phase silent night attack beginning with the diversionary attack by Headquarters Company concurrent with the three rifle companies advancing from Goat Ridge and each seizing a portion of Tumbledown. The general axis of advance was directed at the northern end of the saddle between Tumbledon and Mount William. The ridge was barely wide enough for a platoon to spread out and company dispositions in fire support was going to be critical. Support Company was sited to give maximum support and on call was the Divisional artillery, naval gunfire support from *Arrow* and *Yarmouth* and the 42 Commando and 1/7th Gurkhas mortars. Six sleeping bags per company were to be taken for casualties and the password 'Hey, Jimmy' was adopted because the Argentines could not pronounce the letter J in English. The distinctive khaki berets could be worn to aid identification from the helmeted Argentines, but helmets were to be carried. This seems an extraordinary decision. However the 1944 pattern helmets were awkward and uncomfortable when running, leaping and diving for cover.

5th Marine Infantry Battalion had supported 4th Infantry Regiment and Robacio, knowing he would be attacked next, reinforced O Company with an amphibious engineer platoon. Of Soria's surviving platoons, Lieutenants Silva's 4th Infantry and Mosterin's 12th Infantry Regiments platoons joined Sub Lieutenants Vasquez and Mino on Tumbledown from Mount Harriet, making about ninety men defending the summit. Jimenez-Corvalan, who had also escaped from Mount Harriet, moved on to Mount William and Llambias-Pravaz, from Two Sisters, withdrew to Sapper Hill. Captain Ferrero's 602 Commando Company assault section moved into an anti-tank position south-west of Mount William. On the ridge Vasquez had two major problems – too few radios, which meant orders would have to be relayed by runner, and his positions originally faced south to cover the road from Fitzroy, the expected axis of attack. His men hurriedly adjusted themselves to face west.

Avoiding encirclement when the Outer Defence Zone collapsed, Oscar Jaimet's B Company withdrew to the northern slopes of Tumbledown from its blocking position covering the Estancia track. According to a map later recovered from a prisoner-of-war, the inter-unit boundary between him and the Marines ran along the spine of the central ridge. Major Berazay and A Company, 3rd Infantry Regiment, covered the road to Estancia with orders to support either Tumbledown or Wireless Ridge. Two platoons of 181 Armoured Recce Squadron moved into low ground east of Mount Longdon covering the track from Estancia.

Soon after 4pm Bethell briefed his men at Mount Harriet House, a composite platoon of twelve men from Recce Platoon, an LMG fire support group from A1 Echelon commanded by Company Sergeant Major Braby, Coreth's 4th Troop Blues and Royals, two sappers from 3rd Troop 9 Para Squadron RE and a battalion mortar fire controller, Corporal Miller. An hour later the platoon clambered on to the CVR(T)s. The moon had yet to rise and a nasty cold wind spilled snow through the darkness. The ground was pitted with peat banks and known to be littered with mines, two types identified so far, powerful enough to wreck light armoured vehicles. The two sappers cleared the route and, with Bethell periodically sweeping the ground with his cumbersome night sight, it was inevitable that the march took longer than expected. At about 6.30pm the infantry dismounted and the Blues and Royals moved into cover. Coreth's orders were to give direct fire support on to known Argentine positions at H-30 minutes for one hour.

By about 8.30pm, after three false alerts on positions thought to be Argentine, Bethell knew he had to create some sort of diversion to persuade the Argentines that the attack was coming from the south, as expected, and help G Company get a foothold on Tumbledown. Making another sweep, he saw outlines which suggested trenches about seventy metres ahead and sent Braby to find a fire support position to the south. Bethell cautiously led the assault group toward the shapes and they became three trenches. When sounds were heard from inside one, Bethell told Drill Sergeant Danny White to grenade the left one, while he took the centre and Lance Corporal Pashley RE attacked the right. As the grenades exploded, wounding two marines, positions in depth opened fire almost simultaneously, killing White and Pashley. Braby's group had some difficulty in suppressing the enemy fire as the assault group battled their way into the Argentine

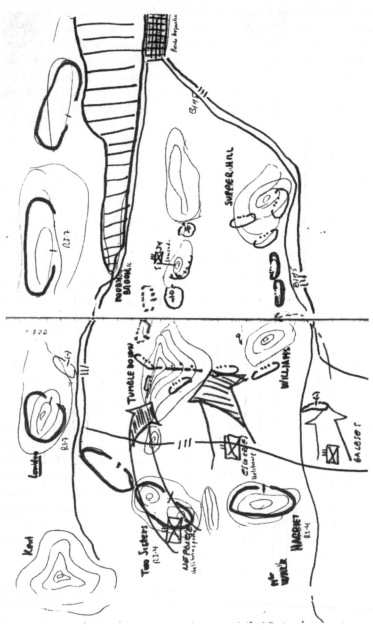

Map captured during search of prisoners on the *St Edmund*. Probably compiled by Commander Robacio as part of an internal inquiry into the performance of the 5th Marine Infantry Battalion. It shows his belief that the Scots Guards (*Escosse*) attacked the saddle in between Tumbledown and Mount William and the Gurkhas (*Nepalese*) attacking Tumbledown. It also shows the Argentines belief of a regimental-size diversionary attack against the platoon west of Pony Pass.

198

position. The fighting was close-quarter, Bethell, Sergeant Coull and Drummer Ward attacking several trenches by crawling underneath the lip of a peat bank and lobbing grenades over the top. It took nearly two hours to fight through eleven positions and Bethell only halted when there was no more return fire. With two killed and four wounded, he had three options – to remain where he was, keep up the diversion or withdraw. Learning that Corporal Miller had lost communications with Battalion headquarters, Bethell radioed Coreth to come forward and, after loosing off a couple of LMG magazines, he returned to the three trenches where the pipers were dealing with the casualties.

Bethell was about to withdraw when an Argentine survivor in the right trench was shot dead as he threw a grenade which exploded, wounding Piper Duffy in the chest and Bethell in the legs. Covered by Sergeant Coull and in the knowledge they could be counter-attacked at any time, the platoon set off, but Sergeant Ian Miller trod on a mine and four more casualties were taken, all of whom had been carrying the dead and wounded. The detonations prompted intense shelling of the area for forty minutes and more casualties would have been taken had not the soft peat absorbed the impact of the shells; nevertheless debris flew all over the place. In view of the priority to get the wounded to safety, the two dead were abandoned. Using a torch, Bethell and Duffy carved a path out of the minefield. According to Richard Bethell, they had some interesting discussions on what was a mine and what was not; fortunately most were either surface-laid or could be seen underneath the turf when approached from the Argentine defences.

For Coreth the hours had ticked by slowly. Nothing was heard from Bethell; indeed, communications with him became progressively worse. He had heard the outbreak of firing and the bark of grenades and, from intermittent radio transmissions, it was obvious the guardsmen were in trouble, so he was relieved to be called forward. As the vehicles broke cover a flare exposed them, which was quickly followed by shelling. Coming across a 155mm crater in the middle of the road, Coreth by-passed it to the left, but his Scorpion had barely moved off the track when it hit an anti-tank mine which, according to Corporal of Horse Paul Stretton in the following CVR(T), lifted the 8.5-ton armoured vehicle three feet into the air, severing the engine mountings, shredding both tracks and blowing off most of the roadwheels. Coreth knew it was vital to provide Bethell's battered infantry with fire support, but the threat of mines confined the CVR(T)'s to the road. In spite of Argentine shelling plastering the area, with considerable gallantry he organized the Troop to fire at the positions on Tumbledown and Mount William. Coreth describes the situation: 'It became a crazy shoot from one vehicle, sitting on the outside, reverse him, climb onto another, bring him forward, fire and so on till the last. There was some excellent shooting by all vehicles.' The next day sappers removed fifty-seven mines from the vicinity of his wrecked Scorpion, although the turret was in working order. It is probable that it was sufficiently robust to withstand the blast and light enough to absorb the shock of being thrown into the air.

At about 10.30pm, just as Major John Kiszely's Left Flank Company had their first contact on Tumbledown, as we shall see, Bethell's bruised and battered platoon reached Coreth's troop and were taken back to the 42 Commando A Echelon at Mount Harriet House where the wounded were flown to Ajax Bay and most then transferred to the *Uganda*. In human terms, it was an expensive operation, nearly fifty per cent of the platoon having been wounded and counting themselves lucky to suffer only two dead. However, in strategic terms the diversion focused the attention of the 5th Marine Infantry Battalion on to the Fitzroy track, suggesting to Army Group Puerto Argentino that the main assault was coming from the south and allowed the Scots Guards to gain a foothold on the mountain. In many respects it was a decisive action. Moro, who flew with 1st Transport Group (Hercules) in the campaign, claims the Scorpion was mined before the infantry attack and that the diversion cost sixty men 'littered about the field' as they withdrew to the south but ran into a heavy artillery bombardment. Surprisingly, there were few awards, Corporal John Foran RE receiving the Military Medal for his gallantry in clearing paths through the minefields. Richard Bethell was only Mentioned in Despatches.

Meanwhile, guided by the occasional shell fired by 29 Battery, Major Ian Dalzell-Job's G Company crossed the start line, a wire fence, and advanced without incident across the 2500 yards of open ground to the western slopes of Tumbledown. Progress was deliberate and interrupted only by the occasional flare soaring high into the darkness and shells and mortar bombs thumping into the peat. Several abandoned Argentine positions were cleared and by 10.30pm G Company were firm. Phase two was complete.

Left Flank took over the advance, its objective being the highest point of Tumbledown. Second Lieutenant John Stuart's 13 Platoon moved through the crags on the left, ready to support Lieutenant Alisdair Mitchell's 15 Platoon cautiously advancing across the open ground below them with Company HQ and 14 Platoon in reserve. On the main feature, about 400 yards ahead of them, Mino's engineers, Vasquez' marines and Silva's and Mosterin's infantry watched through their sights and then opened fire. The darkness ahead of the advancing guardsmen lit up in a ripple of white flashes as tracer split the night, bullets cracked and thumped overhead and rock splinters whizzed all over the place. Caught in the open, they sought cover wherever they could. Mitchell recalled, 'We recovered rapidly and the Argentinians never again put down quite that weight of fire. Even so, our first introduction was slightly shocking. It just showed how much firepower they had.' Immediate section attacks were defeated by the sheer weight of fire. Guardsman Ronald Tabini died respectfully telling Company Sergeant Major Bill Nicol, 'I've been shot, sir'. Nicol then went to the aid of the mortally wounded Platoon Sergeant Simeon and was also wounded, all three probably shot by the same rifleman. B Battery Marine Field Artillery then shelled Tumbledown, adding to the Scots Guards' discomfort.

The shock of the firestorm brought the company to a halt but the guardsmen knew it was vital to win the firefight before an advance could be made. Following a cable, Lance Sergeants McGuiness and Davidson's section destroyed a number of sangars. Guardsman James Reynolds organized several attacks. The fighting then became personal when the Argentines began to taunt the guardsmen. For three hours Left Flank was pinned down. It began snowing heavily and clouds drifted across the full moon, alternately throwing the battlefield into darkness and then casting eerie shadows across the rocks. The gunners' forward observation party had become separated from Kiszely in the scramble to find cover and Lieutenant Colonel Scott had trouble organizing artillery support. The Support Company machine gunners were operating at extreme range and the 81mm mortar crews fought to keep their tubes on a stable platform. At about 2.30am Robacio brought O Company back to a position on the saddle between Tumbledown and Mount William. The Scots Guards were now faced with two companies.

Over the radio Scott and Kiszely planned to break the Argentine resistance in a simple and classic strategy – a short barrage followed by a standard fire and movement infantry attack. Because they were high up and could use the rocks for cover, 13 Platoon were best placed to provide fire support and wormed their way into positions overlooking Vasquez's infantry. With Nicol's help, Stuart divided his guardsmen into groups of machine gunners, anti-tank men and riflemen. As the third artillery salvo smashed into the peat and rocks 13 Platoon opened fire, which was the signal for Left Flank to advance. In spite of the fusillade, Vasquez was surprised when Mino's engineers, fighting in the rocks behind his marine infantry, began to leave their positions because he had not been told they were pulling out. In fact they had broken under the weight of fire.

Kiszely found himself in front of 15 Platoon and was heard to shout, 'Are you with me, 15 Platoon?' Silence. 'Come on, 15 Platoon, are you with me?' Silence, and then a reluctant 'Och, aye, sir. I'm with you!' and 'Aye, sir. I'm f........ with you!' from the other side. Led by their company commander, 15 Platoon surged up the slope and charged the marines with bayonets fixed. Kiszely stabbed a dark figure who collapsed back into his trench holding his chest. The Argentine marines and army were slowly overwhelmed, losing seven marines and five army killed, several wounded and others missing. Left Flank bit deep into Vasquez' defences and eventually Kiszely and seven men reached the summit. There was a violent scuffle in the darkness among the rocks before the last of the defenders were driven off. Far below the British saw the lights of Stanley, the ultimate objective. But the fighting was far from over.

Major Jaimet had moved on to the saddle and, leaving his 81mm mortar platoon with the marines, at about 4.30am he launched Second Lieutenant

Augusto La Madrid's 1st Platoon at Left Flank to relieve the pressure on Vasquez. La Madrid knew the theory of night fighting and, although several of his men had helmet-mounted night-vision devices and they were willing, none of them had seen the ground over which they were about to advance. His orders were simple – advance and allow no one to pass. Any withdrawing Argentines were to join his platoon. A machine gunner opened fire on the summit, felling three of the Scots Guards, including Mitchell, who was badly wounded in the legs. While Kiszely anxiously waited for Right Flank to take over the advance, several 15 Platoon, Company HQ and 14 Platoon, still almost at full strength, arrived. It had taken seven hours to reach the summit. Behind them Piper Ridges, the company medic, worked on the wounded from both sides. By the time Right Flank arrived Mitchell's wounds were beginning to hurt and shock was setting in. Of his platoon of twenty-nine two were killed and twelve wounded.

After receiving a situation report from Kiszely, Major Price ordered 2 and 3 Platoons to advance in a right hook aimed at the eastern end. Artillery support was again unavailable. In the saddle between centre and eastern summits Right Flank and La Madrid's platoon clashed with Corporal Marco Palomo's section taking the brunt. Private Montoya is said to have wrestled with a guardsman. 2 Platoon was held up by Argentines on a narrow ridge, but yard by yard 3 Platoon seeped around the Argentines' right flank and briefly cut La Madrid off from Jaimet. Covered by Palomo's section La Madrid withdrew, but the Scots Guards advanced quickly and the fighting was close-quarter.

At about 8am as a grey dawn crept over Stanley, Robacio was organizing a counter-attack by Quiroga's O Company and Jaimet's company when he was ordered by Brigadier General Jofre's Chief of Staff, Colonel Felix Aguiar, to evacuate Tumbledown. Robacio and Jaimet were furious because they believed they were holding the Scots Guards although it was six years before the latter openly criticized the decision.

First Sergeant Lucero's platoon counter-attacked to relieve the pressure of La Madrid's hard-pressed infantry and then covered the Argentine with-drawal, first to Mount William and then Sapper Hill, leaving Tumbledown to the Scots Guards. Five Scots Guards were wounded, including Lieutenant Robert Lawrence, who was shot in the head in the final stages of the battle, possibly during Lucero's counter-attack. His recovery was miraculous. Of his engineer platoon, Mino was the only one wounded during the night. When La Madrid reorganized to retire, he mustered just sixteen left from the forty-five who had started the counter-attack; several had been captured. One of his men was so impressed with the Scots Guards that he described them as 'panthers in the dark'. The counter-attack on Tumbledown was too weak and too late. Had the radios and night-sights of Jaimet's platoons been fully charged and mortar and machine gun ammunition not been wasted supporting Wireless Ridge, all B Company could have counter-attacked and bought time to allow M Company to be moved from Mount William on to Tumbledown. It was another missed opportunity.

N Company lost seven killed, the two 4th Infantry Regiment platoons five and Jaimet's company eight in the counter-attack. About fifty were wounded. The cost to the Scots Guards was also high, nine killed and forty-three wounded, but the battle was not quite over. Right Flank moved forward to secure the eastern slopes but had trouble re-organizing because platoons and sections had become hopelessly muddled in the final attack. This attracted long-range but effective machine-gun and mortar fire on to the eastern summit.

Apart from capturing ten Argentines near Egg Harbour, the 1/7th Gurkhas' war had been uneventful. But Lieutenant Colonel David Morgan was anxious. The longer the Argentines on Tumbledown held out, the less chance his strong battalion of four companies would have of attacking Mount William under cover of darkness. His offer to help the Scots Guards was turned down by Scott and, after waiting all night in their assembly area on Goat Ridge, Brigadier Wilson at last let the Gurkhas loose. Led by 9 Para RE and under shelling which cost eight wounded, the long column picked up a sheep's path north of Tumbledown, bypassed a minefield and then the assault engineers probed their way through another. B Company swung right and captured a few 6th Infantry Regiment still on the eastern slopes of Tumbledown. A and Support Companies set up a fire base on Tumbledown Mount to shoot D Company on to Mount William, then advancing across the saddle. By now 5th Marine Infantry Battalion had withdrawn to Sapper Hill and 1/7th Gurkhas captured Mount William with barely a shot fired but found a dead marine mortarman.

Casualty evacuation is a precarious business at the best of times, never more so than under fire. It was not until daylight that stretcher-bearers arrived to collect Alisdair Mitchell. Tumbledown was being mortared and a bomb landed near the party, hurling them to the ground. Guardsman Reynolds, who had already been wounded carrying Mitchell, was one of two killed instantly and eight wounded; for his gallantry during the night he was posthumously awarded a Distinguished Conduct Medal. The stretcher in tatters, Guardsman Findley let Mitchell use his SLR as a crutch and helped him hobble down the slope. It was later suggested that the Argentines deliberately attacked stretcher-bearers on Tumbledown. A mortar is an area weapon and the Argentines on Sapper Hill were bombarding movement on Tumbledown in much the same way their gunners were shelling the Outer Defence Zone. It is also of interest that while Argentine medical personnel were clearly identified with the Red Cross on brassards and helmets, British medics wore no such insignia.

When the Argentines believed that a British landing might be at Berkeley Sound, Wireless Ridge, known to the Argentines as *Cordon de la Radio*, had a major role for the defence of Stanley. It was also seen to be key to the approach to Stanley by the British and consequently it was bombarded by ships, shelled by artillery and raided by Harriers. By early June the men of the 7th Infantry Regiment, considered to be the best unit in 10th Infantry Brigade, and who now occupied Wireless Ridge, were tired, demoralized and, with defeat inevitable, were in no mood to fight and just wanted to survive.

After losing Longdon, Lieutenant Colonel Gimenez knew Wireless Ridge would be the next, but he had lost B Company and several key officers. He later commented, 'We had the doubtful honour of fighting the British twice'. More strongly held than Mount Longdon, his defence lay behind a stream in low boggy ground which spilled into the Murrell River. On the 250-foot-high marshy feature known to the British as *Rough Diamond* was First Lieutenant Hugo Garcia's C Company. Sandwiched between Recce Platoon, in low ground north of the Stanley to Estancia track, was its 1st Platoon. During the night of 12/13 June two platoons of 10th Armoured Recce Squadron, commanded by Lieutenant Luis Bertolini and Second Lieutenant Diego Harrington, who had been covering the road and directing the shelling of Mount Longdon, were pulled back behind Recce Platoon. On *Apple Pie*, across a saddle, was First Lieutenant Jorge Calvos' A Company with a platoon on a small feature known as Position X, which overlooked the Murrell River. South across the road was Major Guillermo Berazay with A Company 3rd Infantry Regiment, on call to 5th Marine Infantry Battalion but available to 7th Infantry Regiment. Spread along Wireless Ridge itself, known as *Blueberry Pie,* was Command Company and the 2nd Airborne Infantry Regiment platoon. Gimenez placed his HQ east of the rocky summit of Wireless Ridge.

On 10 June 2 Para reverted to 3rd Commando Brigade. The parachute and commando sapper recce sections linked up with the battalion assault engineers to form a composite engineer organization commanded by Lieutenant Livingstone. Next night the battalion, in reserve to 3 Para and 45 Commando, huddled in a re-entrant not far from the commando regimental aid post and next day moved to an assembly area at Furze Bush Pass expecting to attack Wireless Ridge that night. The paras dozed in the bright sunshine, although many would have welcomed their sleeping bags and a proper sleep. Brigadier Thompson's attack on Wireless Ridge was planned as a preliminary to launching his brigade across Moody Brook Valley and deep into Argentine positions on Stanley Common.

Lieutenant Innes-Ker's 3rd Troop, Blues and Royals, then under command of 2 Para, drove to Fitzroy. When they arrived, each Scorpion was carrying ninety-seven extra rounds of 76mm ammunition and the Scimitars an extra 285 of 30mm. Lieutenant Livingstone found it 'was very reassuring to hear the roar of the Scimitars and Scorpions arriving to support our attack'. Also invited to join 2 Para as the Armoured Liaison Officer was Captain Richard Field of the Blues and Royals, one of two cavalry watchkeepers at HQ 5th

Infantry Brigade advising on the use of armour. Tabbing with the infantry, he recalled that his 'original Sandhurst view of life was utterly correct, namely, that anybody doing what I was now doing when they could be in a nice, warm armoured car, must be mad'.

A Scimitar with gearbox problems and the Samson recovery vehicle were left behind, but the twenty-four-hour delay between the brigade attacks allowed them to rejoin the troop during the night of 13 June. This was the only major engine failure suffered by the Blues and Royals, which speaks much for the reliability of the CVR(T)s and the expert crew maintenance. As the Samson, which was also loaded with spare ammunition, was crossing the rickety Murrell River bridge, it collapsed dumping the vehicle in the stream. The bridge was critical to 3rd Commando Brigade's logistics so the only Airportable Bridge, then at Fitzroy, was released by Lieutenant Colonel Field, Commander Royal Engineers. 1st Section 9 Squadron Para RE assembled it and then Staff Sergeant Yorke convinced the Chinook pilot, 'if you take it easy', to fly it to Murrell Bridge where it was installed by 59 Independent Commando Squadron RE. The Samson was lifted out of the river by the Chinook. A year later Major Davies, working on the principle that if it works in war it ought to work in peace, tried the same trick on exercise, but this time a strop broke, the helicopter wobbled and the bridge crashed into a Scottish wood. It took a week to recover and an inquiry to explain the accident and damage to the trees.

Shortly before dark on 12 June Major Hector Gullen, Thompson's liaison officer, arrived at 2 Para with the instructions, 'It's Wireless Ridge, tonight' and Lieutenant Colonel Chaundler began planning the operation, but he then received a message from Brigade Headquarters that Major General Moore had given 5th Infantry Brigade twenty-four hours' delay before Phase Two. The paras settled down to a second chilly night without sleeping bags, most sleeping fitfully as a sharp frost carpeted the moors.

Chaundler's plan called for a four-phase noisy night attack from the north, not the west as expected by Gimenez, in co-ordinated company attacks supported by close, direct and indirect fire support from 'Black Eight', 79 Commando Battery, the Blues and Royals and *Ambuscade*. The engineers were dispersed in sections with the rifle companies, with 2 Para's Assault Engineer Platoon initially assigned to protect the Blues and Royals. Needless to record, the paras' view on how the armour should be used differed markedly from those who used it. In Phase One D Company were to seize *Rough Diamond* and then, in Phase Two, A and B Companies would attack *Apple Pie*. For Phase Three C Company was to attack Position X, which was also the limit of eastern exploitation, and finally D Company would seize *Blueberry Pie* and advance east toward Cortley Hill. The plan was the nearest the British reached to an all-arms attack, something that had been rejected at Goose Green. The ground was boggy, dotted with ponds and small lakes, indeed, during the advance two men had to be hauled out of deep, ice-

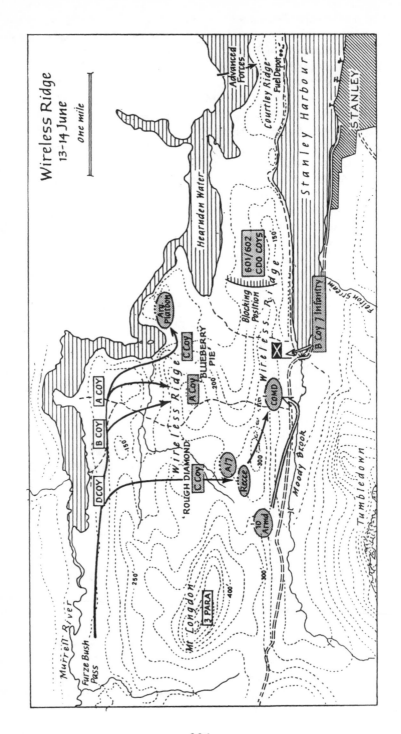

Wireless Ridge
13-14 June

one mile

Advanced
Forces

Courtley Ridge
Fuel Depot

Stanley Harbour

STANLEY

Hearnden Water

601/602
CDO COYS

— 150 —

Blocking
Position

the Wireless Ridge

Fellon Stream

B COY Infantry

Arty
Platoon

C COY

BLUEBERRY
PIE

200

A COY

A COY

B COY

150

D COY

D COY

'ROUGH DIAMOND'

C COY

A11
Recce

CMD

300

Moody Brook

10
Armd

Murrell River

Furze Bush
Pass

250

Mt Longdon

400

3 PARA

300

Tumbledown

covered ponds. Chaundler said that the assault would be supported by an SAS diversionary attack on Cortley Hill, although after 2 Para's experiences before Goose Green, there were some misgivings about what the SAS were meant to do as opposed to what they would do.

During the afternoon Chaundler was given his final orders by Thompson at Brigade Headquarters shortly before it crash-moved after being bombed by the Skyhawks. His communication with Thompson then became difficult and Livingstone's sapper section found itself transmitting messages and relaying reports to Brigade Headquarters via the 59 Commando Squadron RE desk. 2 Para then moved to about 600 metres north of Wireless Ridge. When night fell it was bitterly cold and frequent snow showers shielding a bright full moon behind scudding clouds swept across the dark moors.

C (Patrol) Company, as usual, secured the start line, but were caught by an airburst and some adjustment was made to avoid more shelling. By 10pm everything was ready. Earlier in the evening Major Gullen had arrived with very recent intelligence suggesting that a minefield protected the northern approaches to *Apple Pie,* but Chaundler was not keen to change the plan so late and seems to have told no one about the new information. At 1.45am Wireless Ridge was shelled to soften up the defenders. The Blues and Royals fired on two suspected LVTPs in hull-down positions, although another snowstorm prevented observation of the fall of shot. It is most unlikely the shapes were amtracs or indeed any Argentine vehicles.

At 2am Major Neame's D Company advanced across very boggy ground against limited opposition. On *Rough Diamond* Garcia's C Company was nervous and when they came under heavy fire from 2 Para's Machine Gun Platoon and the Blues and Royals they quickly folded and withdrew in haste. During the night Machine Gun Platoon fired 40,000 rounds and four mortarmen broke their ankles keeping the baseplates steady in the soft peat. The accuracy and high rate of the Scimitar six-clip 30mm Rarden cannon greatly boosted 2 Para's morale. A pre-registered target, D Battery 3rd Artillery Group 155mms forced the paras to shelter in the abandoned positions for the next two phases by accurately shelling *Rough Diamond.* A and B Companies were initially repulsed by Calvo's A Company on *Apple Pie,* but after shelling softened the defenders, it was captured after a short but fierce battle. They were then shelled and lost a man. Meanwhile the teenagers on Position X withdrew, abandoning tents and equipment, shortly before Patrol Company captured it at about 10.45pm. Supported by the remainder of 2 Para and the Blues and Royals on *Apple Pie,* D Company advanced south to its second objective, *Blueberry Pie.* The CVR(T)s had already found the going rough and two vehicles were hauled out of deep 155mm craters. Lance Corporal of Horse Dunkeley was also knocked out when his cupola latch snapped and when Trooper Ford guided the Scimitar to the RAP he met Captain Field, who leapt at the opportunity to command the vehicle, but not the troop. That was Lieutenant Innes-Ker's responsibility.

Beginning Phase Four, Neame's company crossed two small streams, climbed on to the western crags of Wireless Ridge and, advancing east, met stiffening resistance from the airborne infantry platoon in positions covering Gimenez's CP. The Blues and Royals played a key role in suppressing Argentine fire, but, while jockeying between positions, Innes-Ker's Scorpion snapped a sprocket which was repaired under heavy shelling. After a short delay because artillery was diverted to support the withdrawal of the Advanced Forces from Cortley Hill, D Company advanced toward *Blueberry Hill* against the remnants of 7th Infantry Regiment. But resistance stiffened and 12 Platoon became involved in a short and nasty firefight with Second Lieutenant Aristegui's 3rd Infantry Regiment platoon. He had been commissioned in April. While reorganizing, the paras came under rifle and machine-gun fire from Major Jaimet's rifle and Sergeant Lucero's mortar platoons on the northern slopes of Tumbledown, which Neame described as 'an interesting affair'.

Earlier Brigadier-General Jofre instructed Major Berazay to assemble his 3rd Infantry Regiment company, 10th Armoured Recce Squadron and B Company 25th Special Infantry Regiment, who were marching from Stanley Airport, at the ruins of Moody Brook for a regimental-sized counter-attack. In support was 4th Airborne Artillery Group. When Berazay arrived at the shattered barracks there was no sign of the infantry but about seventy cavalrymen from Bertolini's and Harrington's platoons who had retreated after making a stand at the western slopes of Wireless Ridge. Shattered by the weight of fire unleashed on them, they had lost six killed, had nearly fifty wounded and were in disorder after an ineffectual, if confident, unco-ordinated night counter-attack. It was during this action that their Mortar Platoon at Moody Brook engaged the Blues and Royals, technically the only armoured action of the war.

With no sign of the 25th Infantry Regiment company, Jofre told Berazay to wait for the 25th Infantry Regiment company but when they failed to appear, Berazay placed machine guns near a small building and Second Lieutenant Diego Aristegui and Lieutenant Victor Rodriguez-Perez led their platoons of conscripts up the hill in open order. Aristegui was then badly wounded but both platoons carried on and soon became engaged in a lengthy fight with D Company.

Private Patricio Perez, who had just left school, recalls the unnerving experience of 66mm coming straight at them like undulating fireballs. He believes he shot someone and then lost his temper when he heard that his friend Private Horacio Benitez had been killed. Rodriguez-Perez's platoon, growing in confidence, closed with 12 Platoon, now under command of Lieutenant Jonathan Page after the death of Lieutenant Barry at Goose Green, and for the next two hours fighting raged around a line of telegraph poles. Eventually the Argentines were forced to withdraw, leaving four wounded, including one soldier badly burnt by a phosphorous grenade, and three killed in this forlorn hope. Benitez had not been killed, only wounded. Recovering from his wounds after the war, he and the other wounded kept in touch and founded the Malvinas Veterans of the Mutual Co-operative Trading and Social Centre in Buenos Aires. Several British veterans and commentators have met Argentine veterans through this society.

By about 4.30am, Gimenez knew 7th Infantry Regiment had been decisively defeated; 'Communications are lost, my whole regiment is finished' but, with the promise of reinforcements, he continued to defend Wireless Ridge. Near the church in Stanley, intent on helping Berazay, Major Carrizo-Salvadores, helped by army chaplain Father Fernandez, assembled about a platoon, issued each man with a fresh magazine and, with everyone singing the *Malvinas March*, led them at the centre of Wireless Ridge from Moody Brook. When 2 Para saw the Argentine platoon, it caused considerable alarm because the paras weren't sure who they were up against, although some thought it to be a strong patrol. D Company was still reorganizing, small arms and artillery ammunition was very short and orders were passed to fix bayonets. Chaundler sought a fire mission and gave orders to fire anything and everything at the Argentines coming up the hill. Carrizo-Salvadores's last-ditch attack was defeated but it won the admiration of the paras. Reluctantly withdrawing, he joined Gimenez forming a defensive position around the Felton Stream bridge.

By 7am the fighting on Wireless Ridge had died down and with the failure of the counter-attacks, Jofre reluctantly authorized Berazay to abandon his position. Most of the battered 7th Infantry Regiment assembled at the Racecourse where Menendez visited them. During its two battles with the British, most of the officers were either killed, wounded or captured. Of the 130 NCOs, twenty-two had been killed.

Raid on Cortley Hill

While 2 Para were preparing to attack Wireless Ridge, HQ LFFI authorized an Advanced Forces raid on Cortley Hill, the idea being to give the impression of an amphibious landing to link up with 2 Para.

Defending the refinery was Lieutenant Hector Gazollo's 3rd Platoon and part of the Heavy Weapons Platoon, both from H Company, 3rd Marine Infantry Battalion. Brigadier General Jofre allocated them two 2" mortars captured from NP 8901. The defence was later enhanced by B Battery 101st Anti Aircraft Regiment, which had eight 30mm Hispano-Suiza guns and ten .50 Browning machine guns, commanded by Major Monge. The unit formed the northern arc of the Stanley garrison air defence system and had arrived on one of the last three ships to breach the blockade. The sector was largely unaffected by the bombardment of Stanley, although it had stood-by to reinforce the embattled defenders on Mount Longdon. During 12 June the two army commando companies took up a blocking position several hundred yards to the east of the fuel tanks where they remained until the surrender.

The original idea was for an eight-strong 3 SBS patrol to swim across the Murrell River to Wireless Ridge and then advance on the Argentine positions. When this scheme became impractical, two troops of D and one of G Squadron joined for a hurriedly planned raid. The idea was to secure a beach with a recce patrol and then land the assault group. In direct support was a GPMG(SF) team and 60mm mortar on high ground between Weir Creek and Blanco Bay. Hugh McManners, on Beagle Ridge, tried to arrange naval gunfire support but was told there were other priorities.

On 12 June Sergeant Buckle and his coxswains, Lance Corporal Gilbert and Marines Kavanagh and Nordic, left *Fearless* and were towed by the minesweeper-trawler HMS *Cordella* to Berkeley Sound where they lay up on Cochon Island. Next night they met up with the Advanced Forces at Blanco Bay and then, with nine soldiers to each Rigid Raider, they raced across Port William Bay. But they had the misfortune to be heard by a National Gendarmerie commando on board the *Almirante Irizar*. He was part of a Special Forces infiltration operation en route to Beagle Ridge to raid and direct air and 155mm artillery on to the British rear and was on board collecting supplies. The Gendarme not unnaturally switched on a searchlight to find out what was happening and caught the boats full in the beam. Major Monge was alerted and the Argentines opened up, forcing the coxswains to jink and jive between the columns of sea water latticed by machine-gun fire. Splinters ripped into the hulls. Most of the raiding party landed but heavy fire prevented exploitation.

McManners was shivering in his OP when he heard on his radio a report from the raiding party that they had encountered strong opposition and wanted artillery support to cover the withdrawal. He spent a frustrating forty minutes attempting to organize naval gunfire support but without luck, so he switched frequency and asked Captain John Keeling, adjutant of 29 Commando Regiment then supporting 2 Para, if he could help and gave him the grid reference of a suspected battery behind Cortley Hill. The request was greeted with some derision at 3rd Commando Brigade Headquarters where some felt that Advanced Forces activities were taking preference over its operations. Nevertheless Keeling told McManners that thirty-six rounds would be fired for effect.

On the beach the Advanced Forces were in turmoil. Gazollo's marines poured heavy fire on to the beach and anyone who raised his head from cover was liable to have it shot off. An SBS NCO and two SAS were wounded, one in considerable pain after being hit in the groin. On the waterline the coxswains worked frantically to keep the temperamental outboard engines running, and then, as shells bracketed Cortley Hill, nudged their boats forward to collect the raiding party. One Rigid Raider was badly damaged and, creeping past the *Almirante Irizar*, the coxswain made landfall near Watts Bay, where it and two other boats were set on fire. Another sank a few metres offshore and the occupants had to swim ashore.

The Argentines on Cortley Hill were jubilant. In achieving its aim the raid achieved very little, indeed, according to Parker in his book *SBS*, the Advanced Forces admitted they had broken a cardinal rule by carrying out a 'Boys' Own' comic raid, almost because they did not want to miss the fun. Far from diverting Argentine pressure on 2 Para, urgently needed artillery had to be diverted to extract them from the crisis in which the raiders found themselves. But according to Ruiz-Moreno in his book *Commandos in Action,* the raid shattered Argentine plans to insert Special Forces in the British rear areas.

3rd Commando and 5th Infantry Brigades had bitten deep into Army Group Puerto Argentino and, although reorganizing was taking time, there was no evidence that Jofre was contemplating a counter-attack, even though he had virtually a brigade, with armoured recce and four batteries of field artillery, at his disposal around Sapper Hill. 5th Infantry Brigade was probably the most vulnerable to counter-attack. This blunder was decisive and would cost the Argentines dear.

11

Surrender and the Final Battle

14 June to 14 July

"Oh good, the men will be pleased." The Commander at Pebble Island
on being told of the Argentine surrender.

By 7am the Argentines were very close to defeat. Argentine columns were
retreating from Moody Brook to Stanley in such a disorganized manner that
Lieutenant Colonel Comini had to cancel a counter-attack against Wireless
Ridge which hardline elements in his 3rd Infantry Regiment were planning,
using the early morning mist as cover. The remnants of Berazay's 3rd
Infantry Regiment company were withdrawing through 4th Airborne
Artillery Group's gun positions around Felton Stream, which is about one
and a half miles west of Stanley, when three Scout helicopters loosed several
SS-11 missiles at them, wounding several men, before being driven off by
ground fire. 5th Marine Infantry Battalion had retired on to Sapper Hill,
which was being converted into a stronghold. Brigadier General Jofre
planned to create a stronghold around Stanley, and had ordered B Company
25th Infantry Regiment, which had joined B and C Companies 3rd Infantry
Regiment, to form a strong defensive position west of Stanley from the War
Memorial around to the Wind Pump. However, some politically hardline 3rd
Infantry Regiment officers wanted to fight in the town and prepared their
troops for close-quarter fighting, about the last thing the British wanted,
being tired and short of ammunition. However, the British had done some
planning.

A senior Argentine naval officer describes Stanley:

By dawn 5th Marine Infantry Battalion and 7th Infantry Regiment were falling
back toward the naval base around the public jetty, their soldiers a picture of
defeat, stumbling, filthy, tired and dragging themselves along. I heard the King
Edward VII Memorial Hospital was in front of our lines and that casevac helicopters were ferrying wounded to the *Almirante Irizar* [*the Argentine naval
auxiliary now flying Red Cross colours*]. A lieutenant faking serious injury secured
himself passage, not the first instance of desertion in the face of the enemy. A senior
officer had, at the height of the battle, gone to the hospital for a blood test for jaun-
dice, which he had contracted months earlier.

The domination of British artillery is reflected in an intercepted report 'British artillery has complete dominance over Argentine artillery. They are hitting targets on the extreme edge of Stanley. About 140 men have been hit by shrapnel. No more men should attempt to go forward because losses will be too great.' Artillery First Lieutenant Cerezo describes the last night:

The Battery did not have the resources to cover the fire support asked of us. Fatigue, the cold and darkness complicated everything and every change of direction became more difficult. The ground was very soft and did not provide a stable platform. Wheels sank up to the axle and everyone had to help release it from the mud. Number 4 and 5 guns, both facing north, were bogged down but continued to fire in that direction until becoming unserviceable through equipment failures.

The British advanced quickly and the threat against our position increased *[from 2 Para on Wireless Ridge]*. We did not worry about counter-battery fire but continued firing. It seemed the situation became irreversible every minute. The last elevations passed to me by the Fire Control Centre showed we were firing between 1500 and 2000 metres until we received orders to fire over open sights. A small number of men formed local defence. Those not manning the three guns maintained the ammunition supply from the battery ammunition point. The firing mechanism of the third gun broke and minutes later the fourth gun came off its trails when the recuperator failed. During counter-battery fire I found shelter in a water-filled shell hole.

At 9am the CO ordered me to cease fire. Everything seemed to have calmed down but it was cold and snow was falling. At about 11.30am I saw the enemy advancing and was ordered by CO to open fire but a shell was rammed up the breech and the block fell out. The CO ordered us to leave the guns and withdraw into Stanley. At 4pm he told us we had surrendered. This made us cry with the pain of impotence in the face of defeat.

For Julian Thompson, censured at San Carlos by politicians and senior officers thousands of miles from the action, forced against his instinct to fight at Goose Green and who had argued against the adoption of the "narrow front attack" strategy, the Argentine retreat was a sweet moment. He joined Chaundler on Wireless Ridge and saw that there were no enemy between the ridge and the town, and while no white flags could be seen, there was plenty of evidence of Argentines abandoning their positions. Returning to his headquarters, Thompson described the scene to Major-General Moore and told him that 3rd Commando Brigade was on thirty minutes' notice to move in pursuit of the Argentines with 45 Commando tasked to occupy Sapper Hill and 42 Commando and the two parachute battalions ready to advance on Stanley.

5th Infantry Brigade was also advancing against weakening opposition and it was now the turn of the Welsh Guards, now reinforced by A and C Companies and Mortar Troop 40 Commando, which brought the battalion up to strength. So far their campaign had been disastrous, although Support

213

Company had secured the start line for the Mount Harriet attack and the battalion had waited all night in reserve to the attack on Tumbledown but were not committed. Because it was assessed that the Argentine marines would return after Bethell's diversionary attack, the Welsh Guards first dealt with the Pony Pass block and, after extracting themselves from a minefield, they found the position had not been re-occupied. Brigadier Wilson ordered the battalion, by then on Mount Harriet, to be flown to Mount William ready to assault Sapper Hill. However, the pilots made a navigational error and at about 10.30am M Company 5th Marine Infantry Battalion watched as three Sea Kings flew at low level toward their position, reared up and deposited 7 Troop 40 Commando on the metalled track below them. A brisk firefight developed in which two Royal Marines were wounded and three Argentine marines killed in a pointless fight, the last to die in the fighting. 7 Troop was reorganizing when, to their astonishment, a Combat Engineer Tractor and a half-section of 9 Para RE fittingly clattered onto the hill. The previous night they had been asked by the Welsh Guards to rendezvous on Sapper Hill, but, since the Fitzroy bridge could not withstand the weight of the vehicle, this meant a fifteen-mile detour around Port Fitzroy creek in total darkness, but they were on time.

Argentina faced certain defeat and in its wake political factions fractured and internal rivalries surfaced, particularly in the Army, where many in the officer corps were politically hostile to Galtieri. Popular discontent grew as international humiliation and censure beckoned. Army Group Malvinas had been comprehensively defeated and, in a radio conversation with Galtieri, Menendez said that, although his forces were still fighting, should the British continue attacking he doubted he could hold out until nightfall. Losing men in a hopeless situation was worse than surrender. Galtieri encouraged him to counter-attack, citing that his intelligence staff assessed that the British were in an equally precarious position. This was partially correct in that ammunition was low but supplies were still coming forward. One soldier who landed at San Carlos with 250 rounds of 9mm entered Stanley with none. Every round had been donated to keep the front line supplied. Galtieri reminded Menendez that the Argentine code of military conduct demanded that surrender should not be contemplated until 4000 men had been lost and all ammunition expended, but, as Commander Malvinas Joint Command, the final decision was his. Menendez losses of dead, wounded and taken prisoner since 1 May numbered about 1500 and the magazines in Stanley were well stocked. He could withstand a siege in the hope that talks about the future of the Falklands would follow, but the British had superiority at sea, on land and in the air and there was little hope of relief from the mainland. Brigadier General Jofre had already refused an offer of Skyhawks to napalm Wireless Ridge because he believed the British response would be catastrophic.

Navy Captain Melbourne Hussey, senior administrator in Stanley, then contacted the British and agreed with Major General Moore that Lieutenant Colonel Rose and Captain Bell should meet Menendez. Knowing that the Argentines had been listening to the CB and working on an assumption that Menendez had no wish to sustain major casualties among his men or the civilians, both Rose and Bell had adopted a psychological approach, hoping that Menendez would respond. Earlier in the month an Intelligence Corps NCO had waited at Teal Inlet for an officer prisoner to take a cease-fire offer to Menendez but none turned up because none was captured in the patrol skirmishes, although there were at least 100 Argentine officers at Ajax Bay available to take a message. Galtieri was then advised by Major General Garcia that Menendez had accepted an offer for a cease-fire but had been reminded he must commit himself to discussing only the evacuation or with-drawal of Argentine troops from the Falklands.

During the afternoon British negotiators flew into Stanley and persuaded Menendez to surrender all Argentine forces on the Falklands Islands at 12.15am on 15 June. In every respect the surrender was honourable with the word 'unconditional' crossed out by Major General Moore. Units were allowed to retain their colours and officers could keep their sidearms, to pro-tect themselves from the anger of their men. Argentine troops were to assemble at the airport while plans were prepared to repatriate them and working parties were to be formed to lift mines, clear booby traps, treat the wounded and bury the dead. The Argentines did what any beaten army would do – destroyed equipment, material and documents to prevent them falling into enemy hands. British patrols, who at 8.30pm had been told to accept the surrender of opposing forces, found the streets littered with small-arms ammunition, broken weapons and damaged vehicles. Loot left in obvious places was avoided in case it was booby-trapped. Small fires signalled burning documents.

The news flashed around the British units and off came the helmets and on went the berets and comfortable floppy hats. When Moore ordered a general advance as far as the eastern end of the Racecourse, 2 Para climbed on the CVR(T)s, the Blues and Royals broke out their regimental guidon, and, followed closely by 3 Para, raced past abandoned positions and occupied several houses near the cease-fire line. The Welsh Guards, 45 Commando and 4th Troop, the Blues and Royals, occupied Sapper Hill. 42 Commando were flown from Mount Tumbledown to positions on the western edge of Stanley. While the victorious British were asking, 'Where's the transport?' the defeated Argentines were apprehensive. An Argentine naval officer noted:

15 June. I went down to the jetty where a senior naval officer was screaming at conscripts to get off the jetty and accusing them that, because they were no good at fighting, they should clean up the mess that had accumulated in the area. I then heard that senior officers were being taken on board HMS *Fearless* on orders from the British Government and there were some sorrowful goodbyes. That evening Stanley was placed under a curfew.

For the Royal Marines there was just one more thing to do, Operation *Keyhole*, the liberation of South Thule after six years of occupation, and thought to be occupied by 100 troops and scientists. On 16 June Captain Barker on *Endurance* at South Georgia was given M Company 42 Commando for the operation. Captain Chris Nunn, whose brother had been killed at Goose Green, insisted that, if the intelligence was correct, it was unwise to mount the operation without naval gunfire support. Northwood grudgingly approved and *Yarmouth* and the fleet auxiliary *Olmeda* were detached from Falkland Islands operations to join the ocean-going tug *Salvageman* and *Endurance* to reform CTG 317.9. They arrived off Thule on the 19th. The weather was nasty but shortly after midday Sergeant John Napier and nine other experienced winter warfare experts were dropped by helicopter and established an observation post overlooking the scientific base at Morrell Peninsula, a small spit heading east from the central volcano.

During the afternoon it became clear the Argentines were aware a landing had been made and, to encourage them to believe they were hopelessly outnumbered, *Endurance's* helicopters flew around transmitting spurious messages to a non-existent amphibious task force. The weather suddenly took a turn for the worse and communications with Napier faltered. A repetition of the Fortuna Glacier disaster seemed likely. Ashore, Napier roped his patrol into two groups and, crossing large ice-fields and crevasses, reached the observation post just after dark. Conditions were appalling, with whiteout, and windchill dropping to −50 degrees. During the night the BBC again compromised military operations by broadcasting that Thule had been retaken.

Soon after first light the weather improved and when the two Falklands ships arrived Napier gave *Yarmouth* its targets. Barker then radioed to the Argentines that they had until 11.30 to surrender. Nothing was heard all morning and preparations were made to attack. During this lull the Argentines chose to vandalize the base and contaminate their food. Then, two minutes before H-Hour, they radioed that they wished to surrender. Sergeant 'Mac' McLeman reported that a white flag was being flown and, covered by Napier's section, he moved down to the base and captured just nine people. The fourth surrender of the war was signed on *Endurance* and, while the Argentines were being taken to the Falklands, M Company returned to South Georgia where they had Christmas dinner on a snowy 25 June, Midsummer's Day in the northern hemisphere. The shooting war had finished, although Argentina had yet to acknowledge total defeat.

Following the capitulation, Moore's staff were faced with a major logistic and disaster relief problem, namely the collection, assembly and disposal of several thousand Argentines on East and West Falklands and Pebble Island.

216

Stanley was tense. Most of the Argentines were confined to large buildings, warehouses and a neutral zone around the Cathedral, but many were still armed. It was a dangerous situation, particularly if militant officers rejected the cease-fire. Largely forgotten in the euphoria of the victory, a small group of British Intelligence personnel continued to engage the Argentines, not on the battlefield but in an intellectual battle which lasted until mid-July with not a single life lost and only one shot fired.

Late on the afternoon of 15 June, Captain David Chartres' HQ LFFI Intelligence Section, reinforced by the 3rd Commando Brigade Intelligence Section, some of whom had served in Belize and spoke Spanish to a greater or lesser degree, entered Stanley and began the search of Argentine head-quarters for documents and equipment of intelligence interest. Moving into the LADE offices, they enjoyed a meal of scrounged 'compo', swilled down with captured red wine, and then, with the possibility of mutiny among the armed Argentines, pointed a captured MAG machine gun at the door, primed grenades, took up positions in their sleeping bags and promptly fell asleep.

In spite of the best efforts of the Royal Engineers, Stanley was without water and the decision was quickly made to empty it of as many troops as possible to avoid an epidemic. The repatriation of the Argentines was the responsibility of a prisoner-of-war administration team, but since they were still at sea, Chartres' team was instructed to screen each prisoner. Plans were drawn up to select 500 Special Category prisoners from commanders, pilots, intelligence offices, special forces, field security, military police, radar and communications experts, artificers, bomb disposal teams, air force ground crews and air defence and missile operators for further interrogation by Major John Healey's Joint Service Interrogation Unit (JSIU) which was due in theatre within the week. They would be repatriated only when Argentina unconditionally acknowledged the cease-fire. In effect they were hostages. In his *Her Majesty's Interrogator Falklands* former RAF Regiment Flight Lieutenant Guy Bransby wrote a potentially valuable insight into this phase of the conflict but sadly it is factually muddled.

16 June dawned cold. The prisoners in the godowns stayed where they were while the remainder were escorted to the airfield. Very few townspeople were evident but one elderly couple pleaded with a soldier to be gentle with the prisoners: 'After all, they're so young and confused'. The captured Argentine officer continues:

I slept on the floor of the Falkland Islands Company offices and it was very cold, without lighting or heating. At about 9am I was told everyone was to go to the Airport. We marched against a cold wind and freezing rain. People stumbled along under the weight of packs but soon equipment was jettisoned and the road became a scene of total desolation. I persuaded a truck driver to take our baggage, which made life easier. Arriving at the Airport, we found there were no tents or water and people were ripping up corrugated iron to make shelters, while others set vehicles alight to keep warm. I scrounged five tents from 5th Marine Infantry Battalion and after pitching them, we watched those dirty tattered soldiers, about 8000 of them, swarming all over the place. One managed to kill himself when he accidentally fired the ejection seat of an abandoned Pucara. Ammo, rockets and bombs littered the place.

At about mid-afternoon I told some Red Cross we needed tents and water and because there were so many sleeping in the open, there was a danger of some dying from exposure. They told me there was not much they could do because, although General Menendez had surrendered, the Argentine government had not acknowledged the cease-fire. The Red Cross came across as anti-Argentina.

An interesting comment from an officer of a country which had denied so many people their human rights in the Dirty War.

The first priority was to screen about 400 sick and badly wounded prisoners from the civil and field hospitals before they were taken on board the *Almirante Irizar*. She later met the *Uganda* to transfer some Argentines for specialist treatment and care. Earlier on 16 June *Avenger, Cardiff* and two LCUs ferried 8th Infantry and 5th Infantry Regiments, a total of 1,748 troops, to Ajax Bay, and 150 Argentine Air Force ground crew and marines were collected from Pebble Island by the SBS and the ubiquitous Ewen Southby-Tailyour. 1,120 were transferred to the rust-streaked but still majestic *Canberra*, each of whom was given a P&O luggage label and accommodated on B Deck. They also released SAS Sergeant Fonseka, who was captured by 601 Commando Company after Captain Hamilton had been killed near Port Howard. He had spent four days confined to a 4-foot sheep pen. The only other prisoner captured by the Argentines since the British had landed at San Carlos was Flight Lieutenant Jeff Glover, who had been shot down. He was eventually transferred to a military hospital in Argentina.

During the afternoon HQ LFFI issued orders that the repatriation would begin that night from the public jetty on to *Canberra*, which was due in Port William. The prisoners were to jettison all equipment and kit except the uniforms they were wearing, a spoon and washing kit. Originally Captain Chartres had planned to use the Falkland Islands Company offices to screen the prisoners, but, to speed up the process, it was decided the jetty should be used. At first the Royal Marine Police were to search each prisoner before they were ferried to *Canberra*, either in the *Forrest* or by one of the liner's boats. The BAS offices near the jetty were requisitioned to assemble the Special Category. Chartres organized his team into two watches, each under command of a SNCO.

At about 8pm the first column arrived under escort, which, having delivered the prisoners, then disappeared into the darkness. A biting southerly wind whipped up a snowstorm and large wet flakes fled almost horizontally across the single spotlight shining from the captured Argentine Coastguard cutter *Islas Malvinas* moored alongside the jetty. There was no electricity. Weary, battle-stained and wet, the Argentines stood three-deep facing the jetty, the officers and NCOs apprehensive, but the conscripts not entirely unhappy at the thought of going home. Heaps of discarded equipment began to appear on the square. At the order 'Next!' each prisoner doubled forward and stood in front of the screeners: 'Name? Rank? Occupation?' Then either 'Until next time' for those lucky enough to be repatriated or 'Over there!' for the Special Category. On occasion officers organized disruption with prisoners, exchanging identities and uniform. Others tried to smuggle knives, weapon parts and equipment. An extremely angry infantry lieutenant, claiming to be the son of a general, hurled his two pearl-handled silver Colt .45 automatics into the harbour: 'No bloody English are going to have these!' A 601 Commando Company NCO declared, 'It was a boring war'.

A young 4th Infantry Regiment officer, possibly Second Lieutenant Jimenez-Corvalen, described the fighting on Mount Harriet. During the final stages he led his platoon from the west ridge and joined 5th Marine Infantry Battalion on Mount Tumbledown, where, two nights later, he fought another battle. He said the Argentine Army had learnt much from the war, the principal lesson that a conscript army cannot take on a professional army and win. He was happy with his equipment, but considered some of that used by the British inferior, for instance the boots and night sights. He believed Menendez's reliance on helicopters as a prime transporter of troops to have been an error and mentioned their losses as a prime cause of the defeat. The lieutenant was disappointed that the San Carlos beachhead had not been attacked.

At midnight the Royal Marine Police received a message that the crew of the *Forrest* were refusing to sail and the relief crew had not appeared. The relief crew then tottered on to the jetty and the repatriation continued. A conscript fell into the dark, freezing water and was hauled clear by the Argentine lieutenant and an Intelligence Corps SNCO just before the black hull of the coaster smashed into the jetty.

Shortly after midnight an already fraught situation developed into a near mutiny when several civilians and soldiers drinking in the Globe Hotel threw smoke grenades and directed a Panhard at a column of prisoners. For the bitter Argentines this was a golden opportunity to set fire to the Globe Store. The fire brigade, cheered on by British and Argentines, turned on the tap and small fountains of water spilled from rotten hoses. Further disorder erupted when three large columns, each led by a senior officer, barged through the waiting Argentines and demanded to be given priority treatment. A guard force had not yet been assigned to the jetty and it seemed the tiny British team was about to be overwhelmed until an RAF SNCO, examining an automatic pistol, accidentally pulled the trigger. The bullet hit the road and sang off into the darkness. There was silence and then 'Sorry about that, chaps!' A 40 Commando troop arrived complete with fixed bayonets.

To counter the determination of some Argentine officers to disrupt the repatriation process Brigadier General Jofre was told to appoint liaison officers, one of whom was a portly, jolly major. Captain Chartres also appointed a member of his team to mingle with the prisoners, listen to what was being said and counter disruption. It would be a dangerous tactic, particularly as the captured officers were still armed. A tough Spanish-speaking Belizean soldier from the Commando Logistic Regiment, Private Ali Ciasco, was assigned as close escort.

Next morning, while the victors picked over the mountains of abandoned equipment, the Special Category prisoners were escorted to the football field outside Government House and flown by Chinook to Ajax Bay. The Argentine Navy officer recalls:

We were warned to assemble at the football pitch ready to be helicoptered to *Canberra*. When we arrived, we handed in our weapons, boarded a Chinook and were transferred to Ajax Bay, where we were issued with identity cards, escorted into the refrigeration plant, searched and interviewed before being put into a small room. My cellmates included a Canberra pilot, an Air Force SAM-7 observer and a number of Army officers.

Michael Clapp has alluded to the apparent breakdown of discipline in Stanley. From someone who spent the campaign fed, watered, warm and comfortable, this criticism is unfair. In much the same way as the Royal Navy have shared prize money, so soldiers through the ages have collected and used their allies and enemies' equipment. The Falklands was no different and there is no doubt that some Argentine kit was superior to the British issues, particularly boots. Such looting as there was came from abandoned equipment and captured stores. There was also another reason. Most British troops arrived in Stanley with little or no food and near empty waterbottles. Most of the 3rd Commando Brigade units had not had a hot meal for seventy-two hours. There was also no fresh water because the filtration plant had been damaged during the shelling. The alternative was discarded Argentine ration packs and a bottle of rough red wine. And why not? Few sailors had the opportunity to go ashore since leaving England and their ships had played a vital role in the victory. On more than one occasion at San Carlos and Stanley, kitbags of souvenirs were sent to ships, including the Great White Whale. They deserved something to show for it.

More prisoners arrived. The fully qualified German-speaking doctor, who was serving as a medical orderly, and the English-speaking university graduate conscript, who did not want to return to Argentina and interpreted for the intelligence team. 181 Military Police Company turned up with their

220

huge well-groomed Alsatians and there was a suggestion the dogs should be retained. 'Sit!' induced a blank brown-eyed stare and a cocked head until it was realized they understood only Spanish. Prisoners complaining of ill-health or with an urgent requirement to return to Argentina were referred to Red Cross officials. A doctor found concealing a pistol in his medical bag was given a sharp dressing-down by their chief representative, who threatened to remove his retained status. After an unavoidably public consultation by a Swiss doctor, a captain's complaint was pronounced to be genuine and orders were given he should be admitted to the *Almirante Irizar* as soon as possible. As befits their tradition, the Red Cross were impartial and both sides worked with them without undue disagreement.

At midday on the 17th the coxswain of a *Canberra* whaler told the screeners the liner had reached the limit of 4,167 prisoners. Most of the Argentines were confined four to a cabin and completely overwhelmed by the sheer luxury of the ship. As those who returned to the United Kingdom on *Canberra* would later experience, the crew were kindness itself. One steward showed four conscripts how to use the shower. Returning twenty minutes later, he found a fully clothed conscript, blue and shivering, standing under a jet of ice cold water. He and his colleagues couldn't find hot water and had agreed that, not to disappoint the steward, one of them would take a cold shower but would remain dressed to keep warm.

The coxswain's message came as a complete surprise. 500 screened prisoners were on the jetty awaiting embarkation, including several on stretchers, and more columns were on their way from the airport but could not be contacted. The organization had collapsed and a member of the screening team returned to Sulivan House to find it empty except for Brigadier Thompson working alone upstairs. Hearing about the problems – *Canberra* full, no communications, guard fallen out and no LFFI liaison officer – he radioed HQ LFFI 'The prisoners are your problem. Come down and sort it out – now!' Eventually Colonel Ian Baxter, whose organization was responsible for the administration of the prisoners, arrived and issued a stream of orders. News then arrived from Ajax Bay that parts of a rifle had been found among the Stanley prisoners. During the afternoon *Canberra* left Port William and on the 19th arrived at Puerto Madryn where the Red Cross supervised the disembarkation of the weary prisoners, who were loaded into lorries and buses and taken to barracks.

59 Independent Commando and 9 Para Squadrons RE offered thirty-four captured sappers parole to help dismantle the minefields and when they accepted were given white arm bands to denote their status. A major was also selected, but he proved such a nuisance that he was immediately sent to Ajax Bay as Special Category, much to his fury, and was replaced by a useful lieutenant. The team was greatly assisted by WO 1 Canessa, a Spanish-speaking Gibraltarian serving with the Royal Engineers.

Meanwhile a counter-intelligence operation was underway to examine the extent of Argentine influence, espionage and subversion before and during the campaign. A number of Falkland Islanders were interviewed, as well as nine Poles, seamen who had been landed from a Polish fish factory ship and were ashore when the Argentines landed and had been pressed into working for them. As luck would have it, one of the Intelligence Corps was a Polish linguist. Detailed searches of Argentine headquarters were also carried out and several boxes of documents and equipment sent back to the Ministry of Defence.

Lance Corporal Ivor Garcia was still at Ajax Bay and to help him with the influx of Special Category, two screeners were sent to help him. His war had been adventurous. While attached to Y(Electronic Warfare) Troop RM to translate Argentine transmissions, the heavily laden Land Rovers were making difficult progress to Goose Green after the battle when two marauding Mirages suddenly buzzed them. To the astonishment of the drivers, the Royal Signals captain commanding the Troop ordered the vehicles to outrun the aircraft. One aircraft settled down on a low strafing run and the Royal Marines cheerfully disobeyed orders seeking cover. Garcia dived to the beautiful soft peat face first and 'hit the only blinking stone for miles around costing me my dentures!' He searched for the pieces in vain, and thereafter was blessed with a piratical appearance. Transferred to the *Norland* with repatriated Goose Green prisoners, Garcia worked for two days non-stop until ordered to rest, and discovered from coded signals tapped from cabin to cabin and between decks, a plot to hijack the ship. He intercepted the chain, fed duff information and effectively ruined the plan. During the approach to Puerto Madryn he interpreted the Uruguayan pilot's orders for Captain Ellerby and dealt with the authorities on matters far beyond his rank. Returning to Ajax Bay, Garcia had since been deluged with intelligence requirements from HQ LFFI staff such as 'Where and what types are the minefields?' 'Is there a map of them?' Faced with bitter prisoners whose heads were full of information, he now needed expert help. Garcia eventually received a Commander Task Force 317 Commendation for his work. He deserved more.

19 June dawned bright. Stanley was still without water, the Globe Store was still burning and Argentine work parties were collecting the abandoned equipment, ammunition and debris littering the roads. 3rd Commando Brigade handed over its positions to 5th Infantry Brigade and the heavily laden 45 Commando silently plodded along Ross Street in one long snake to a LSL tied up alongside the jetty. Captain Gardiner later wrote

As if in answer to a Royal Marine's prayer, the whole thing ended up, unbelievably, in a pub called the Globe Hotel. Having marched into Stanley to go on board a ship for a wash, we found ourselves in a smoky wooden bar-shaped room. 150 Marines, unshaven, dirty, tired, stinking and very lightly boozed – every man a can of beer in his hands.

222

Just like the end of a map-reading exercise.

During the afternoon, the prisoner administration team finally arrived at the jetty. A screener recalls:

We had nearly finished when a major appeared sporting French parachute wings above his right breast pocket of his incredibly clean combat jacket. His new full webbing included a holstered pistol, bayonet and large hunting knife; his SLR was hooked under his arm.

'Who is in charge here?"

'I suppose I am. What can I do for you?' I replied.

'I am to organize the repatriation,' he said. 'I have a team of sixty-nine and a computer to help.' This was completely unexpected and I was nonplussed after all the problems we had encountered. 'Our system has been working satisfactorily so far and I have no intention of changing. If you want to work, go behind the searchers and do your business on the jetty' I replied. Perhaps he sensed our irritation and set up on some forty-gallon oil drums on the jetty. Soon there was a chattering group of Argentines gathered around the drums awaiting documentation and a coaster awaiting the next load. The trouble was that not all of his team could speak Spanish. And then it snowed heavily. 'Where can we go? Our pens and pencils are running,' asked a Royal Engineer Warrant Officer.

'There is nowhere' I replied and with that the major and his team left the jetty. We breathed a sigh of relief. I learnt later the team had been created to run a prison camp; indeed it had exercised prisoners prior to coming south. Unfortunately the prison camp was now floating around in the holds of the sunken *Atlantic Conveyor*.

During the afternoon 2 Para barged three abreast along the sea front to hold their famous church service in the Cathedral. Royal Marines escorting prisoners sat on the grass to let them pass. The paras had arrived, but it seemed a little ostentatious and unnecessary. *Norland* then arrived in Port William and the screening began again. The night was foul, with snowstorms sweeping down the mountains. As each column arrived, it was given an amnesty by one of Jofre's liaison officers, but, in spite of several warnings, a hacksaw and knife was found tucked into the boots of a 3rd Infantry Regiment conscript. In the freezing cold, while the anxious young soldier was strip-searched down to his underpants, Jofre and his two liaison officers were given an traditional sergeant-major's dressing down by Captain Barclay, 106th Provost Company RMP, and warned that the smuggling of weapons was intolerable and in future any prisoners caught with prohibited items would be dealt with severely, as would Brigadier General Jofre for not co-operating. It seemed to work for soon afterwards a dumped pistol was found. The conscript was taken into the BAS offices for a cup of tea by the military police, who had relieved the Royal Marine Police searching the prisoners.

When the green-bereted 25th Infantry Regiment marched into the square under escort, Lieutenant Colonel Seineldin and his adjutant brushed past

223

Jofre's liaison officers and presented themselves to the screeners, who told them what the soldiers were allowed to take on board the ship. The adjutant translated and all those with a problem doubled on to the road and, to his horror, the regimental war diary was surrendered by a conscript. It seems the young man had been ordered to smuggle it to Argentina. By about midnight *Norland* had taken her capacity and next morning she sailed for Puerto Madryn with 2,047 prisoners. The *Bahia Paraiso* collected several hundred lightly wounded and sick prisoners, mainly ill with dysentery, stomach and painful foot ailments. There were three gastro-enteritis stretcher cases and a conscript had a serious head wound in a godown. The column also included an unusually large number of healthy pilots, who were quickly sifted out as Special Category.

The officers generally accepted surrender as inevitable and seemed pleased with the settlement. Most field and senior officers were, however, adamant that they would be back in the future; some said within twenty years, others within five and one within the year, which seemed a little unrealistic. Most agreed they had been defeated by an outnumbered army, but superior in experience, training and equipment. Many criticized the conscript nature of their army but most accepted that politics prevented the creation of professional armed forces. The junior officers appeared to have genuine concern for their men and in more than one instance witnessed their units being processed before embarking themselves. One, amazed by the stockpiles in Stanley, correctly concluded that the Harriers, the virtual neutralization of 601 Combat Aviation Battalion and poor roads had prevented regular supplies arriving at the front.

Virtually all the NCOs expressed dissatisfaction with the leadership of the senior officers and felt badly let down. The conscripts looked upon captivity with stoicism and disinterest, although they obviously all wanted to go home; who could blame them? Their intellect ranged from well-educated graduates to peasants. Very few civilians were captured, although a television war correspondent was selected for Special Category, much to his disgust. Two alleged priests named by some Argentine soldiers as propaganda experts slipped through the net onto the *Canberra*.

By 20 June, an estimated 10,250 Argentines had been repatriated through Stanley and Ajax Bay. 593 Special Category, thirty-five engineers on parole and about 200 other conscripts remained. After some initial success in causing disruption, the Argentines had been outwitted by a small group. Captain Chartres' team wound down its operations and handed over to Major John Healey's JSIU which had arrived at Ajax Bay on the Offshore Patrol Vessel HMS *Dumbarton Castle*.

Living in primitive conditions inside the bomb-damaged refrigeration plant, Healey found several hundred prisoners guarded by Royal Marine battle casualty replacements. A dilapidated Nissen hut offered some privacy for questioning and the inevitable battle of wits developed as his team

Los 6 de San Carlos

A cartoon of six NCOs unearthed during a search of prisoners at Ajax Bay showing their names, their signatures, addresses and date of capture. They are Marine Corporal Carrasco, airborne gunner Sergeant Moreno, captured at Goose Green, Sergeant Major Riveros, First Sergeants Potocsnyak and Rivas, both 12th Infantry Regiment and also captured at Goose Green, and First Sergeant Flores, a member of 602 Commando Company captured during the skirmishes on Mount Kent.

struggled to gain information from prisoners becoming more resistant, less co-operative and critical of a government that had yet to acknowledge the futility of the Argentine expedition to the Falklands and accept unconditional defeat. In total about 90 prisoners were questioned, some more than once, but the interrogators found it difficult to provide answers on the performance of British equipment, which was being sought by Technical Intelligence in the United Kingdom. The Argentine naval officer described conditions and his thoughts:

17 June. Although I managed to sleep that night, the room was hot and damp. The light remained on although every so often the generator would run out of fuel; we remained very quiet in the darkness until the light came back on in case the guards became frightened and shot us. Breakfast was stew but because only a few us had utensils, most had to use empty drink cans. The toilet was screened off in the corner with one bucket for a urinal and another filled with a liquid that decomposes matter.

'In the mid-morning we were allowed into the Pig Pen for an hour, a 20×20 metre quagmire, full of rubbish from previous occupants, where we were gazed at by the British and occasionally jeered. When we returned to our cell, we found that it had been cleaned by Argentine other rank prisoners. Water was in a small tub that was replaced infrequently but I later learnt that water was scarce anyway. In the evening we were given supper and then we listened on a smuggled radio that President Galtieri had resigned. About 200 officers arrived that evening from Stanley.

18 June. Another uncomfortable night, but at breakfast, we were advised by the British to eat because we would be transferring to a ship and nobody knows when the next meal will be. It had become unbelievably hot in our cell and we persuaded the guards to let us get some fresh air. I met the same Red Cross official and he told me that Britain wanted Argentina to accept the cease-fire and in return would repatriate all the captured forces apart from four hundred officers who would be held as hostages to ensure safe passage for the return of the victors to England. I later learnt that soon after this conversation the *Canberra* departed for Puerto Belgrano with 4500 soldiers.

In the afternoon, a padre held Mass. I sat next door to Lieutenant-Colonel Gimenez who was very angry because he feared court-martial for retreating and was worried that he would be accused of having left the front line. Later some of the more senior officers accepted an invitation to attend a mass burial of some Argentines at the San Carlos cemetery. That evening we listened to the radio and heard Anaya bidding farewell to Galtieri.

19 June. We had no breakfast until after we had exercised in the Pig Pen, when we were given some biscuits and soup but everyone complained about the lack of food. More prisoners arrived overnight, including some from Stanley. They reported that all those who went on the *Canberra* had been ordered by the British to leave everything behind and that it then was all set alight. There was some harsh words said of the Navy when we learnt the *Canberra* had been escorted into Puerto Madryn by an Argentine destroyer. One Navy officer came in for considerable criticism for accepting a dinner invitation with a Royal Navy officer.

226

20 June. The news on the illegal radio from Argentina is very discouraging. Britain had declared she would retain prisoners until Argentina recognised the cease-fire agreement. Argentina would not respond until Britain accepts UN Resolution 509 on the withdrawal of forces, including nuclear submarines, and the lifting of the blockade. It was Father's Day and I was without my children. When we went out to the Pig Pen, it was very cold.

21 June. By now I was becoming more used to our confinement, although I thought that the lack of vitamins was beginning to take effect. Nevertheless the strain of living in a small and crowded space was beginning to tell. There was a serious disagreement between the Army prisoners but I suspect it was more a loss of dignity than anything else. When we went to the Pig Pen, it was pouring with rain. On our return I was taken for interrogation. I told them I was only required to give name, surname, number and date of birth and name of father as required by the Geneva Convention. This annoyed the interrogators and I was told that unless I co-operated, repatriation could be delayed. Some officers managed to retain dignity in their dealings with the British, particularly "Los Anglos". Our radio was found, which was a great loss.

22 June. My mood had changed and it was now the Black Hole of Ajax Bay. For exercise the guards took us to the part of the refrigeration plant that had been bombed (on 25 May) and there lodged in the masonry were two unexploded bombs. I was then taken away for more interrogation and played dumb to all their questions. When I returned more officers had arrived and our cell was very crowded'.

On 23 June the Scots Guard's Right Flank Company took over from the Royal Marines. A Red Cross delegation headed by Monsieur Claude Dietrich demanded better conditions for the prisoners, which was immediately actioned. The Argentine naval officer continued:

25th June. Two philosophies had developed to fit our lifestyle and both totally opposite to each other. The Los Anglos spoke good English, read English novels and essentially co-operated. Those of Latin descent, mainly Army officers, played dumb and pretended not to understand English and said derogatory things about them. During one argument a Latino said to a Los Anglos naval officer 'That depends on your superiors'. The officer replied 'I do not have any superiors. I have a high ranking face starting with Anaya' (sic). Someone then said, 'Watch out because his son is an Army lieutenant and is somewhere around'.

When this was realized, the British hauled out the well-groomed, articulate and immaculately dressed, prisoner named First Lieutenant Guillermo Anaya but he refused to confirm his relationship with Admiral Anaya. It later turned out he was Anaya's son and was an Iroquois helicopter pilot with 601 Combat Aviation Battalion.

29 June. In the afternoon we were given a medical inspection in preparation for boarding the ship St Edmund but loading was cancelled until the following day.

This sounded like a lie. The problem was still the refusal of Argentina to accept the cease-fire.

Before his diary was found during the search for embarkation, the naval officer commented on the value of intelligence. He notes that information was lost when Governor Hunt destroyed papers, his secretary was allowed to burn code books and English journalists photographed the surrender in April, which harnessed British opinion, while Argentine photographers took photographs of Argentine 'heroes', which became of intelligence interest.

The next day the JSIU and the prisoners were transferred to the Sealink Ro-Ro ferry *St Edmund* where a complete nominal role was taken. A systematic search unearthed two automatic pistols, parts of a FAL rifle, ammunition and diaries, including the senior naval officer's. The Naval Party 2060 on board insisted on the maximum security of the prisoners seemingly without appreciating John Healey's requirements. The ship was not ideal for the separation of the prisoners, but this was resolved by confining the officers three to two-person and six to four-person cabins. The SNCOs were accommodated in other cabins and the remainder were confined in five pens on the car deck. This area had no ablutions except urinal buckets, which often overflowed as the ship pitched.

On 2 July the *St Edmund* embarked twenty-five more prisoners, including Brigadier General Menendez, and a stiffening of resistance was noted as he and his senior officers made their presence felt. Also transferred on board were the detainees and prisoners captured at South Thule and the paroled sappers, one of whom, Corporal Cattay, had lost part of his leg when a mine exploded.

Major Drewry's Welsh Guards No 1 Company took over as Guard Force and settled into a routine of three fifty-strong platoon shifts doing six hours on duty manning thirteen three-man piquet posts, followed by six hours' rest and six hours' on two minutes notice to move. Drewry endeavoured to keep everyone occupied by holding Sunday Mass, organizing football matches and deck hockey, until all the pucks had been hit over the side, and the most popular social event on any ship, the two meals a day. To escape the confines of the car deck, the conscripts did fatigues. Daily meetings were held between Drewry, the Prisoners' Representatives and the multi-lingual Dietrich. Drewry found these meetings valuable barometer of prisoner morale, but also tricky as he struggled to avoid thoroughly prepared traps aimed at setting precedents.

For the next ten days, the *St Edmund* slowly plied between Stanley and Berkeley Sound. Argentina then acknowledged the futility of refusing to concede that she had lost the war and on 12 July Major Healey ceased operations and the Guard Force prepared the prisoners for repatriation at Puerto Madryn. Over the next two days, in an atmosphere of carnival, the prisoners' carefully labelled property was returned and their quarters cleaned. On

228

14 July at 4am, the prisoners were woken to the shrill blast of the Duty Drummer beating Reveille and then after breakfast were paraded by Drill Sergeant Cox. Major Drewry was anxious – his headcount was for 591 Special Category prisoners whereas the Argentines were expecting 593, a figure agreed by Dietrich.

The *St Edmund* edged alongside a fruity fish jetty. The welcome for the prisoners was very low key. Corporal Cattay was first stretchered by the ship's medical detachment to a waiting ambulance and then Brigadier General Menedez led the prisoners through the checkpoints. Two hours later Drewry consulted his counting machine and to his horror it registered 589 – four missing. He consulted the Argentine sergeant at the foot of the gangway, who also registered 589. Drewry did what all sensible people do and arranged for a bottle of whisky and six glasses for the Red Cross delegation and the Argentine general in command of the reception committee. Everyone agreed that 593 prisoners had passed through the checkpoints but the missing four had not been registered because of a fault with the counting machine. It was also agreed that the Argentine sergeant at the base of the gangway on the quay had also lost count several times. Handover certificates were given to the Argentine delegation signalling the completion of the repatriation of the Argentines involved. Captain Stockman signalled the Ministry of Defence 'From MV *St Edmund*. At 10.00 hrs local this morning we completed the release of the last 593 Special Category prisoners under the supervision of the International Committee of the Red Cross at Puerto Madryn, Argentina. In so doing, we have fulfilled the Company motto – Sealink sets you free'. It was a fitting epitaph to the Falklands War.

12

Postscript

With the recovery of the Falkland Islands and its dependencies British international prestige had been recovered. Those in the Task Force wondered how on earth they had sailed nearly 8000 miles with little interference from the Argentines and defeated an army slightly larger than the combined strength of the 3rd Commando and 5th Infantry Brigades. Compared to other twentieth century wars, it had been a relatively gentlemanly affair – no atrocities, no great long lasting hatred for the Argentines, mercifully short and certainly not as vicious and voracious as the Israeli invasion of Beirut or Iran/Iraq War to which many of the participants returned to watch on television and read about in their newspapers. Ironically within ten years British and Argentines serve alongside each other in the United Nations Forces in Cyprus.

The Task Force had given Great Britian something to celebrate and the welcome home was a surprise but most admitted they had merely done their job. For some there were glittering careers ahead but many who were outspoken about the war, not the necessity, but about systems, tactics and equipment performance, were passed over in the promotion stakes and served until natural retirement, their combat experience not required.

For Argentina, politically the war was not exactly a disaster but was a major embarrassment. It removed the threat of military dictatorship probably forever and although she still claims the '*Malvinas es Argentina*', her direct action virtually ruined any chance of a political negotiation, particularly as the only country to support her was Libya and some South American neighbours. Argentina's claim to the Falkland Islands has continued to simmer. In the summer of 1998, the French novelist, Jean Raspail, acting in the name of King Orelie-Antoine the First, self-styled King of Patagonia in 1860, bizarrely seized the Channel Islands islet, Les Minquiers. Raspail first laid claim to the islet in 1984 in response to Britain's 'prolonged occupation of the Malvinas, a territory of Patagonia.'

Argentina's Armed Forces had tried very hard but had been outclassed by highly professional soldiers and led by inept and inexperienced commanders. The euphoria of the victory on 2nd April dissipated into national humiliation and self-interest on 14th June and the repatriated servicemen returned to a demoralized and defeated nation and suffered unemployment, lack of access to the Patriotic Fund and, for many, post combat trauma. Materially three infantry brigades were stripped of everything they had except for the clothes the soldiers were wearing. As a consequence of the defeat an inquiry chaired by retired General Rattenbach, several senior officers were formally blamed for the defeat although Brigadier General Jofre, ineffective defender of Stanley who took very little offensive action, was absolved. The one man left isolated and ill-equipped to fight the British at Goose Green, Lieutenant Colonel Piaggi, was forced not only to resign his commission but retire.

Because Argentina still claims the islands to be Argentine territory, the dead left behind lie buried in a cemetery at Darwin. Although President Menem had the graciousness to attend a remembrance service in front of the Falklands War memorial during his state visit in 1998, to their shame the Falkland Islanders, defying the forgiveness due for soldiers killed on active service, refuse to allow Argentine families to visit the graves of their husbands, sons and friends. This attitude is not what I and others who fought the war want.

Perhaps the most dramatic change was for the Falkland Islands. The group of isolated islands and sleepy settlements was converted from one fortress to another in a matter of weeks. The Services pulled out of Stanley to a large base built at Mount Pleasant by contractors and engineers imported from the United Kingdom. The quiet 'camp' thunders to the roar of fast aircraft screaming across the moor, artillery shelling and to the crackle of small arms fire as British Forces Falkland Islands prepare for an invasion that is unlikely to happen. Meanwhile British engineers continue to search for and lift mines left behind by the Argentines. An offer by Argentina to help clear the islands of landmines was rejected. The Falkland Islanders have been able to keep the islands very much in the public eye in Great Britain but at a cost to their traditional way of life.

COMPOSITION OF COMBINED TASK GROUP 317.8 (THE TASK FORCE)

CTG 317.8 (FOF1 in ANTRIM)

TG 317.8

CTU 317.8.1 (FOF1 in ANTRIM)	CTU 317.8.2 (FORT AUSTIN)	CTU 317.8.3 (COMAW in FEARLESS)	CTU 317.8.4 (Comd 3 Cdo Bde RM)	CTU 317.8.5 (ENDURANCE)
TU 317.8.1	TU 317.8.2	TU 317.8.3	TU 317.8.4	TU 317.8.5
HMS ANTRIM*	RFA FORT AUSTIN	HMS FEARLESS+	3 Cdo Bde RM	HMS ENDURANCE
GLASGOW		INVINCIBLE	HQ 3 Cdo Bde RM	
BRILLIANT*		HERMES	40 Cdo RM	
SHEFFIELD+		ALACRITY	42 Cdo RM	
COVENTRY+		ANTELOPE+	45 Cdo RM	
PLYMOUTH*		RFA PEARLEAF	3 Para	
ARROW		OLMEDA	29 Cdo Regt + 148 Cdo LO Bty	
RFA TIDESPRING		STROMNESS	59 Indep Cdo Engr Sqn	
		RESOURCE	M & AW Cadre RM	
HMS BROADSWORD*		SIR GALAHAD+	RL Det 30 Sig Regt	
HMS ARGONAUT*		GERAINT	LSL/Mexi Det 17 Port Regt RCT	
HMS ARDENT		TRISTRAM*	RAF Det SF	
HMS GLAMORGAN*		LANCELOT*	Det 47 Air Despatch Sqn RCT	
HMS YARMOUTH*		PERCIVAL	Cdo Log Regt RM	
			T Bty 12 AD Regt	
		TE 317.8.3.1 (Embarked RNLO)	3 Air Sqn RM	
		SS CANBERRA	3 Cdo Bde Sig Sqn RM	
			2 Med Recce Tp B Sqn RHG/D	
		TE 317.8.3.2 (Embarked RNLO)	1 RSRM	
		MV ELK	2,3,6 SBS	
			D Sqn 22 SAS	
			Air Maint GP	
			845 NACS	
			846 NACS	
			SST	
			PCCU Det 1 PC Regt	
			Det 49 EOD Sqn	
			Y Tp RM	
			Cdo Forces Band	

NOTES

+ denotes ships sunk

* denotes ships hit by bombs

Contemporary order of battle of CTG 317.8. It is incorrect in that 2 Para has not been included in CTU 317.8.4 (Comd 3 Cdo RM) and 845 and 846 NACS should be with CTU 317.8.3 (COMAW)

COMBINED TASK UNIT 317.8.4 (3rd COMMANDO BRIGADE RM)

TU 317.8.4

HMS FEARLESS	LSL SIR GERAINT	LSL SIR GALAHAD	SS CANBERRA	RFA STROMNESS
HQ 3 Cdo Bde RM	29 Cdo Regt	59 Indep Cdo Engr Sqn	40 Cdo RM	45 Cdo RM
3 Cdo Bde Sig Sqn RM	T Bty 12 AD Regt	1 RSRM	42 Cdo RM	3 SBS
3 Cde Bde Air Sqn RM	Air Maint Cp	LSL Det	3 Para	
D Sqn 22 SAS	LSL Det		B Sqn RHG/D	
RL Det 30 Sig Regt			Det 49 EOD Sqn	
47 AD Sqn RCT			SST	
CO 29 Cdo Regt			PCCU	
OC 59 Indep Cdo Engr Sqn			Cdo Forces Band	
OC T Bty 12 AD Regt				
OC 148 Cdo Bty				
AD Tp RM				
Y (EW) Tp RM				
SB Comd				
RAF SF Det				

LSL SIR LANCELOT	RFA RESOURCE
Cdo Log Regt RM	M & AW Cadre
LSL Det	
Mexefloat Det 17 Port Regt RCT	

233

COMPOSITION OF LAND FORCES FALKLANDS ISLANDS 2 APRIL TO 14 JUNE 1982

CTU 317.1
Commander
Land Forces Falkland Islands
(Major-General Jeremy Moore)

CTU 317.1
Land Forces Falkland Islands
Royal School of Artillery Support Regiment
49 (EOD) Squadron 33 Engineer Regiment
RHQ and Workshop 36 Engineer Regiment
11 and 61 Field Support Squadrons 38 Engineer Regiment
50 (Construction) Squadron
Military Works Force
2 Postal and Courier Regiment RE
14th (Electronic Warfare) Signal Regiment
205 Signal Squadron 30 (Rear Link) Signal Squadron
602 Signals Troop
29 Transport and Movements Regiment RCT
47 Air Despatch Squadron RCT
407 Troop RCT
The Joint Helicopter Unit

CTU 317.1.1
3rd Commando Brigade
(Brigadier Julian Thompson)
See Annex ......for composition
of the Landing Force. Some
units reverted to LFFI when the
Division landed.

Not included in the Annex are 605,
611 and 612 (RM) and 613 Tactical
Air Control Parties.

CTU 317.1.2
5th Infantry Brigade
(Brigadier Tony Wilson)
2nd Scots Guards
Welsh Guards
1/7th Gurkha Rifles
4th Field Regiment RA
Element 49th Field Regiment RA
9 Parachute Squadron RE
20 Field Support Squadron RE
656 Squadron AAC
HQ 5th Infantry Brigade and Signal Squadron
566 Rear Link Detachment
9 Ordnance Battalion RAOC
81 Ordnance Company RAOC
10 Field Workshops REME
70 Aircraft Workshops REME
16 Field Ambulance RAMC
19 Field Ambulance RAMC
Elements 2 Field Hospital RAMC
160 Provost Company RMP
6 Field Cash Office RAPC
172 Intelligence Section

ARMY GROUP MALVINAS
(Brigadier-General Mario Menendez)

SPECIAL FORCES GROUP
601 Commando Company
602 Commando Company
601 National Guard Special Forces Squadron
Special Operations Group (Air Force)

ENGINEER GROUP MALVINAS
1st Amphibious Company
601 Combat Engineer Company
10th Engineer Company

LOGISTIC CENTRE MALVINAS
9th Logistic Battalion
10th Logistic Battalion

235

Z RESERVE
Task Force Reconquest - Port Howard
Task Force Mercedes - Goose Green
Task Force Monte Caseros - Mt Wall/Two Sisters
Task Force Solari - Mount Kent

ARMY GROUP PUERTO ARGENTINO
HQ 10th Infantry Brigade
(Brigadier-General Oscar Jofre)

ARMY HEADQUARTERS
Troop 1st Cavalry Regiment
A Company 1st Infantry Regiment
601 Commando Company
602 Commando Company
601 Combat Aviation Company
601 Air Maintenance Company
601 Communication Company
602 Electronic Warfare Company
601 Combat Engineer Company
601 Air Defence Group (35mm)
602 Air Defence Group (30mm)

3rd ARMY CORPS
4th Airborne Brigade
4th Airborne Artillery Group (105mm)
Platoon 2nd Airborne Infantry Regiment

NATIONAL GUARD
601 Special Forces Squadron

1st ARMY CORPS
101 Artillery Group (155mm)
101 Air Defence Group (35mm)

10th Infantry Brigade
3rd Infantry Regiment
6th Infantry Regiment
7th Infantry Regiment
10th Armoured Recce Squadron
10th Logistic Battalion
10th Engineer Company
10th Communications Company

5th ARMY CORPS
Troop 181 Armoured Recce Squadron
181 Communications Company
181 Military Police Company
181 Intelligence Company

9th Infantry Brigade
25th Infantry Regiment

2nd ARMY CORPS
3rd Infantry Brigade
Task Force Monte Caseros
B Company 4th Infantry Regiment
C Company 4th Infantry Regiment

Task Force Solari
B Company 12th Infantry Regiment

3rd Artillery Group (105mm)

MARINE SUPPORT FORCE
5th Marine Infantry Battalion
B Battery Marine Field Artillery Battalion (105mm)
Marine Anti-Aircraft Battalion
Marine Engineer Company
12.7mm Marine Machine-Gun Company

AIR FORCE

1 Air Brigade
Command and Control Team
7 Air Brigade
Special Operations Group
10 Air Brigade
2nd Early Warning and Control Group

Air Defence Command
1st Anti-Aircraft Command
Training Command
Security Company Military Aviation School

ARMY GROUP LITTORAL
HQ 3rd Infantry Brigade
(Brigadier-General Omar Parada)

EAST FALKLANDS

TASK FORCE MERCEDES - GOOSE GREEN
Army Headquarters
2 Section B Battery 601 Air Defence Group (35mm)
Detachment 602 Electronic Warfare Company
2nd Army Corps/3rd Infantry Brigade
A Company (-) 12th Infantry Regiment
C Company 12th Infantry Regiment
3rd Communications Company
3rd Army Corps/4th Airborne Brigade
Troop A Battery 4th Airborne Artillery Regiment (105mm)
5th Army/9th Infantry Brigade
3rd Platoon C Company 8th Infantry Regiment
C Company 25th Infantry Regiment
9th Engineer Company

AIR FORCE
Air Defence Command
Battery 1st Anti-Aircraft Group (20mm)
Training Command
Security Company School of Military Aviation

COMBAT TEAM EAGLE - PORT SAN CARLOS
2nd Army Corps/3rd Infantry Brigade
Section Command Company 12th Infantry Regiment
Section Service Company 12th Infantry Regiment
5th Army/9th Infantry Brigade
1st Platoon C Company 25th Infantry Regiment

WEST FALKLANDS

TASK FORCE RECONQUEST
Army Headquarters
1st Section 601 Commando Company
5th Army/9th Infantry Brigade
PORT HOWARD
5th Infantry Regiment
9th Engineer Company
9th Medical Company

FOX BAY
8th Infantry Regiment

NAVAL AIR BASE PEBBLE ISLAND
Marine Support Force
1st Platoon H Company 3rd Marine Infantry Battalion

ORDERS OF BATTLE

BATTLE OF STANLEY - 2 APRIL

Royal Marines Naval Party 8901 (1981/82)
Royal Marines Naval Party 8901 (1982/83)
Royal Navy Naval Party HMS Endurance
Platoon, Falklands Islands Defence Force

2nd Marine Infantry Battalion
1st Platoon, C Company, 25th Infantry Regiment
1st Amphibious Commando Company
1st Amphibiuos Vehicle Company
1st Amphibious Engineer Company
A Battery, Marine Field Artillery Battalion (105mm MRL)
Marine Air Defence Battery
Tactical Divers
ARA *Santisima Trinidad*
ARA *Cabo San Antonio*
ARA *Santa Fe*

Naval Party 8901 captured

One 1st Marine Infantry Battalion officer, two Amphibious wounded and three captured and later released.

Result: *Argentina completes first stage of Operation 'Rosario'.*

FIRST BATTLE OF GRYTVIKEN - 3 APRIL

Ship's Detachment, *HMS Endurance*

Composite Platoon, A Company, 1st Marine Infantry Battalion
Puma, 601 Combat Aviation Battalion
Alouette, Antarctic Squadron
ARA *Guerrico*
ARA *Bahia Paraiso*

One Royal Marine wounded and Ship's Detachment captured.

Two Argentine marine infantry killed
Unknown number wounded

Result: *Argentina occupies all Falkland Island and its Dependencies*

SECOND BATTLE OF GRYTVIKEN - 25 APRIL

Section, Recce Troop, 42 Commando
Section, Mortar Troop, 42 Commando
2 SBS
D Squadron, 22 SAS
NGFO 2, 148 Commando Forward Observation Battery
NGFO 5, 148 Commando Forward Observation Battery
HMS Antrim
HMS Plymouth
HMS Brilliant
HMS Endurance
HMS Tidespring

Tactical Divers
Composite Platoon, A Company, 1st Marine Infantry Battalion
Anti-Tank Det, 1st Marine Infantry Battalion
ARA Santa Fe

Two SAS injured in helicopter crash
One naval steward wounded on Santa Fe
Result: *Britain begins recovery of lost territories.*

RAID ON PEBBLE ISLAND - 15 MAY

D Squadron, 22 SAS
NGFO 5, 148 Commando Forward Observation Battery
HMS Hermes
HMS Glamorgan
HMS Brilliant

1st Platoon, H Company, 3rd Marine Infantry Battalion

Two SAS wounded
Result: *Naval air threat in West Falklands removed and therefore San Carlos safer.*

BATTLE OF PORT SAN CARLOS - 21 MAY

3 Para
4th Troop, B Squadron, Blues and Royals
79 Commando Battery (Light Gun)
NGFO 1, 148 Commando Forward Observation Battery
3rd Commando Brigade Air Squadron
846 Naval Air Squadron

Combat Team Eagle

Three 3rd Commando Brigade Air Squadron killed and one NCO wounded.
Result: *Argentine threat, if minimal, to San Carlos beachhead neutralised.*

240

BATTLE OF GOOSE GREEN - 28 MAY

2 Para
Troop, 8 Commando Battery (Light Gun)
Recce Troop, 59 Independent Commando Squadron
3rd Commando Brigade Air Squadron
Air Defence Troop RM
Section, 43 Battery, 32 Guided Weapon Regiment
NGFO 4, 148 Commando Forward Observation Battery
HMS Arrow
No 1 (F) Squadron (Harriers)

A and C Company, 12th Infantry Regiment
3rd Platoon, C Company, 8th Infantry Regiment
Troop, A Battery, 4th Airborne Artillery Regiment (105mm)
3rd Section B Battery 601 Air Defence Group (35mm)
Combat Team Eagle
Combat Team Solari (-)
1st Anti-Aircraft Group (Rh 202s)
Security Company, Military Aviation School
Pucara Squadron Falklands
1st Naval Attack Squadron (MB-399 Aeromacchis)

Sixteen 2 Para, one 59 Independent Commando Squadron RE
NCO and one 3rd Commando Brigade Air Squadron pilot
killed and thirty-three 2 Para wounded.

Five 8th Infantry Regiment, thirty-one 12th Infantry Regiment,
twelve 25th Infantry Regiment, two 1st AA Group, four Security
Company, Military Aviation School and one Pucara pilot killed.
Fifty-two wounded and about 1007 taken prisoner

Result: Threat to British operations against Stanley removed.

SKIRMISH ON MOUNT KENT - 30 MAY

D Squadron, 22 SAS

1st Assault Section, 602 Commando Company
3rd Assault Section, 602 Commando Company

Four SAS wounded.
Result: Strategically important feature of Mount Kent denied to Argentines.

BATTLE OF TOP MALO HOUSE - 31 MAY

Mountain and Arctic Warfare Cadre RM

2nd Assault Section, 602 Commando Company

Three NCOs wounded.
Result: Argentine Special Forces Group operations in front of 3rd Commando Brigade's advance neutralised.

BATTLE OF THE OUTER DEFENCE ZONE - 11/12 JUNE

Battle of Mount Longdon

3 Para
79 Commando Battery (Light Guns)
FOO 2, 41 Battery
NGFO 2, 148 Commando Forward Observation Battery
2 Troop, 9 Parachute Squadron
HMS Avenger

Eighteen 3 Para killed
Result: Important feature captured and B Company 7th Infantry Regiment destroyed.

Battle of Two Sisters (Dos Hermanos)

45 Commando
Milan Troop, 40 Commando
8 Commando Battery (Light Gun)
NGFO 5, 148 Commando Forward Observation Battery
Condor Troop, 59 Independent Commando Squadron
HMS Glamorgan

Four 45 Commando killed.
Result: Centre of Outer Defence Zone captured and part of Argentine 4th Infantry Regiment destroyed.

Battle of Mount Harriet (Monte Enriqueta)

42 Commando
Recce Platoon, Welsh Guards
7 Commando Battery (Light Gun)
NGFO 3, 148 Commando Forward Observation Battery
2 Troop, 59 Independent Commando Squadron
HMS Yarmouth

Two 42 Commando killed and seven wounded.
Result: Classic night attack overwhelms third sector of Outer Defence Zone and 4th Infantry Regiment destroyed.

Silver Sector 2

B Company, 7th Infantry Regiment
1st Platoon, C Company, 7th Infantry Regiment
Platoon, 10th Engineer Company
4th Airborne Artillery Group (Pack Howitzers)
D Battery, 3rd Artillery Group (155mm)
Platoon, Marine 12.7 Machine Gun Company

Thirty-six Argentines killed and about eighty wounded.

C Company, 4th Infantry Regiment
2nd and 3rd Platoons, A Company, 4th Infantry Regiment
B Company, 6th Infantry Regiment
Section, Mortar Platoon, 4th Infantry Regiment
3rd Artillery Group (Pack Howitzers)
B Battery, Marine Field Artillery Battalion (Pack Howitzers)

Nineteen 4th Infantry Regiment killed and forty-four captured

RHQ 4th Infantry Regiment
B Company, 4th Infantry Regiment
Combat Team Solari(-)
Defence Platoon, HQ 3rd Infantry Brigade
Machine Gun Troop, 1st Cavalry Regiment
3rd Artillery Group (Pack Howitzers)
B Battery, Marine Field Artillery Battalion (Pack Howitzers)

Eight 4th Infantry Regiment killed and over 300 captured.

DEFENCE OF THE INNER DEFENCE ZONE - 13/14 JUNE

Battle of Mount Tumbledown (Cerro Destartalado)

2nd Scots Guards
4th Field Regiment (Light Gun)
NGFO 5, 148 Commando Forward Observation Battery
3 Troop, 9 Parachute Squadron
HMS Avenger
HMS Active
HMS Glamorgan

N Company, 5th Marine Infantry Battalion
O Company, 5th Marine Infantry Battalion
B Company, 6th Infantry Regiment
2 Platoon, A Company, 4th Infantry Regiment
Platoon, B Company, 12th Infantry Regiment
Platoon, Amphibious Engineers
B Battery, Marine Field Artillery Battalion (Pack Howitzers)

Nine 5th Marine Infantry Battalion, five 4th Infantry Regiment and eight 6th Infantry Regiment killed and about fifty wounded.

Nine Scots Guards killed and forty-three wounded.

Result: *Key feature of defence of Stanley captured and N Company destroyed.*

Battle of Wireless Ridge (Cordon de la Radio)

Silver Sector 1

2 Para
3rd Troop, B Squadron, Blues and Royals
79 Commando Battery (Light Gun)
NGFO 2, 148 Commando Forward Observation Battery
Recce Troop, 59 Independent Commando Squadron

Command Company, 7th Infantry Regiment
A and C Company (-), 7th Infantry Regiment
2nd Platoon, A Company, 2nd Parachute Infantry Battalion
10th Armoured Recce Squadron
4th Airborne Artillery Group (105mm)

Fifteen 7th Infantry Regiment, six 10th Armoured Recce Squadron and three 3rd Infantry Regiment killed. Wounded not known although 10th Armoured Recce is thought to have had sixty.

Two 2 Para killed and eleven wounded.

Result: *Stanley surrounded and destruction of 7th Infantry Regiment complete.*

Raid on Cortley Ridge

D Squadron, 22 SAS
G Squadron, 22 SAS
1st Raiding Squadron Royal Marines
NGFO1, 148 Commando Forward Observation Battery

3rd Platoon, H Company, 3rd Marine Infantry Battalion
B Battery, 101 Air Defence Group

Two SAS wounded
Result: *No strategic or tactical value.*

Battle of Mount William (Cerro Guillermo) - 14 June

1/7th Gurkha Rifles
4th Field Regiment (Light Gun)
1 Troop, 9 Parachute Squadron

M Company, 5th Marine Infantry Regiment

Result: *Capture of principal features south of Stanley completed.*

Capture of Sapper Hill (Monte de Ingenerio)

7 Troop, C Company, 40 Commando

M Company, 5th Marine Infantry Regiment

Two 42 Commando wounded.
Result: *Major incursion by 5th Infantry Brigade into Army Group Stanley's southern defences.*
and Argentines surrender

Three 5th Marine Infantry Battalion killed.

BRITISH CASUALTIES IN DIRECT SUPPORT OF GROUND OPERATIONS 2 APRIL - 14 JUNE 1982

	KILLED				WOUNDED				NON-BATTLE				TOTAL
	Offrs	NCO's	OR's	Total	Offrs	NCO's	OR's	Total	Offrs	NCOs	ORs	Total	
ROYAL NAVY													
HMS Glamorgan	1	5	8	14	0	3	10	13	0	0	0	0	27
4th Assault Squadron RM	0	2	2	4	0	0	0	0	0	0	0	0	4
Royal Navy	0	1	1	2	0	0	0	0	0	0	0	0	2
Royal Marines	0	1	1	2	0	0	0	0	0	0	0	0	2
846 Naval Air Squadron	0	1	0	1	0	1	0	1	0	0	0	0	2
Royal Marines	0	1	0	1	0	0	0	0	0	0	0	0	1
TOTAL	1	8	10	19	0	4	10	14	0	0	0	0	33
ROYAL MARINES													
40 Commando	0	1	0	1	0	1	5	6	1	0	7	8	15
42 Commando	0	1	1	2	1	2	19	22	0	0	22	22	46
Argyll and Sutherland Highlanders	0	0	0	0	0	0	1	1	0	0	0	0	1
45 Commando	0	3	9	12	1	2	20	23	0	0	23	23	58
SBS	0	0	1	1	0	0	0	0	0	0	0	0	1
3rd Commando Brigade HQ and Signal Squadron	0	0	0	0	1	1	0	2	0	3	0	3	5
Mountain and Arctic Warfare Cadre RM	0	1	0	1	0	2	0	2	0	0	0	0	3
Commando Logistic Regiment	0	0	2	2	0	2	4	6	0	2	1	3	11
3rd Commando Brigade Air Squadron	2	0	0	2	1	1	4	6	0	0	0	0	8
Ship's Detachment HMS Endurance	0	0	0	0	0	0	1	1	0	0	0	0	1
TOTAL	2	6	13	21	4	11	53	68	1	5	53	59	148

ARMY

B Squadron, Blues and Royals	0	0	0	0	1	1	0	0	1	1	2
2nd Battalion Scots Guards	0	8	3	4	32	39	0	0	14	14	61
1st Battalion Welsh Guards	0	33	1	2	25	28	0	1	8	9	70
Argyll and Sutherland Highlanders	0	0	1	0	0	1	0	0	0	0	1
42 Commando	0	0	1	0	0	1	0	0	0	0	1
2nd Battalion Parachute Regiment	3	17	1	2	36	39	0	0	45	48	104
3rd Battalion Parachute Regiment	0	21	3	1	52	56	0	3	20	20	97
1/7th Gurkha Rifles	0	1	1	0	14	15	0	0	0	0	16
22 SAS	1	0	1	0	4	4	0	0	0	0	18
Royal Artillery	0	14	1	1	7	9	0	2	13	15	24
29 Battery, 4th Field Regiment RA	0	0	0	0	1	1	0	0	0	0	1
97 Battery, 4th Field Regiment RA	0	0	0	0	1	1	0	0	3	3	4
12th (Air Defence) Regiment RA	0	0	0	0	0	0	0	3	3	3	3
29th Commando Regiment RA	0	0	1	1	3	4	0	0	5	6	9
43 Battery, 32nd (Guided Weapon) Regiment RA	0	0	0	0	0	0	0	0	1	1	1
49th Field Regiment RA	0	0	0	0	1	1	0	1	1	1	3
Royal School of Artillery Support Regiment	0	0	1	0	2	3	0	0	1	2	4
Royal Engineers	0	8	1	10	22	33	0	0	4	4	45
9th Parachute Squadron RE	0	3	1	0	2	3	0	0	2	2	8
11th Field Squadron, 38 Engineer Regiment RE	0	0	0	0	0	0	0	0	2	2	2
20th Field Squadron, 38 Engineer Regiment RE	0	0	0	8	12	20	0	0	2	2	20
49th (EOD) Squadron, 33 Engineer Regiment RE	0	1	0	0	0	0	0	0	0	0	1
59th Independent Commando Squadron RE	0	4	1	2	5	7	0	1	0	0	11
Royal Signals	2	8	0	0	0	0	0	0	0	0	8
5th Infantry Brigade HQ & Signal Squadron	1	0	0	0	0	0	0	0	0	0	2
264 Signal Squadron	0	4	0	0	0	0	0	0	0	0	4
2nd Battalion Parachute Regiment	1	1	0	0	0	0	0	0	0	0	1
605 Tactical Air Control Party	1	0	0	0	0	0	0	0	0	0	2
81 Ordnance Company RAOC	0	0	0	0	0	0	0	0	0	0	2
656 Squadron AAC	0	3	0	0	1	1	0	0	2	2	5
16th Field Ambulance RAMC	1	3	0	2	2	4	0	0	1	1	8

												Total
Royal Electrical and Mechanical Engineers	0	2	2	4	0	0	0	0	0	0	0	4
Welsh Guards	0	2	1	3	0	0	0	0	0	0	0	3
3rd Battalion Parachute Regiment	0	0	1	1	0	0	0	0	0	0	0	1
Army Catering Corps	0	0	2	2	0	0	0	0	0	0	0	2
Welsh Guards	0	0	2	2	0	0	0	0	0	0	0	2
TOTAL	7	58	58	123	12	22	189	231	0	6	108	114	467
ROYAL AIR FORCE												
No 1 (Fighter) Squadron (Harrier GR3s)	0	0	0	0	2	0	0	2	0	0	0	2
RAF Upavon	1	0	0	1	0	0	0	0	0	0	0	1
605 Tactical Air Control Party	1	0	0	1	0	0	0	0	0	0	0	1
TOTAL	1	0	0	1	2	0	0	2	0	0	0	3
ROYAL FLEET AUXILIARY												
LSL Sir Galahad	3	2	2	5	0	0	0	0	0	0	0	5
LSL Sir Tristram	0	1	1	2	0	0	0	0	0	0	0	2
TOTAL	3	3	3	7	0	0	0	0	0	0	0	7
GRAND TOTAL	14	73	84	171	19	36	252	308	0	7	161	173	656

Notes

Some of the basic information on British casualties came from the Royal Navy, Army and RAF Historical Branches of the Ministry of Defence but one difficulty is that, unlike the Argentines, who list their casualties by unit irrespective of their arm or service, casualties are listed by parent arm e.g. Royal Engineers. However it has been possible, by trawling through public, semi-official and private sources, to calculate to which units casualties belonged but not necessarily the rank ratio. For instance twenty 20 Field Squadron RE were wounded in the attack on the *Sir Galahad*, which essentially wrote the unit out of the campaign, but it has not been possible to sub-divide them into NCOs and Sappers and therefore the 8:12 is an estimate. The four members of the SAS who were injured/wounded in the South Georgia and Pebble Islands operations have not been included under wounded because three of them were killed when the Sea King ditched on the 19 May.

A total of 255 British were killed during the war of which eighty-eight were Royal Navy, ten Royal Fleet Auxiliary and nine in the Merchant Navy. Of the twenty-five Royal Marines killed, all died in the fighting after 21 May, the twenty-fifth being killed when the Sea King ditched, as did the one RAF fatality. All ground 123 Army were killed after 21 May as were three female civilians in Stanley on the last day of the fighting. The one SAS and four Royal Marines who lost their lives in 'blue on blue' incidents are included in the 'killed' column. The most senior rank killed was Lieutenant Colonel Jones VC while leading his battalion at Goose Green.

A total of 777 wounded in the war of whom 581 were evacuated to the hospital ship *Uganda* and 569 were repatriated to the United Kingdom through Montevideo. By 1983, over 700 were fully employed. Of the 253 British servicemen killed, this was less than in Korea, Malaya and Northern Ireland until 1982 but more than in Cyprus, Aden and Confrontation in Borneo. 3 Para lost the most, 23 killed, during Mount Longdon and two days of shelling. Most of the dead were returned to the United Kingdom with twenty-three being buried in a military cemetery at San Carlos, not far from where 3rd Commando Brigade had its headquarters until the breakout.

ARGENTINE CASUALTIES IN DIRECT SUPPORT OF GROUND OPERATIONS 2 APRIL - 14 JUNE	KILLED				WOUNDED				CASUALTIES	
	Offrs	NCOs	ORs	Total	Offrs	NCOs	ORs	Total	Total	Stanley
ARMY										
Military Governor's Office	0	0	0	0	0	0	0	0	0	10
HQ 5th Army Corps	0	0	0	0	0	0	0	0	0	1
Civil Affairs Office	0	0	0	0	0	0	0	0	0	24
HQ 3rd Mechanised Infantry Brigade	0	0	4	4	3	4	6	13	17	x
HQ 10th Motorised Infantry Brigade	0	0	2	2	0	2	2	4	6	179
A Company 1st Infantry Regiment	0	1	1	2	0	0	0	7	9	x
3rd Motorised Infantry Regiment	0	0	5	5	0	6	78	84	89	917
4th Mechanised Infantry Regiment	2	4	17	23	8	24	89	122	145	328
5th Mechanised Infantry Regiment	0	0	7	7	3	2	62	67	74	x
6th Motorised Infantry Regiment	0	2	9	11	0	1	34	35	46	749
7th Motorised Infantry Regiment	1	2	33	36	7	20	125	152	188	816
8th Mechanised Infantry Regiment	0	1	4	5	2	3	46	51	56	814
12th Mechanised Infantry Regiment	0	4	31	35	3	17	52	72	107	x
25th Special Infantry Regiment	1	4	8	13	0	8	45	53	66	639
Platoon 181 Armoured Recce Squadron	0	1	0	1	1	1	0	2	3	43
10th Armoured Recce Squadron	0	3	3	6	0	14	54	68	74	216
8th Armoured Regiment	0	0	1	1	0	0	0	0	1	x
601 Combat Aviation Battalion (Helicopters)	1	0	0	1	0	0	0	0	1	x
601 Commando Company	0	0	0	0	0	0	0	0	0	43
602 Commando Company	2	3	0	5	3	0	4	7	12	32
30th Mountain Infantry Regiment	1	x	x	x	x	x	x	x	1	x
143 Intelligence Company	x	1	x	x	x	x	x	x	1	x
161 Intelligence Company	x	1	1	x	x	x	x	x	1	x
G5 HQ Army	x	1	x	x	x	x	x	x	1	x
General San Martin Military College	1	x	x	x	x	x	x	x	1	x
3rd Artillery Group	1	1	0	2	3	6	12	21	23	215
4th Airborne Artillery Group	0	0	3	3	0	4	38	42	45	294
101 Artillery Group	1	1	0	2	0	0	0	0	2	x

Unit										Total
101 Air Defence Group	0	1	2	3	0	1	8	9	12	X
601 Air Defence Group	1	1	4	6	1	5	17	23	29	465
3rd Mechanised Engineer Company	0	0	0	0	1	0	2	3	3	3
9th Mechanised Engineer Company	0	0	0	1	0	1	3	4	4	4
10th Motorised Engineer Company	0	0	1	1	0	4	13	17	18	271
601 Combat Engineer Battalion	0	0	1	1	0	1	9	10	11	228
601 Logistic Construction Battalion	0	0	0	0	0	0	0	0	1	X
3rd Mechanised Communications Company	0	0	0	1	1	0	1	1	1	X
10th Motorised Communications Company	0	0	1	1	1	1	0	2	3	244
181 Communications Company	0	0	0	0	0	0	1	1	2	X
601 Communications Company	0	0	0	3	0	0	0	0	0	7
601 Combat Aviation Battalion	2	1	0	0	1	1	0	1	4	65
601 Air Maintenance Company	0	0	0	0	0	0	0	0	0	9
181 Military Police Company	0	0	0	1	0	0	0	0	0	64
3rd Mechansied Logistic Battalion	1	0	0	0	0	0	0	0	1	X
9th Mechanised Logistic Battalion	0	0	0	3	0	1	1	2	2	94
10th Motorised Logistic Battalion	0	2	1	2	0	3	2	5	8	133
3rd Mechanised Medical Company	1	1	0	0	0	1	4	5	7	X
Military Hospital Comodoro Rivadavia	0	0	0	7	0	0	0	0	0	65
General Roca Military Institute	2	0	5	7	0	0	0	0	7	X
TOTALS	16	35	141	193	29	121	561	883	1077	7087

MARINES

Unit										Total
1st Marine Infantry Battalion	1	2	0	3	1	0	2	2	5	
2nd Marine Infantry Battalion	0	0	0	0	0	1	0	1	1	
5th Marine Infantry Battalion	2	0	14	16	0	0	4	4	20	
B Battery Marine Field Artillery Battalion	0	0	0	0	0	0	2	2	2	
Marine Anti-Aircraft Battalion	0	0	7	7	0	0	7	7	14	
Marine 12.7mm Machine Gun Company	1	1	2	4	0	1	3	4	8	
TOTALS	4	3	23	30	1	2	18	20	50	

ARGENTINE AIR FORCE									
1st Air Photographic Group (Learjets)	3	2	0	5	0	0	0		5
2nd Bomber Group (Canberras)	1	0	0	3	0	0	0		3
3rd Attack Group (Malvinas Pucara Squadron)	2	0	0	2	0	0	0		2
4th Attack Group (Pucaras)	1	0	0	1	0	0	0		1
1st Anti-Aircraft Group	1	7	3	11	0	0	0		11
Security Company, Military Aviation School	0	1	2	3	0	0	0		3
TOTALS	8	10	5	25	0	0	0		25
NAVAL AIR COMMAND									
1st Attack Squadron (MB-339s)	2	0	0	2	0	0	0		2
TOTAL	2	0	0	2	0	0	0		2
NATIONAL GENDARMERIE									
601 National Gendarmerie Special Forces Squadron	1	5	0	6	8	8	8		14
TOTAL	1	5	0	6	8	8	8		14
MARITIME									
Argentine Navy	0	0	1	0	0	0	0		1
Argentine Coastguard	0	0	2	2	0	0	0		2
Naval Transport Service	2	13	0	15	0	0	0		15
TOTALS	2	13	3	17	0	0	0		18
GRAND TOTAL	33	66	172	271	30	131	587	746	1186

Notes

Details of Argentines casualties in direct support of the ground forces has been calculated from public sources, in particular from *Lista de Bajas de Combatientes del Conflicto del Atlantico Sur que incluyu: Oficiales, Suboficiales y Soldados del Ejercito Argentino* and the Marine Corps *Desembarco No 145*. Non-battle casualties were not available. The column headed 'Stanley' gives details of Argentine strengths taken from a document dated 3 June. Not listed are one Argentine Navy, two Coastguard, fourteen non-aircrew Argentine Air Force and several merchant seamen killed fighting and supporting the Argentine ground forces.

Of the Argentine Army killed, a reservist of the 1954 induction died as did two each from 1959 and 1960 and 101 from those who entered the Army in 1981. Of the serving conscripts, i.e. those inducted in February 1982, thirty-three were killed, most with 12th Infantry Regiment at Goose Green. 7th Infantry, which according to its CO, Lieutenant Colonel Gimenez, 'had the dubious honour of fighting the British twice' (at Mount Longdon and on Wireless Ridge) suffered the heaviest casualties losing thirty-six killed and 152 wounded. The most senior rank killed was Colonel Clodoveo Arevalo, who was on the staff of HQ 5th Army Corps and was serving with the General Roca Military Institute. Julio Roca formed 10th Infantry Brigade in 1880 and became an Argentine hero in the war against the Indian tribes in Patagonia.

TRANSLATION OF CAPTURED DOCUMENT - 3 JUNE 1982

Serial	Name	Number of Personnel	Comment
1	GOB	10	'Gobiniero' Governor probably GHQ. Located at Government House. Governor General de Brigade M B Menendez.
2	Col	24	No identification
3	CDO CPO EJ V	1	No identification although 'CDO' is probably 'Command', 'EJ' is Ejercito which is Army and 'V' is Roman numeral for figure five.
4	CDO Br I IX	8	'Brigade de Infantera'. Probably in Stanley now less 12 Infantry Regiment captured at Goose Green (9 Infantry Brigade).
5	RI 25	639	'Regimentio de Infantera 25', of 9 Brigade. Based at Port Stanley less ECG captured Fanning Head. (25 Infantry Regiment).
6	RI 8	814	'Regimentio de Infantera 8' of 9 Brigade. Based at Fox Bay. (8 Infantry Regiment).
7	Dest C BI 181	34	' de Caballeria Blindado 181'. Possibly the LTVP 7 unit 181 indicated Army level unit.
8	Co Ing 9	124	'Compania de Ingenerio 9' of 9 Brigade. Detachments at Fox Bay and Port Howard (9 Engineer Company).
9	Co Ing 601	228	'Companie de Ingenerio 601'. An Army level unit. (601 Engineer Company).
10	Arg Com 601	7	'Argentina Communicion 601'? Rear link communication unit to Argentina Army level unit.

Contemporary interpretation of a document captured on 3rd June the unit strengths in Stanley in early June is at Annex. In hindsight there are translation errors, for instance:

Serial 2
Serial 7
Serial 10

COL=Civil Affairs Department
This detachment had Panhards, not LVTP's
"Arg" = Agrupacion = Group.

Serial	Name	Number of Personnel	Comment
22	Esc Expl C Bl 10	216	'Escuadron de Exploracion de Caballenia Blindado 10' - based at Port Stanley and probably equipped with PANHARD AML 90 armoured cars. The armoured reconnaissance unit at 10 Mechanised Infantry Brigade. (Armoured Reconnaissance Sqn)
23	Co Ing MEC 10	271	'Companies de Ingeniero Mecanizada 10' - Based at Port Stanley and part of 10 Mechanised Infantry Brigade (10 Mechanised Engineer Company).
24	Co Com MEC 10	244	'Compania de Communicion Mecanizada 10' - the signals element of 10 Mechanised Infantry Brigade (10 Mechanised Communication Company).
25	B LOG 10	133	'Batallon de Logistique 10'. Logistic element of 10 Mechanised Infantry Brigade. (10 Logistic Battalion).
26	GA 3	215	'Grupo de Artilleria 3' - at Port Stanley and equipped with the Italian 105m Pack Howitzer (3 Artillery Group).
27	GA/RI 4	176	'Grupo de Artilleria/Regimentio de Artilleria 4'. Artillery unit organic to 4 Infantry Regiment. This helped to confirm that the four guns captured at Goose Green were probably organic to 12 Infantry Regiment. (4 Infantry Regiment artillery group).
28	RI 4 (-)	326	'Regimentio de Infanteria 4' not at full strength. At Port Stanley. Part of 3 Mechanised Infantry Brigade (4 Infantry Regiment).
29	Co CDOS 601	43	'Compania de Commandos 601' - Army level Special Forces unit. Had been in the Falklands for some time and had probably patrolled the San Carlos area prior to the landings. (601 Commando Company).
30	Co CDOS 602	32	'Compania de Commandos 602' - Army level Special Forces unit. Recently assigned to the Falkland Islands on 24 May '83. Had already been in contact with the Mountain and Arctic Warfare Cadre at Top Malo House. (602 Commando Company).

Serial	Name	Number of Personnel	Comment
11	B Log 9	94	Batallon de Logistique '9 Logistic Battalion' of 9 Infantry Brigade.
12	HMCR	65	Unidentified.
13	Ca Ab Mant Aeron 601	9	'Compania ___ 601. Unidentified but possibly '601 Aircraft Maintenance Company' for army helicopters. Port Stanley airfield.
14	Co PM 181	64	Compania de Policia Militar – 601 Military Police Company – Army level unit. At Port Stanley.
15	GA AEROT 4	294	'Grepo de Artilleria – Aerot 4' possibly 4 Anti-Aircraft Group. Probably Po t Stanley.
16	GADA 601	465	Grepo de Artilleria de Defense Anti-Aeria 601 – Army level unit. Probably at Port Stanley. Elements of GADA 601 had been killed or captured at Goose Green (601 Army Defence Group).
17	B Ar Comb Ej 601	65	Batallon de Avion Combat Ejerito 601. Army aviation unit – possibly equipped with helicopters. An Army level unit.
18	CDO Br 1 Mec X	179	'Commando Brigade de Infanteria Mecanizade' – now at Port Stanley and probably at full strength (10 Mechanised Infantry Brigade).
19	RI Mec 3	917	'Regimentio de Infanteria Mecanizada 3' – at Port Stanley. Part of 10 Mechanised Infantry Brigade (3 Mechanised Infantry Regiment).
20	RI Mec 6	749	'Regimentio de Infanteria Mecanizada 6' – at Port Stanley. Also part of 10 Mechanised Infantry Brigade (6 Mechanised Infantry Regt.)
21	RI Mec 7	819	'Regimentio de Infanteria Mecanizada 7' at Port Stanley. Also part of 10 Mechanised Infantry Brigade (7 Mechanised Infantry Regiment).

Bibliography

Adams, James; *Secret Armies*; London; Hutchinson; 1987.

Adkin, Mark; *Goose Green*; London; Leo Cooper; 1992.

Aristu, Javier; *Argentine Elite Combined Special Ops in Las Malvinas*; Soldier of Fortune; December 1985

Beadle, Jeff; *The Light Blue Lanyard: Fifty Years with 40 Commando*; London; Square One Publications; 1992

Bilton, Michael and Kosminsky, Peter; *Speaking Out*; London; Andre Deutsch; 1989.

Blakeway, Dennis; *The Falklands War*; TV Channel 4; London; Sidgewick and Jackson; 1992

Bransby, Guy; *Her Majesty's Interrogator Falklands*; London; Leo Cooper; 1996.

Carr, Jean; *Another Story*; London; Hamish Hamilton; 1984

Clayton, Anthony; *Forearmed*; London; Brassey's; 1993.

Brown, David; *The Royal Navy and the Falklands War*; London; Leo Cooper; 1987.

Burdon Rodney, Draper Michael, Rough Douglas, Smith Colin and Wilton David; *Falklands – The Air War*; London; Arms and Armour; 1986.

Clapp, Michael and Southby-Tailyour, Ewen; *Amphibious Assault Falklands*; London; Leo Cooper;1996.

Farwell, Byron; *The Gurkhas*; New York; Norton; 1984

Fitz-Gibbon, Spencer; *Not Mentioned in Despatches*; Cambridge; The Lutterworth Press; 1995.

Freedman, Lawrence and Gamba-Stonehouse, Virginia; *Signals of War*; London; Faber and Faber; 1990.

Frost, Major-General John; *2 Para Falklands – The Battalion At War*; London; Buchan and Enright; 1983.

Geraghty, Tony; *Who Dares Wins: The Special Air Service 1950 to the Gulf War*; London; Little, Brown and Co; 1992.

Hastings, Max and Jenkins, Simon; *The Battle for the Falklands*; London; Michael Joseph; 1983

HMSO; *The Disputed Islands. The Falklands Crisis: A History & Background*; London; HMSO; 1982

Sunday Times Insight Team; *The Falklands War*; London; Sphere Books Ltd; 1982.

Kon, Daniel; *Los Chicos de la Guerra/Children of the War*; New English Library; 1984

Lawrence, John and Robert; *When the Fighting is Over: The Battle for Tumbledown Mountain and its Aftermath*; London; Bloomsbury Publishing Ltd; 1988.

London Gazette; *Honours and Awards*; London; HMSO; 8th October 1982.

McManners, Hugh; *Falklands Commando*; London; Kimber; 1984.

Middlebrook, Martin; *The Fight For The Malvinas;* London; Viking; 1989.
Middlebrook, Martin; *Operation Corporate;* London; Viking; 1985.
Moro, Ruben O; *The History of the South Atlantic Conflict;* New York; Preager; 1989.
Norden, Deborah; *Military Rebellion in Argentina;* Nebraska, University of Nebraska; 1996
Oakley, Derek; *The Falklands Military Machine;* Tunbridge Wells; Spellmount; 1989.
Parker, John; *SBS;* London; Headline Books; 1997
Perkins, Roger; *Operation Paraquat;* Chippenham; Picton Publishing (Chippenham) Ltd; 1986.
Ramsey, Jack; *SAS: Soldiers' Story;* London; Mcmillan Publishers; 1996
Reed, John; *Commando Logistic Regiment Royal Marines;* Armed Forces; June 1983.
Rock, David; *Argentina 1516–1987;* London; IB Tauris & Co Ltd; 1986.
Southby-Tailyour, Ewen; *Reasons in Writing;* London; Leo Cooper; 1993.
Stewart, Nora Kinzer; *Mates and Muchachos;* Washington; Brassey's (US); 1991.
Swanson, John; *A History of the SAS Regiment;* London; Secker and Warburg; 1984.
Thompson, Julian; *No Picnic;* London; Leo Cooper; 1985.
Turolo, Carlos; *Asi Lucharon;* Buenos Aires; Editorial Sudamericana; 1982
Vaux, Nick; *March to the South Atlantic;* London; Buchan and Enright; 1986.
van der Bijl, Nick; *Argentine Forces in the Falklands;* London; Osprey No 250; 1992.
Villarno Emilio; *Batallon 5;* Aller Atucha y Asociados; Buenos Aires; 1992
Woodward, Admiral Sandy; *One Hundred Days;* London; HarpurCollins; 1992.

Articles

"Gunner"; *29th Commando Regiment RA in the Falklands* and *148 (Meiktila) Commando Forward Observation Battery RA;* Issue Number 142, September 1982.
International Defence Review 9/1982, *T Air Defence Battery (Shah Shujah's Troop) RA in the Falklands;* September 1982.
Reed, John; *Commando Logistic Regiment Royal Marines;* Armed Forces; June 1983.

Unpublished Material

Davies, Chris; *A Memoir of 9 Parachute Squadron Royal Engineers in the Falklands Campaign.*
Falkland Island Logistic Unit Battlefield Tour packs
  Mt Harriet Battlefield Tour.
  2 Para – Goose Green
  3 Para – Mount Longdon.

2 Scots Guards – Tumbledown
Jolly, Rick; *Ajax Bay – A Visitor's Guide.*
van der Bijl; *Down South* and *My Friends The Enemy;* 1983.
van der Bijl, Nick and Aldea, David; *The Falklands War*

Post Operation Reports

Post Operations Corporate, Sutton and Paraquat Reports.
  Blues and Royals.
  2nd Battalion The Parachute Regiment.
  3rd Battalion The Parachute Regiment.
  4th Regiment Royal Artillery.
  29th Commando Regiment Royal Artillery.
  59th Independent Commando Squadron RE.

Argentine Sources

Armas y Geoestrategia; *Argentina en la guerra de Malvinas; Incursiones de los Comandos;* Septiembre 1983.
Busser, Carlos; *Operacion Rosario*
Calvi Report; the official Argentine report into the Falklands campaign.
Carrizo-Salvadores, Carlos E; *Other Side of the Hill – Mount Longdon.* Originally appeared in *Malvinas: Testimonios de soldados';* Buenos Aires, 1983. Published in the April 1988 edition of *Pegasus,* the journal of the Parachute Regiment.
Castagneto, Mario Luis and Spadaro, Jose Ricardo; *La Guerra de las Malvinas;:* Buenos Aires; Editorial Oriente; 1987
Conflicto Malvinas; Informe Oficial del Ejercito Argentino; Buenos Aires; Ejercito Argentina; 1983
Jofre, Oscar and Aguiar, Felix; *La Brigada X de Infanteria Mecanizada 'General Nicolas Levalle' en Accion en Malvinas;* Buenos Aires; Circulo Militar; 1992
Kasanzew, Nicolas; *Malvinas: A Sangre y Fuergo;* Buenos Aires; Editorial Abril 1982.
Malvinas; La Trama Secreta; Editorial Sudamericana-Planeta; 1983
Menendez, Mario and Turolo, Carlos; *Malvinas: Testimonio de su Gobernador;* Argentina, Sudamericana-Planeta; 1983
Piaggi, Italo Angel; *Goose Green, Revealing War Diary of the Argentinian 12th Infantry Regiment Commander;* Sudamericana-Planeta; 1989
Rattenbach, Lt-Gen Benjamin; *The Rattenbach Report: The Commission for the Political and Strategic Evaluation of the Conflict in the South Atlantic Report.*
Testimonio de Oficiales Superiors y Jefes de la Guerra de las Malvinas; Buenos Aires; Circulo Militar; 1988
Extracts from War Diary 601st Commando Company
Extracts from War Diary 602nd Commando Company

258

Further Reading

Arostequi, Martin; *Twilight Warriors: Inside The World's Special Forces*; London; Bloomsbury; 1995

Burns, Jimmy; *The Land That Lost Its Heroes*; London; Bloomsbury; 1987

English, Adrian J; *Latin American Armed Forces*; Jane Publishing; 1984

Keegan. John; *World Armies*; MacMillans; 1983.

Keesing Publications; *Contemporary Archives 1982*; Longman

Rice, Desmond and Gavshon, Arthur; *The Sinking of the Belgrano*; London; Secker and Warburg; 1984

Ruiz-Moreno, Isidoro; *Commandos in Action, The Argentinian Army in Malvinas*; Buenos Aires; Emece; 1998

Scheina, Robert; *Latin America: A Naval History 1810–1987*; Annapolis; Naval Institute Press; 1987

Ward, Sharkey; *A Maverick at War over the Falklands*; London; Leo Cooper; 1992

Index

Galtieri, General Leopoldo, 215
appointed President of Argentina
(1981), 5
forms Junta with Anaya and Lami
Dozo, 5
rejects counter offensive plan, 168
visits Stanley, 52–53
Garcia, Major General, 12, 15,
23–24, 122, 166
Glamorgan, HMS, destroyer, 89–90,
180
Glasgow, HMS, destroyer, 84
Goose Green
advance on, 123–29
Argentine defence of, 115–17
Argentine surrender, 139
attack plans, 122
battle, 129–40
Government House, Stanley
attacked, 20–23
Guatemala offers support to
Argentina, *141*
Guerrico, Argentine frigate, 27–30

Haig, General Al, US Secretary of
State, 34, 69
Hamilton, Captain John, SAS, 68, 71,
89, 143
helicopters, 57–58
Gazelles lost at Port San Carlos,
110–11
Wessex lost at Fortuna Glacier,
71–72
Hermes, HMS, 68, 84, 89, 117
Hunt, Sir Rex, Governor, 7, 16
surrenders to Admiral Busser, 23
see also Government House

intelligence, 119–22, 128
screening, 218–21, 223–24
Intelligence Corps, 34, 120
Intrepid, HMS, 99, 102, 108, 111,
192
Invincible, HMS, carrier, 84, 144
Islas Malvinas, Argentine cutter, 83,
219

Jofre, Brigadier General Oscar, 13,
36, 50, 208–9
discounts use of napalm, 214
organizes Army Group Puerto
Argentino, 52
John Biscoe, RRS, 14
Jolly, Commander Rick, RN, 59
Jones, Lieutenant Colonel 'H,' 2
Para, 119, 122–24, 128, 131–34
killed, 134
Kent, Mount, battle, 147–49

LADE (Linea Aerea Del Estado), 9,
18, 23, 50
Lami Dozo, Brigadier, 5, 113
landings at San Carlos, 99–112
linguists, Spanish, 121
logistics, 59
Lombardo, Vice Admiral, 46
Longdon, Mount
attacked, 171
evacuated, 178

Maritime Exclusion Zone (MEZ),
47–48, 62, 84
imposed, 39
McKay, Sergeant Ian, 3 Para, 173–74
M Coy RM, 65
see also South Georgia
medical, 59–60
Menendez, Brigadier General Mario,
13, 39, 113, 122, 125, 138,
228–29
Mercedes, Task Force, 60, 116,
118–19, 140
MEZ *see* Maritime Exclusion Zone
military culture, 43–45
Mills, Lieutenant Keith, RM, 8, 15,
25, 66
surrenders detachment, 31
minefields dismantled, 221
Moody Brook barracks
attacked, 19–20
Moore, Major General Jeremy MC,
65, 118
appointed Commander LFFI, 33

263

takes command of LFFI in the field, 190

Mount Harriet
 attacked, 183–86
Murrell River bridged, 205

napalm, use discounted by Jofre, 214
Narwal, trawler, 84
Naval Party 8901, 5, 13–15, 24
 deploys to defend Falkland Islands, 17–22
 surrenders, 23
Naval Transport Service, 58
Noott, Major Gary, RM, 17, 23
Norland, MV, 96–103, 106, 108
Norman, Major Mike, RM, 14, 17
Nunn, Captain Chris, RM, 65

Olmeda, RFA, 216
Outer Defence Zone
 attacked by British, 170–88
 defended by Argentine forces, 156–62

Parada, Brigadier General, 105, 125
Paraquet, Operation, 65–76
 see also South Georgia
Pebble Island, 83, 86–88
 raid, 88–92
People's Revolutionary Army (ERP), 41
Perón, Juan, President, 41
Pike, Lieutenant Colonel Hugh, 3 Para, 170–72
Plymouth, HMS, frigate, 67, 69, 77, 111
Port Howard, 118, 142–43
Price, Annie, 27, 64, 69
prisoner administration, 217–29

QE2, RMS, 190

RAF *see* Royal Air Force
'Red Plum' *see* Endurance, HMS
Resource, RFA, 82

Ridley, Nicholas, Under–Secretary of State, Foreign Office, 6
Rio Carcarana, 143
Rio de Plata, Argentine merchant ship, 79
Rio Iguazu, cutter, 118
Rosario, Operation, 15–24
 see also Falkland Islands
Royal Air Force, 79, 81, 146–47
 recce South Georgia, 68
Royal Electrical and Mechanical Engineers, 57
Royal Engineers, 156, 163

Salvageman, tug, 216
San Carlos
 break out, 142
 consolidation, 112–14
 landings at, 99–112
Santa Fe, Argentine submarine, 12, 19, 73–77
 see also Astiz; South Georgia
Santisima Trinidad, Argentine destroyer, 12, 15, 23
SAS *see* Special Air Service
SBS *see* Special Boat Service
Seineldin, Lieutenant Colonel Mohammed, 13, 15, 24, 43, 60
Sheffield, HMS, destroyer, 92
Sir Galahad, LSL, 110
 attacked, 164–65
Sir Geraint, LSL, 56
Sir Lancelot, LSL, 125
Sir Percivale, LSL, 140
Sir Tristram, LSL, 192
 attacked, 164–65
Sollis, Jack, skipper of MV Forrest, 19, 21
South Atlantic Medal Association, 187
Southby–Tailyour, Major Ewan, RM, 18, 95, 102–6, 192–94
Southern Thule, liberation, 216
South Georgia, 53
 battle of Grytviken, first, 25–31
 battle of Grytviken, second, 64–78